CONTENTS

D0108104

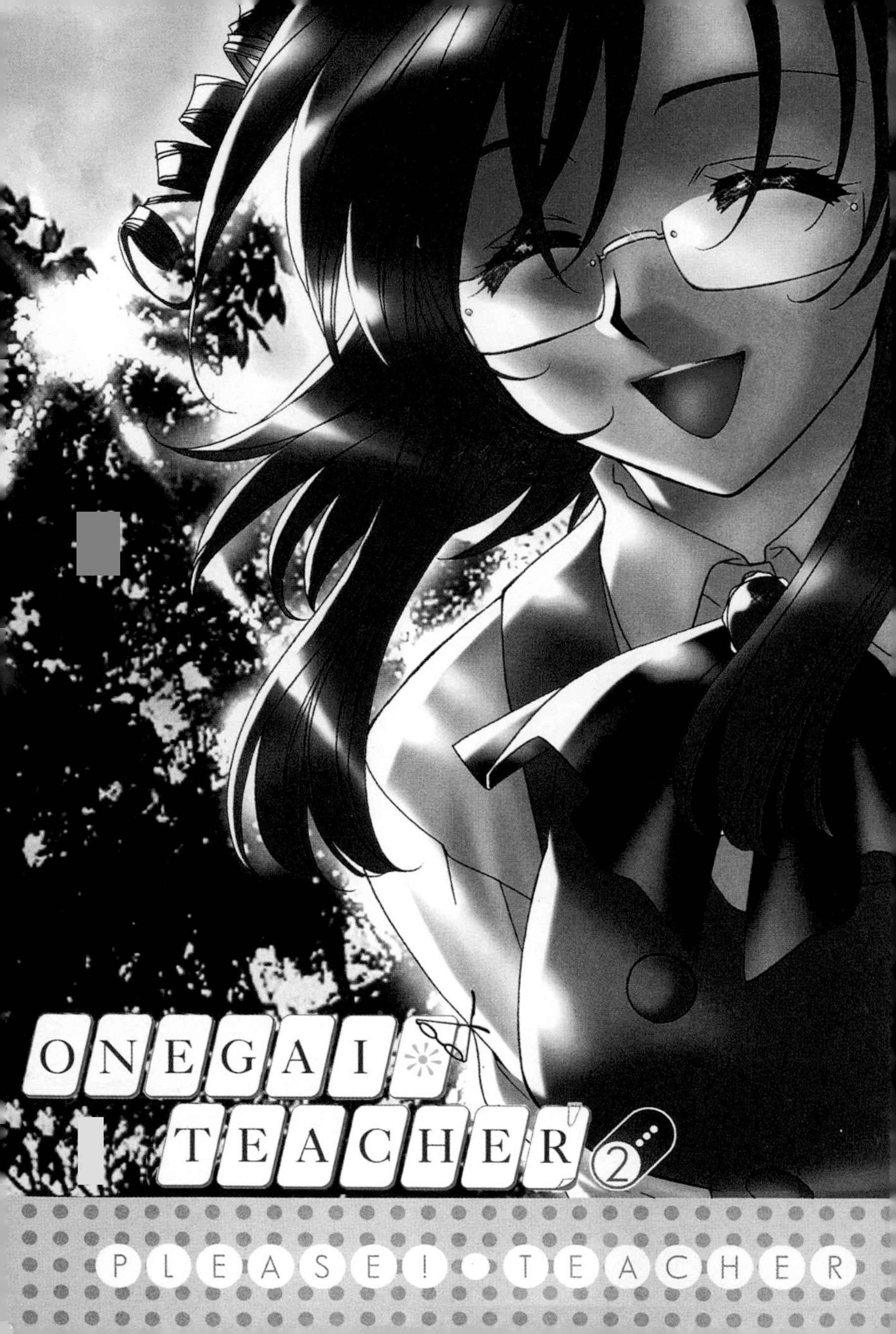
ONEGAI TEACHER 2
PLEASE! · TEACHER

You hold in your hand a comic that is as faithful as possible to the original Japanese work. None of the images have been rearranged or altered. This work truly represents the vision of the original author.

Confused?

Simply read the work from right to left. Start with what you'd traditionally consider the "last page" and continue through the book from right to left, page by page. Within each page, start with the rightmost top panel, and continue right to left, top to bottom. We hope that you enjoy this work in its original format.

Directions:

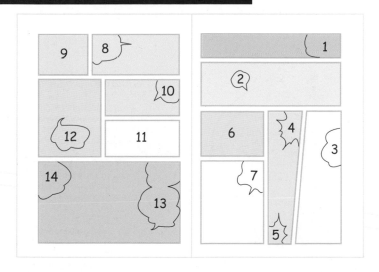

ONEGAI TEACHER

Translator: Sahe Kawahara

Editors: Shawn Sanders / Duncn Cameron / Angel Cheng

Production Artist: Wan-Ju Lee

US Cover Design: Yuki Chung

Production Manager: Janice Chang

Art Director: Yuki Chung

Marketing: Nicole Curry

© Please! / Bandai Visual
© SHIZURU HAYASHIYA 2003

First published in 2003 by
Media Works Inc., Tokyo, Japan.
English translation rights arranged
with Media Works Inc.

ONEGAI TEACHER
English translation © 2003
ComicsOne, Corp.
All rights reserved.

Publisher
ComicsOne Corporation
48531 Warm Springs Blvd., Suite 408
Fremont, CA 94539
www.ComicsOne.com

First Edition: May 2003
ISBN 1-58899-294-2

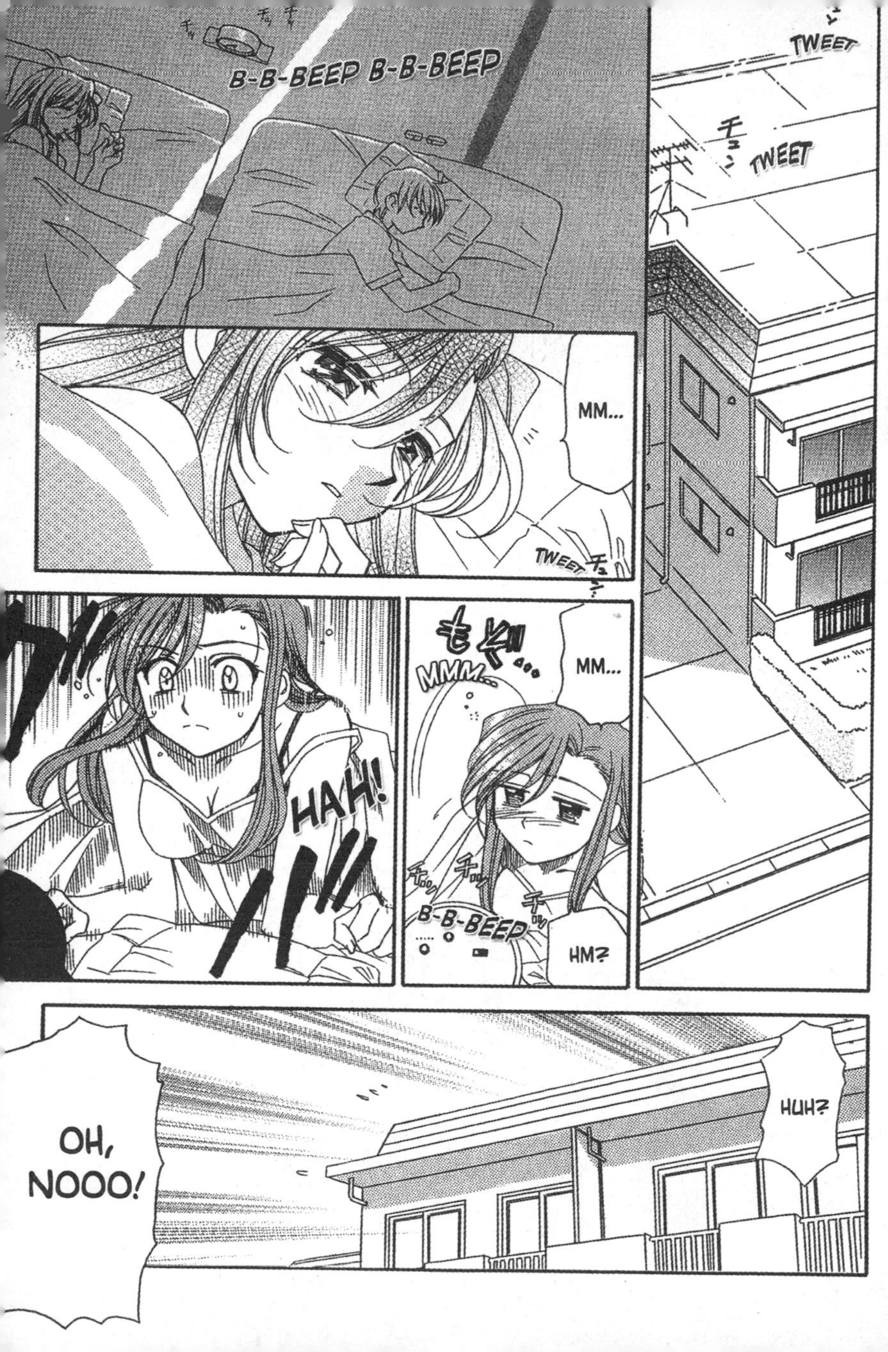
TWEET
TWEET
B-B-BEEP B-B-BEEP
MM...
TWEET
MM...
MMM...
B-B-BEEP
HM?
HAH!
HUH?
OH, NOOO!

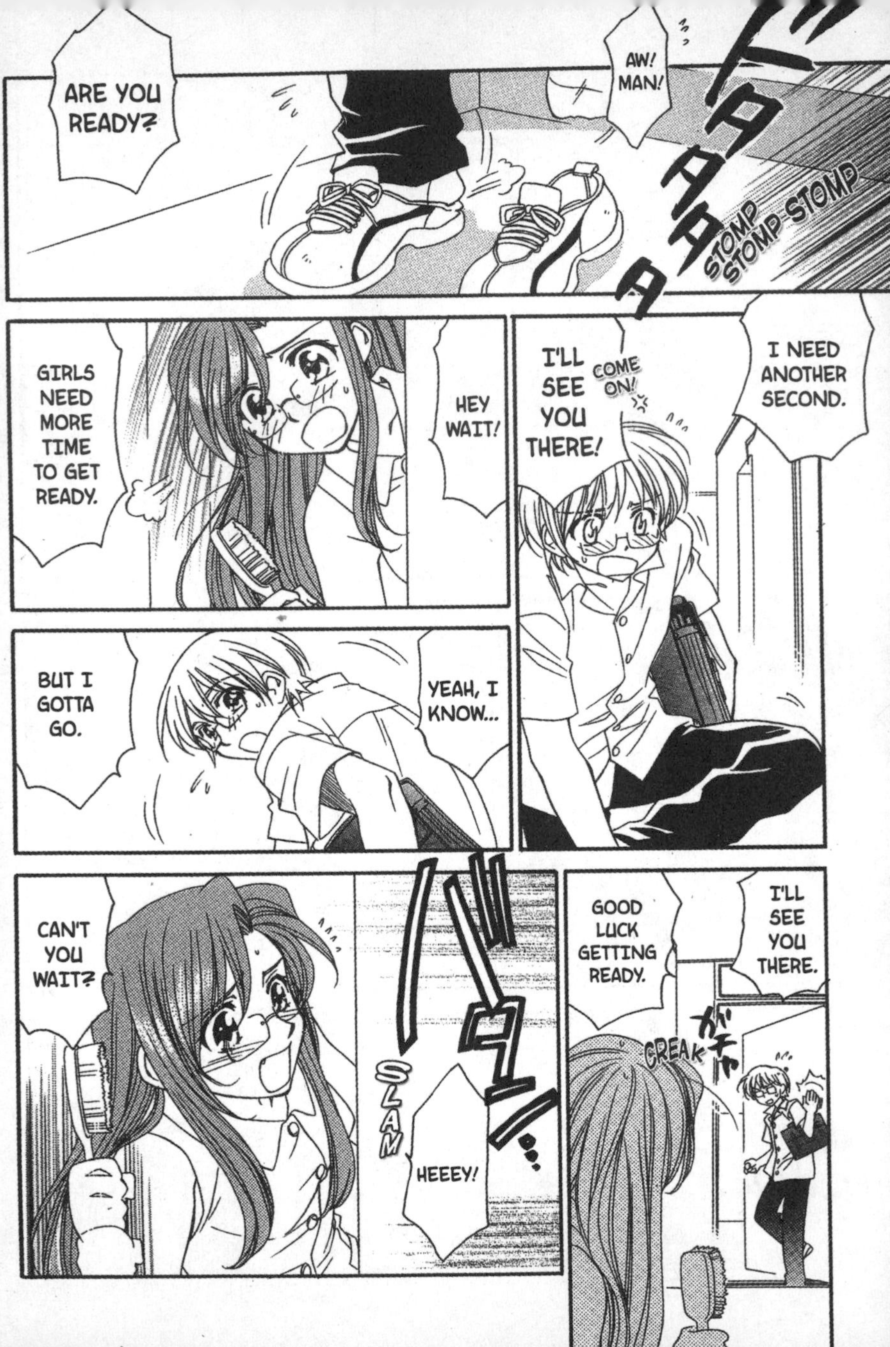
AW! MAN!
ドタタタタ
STOMP STOMP-STOMP
ARE YOU READY?
I NEED ANOTHER SECOND.
COME ON!
I'LL SEE YOU THERE!
HEY WAIT!
GIRLS NEED MORE TIME TO GET READY.
YEAH, I KNOW...
BUT I GOTTA GO.
I'LL SEE YOU THERE.
GOOD LUCK GETTING READY.
ガチャ
CREAK
バタン
SLAM
HEEEY!
CAN'T YOU WAIT?

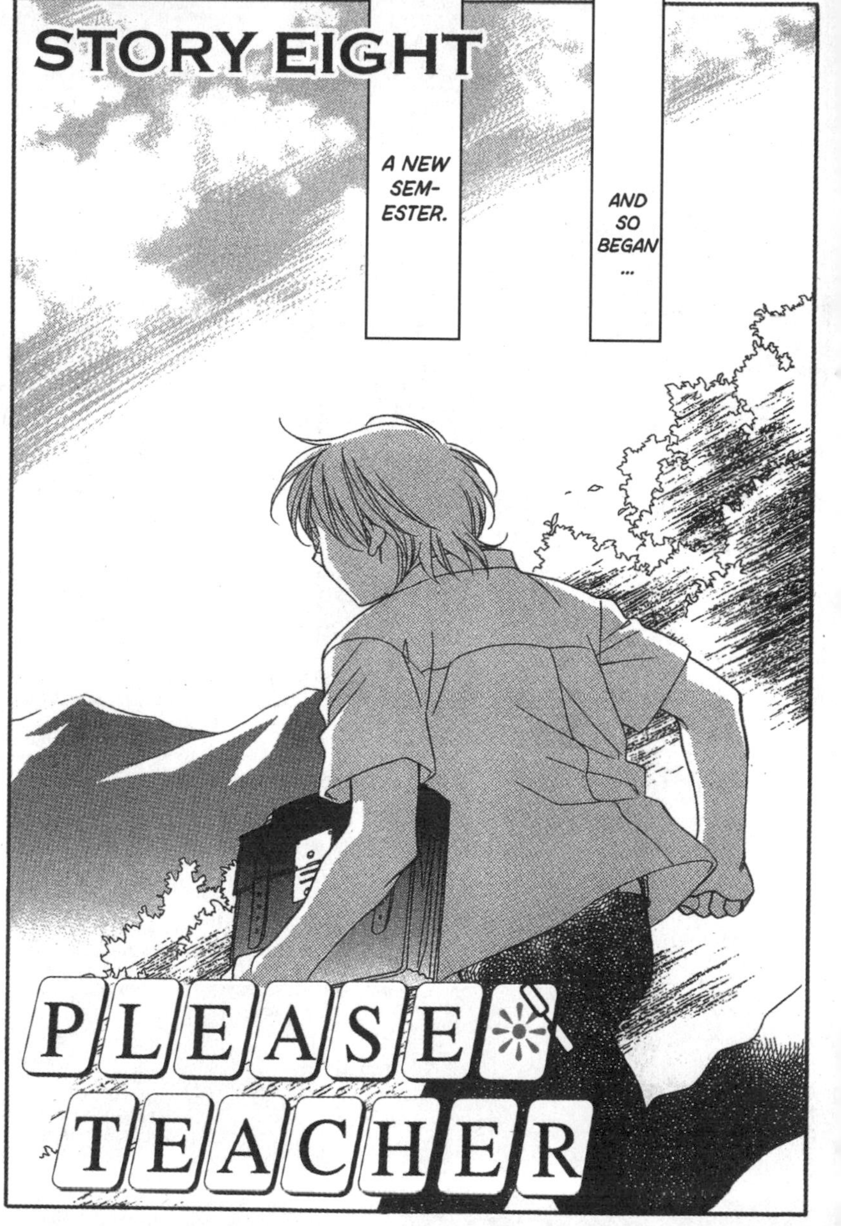
AND SO BEGAN ...
A NEW SEMESTER.
STORY EIGHT
PLEASE TEACHER

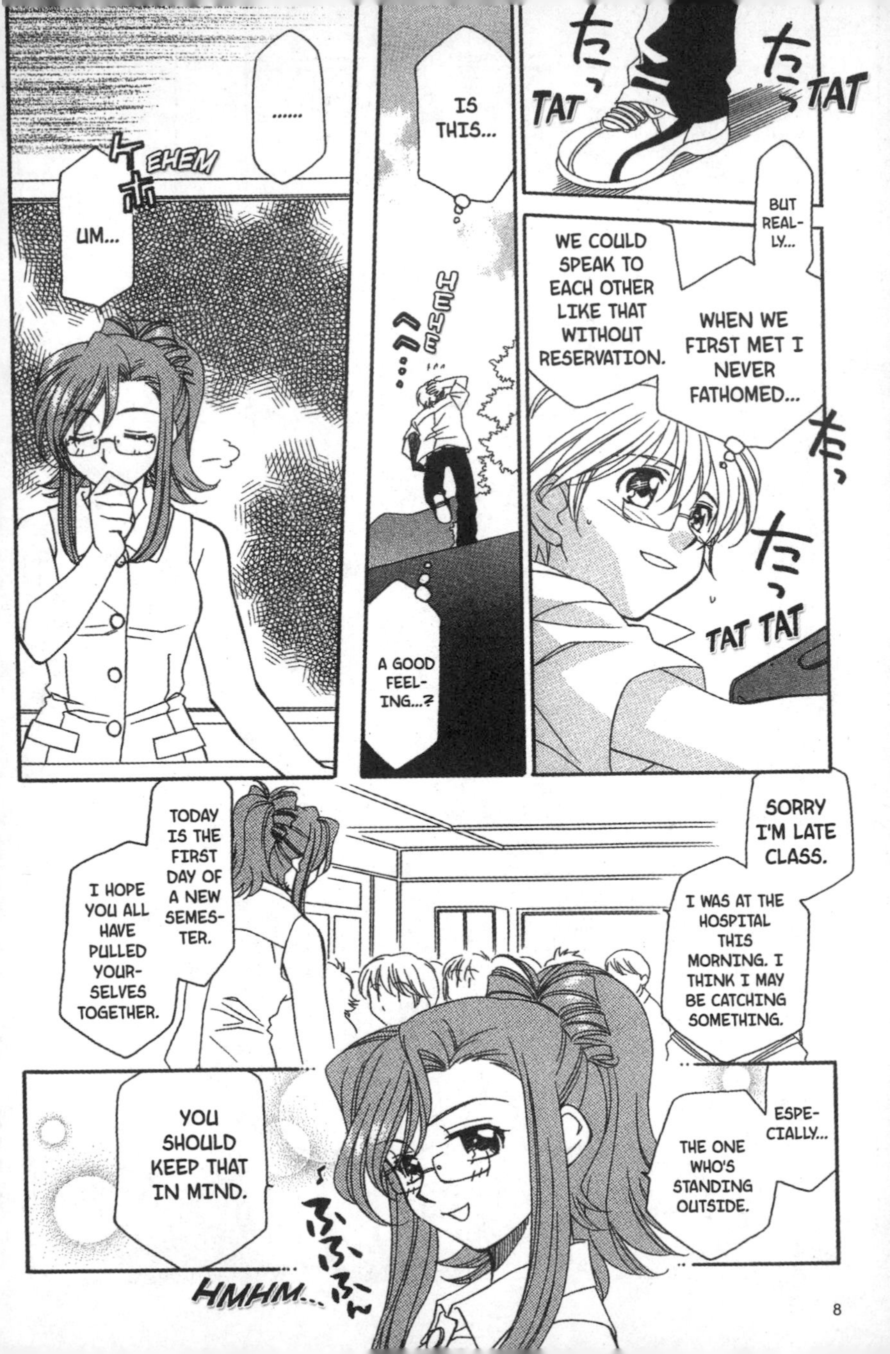
TAT
TAT
BUT REALLY...
WHEN WE FIRST MET I NEVER FATHOMED...
WE COULD SPEAK TO EACH OTHER LIKE THAT WITHOUT RESERVATION.
TAT TAT
IS THIS...
HEHE
A GOOD FEELING...?
......
EHEM
UM...
SORRY I'M LATE CLASS.
I WAS AT THE HOSPITAL THIS MORNING. I THINK I MAY BE CATCHING SOMETHING.
TODAY IS THE FIRST DAY OF A NEW SEMESTER.
I HOPE YOU ALL HAVE PULLED YOURSELVES TOGETHER.
ESPECIALLY...
THE ONE WHO'S STANDING OUTSIDE.
YOU SHOULD KEEP THAT IN MIND.
HMHM...

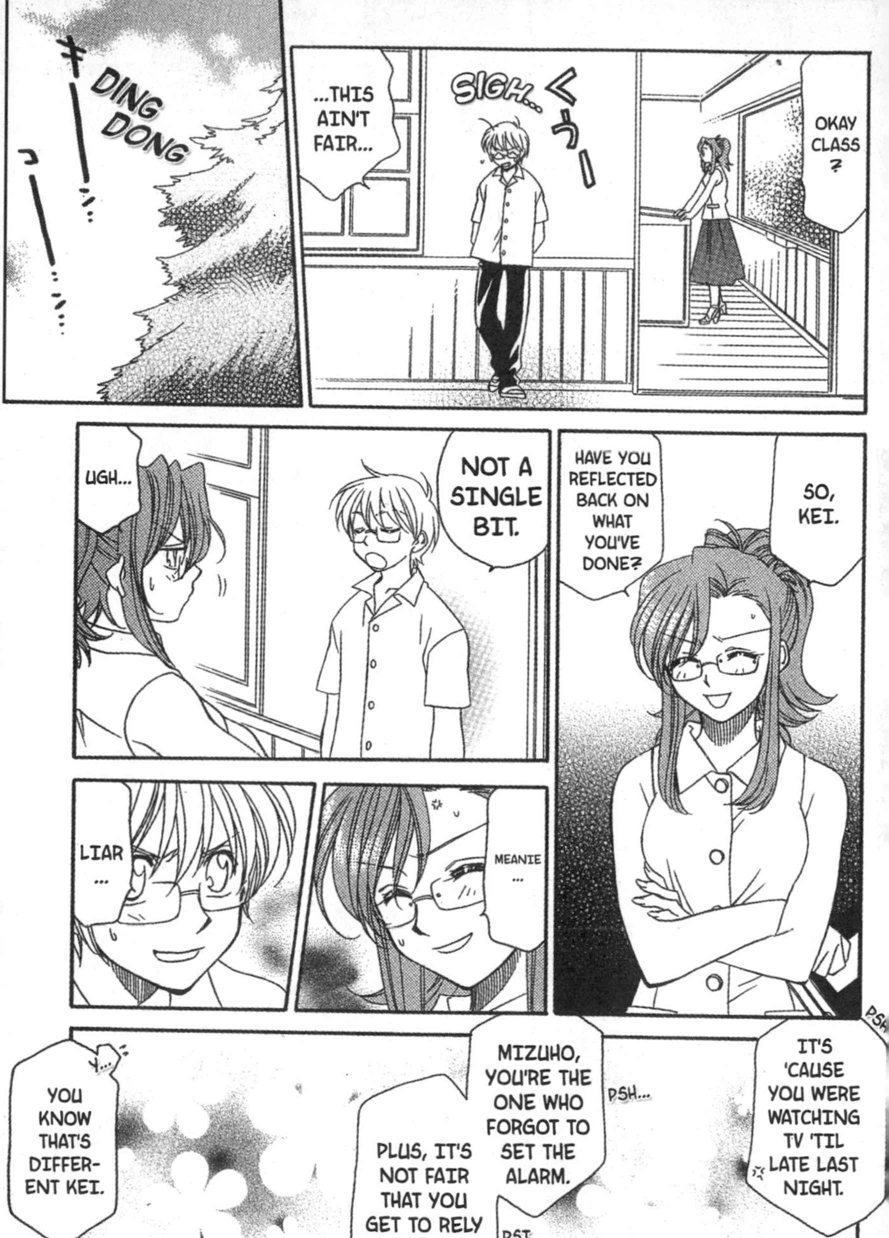
OKAY CLASS?
...THIS AIN'T FAIR...
SIGH... くぅー
DING DONG
キーン…コーン…
SO, KEI.
HAVE YOU REFLECTED BACK ON WHAT YOU'VE DONE?
NOT A SINGLE BIT.
UGH...
MEANIE...
LIAR...
IT'S 'CAUSE YOU WERE WATCHING TV 'TIL LATE LAST NIGHT.
PSH
MIZUHO, YOU'RE THE ONE WHO FORGOT TO SET THE ALARM.
PSH...
PLUS, IT'S NOT FAIR THAT YOU GET TO RELY ON MARIE.
PST...
Y...
YOU KNOW THAT'S DIFFER-ENT KEI.

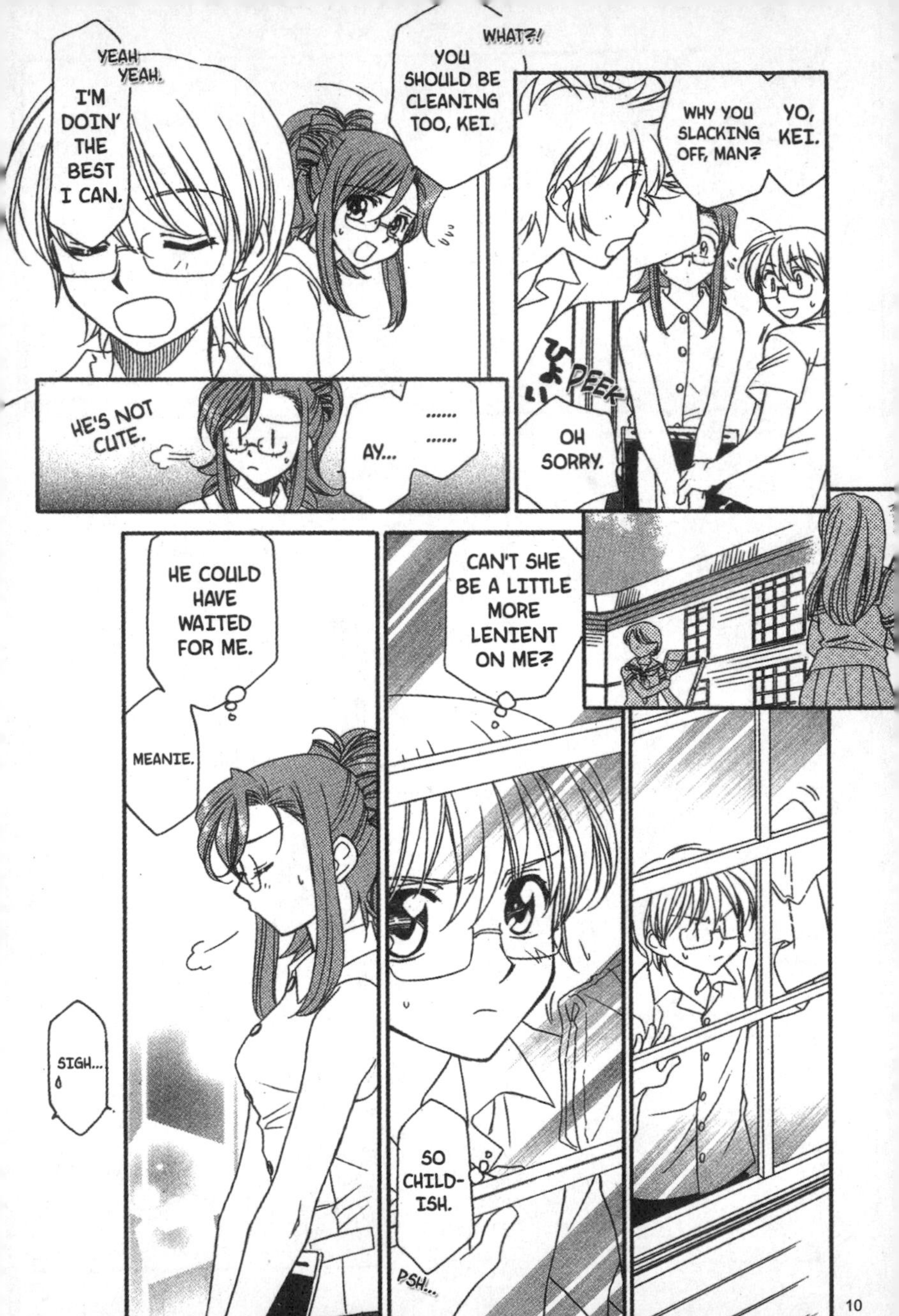
YO, KEI.
WHY YOU SLACKING OFF, MAN?
PEEK
OH SORRY.
WHAT?!
YOU SHOULD BE CLEANING TOO, KEI.
YEAH YEAH.
I'M DOIN' THE BEST I CAN.
......
......
AY...
HE'S NOT CUTE.
CAN'T SHE BE A LITTLE MORE LENIENT ON ME?
SO CHILD-ISH.
PSH...
HE COULD HAVE WAITED FOR ME.
MEANIE.
SIGH...

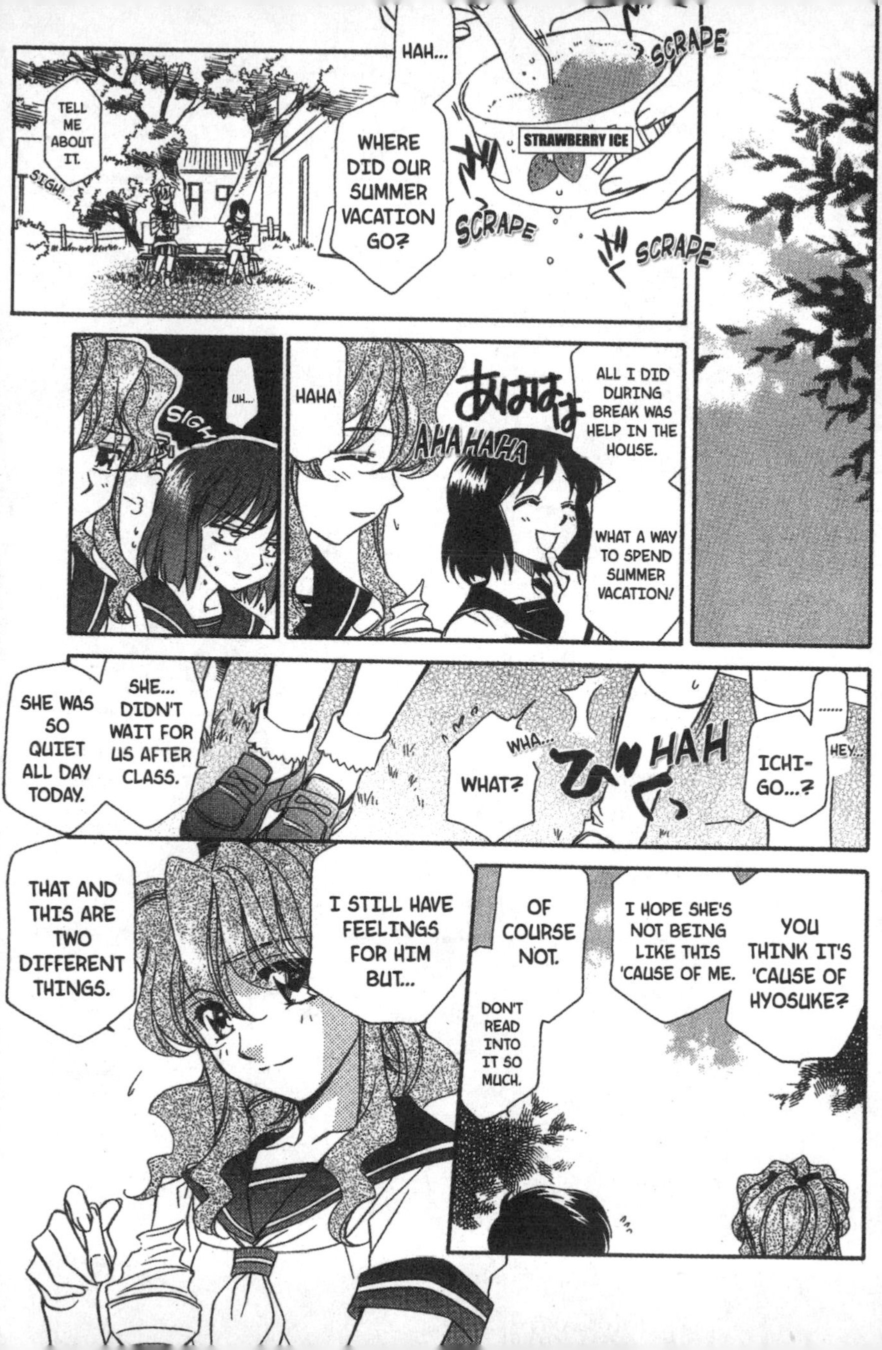

SCRAPE
SCRAPE
SCRAPE
STRAWBERRY ICE
HAH...
WHERE DID OUR SUMMER VACATION GO?
TELL ME ABOUT IT.
SIGH...
ALL I DID DURING BREAK WAS HELP IN THE HOUSE.
あははは
AHAHAHA
WHAT A WAY TO SPEND SUMMER VACATION!
HAHA
UH...
SIGH
......
HEY...
ICHI-GO...?
HAH
WHA...
WHAT?
SHE... DIDN'T WAIT FOR US AFTER CLASS.
SHE WAS SO QUIET ALL DAY TODAY.
YOU THINK IT'S 'CAUSE OF HYOSUKE?
I HOPE SHE'S NOT BEING LIKE THIS 'CAUSE OF ME.
OF COURSE NOT.
DON'T READ INTO IT SO MUCH.
I STILL HAVE FEELINGS FOR HIM BUT...
THAT AND THIS ARE TWO DIFFERENT THINGS.

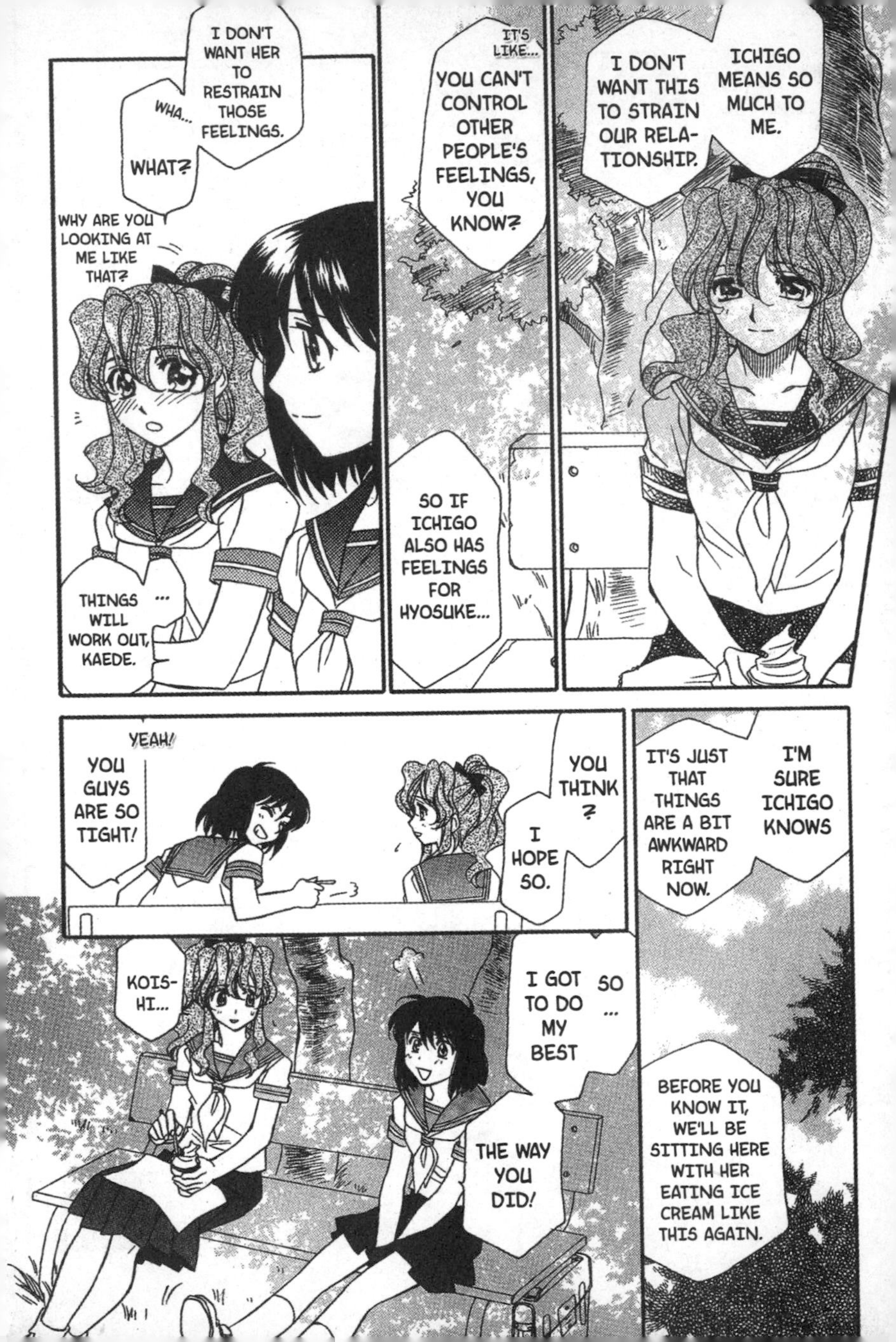
ICHIGO MEANS SO MUCH TO ME.
I DON'T WANT THIS TO STRAIN OUR RELA-TIONSHIP.
IT'S LIKE...
YOU CAN'T CONTROL OTHER PEOPLE'S FEELINGS, YOU KNOW?
SO IF ICHIGO ALSO HAS FEELINGS FOR HYOSUKE...
I DON'T WANT HER TO RESTRAIN THOSE FEELINGS.
WHA...
WHAT?
WHY ARE YOU LOOKING AT ME LIKE THAT?
... THINGS WILL WORK OUT, KAEDE.
I'M SURE ICHIGO KNOWS
IT'S JUST THAT THINGS ARE A BIT AWKWARD RIGHT NOW.
BEFORE YOU KNOW IT, WE'LL BE SITTING HERE WITH HER EATING ICE CREAM LIKE THIS AGAIN.
YOU THINK?
I HOPE SO.
YEAH!
YOU GUYS ARE SO TIGHT!
SO...
I GOT TO DO MY BEST
KOIS-HI...
THE WAY YOU DID!

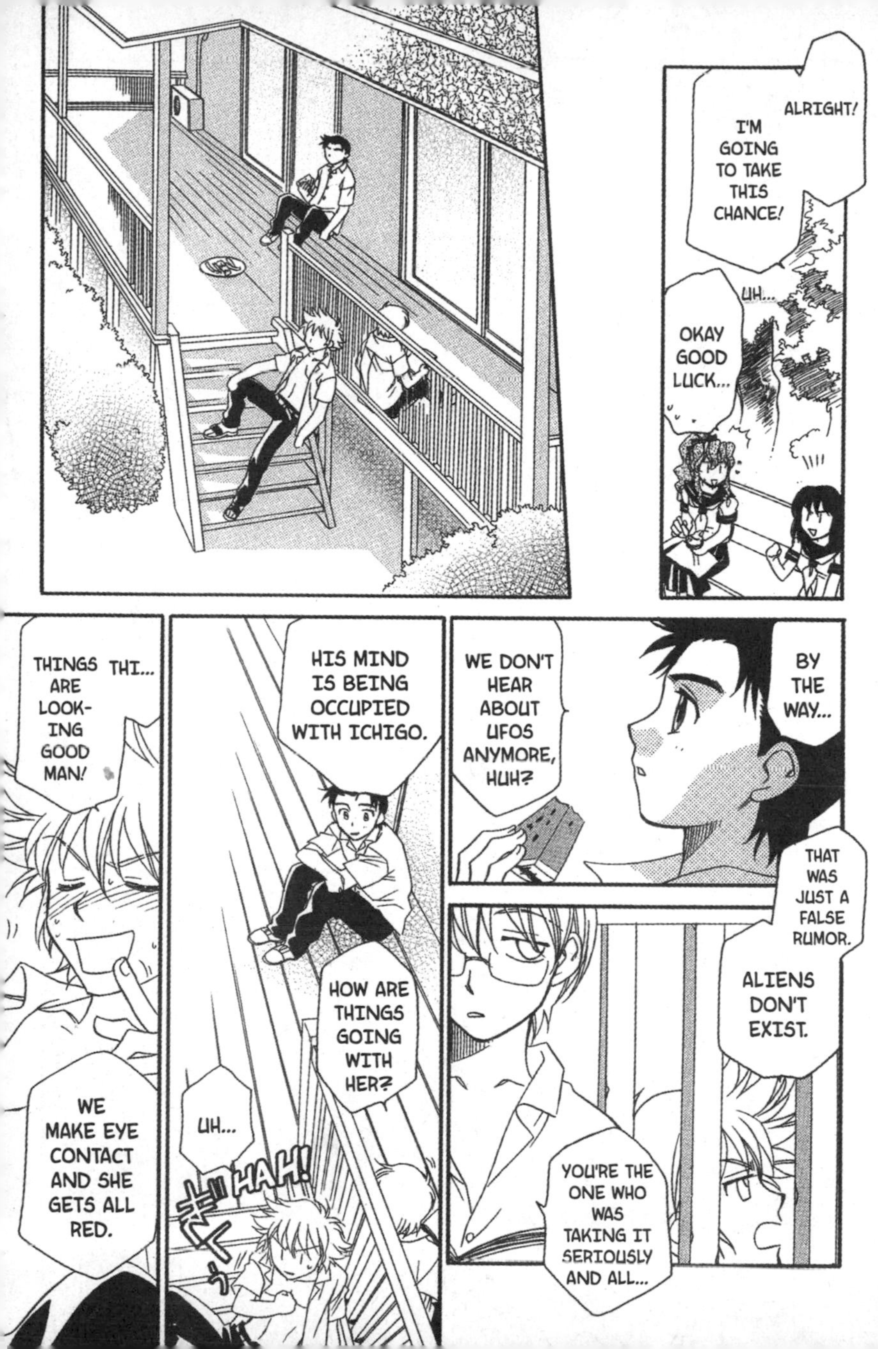
ALRIGHT! I'M GOING TO TAKE THIS CHANCE!
UH...
OKAY GOOD LUCK...
BY THE WAY...
WE DON'T HEAR ABOUT UFOS ANYMORE, HUH?
THAT WAS JUST A FALSE RUMOR.
ALIENS DON'T EXIST.
YOU'RE THE ONE WHO WAS TAKING IT SERIOUSLY AND ALL...
HIS MIND IS BEING OCCUPIED WITH ICHIGO.
HOW ARE THINGS GOING WITH HER?
UH...
HAH!
THI...
THINGS ARE LOOKING GOOD MAN!
WE MAKE EYE CONTACT AND SHE GETS ALL RED.

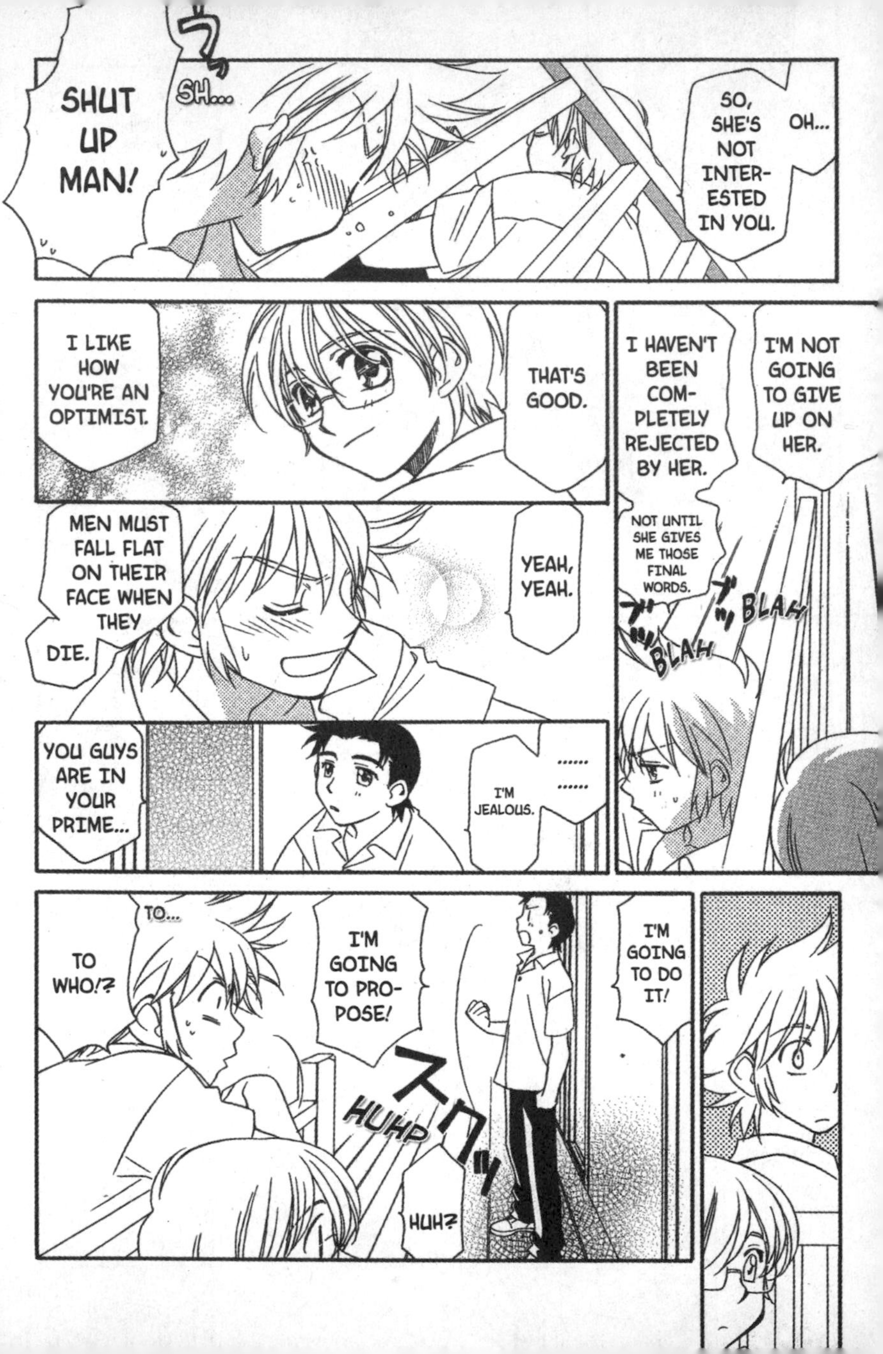
OH...
SO, SHE'S NOT INTERESTED IN YOU.
SH...
SHUT UP MAN!
I'M NOT GOING TO GIVE UP ON HER.
I HAVEN'T BEEN COMPLETELY REJECTED BY HER.
NOT UNTIL SHE GIVES ME THOSE FINAL WORDS.
BLAH
BLAH
THAT'S GOOD.
I LIKE HOW YOU'RE AN OPTIMIST.
YEAH, YEAH.
MEN MUST FALL FLAT ON THEIR FACE WHEN THEY DIE.
......
......
I'M JEALOUS.
YOU GUYS ARE IN YOUR PRIME...
I'M GOING TO DO IT!
I'M GOING TO PROPOSE!
TO...
TO WHO!?
HUHP
HUH?

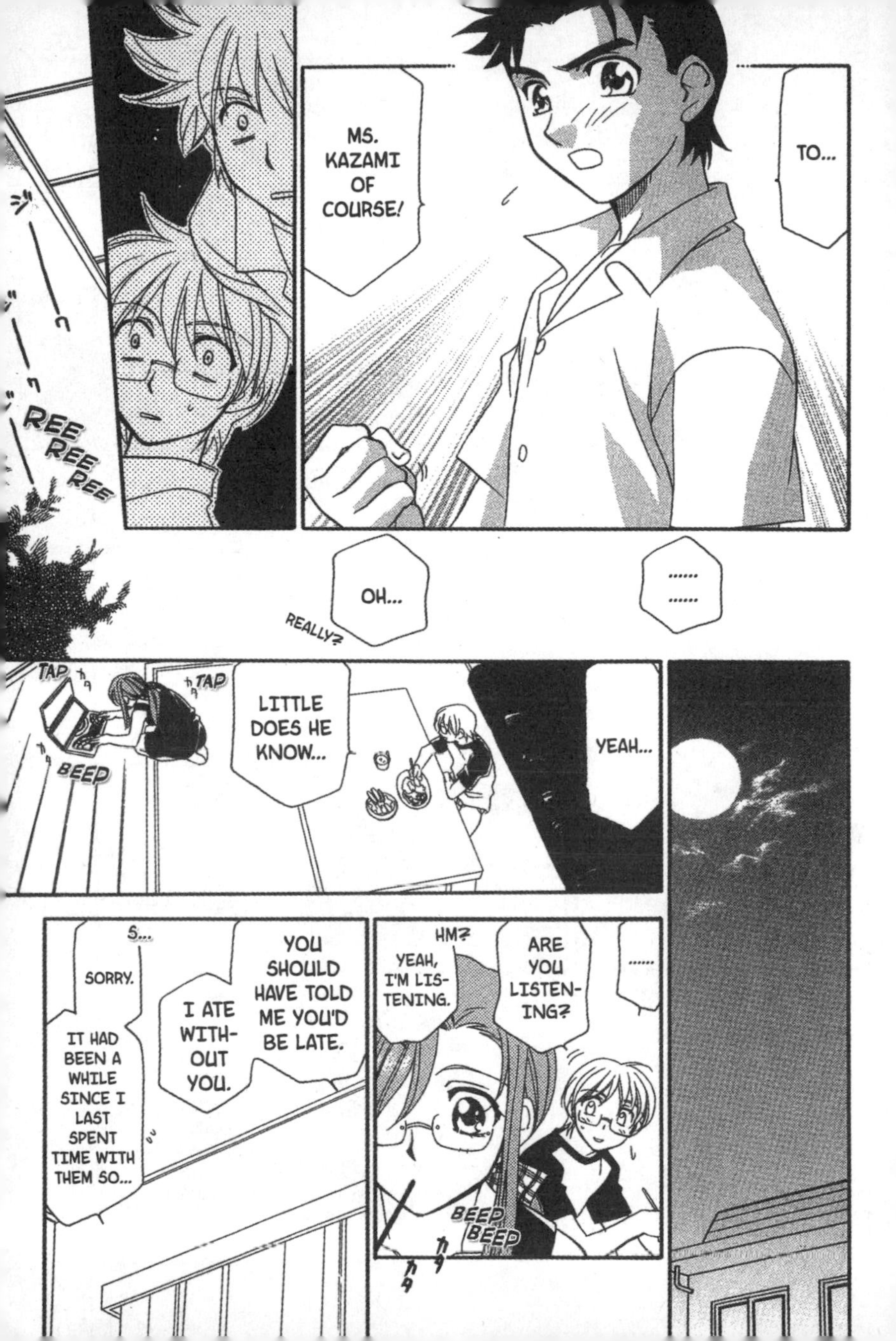
TO...
MS. KAZAMI OF COURSE!
REE REE REE
......
......
OH...
REALLY?
YEAH...
LITTLE DOES HE KNOW...
TAP
TAP
BEEP
......
ARE YOU LISTEN-ING?
HM?
YEAH, I'M LIS-TENING.
BEEP BEEP
YOU SHOULD HAVE TOLD ME YOU'D BE LATE.
I ATE WITH-OUT YOU.
S...
SORRY.
IT HAD BEEN A WHILE SINCE I LAST SPENT TIME WITH THEM SO...

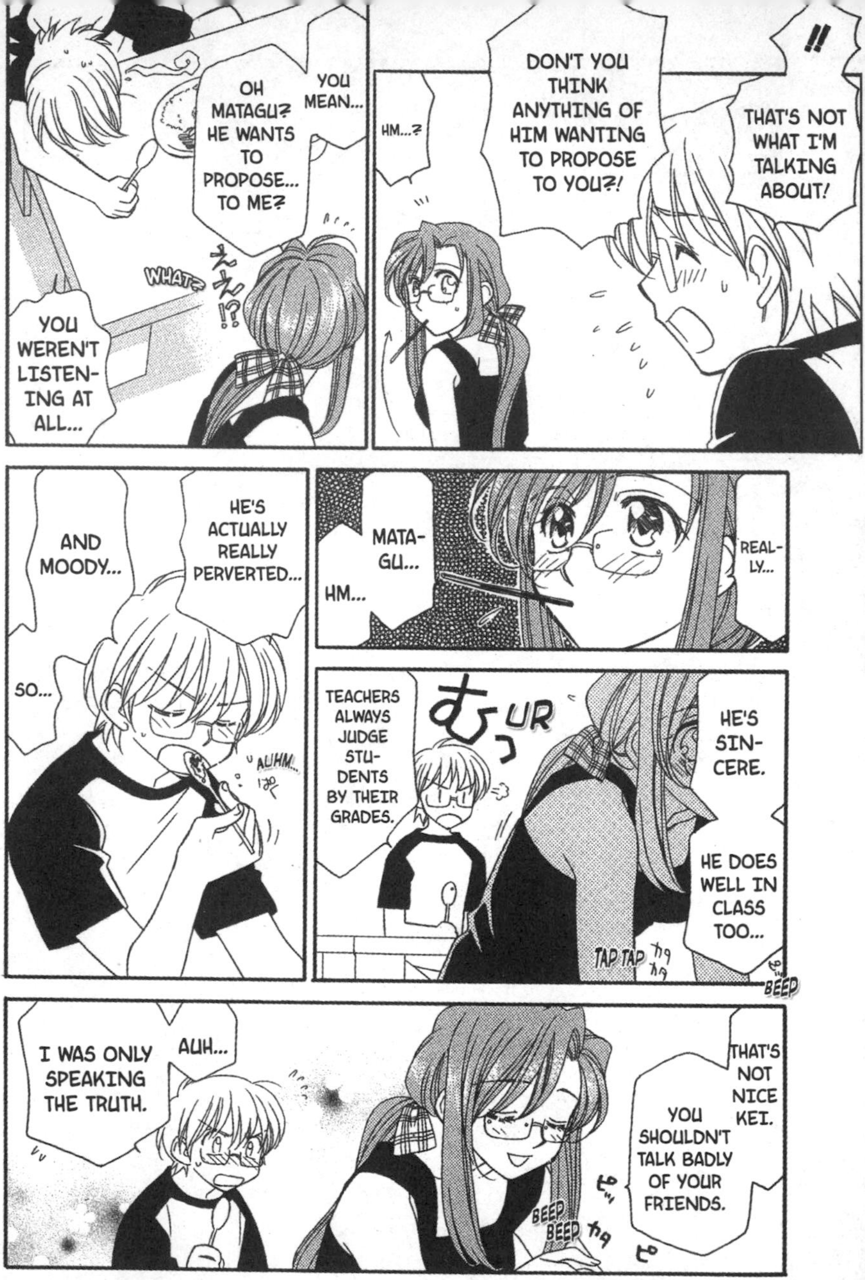
!!
THAT'S NOT WHAT I'M TALKING ABOUT!
DON'T YOU THINK ANYTHING OF HIM WANTING TO PROPOSE TO YOU?!
HM...?
YOU MEAN...
OH MATAGU? HE WANTS TO PROPOSE... TO ME?
WHAT?
ええ!?
YOU WEREN'T LISTEN-ING AT ALL...
REAL-LY...
MATA-GU...
HM...
HE'S SIN-CERE.
HE DOES WELL IN CLASS TOO...
BEEP
TAP TAP
TEACHERS ALWAYS JUDGE STU-DENTS BY THEIR GRADES.
UR
HE'S ACTUALLY REALLY PERVERTED...
AND MOODY...
SO...
AUHM...
THAT'S NOT NICE KEI.
YOU SHOULDN'T TALK BADLY OF YOUR FRIENDS.
BEEP BEEP
AUH...
I WAS ONLY SPEAKING THE TRUTH.

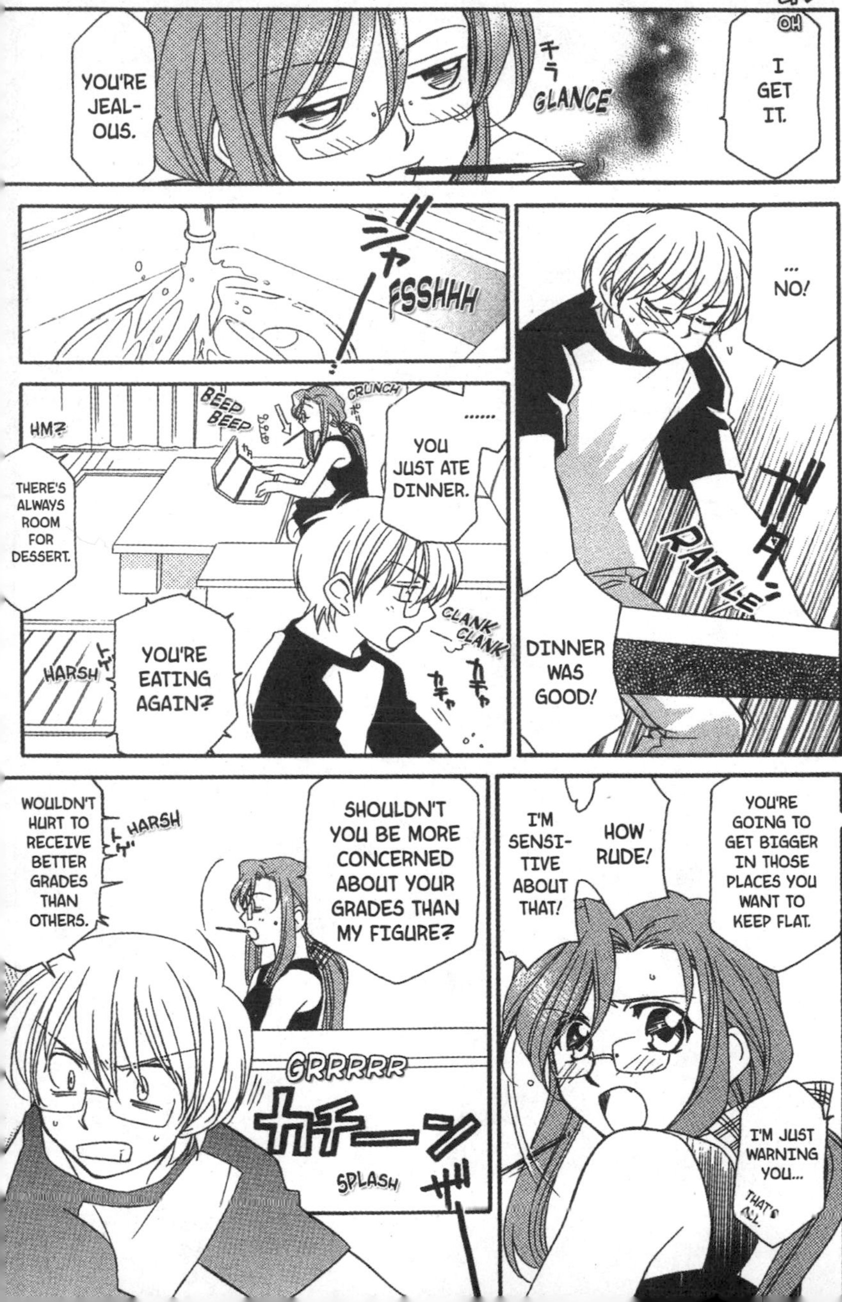
OH
I GET IT.
GLANCE
YOU'RE JEAL-OUS.
... NO!
RATTLE
DINNER WAS GOOD!
FSSHHH
CRUNCH
......
YOU JUST ATE DINNER.
BEEP BEEP
HM?
THERE'S ALWAYS ROOM FOR DESSERT.
CLANK CLANK
YOU'RE EATING AGAIN?
HARSH
YOU'RE GOING TO GET BIGGER IN THOSE PLACES YOU WANT TO KEEP FLAT.
HOW RUDE!
I'M SENSI-TIVE ABOUT THAT!
I'M JUST WARNING YOU...
THAT'S ALL.
SHOULDN'T YOU BE MORE CONCERNED ABOUT YOUR GRADES THAN MY FIGURE?
WOULDN'T HURT TO RECEIVE BETTER GRADES THAN OTHERS.
HARSH
GRRRRR
SPLASH

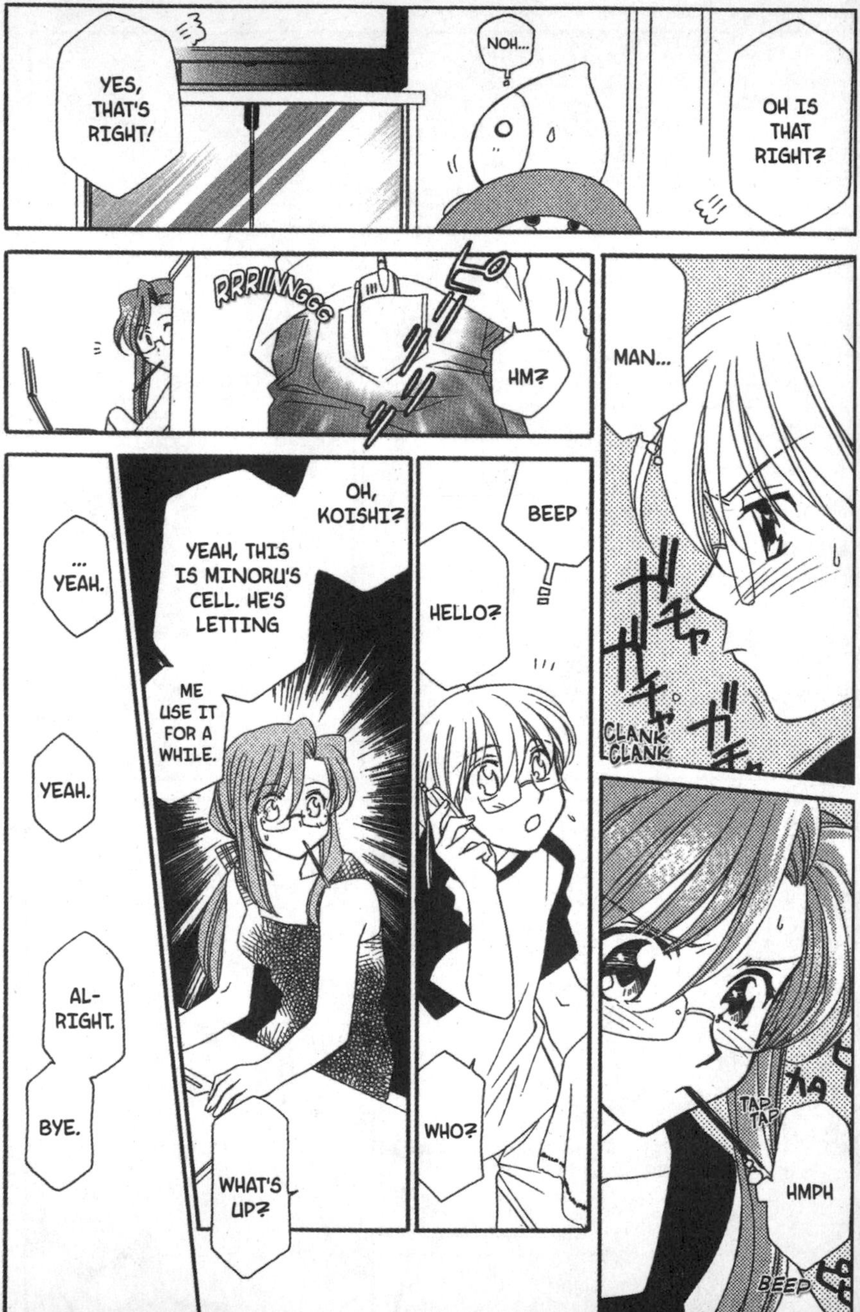
OH IS THAT RIGHT?
NOH...
YES, THAT'S RIGHT!
MAN...
CLANK CLANK
TAP TAP
HMPH
BEEP
RRRIINNGGG
HM?
BEEP
HELLO?
WHO?
OH, KOISHI?
YEAH, THIS IS MINORU'S CELL. HE'S LETTING
ME USE IT FOR A WHILE.
WHAT'S UP?
... YEAH.
YEAH.
AL-RIGHT.
BYE.

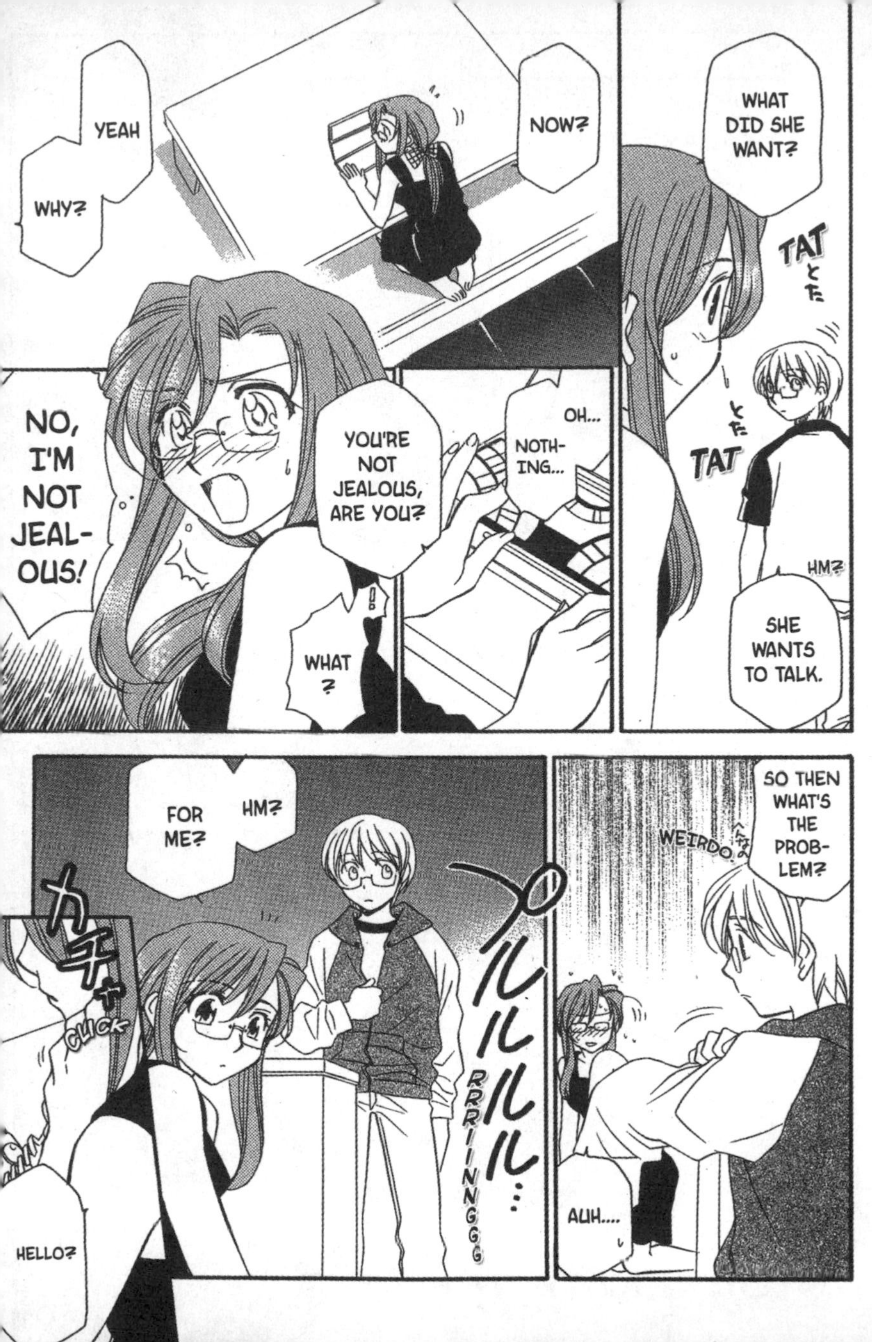
WHAT DID SHE WANT?
TAT とた
とた TAT
HM?
SHE WANTS TO TALK.
NOW?
YEAH
WHY?
OH... NOTHING...
YOU'RE NOT JEALOUS, ARE YOU?
WHAT ?
NO, I'M NOT JEALOUS!
SO THEN WHAT'S THE PROBLEM?
WEIRDO. へんなの
AUH....
HM?
FOR ME?
プルルル…
RRRIINNGGG
カチャ
CLICK
HELLO?

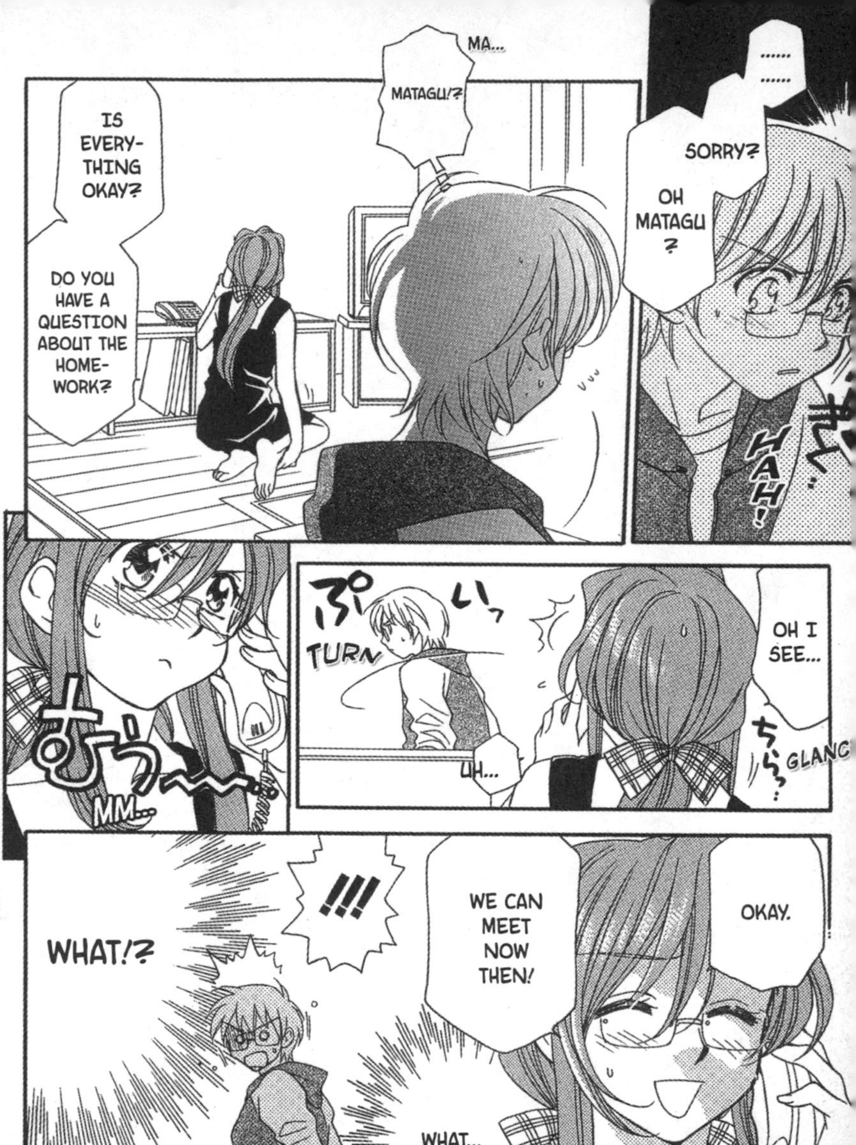
......
......
SORRY?
OH MATAGU ?
HAH!
MA...
MATAGU!?
IS EVERY-THING OKAY?
DO YOU HAVE A QUESTION ABOUT THE HOME-WORK?
OH I SEE...
GLANC
TURN
UH...
MM...
OKAY.
WE CAN MEET NOW THEN!
!!!
WHAT!?
WHAT...

STORY EIGHT - THE END

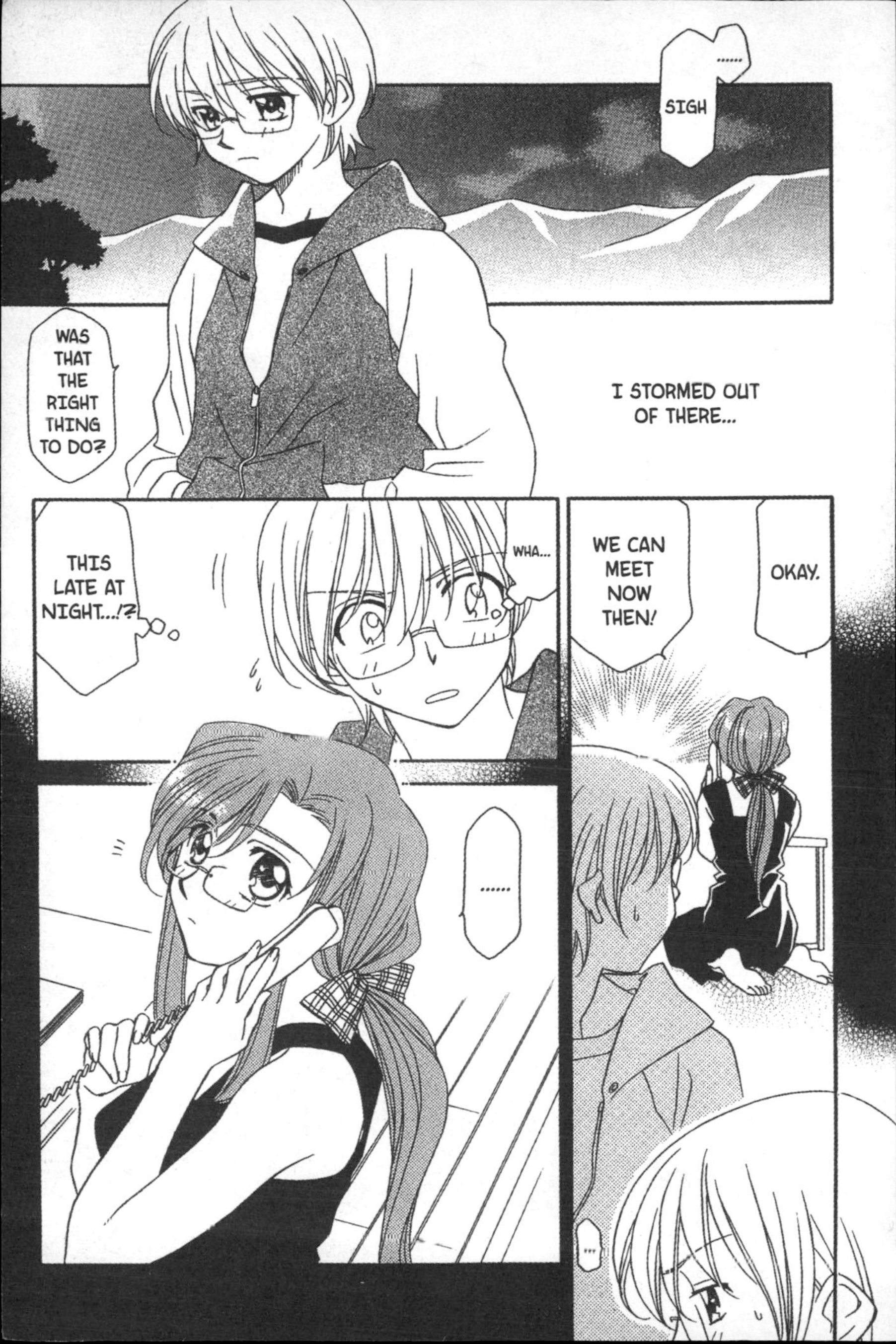

......
SIGH
I STORMED OUT OF THERE...
WAS THAT THE RIGHT THING TO DO?
OKAY.
WE CAN MEET NOW THEN!
...
WHA...
THIS LATE AT NIGHT...!?
......

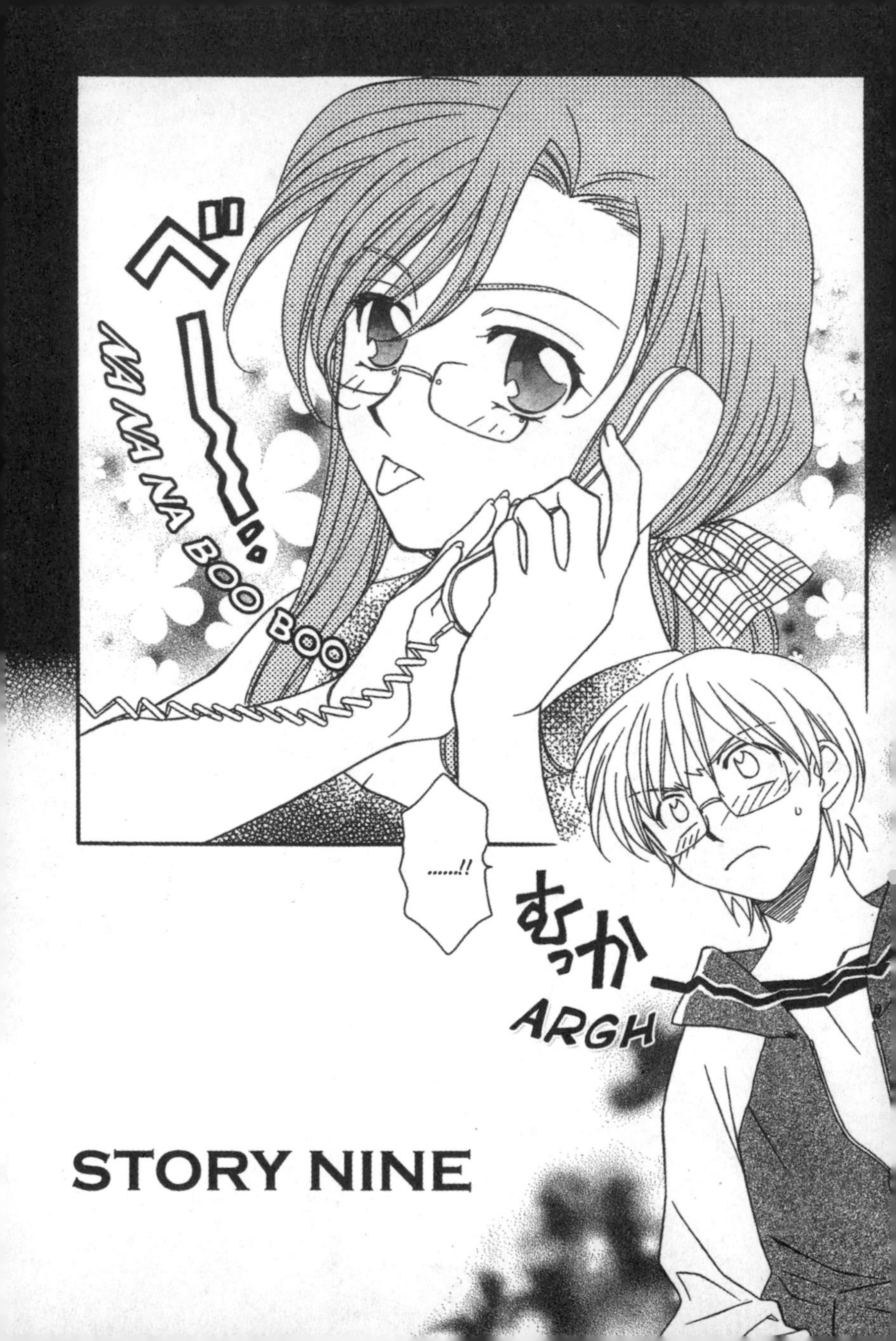
べーーー!!
AH NA NA BOO BOO
むっかー
ARGH
......!!

STORY NINE

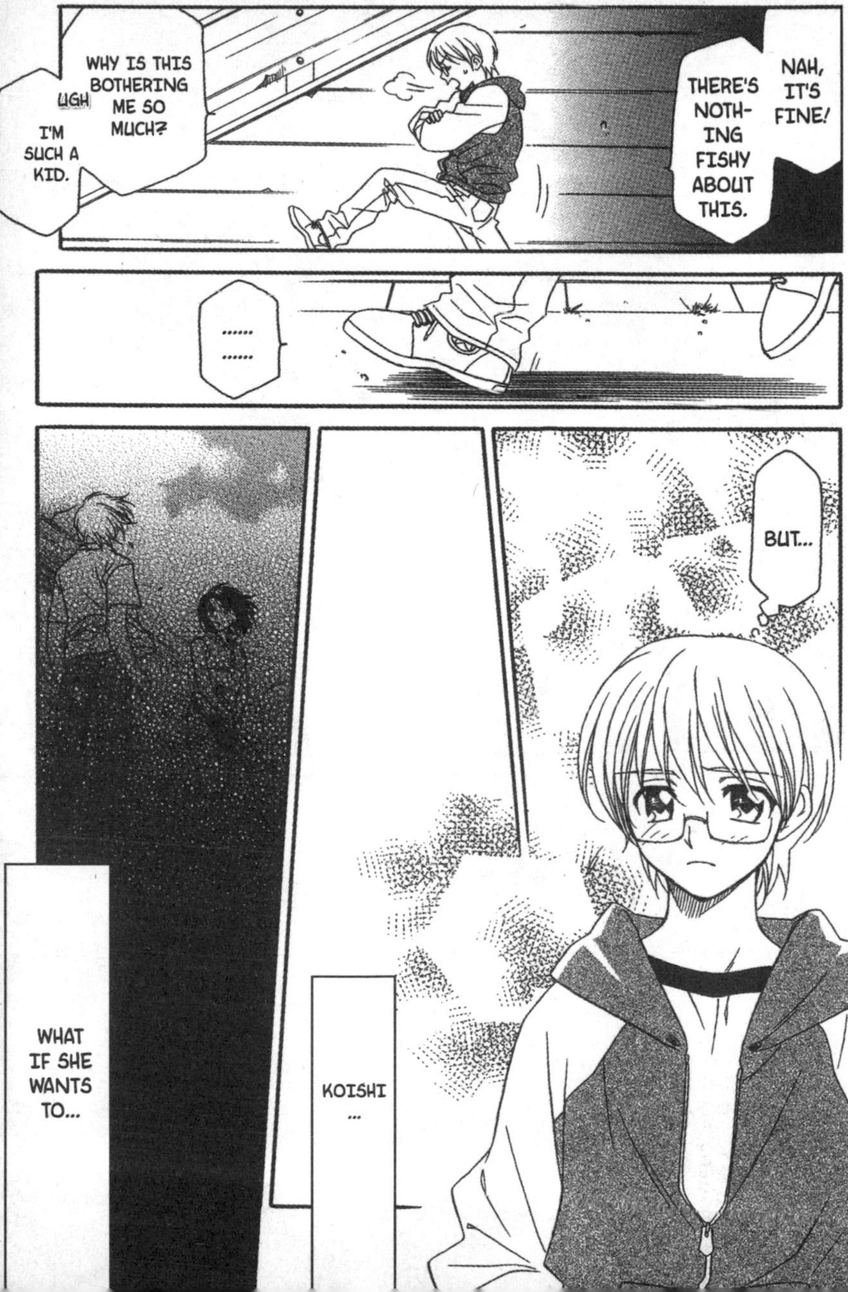
NAH, IT'S FINE!
THERE'S NOTH-ING FISHY ABOUT THIS.
WHY IS THIS BOTHERING ME SO MUCH?
UGH
I'M SUCH A KID.
......
......
BUT...
KOISHI ...
WHAT IF SHE WANTS TO...

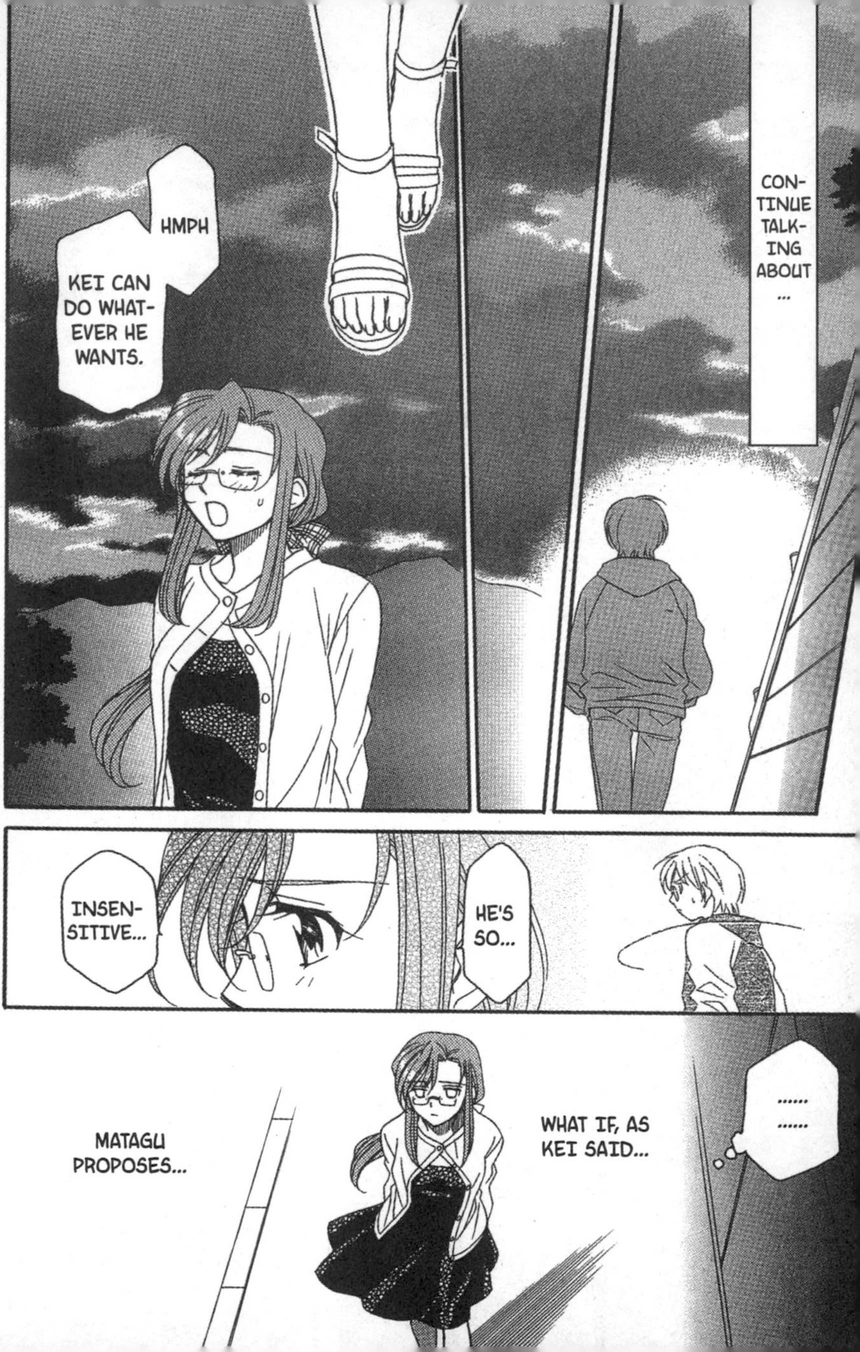
CON-
TINUE
TALK-
ING
ABOUT
...
HMPH
KEI CAN DO WHAT-EVER HE WANTS.
HE'S SO...
INSEN-SITIVE...
......
......
WHAT IF, AS KEI SAID...
MATAGU PROPOSES...

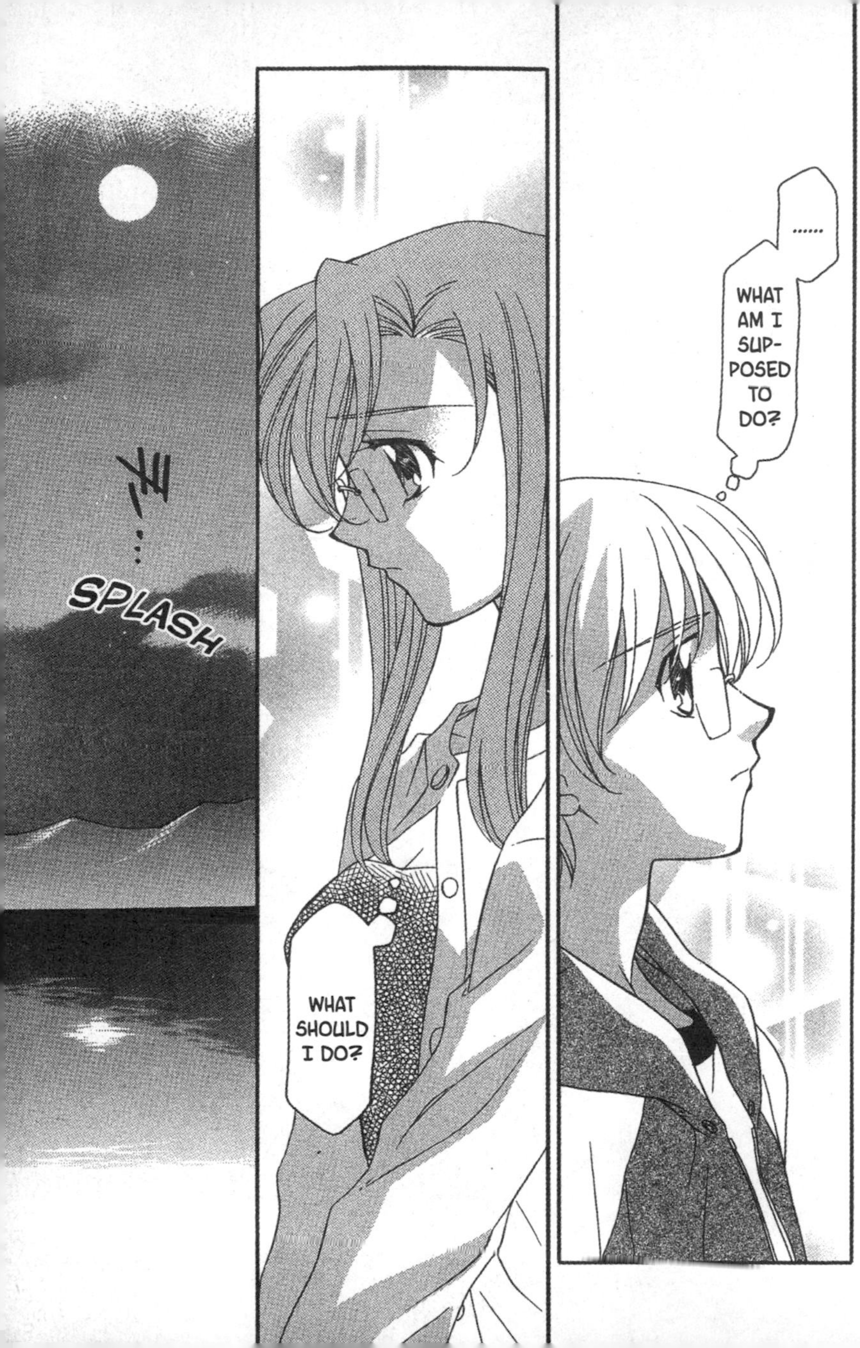
...... WHAT AM I SUP-POSED TO DO?
WHAT SHOULD I DO?
SPLASH

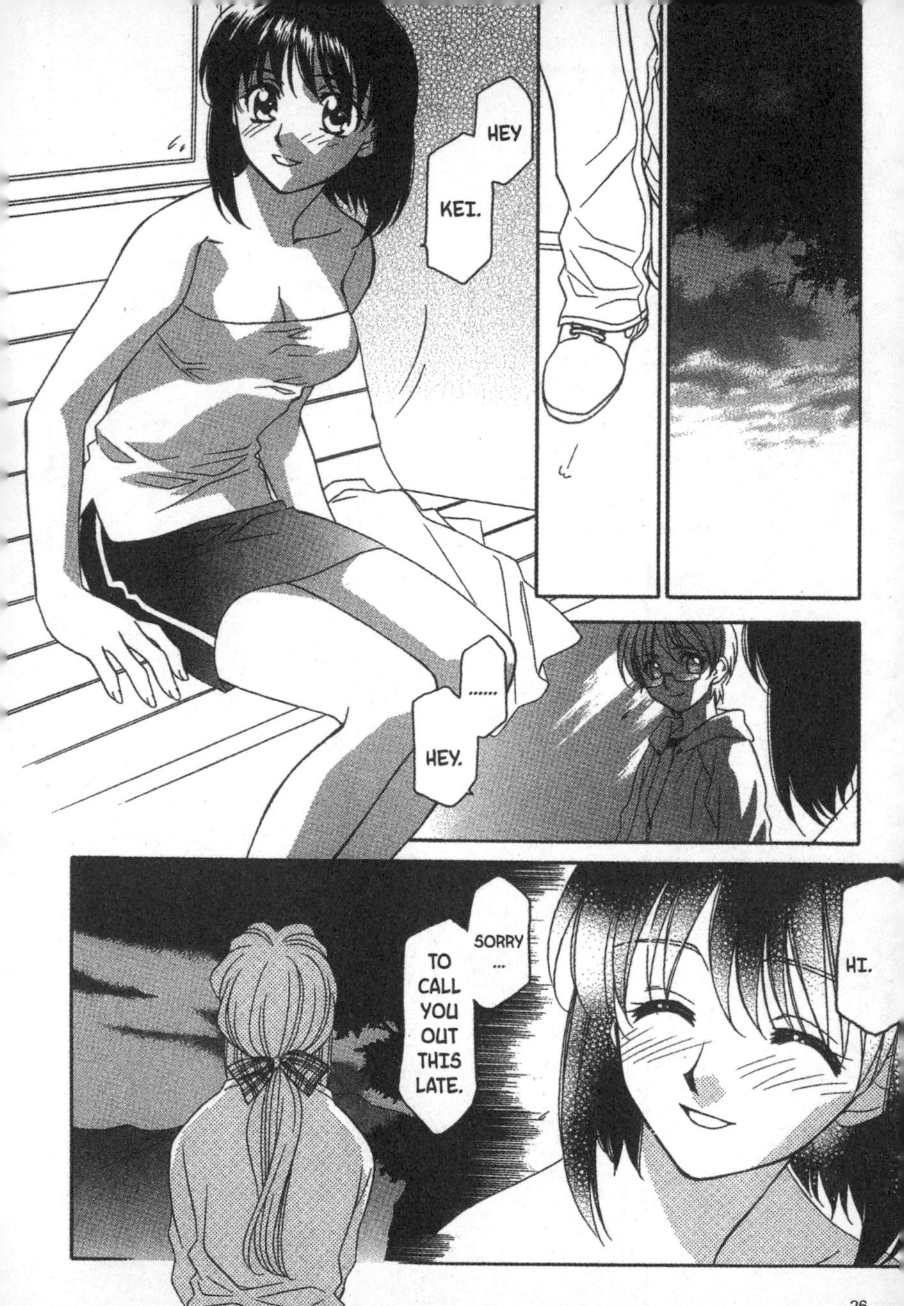
HEY KEI.
...... HEY.
HI.
SORRY ...
TO CALL YOU OUT THIS LATE.

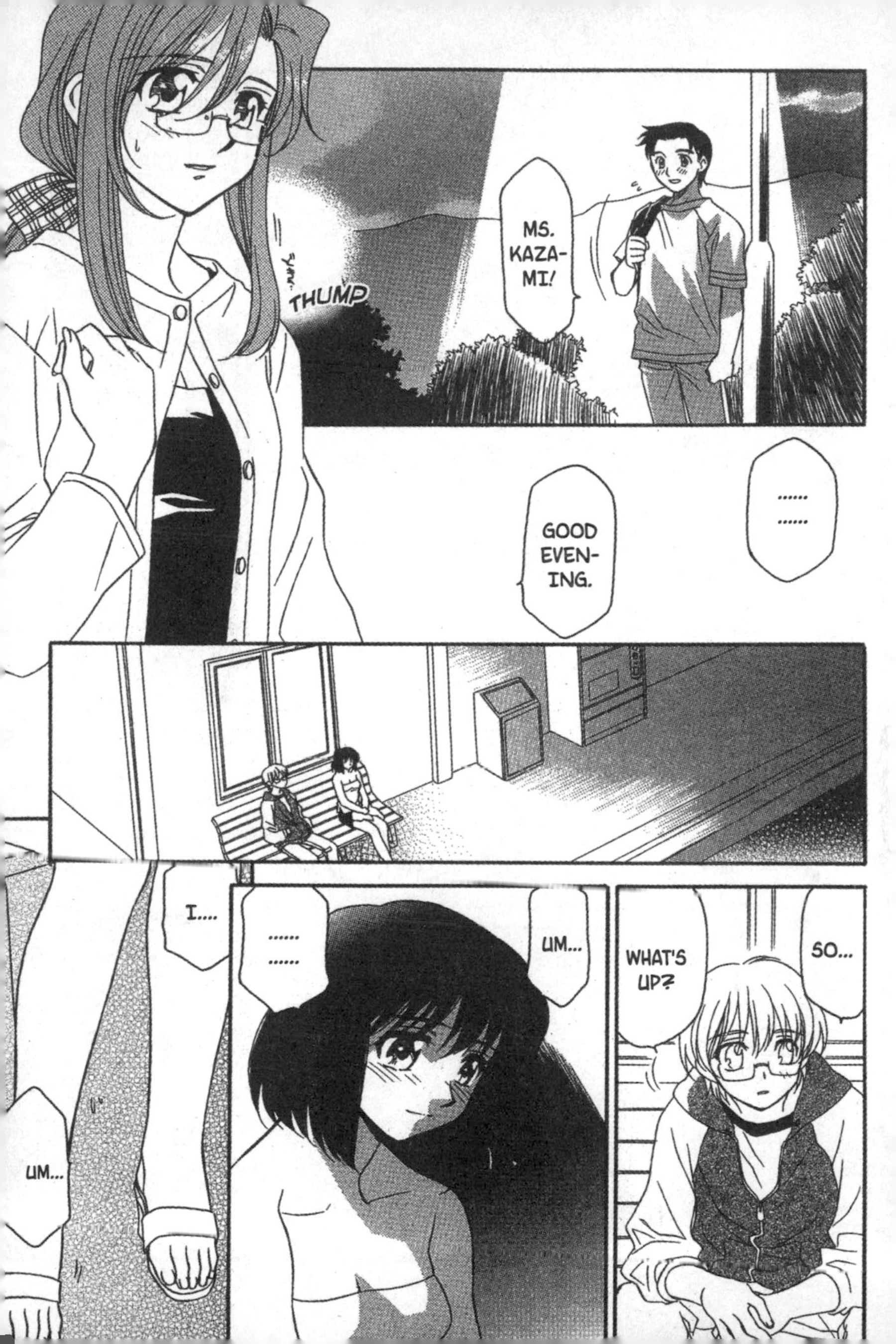
MS. KAZAMI!
THUMP
......
......
GOOD EVENING.
SO...
WHAT'S UP?
UM...
......
......
I....
UM...

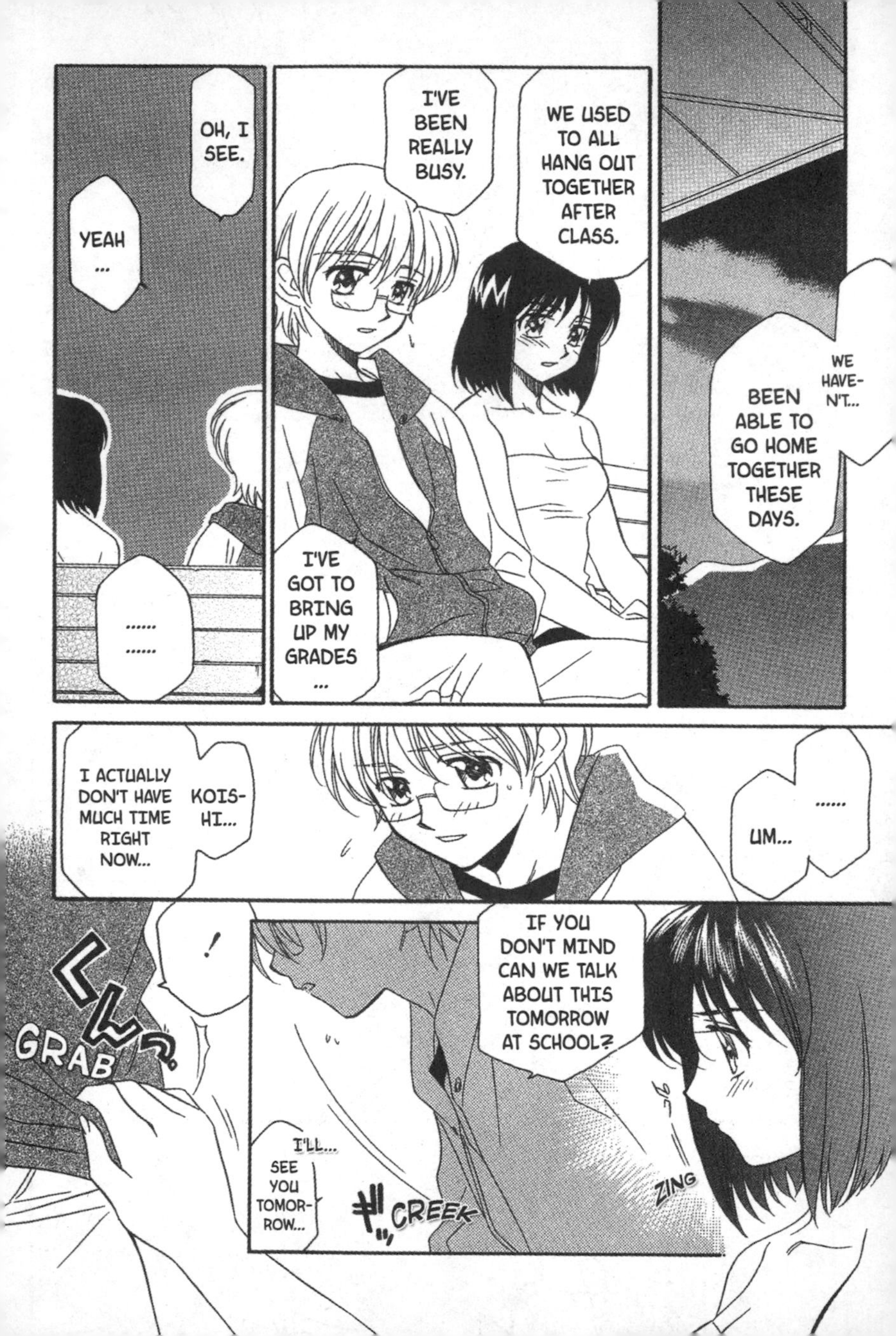
WE HAVEN'T... BEEN ABLE TO GO HOME TOGETHER THESE DAYS.
WE USED TO ALL HANG OUT TOGETHER AFTER CLASS.
I'VE BEEN REALLY BUSY.
I'VE GOT TO BRING UP MY GRADES ...
OH, I SEE.
YEAH ...
....
...... UM...
KOISHI...
I ACTUALLY DON'T HAVE MUCH TIME RIGHT NOW...
IF YOU DON'T MIND CAN WE TALK ABOUT THIS TOMORROW AT SCHOOL?
ZING
CREEK
I'LL... SEE YOU TOMORROW...
!
GRAB

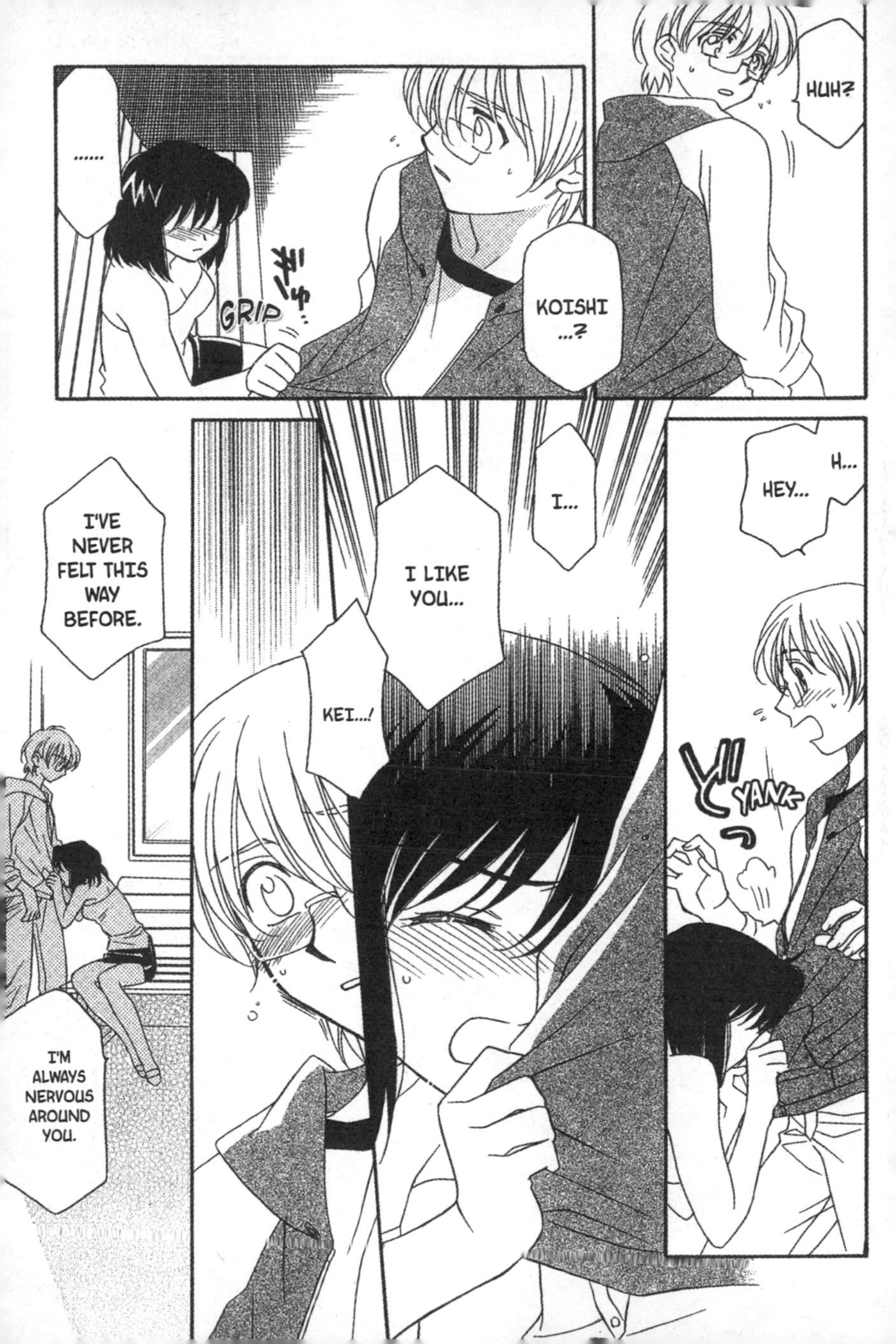
HUH?
KOISHI ...?
......
GRIP
H... HEY...
YANK
I...
I LIKE YOU...
KEI...!
I'VE NEVER FELT THIS WAY BEFORE.
I'M ALWAYS NERVOUS AROUND YOU.

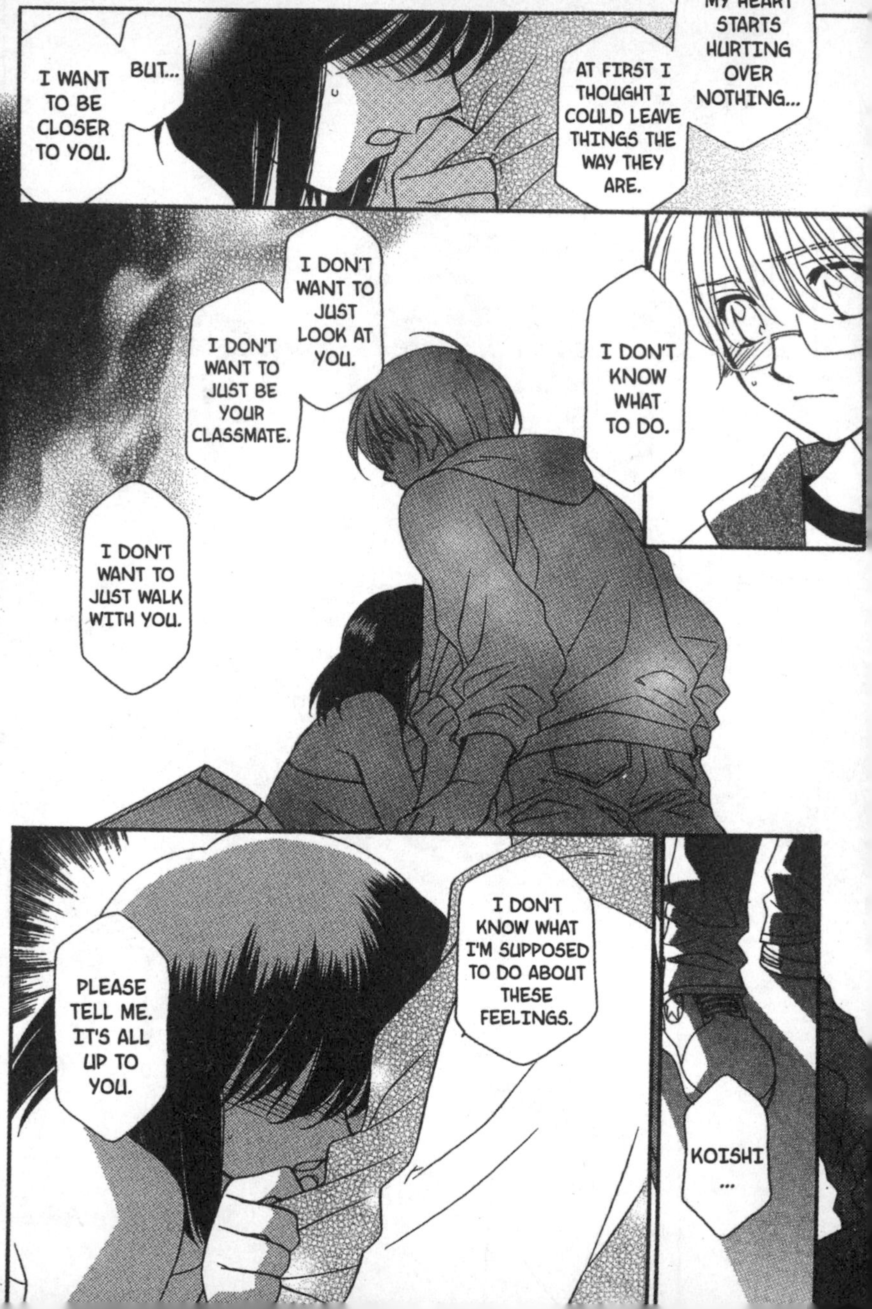
MY HEART STARTS HURTING OVER NOTHING...
AT FIRST I THOUGHT I COULD LEAVE THINGS THE WAY THEY ARE.
BUT...
I WANT TO BE CLOSER TO YOU.
I DON'T KNOW WHAT TO DO.
I DON'T WANT TO JUST LOOK AT YOU.
I DON'T WANT TO JUST BE YOUR CLASSMATE.
I DON'T WANT TO JUST WALK WITH YOU.
KOISHI ...
I DON'T KNOW WHAT I'M SUPPOSED TO DO ABOUT THESE FEELINGS.
PLEASE TELL ME. IT'S ALL UP TO YOU.

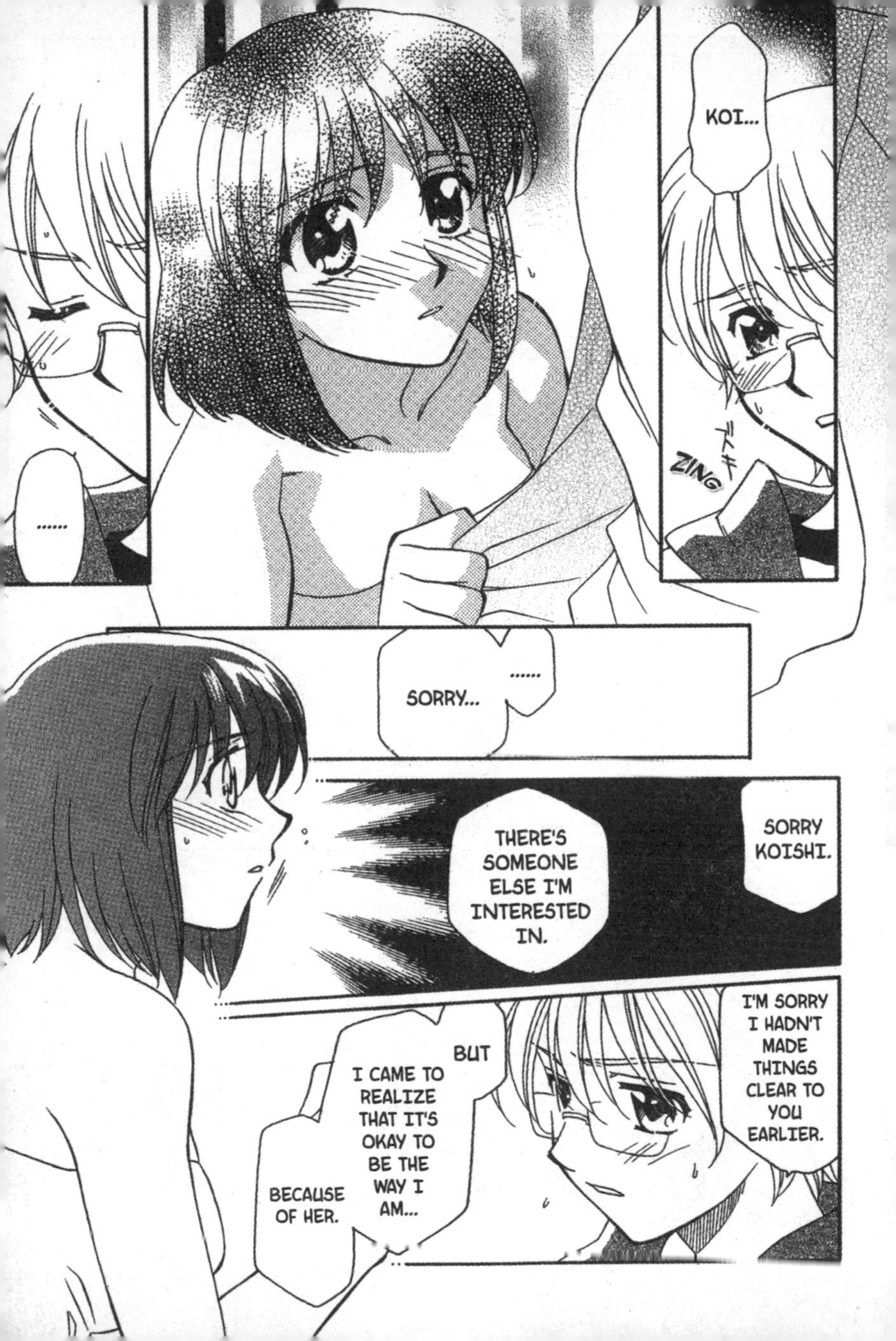

KOI...
ズキ
ZING
......
......
SORRY...
SORRY KOISHI.
THERE'S SOMEONE ELSE I'M INTERESTED IN.
I'M SORRY I HADN'T MADE THINGS CLEAR TO YOU EARLIER.
BUT
I CAME TO REALIZE THAT IT'S OKAY TO BE THE WAY I AM...
BECAUSE OF HER.

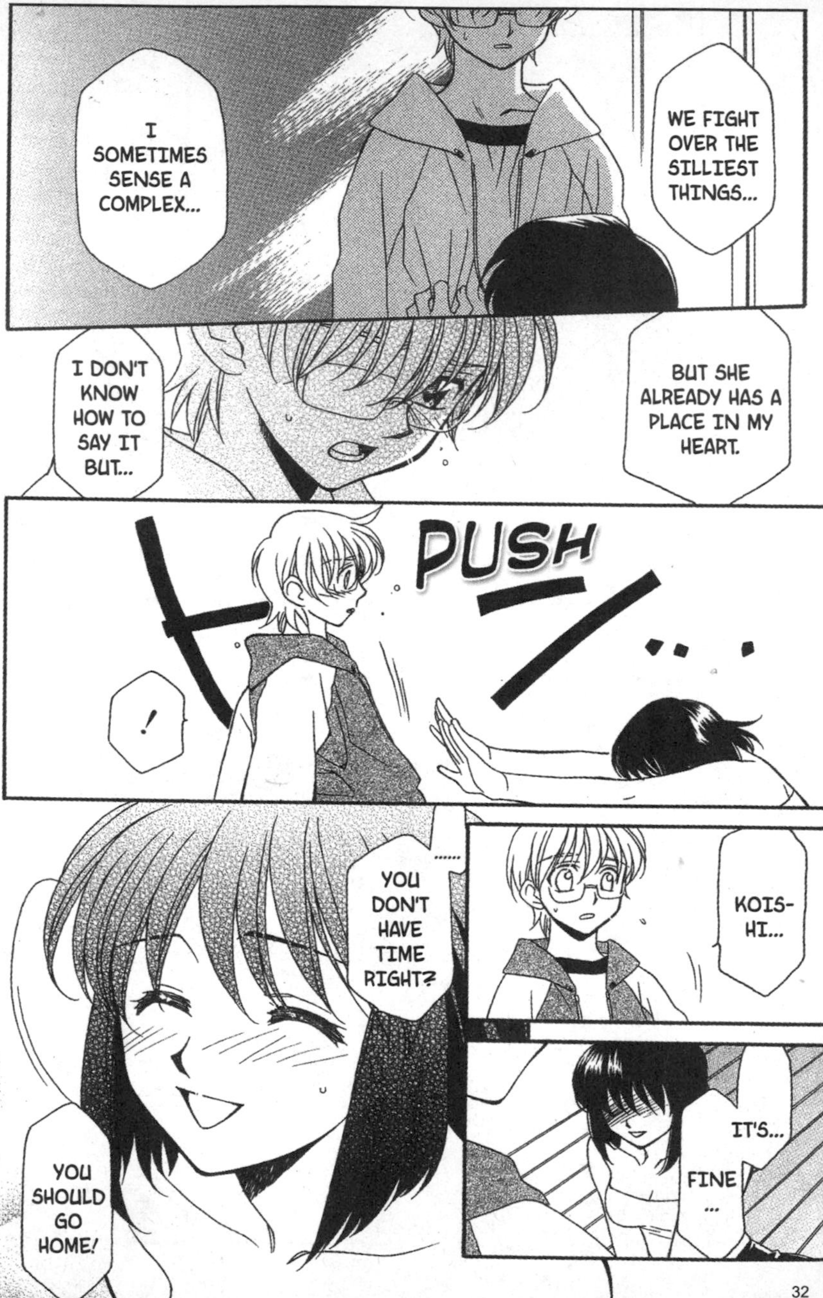
WE FIGHT OVER THE SILLIEST THINGS...
I SOMETIMES SENSE A COMPLEX...
BUT SHE ALREADY HAS A PLACE IN MY HEART.
I DON'T KNOW HOW TO SAY IT BUT...
PUSH
!
KOIS-HI...
IT'S...
FINE ...
...... YOU DON'T HAVE TIME RIGHT?
YOU SHOULD GO HOME!

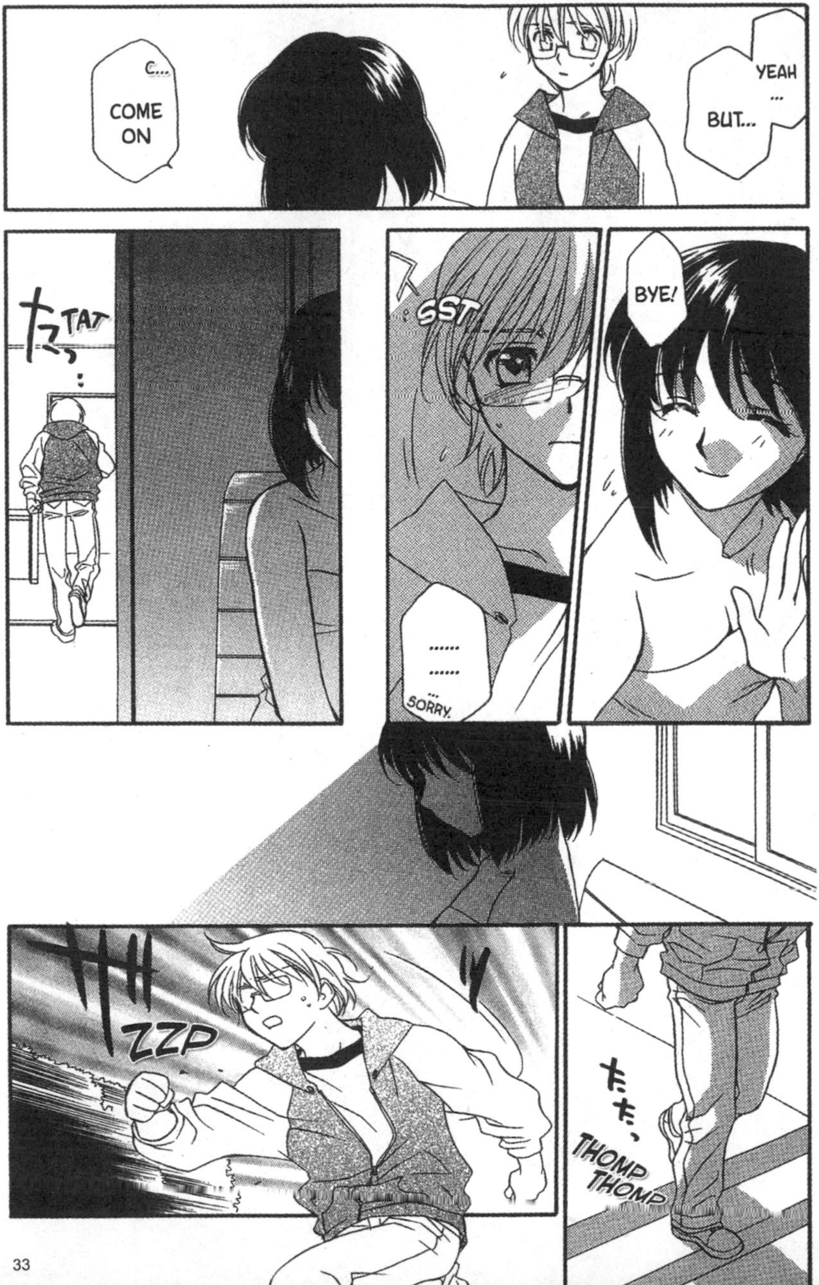
YEAH ... BUT...
C... COME ON
BYE!
SST
.... SORRY.
TAT
THOMP THOMP
ZZP

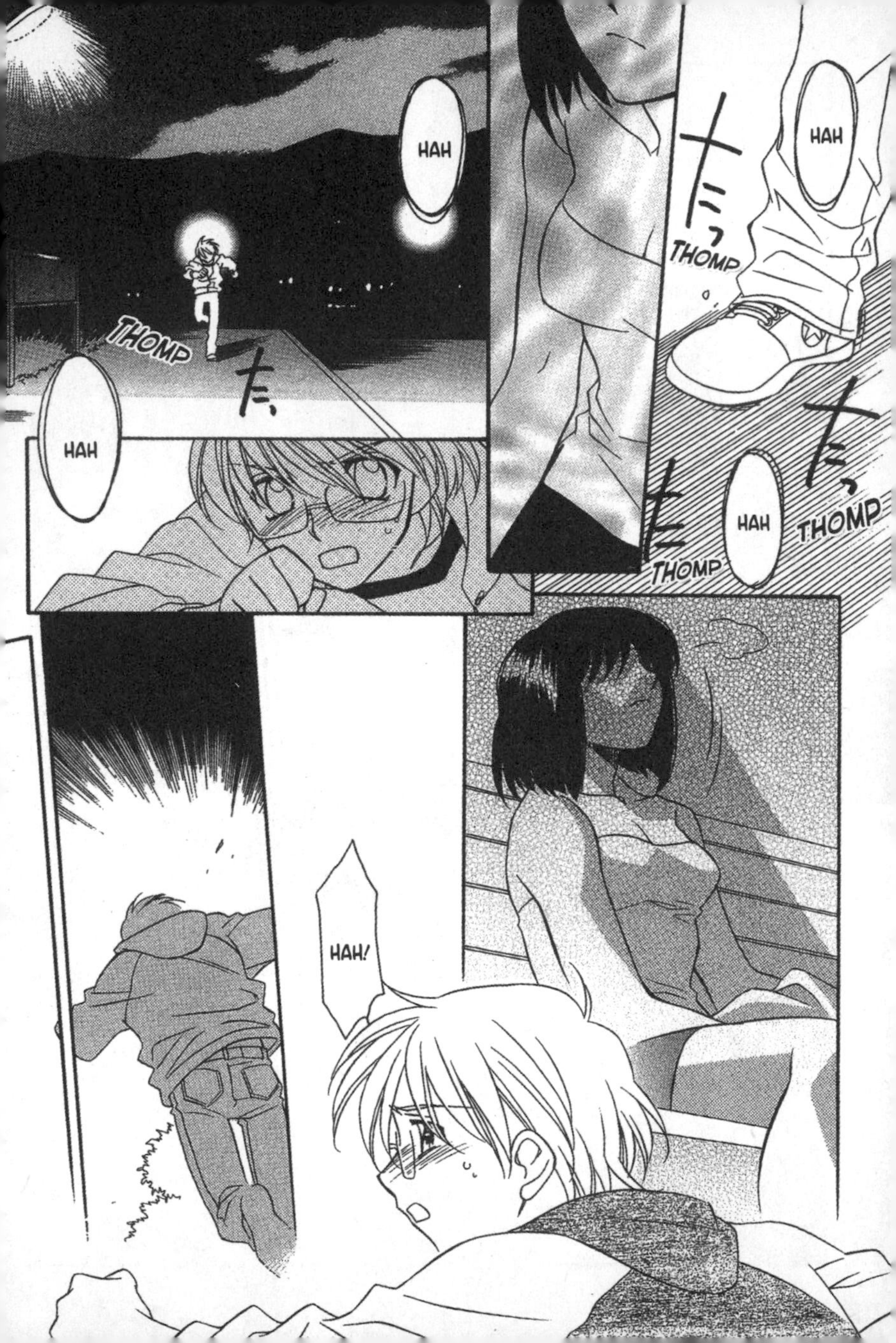
HAH
THOMP
THOMP
HAH
THOMP
HAH
THOMP
HAH
HAH!

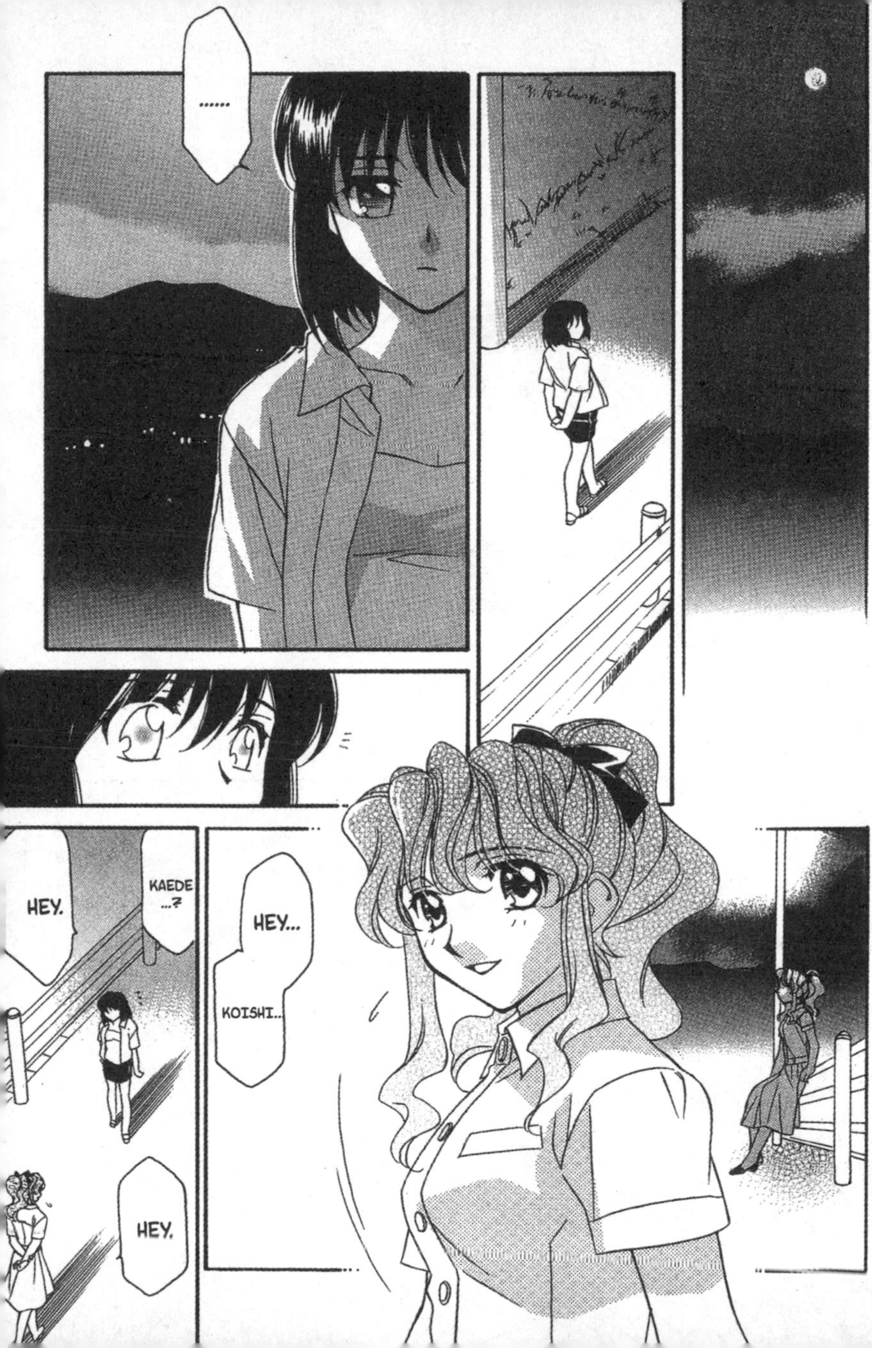
......
HEY...
KOISHI...
KAEDE ...?
HEY.
HEY.

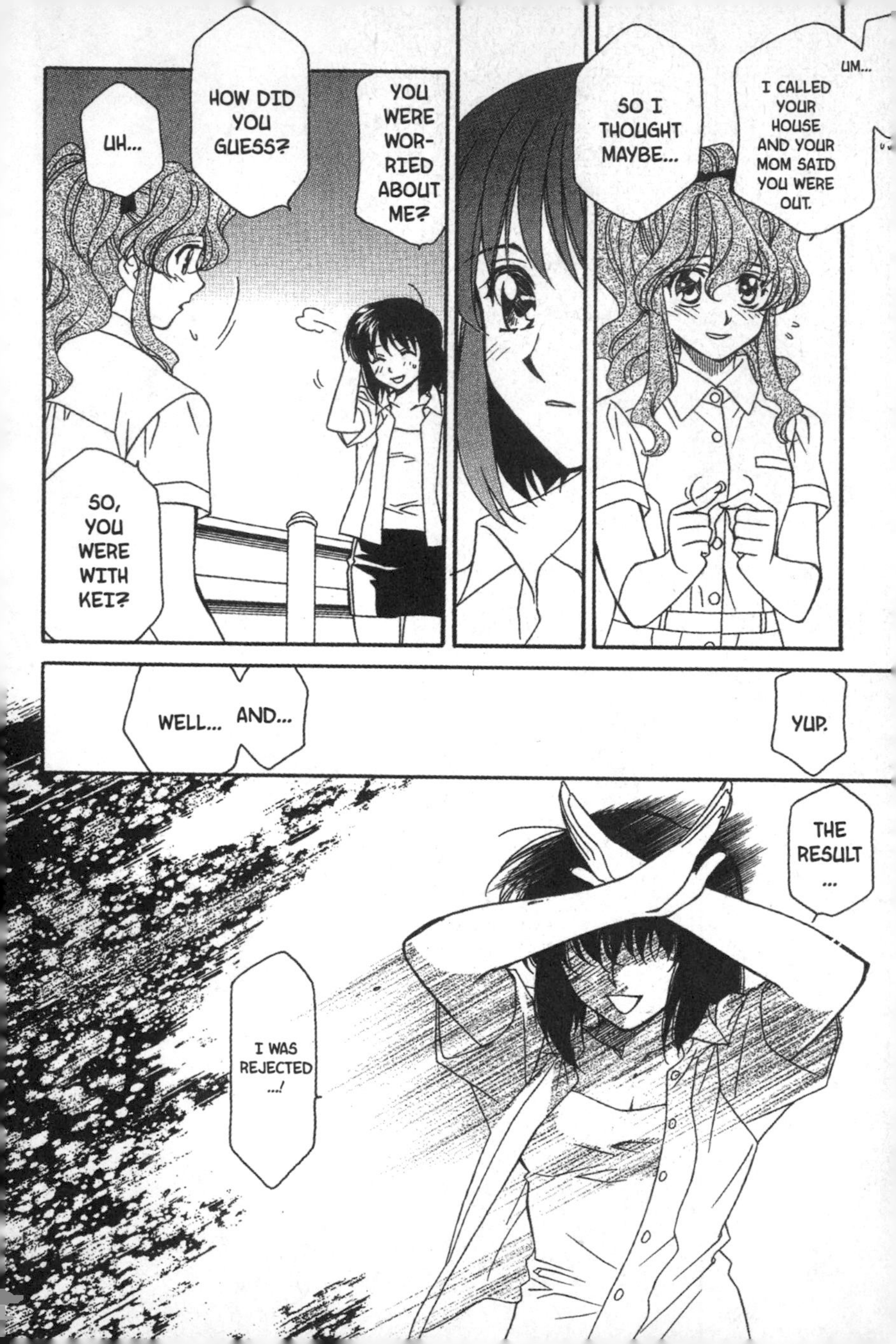
UM...
I CALLED YOUR HOUSE AND YOUR MOM SAID YOU WERE OUT.
SO I THOUGHT MAYBE...
YOU WERE WOR-RIED ABOUT ME?
HOW DID YOU GUESS?
UH...
SO, YOU WERE WITH KEI?
YUP.
WELL... AND...
THE RESULT ...
I WAS REJECTED ...!

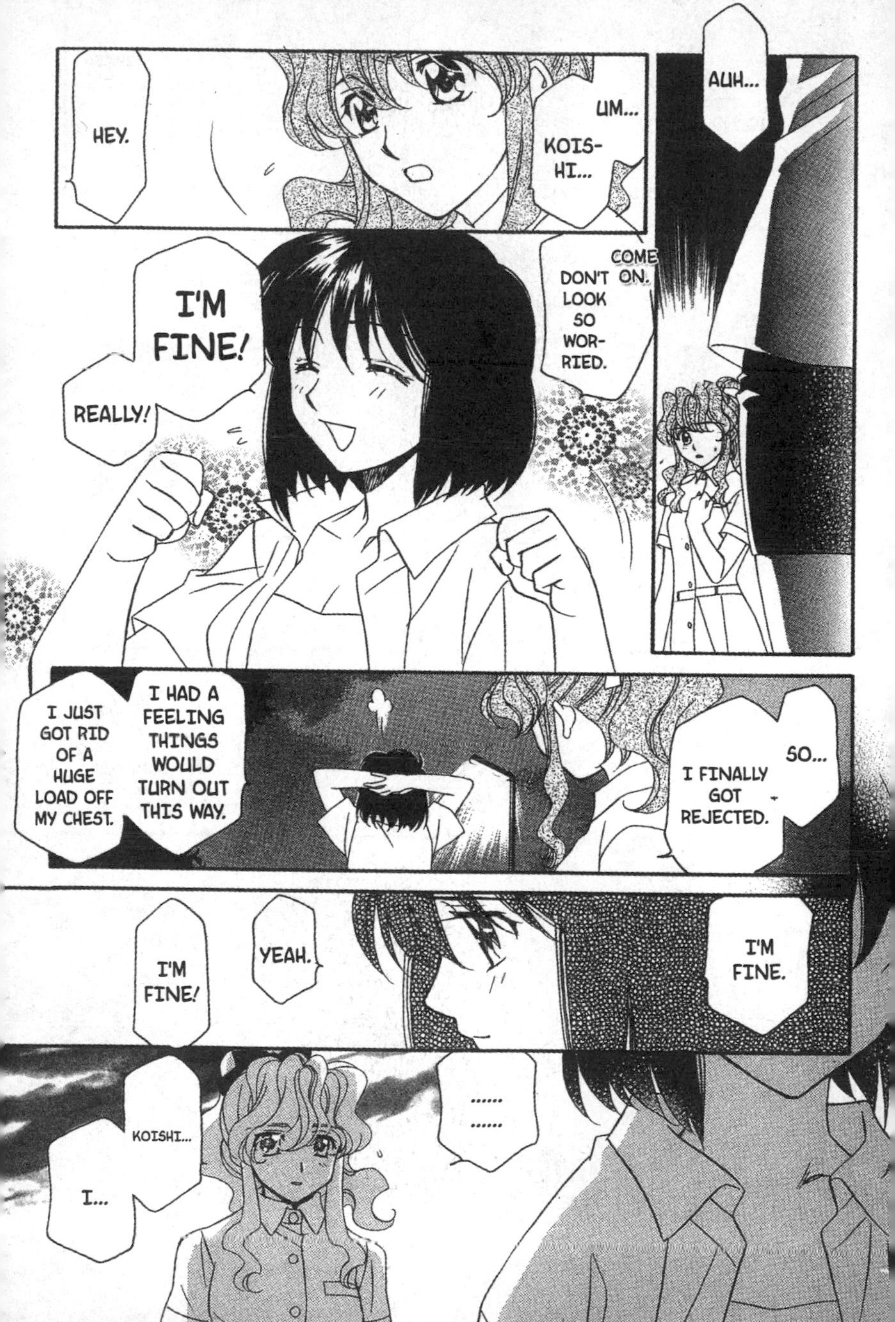
AUH...
UM... KOIS-HI...
HEY.
COME ON. DON'T LOOK SO WOR-RIED.
I'M FINE!
REALLY!
SO... I FINALLY GOT REJECTED.
I HAD A FEELING THINGS WOULD TURN OUT THIS WAY.
I JUST GOT RID OF A HUGE LOAD OFF MY CHEST.
I'M FINE.
YEAH.
I'M FINE!
......
......
KOISHI...
I...

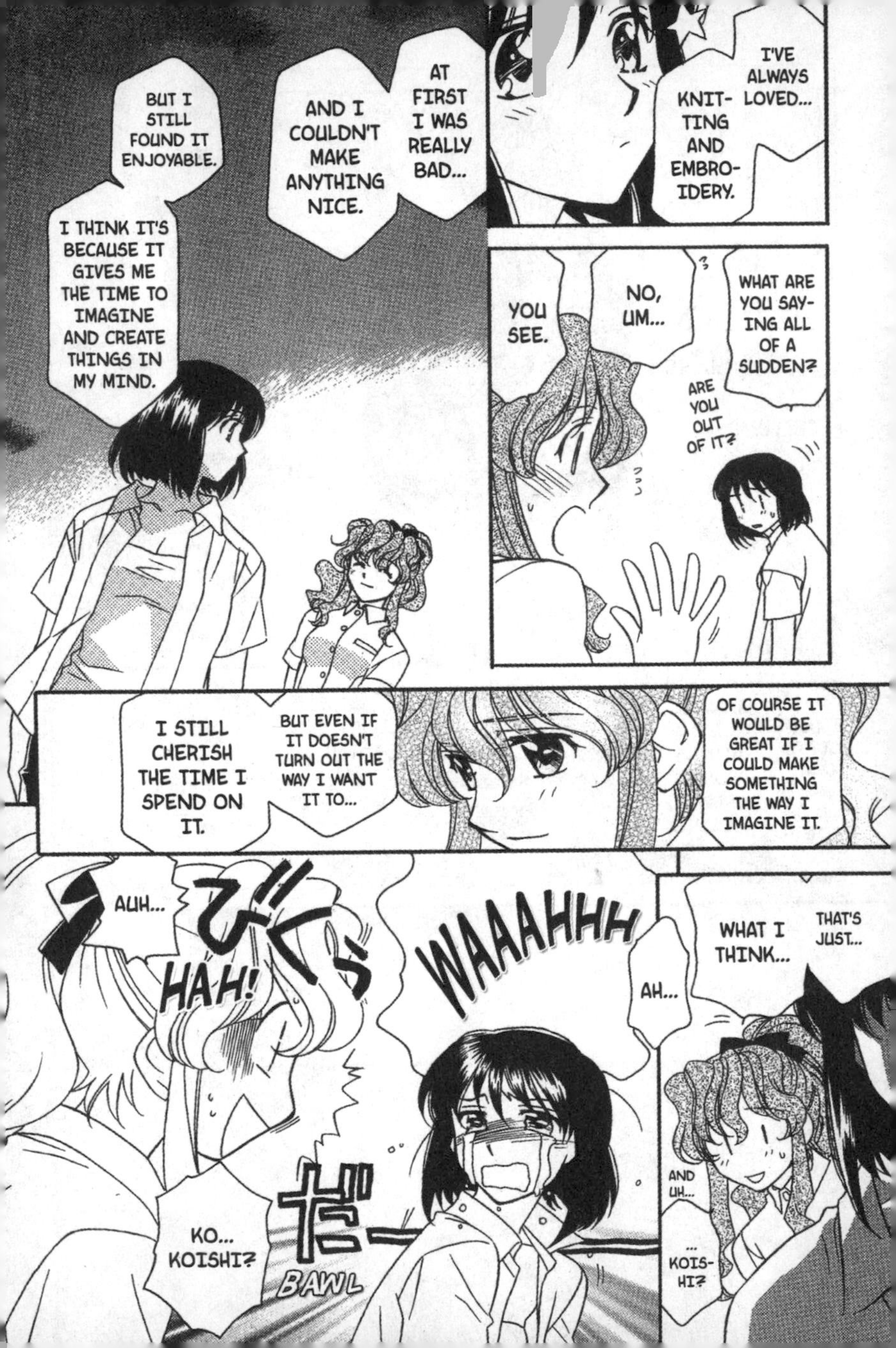

I'VE ALWAYS LOVED...
KNITTING AND EMBROIDERY.
WHAT ARE YOU SAYING ALL OF A SUDDEN?
ARE YOU OUT OF IT?
NO, UM...
YOU SEE.
AT FIRST I WAS REALLY BAD...
AND I COULDN'T MAKE ANYTHING NICE.
BUT I STILL FOUND IT ENJOYABLE.
I THINK IT'S BECAUSE IT GIVES ME THE TIME TO IMAGINE AND CREATE THINGS IN MY MIND.
OF COURSE IT WOULD BE GREAT IF I COULD MAKE SOMETHING THE WAY I IMAGINE IT.
BUT EVEN IF IT DOESN'T TURN OUT THE WAY I WANT IT TO...
I STILL CHERISH THE TIME I SPEND ON IT.
THAT'S JUST...
WHAT I THINK...
AND UH...
...KOISHI?
AH...
WAAAHHH
だーっ
BAWL
KO... KOISHI?
びくっ
AUH...
HAH!

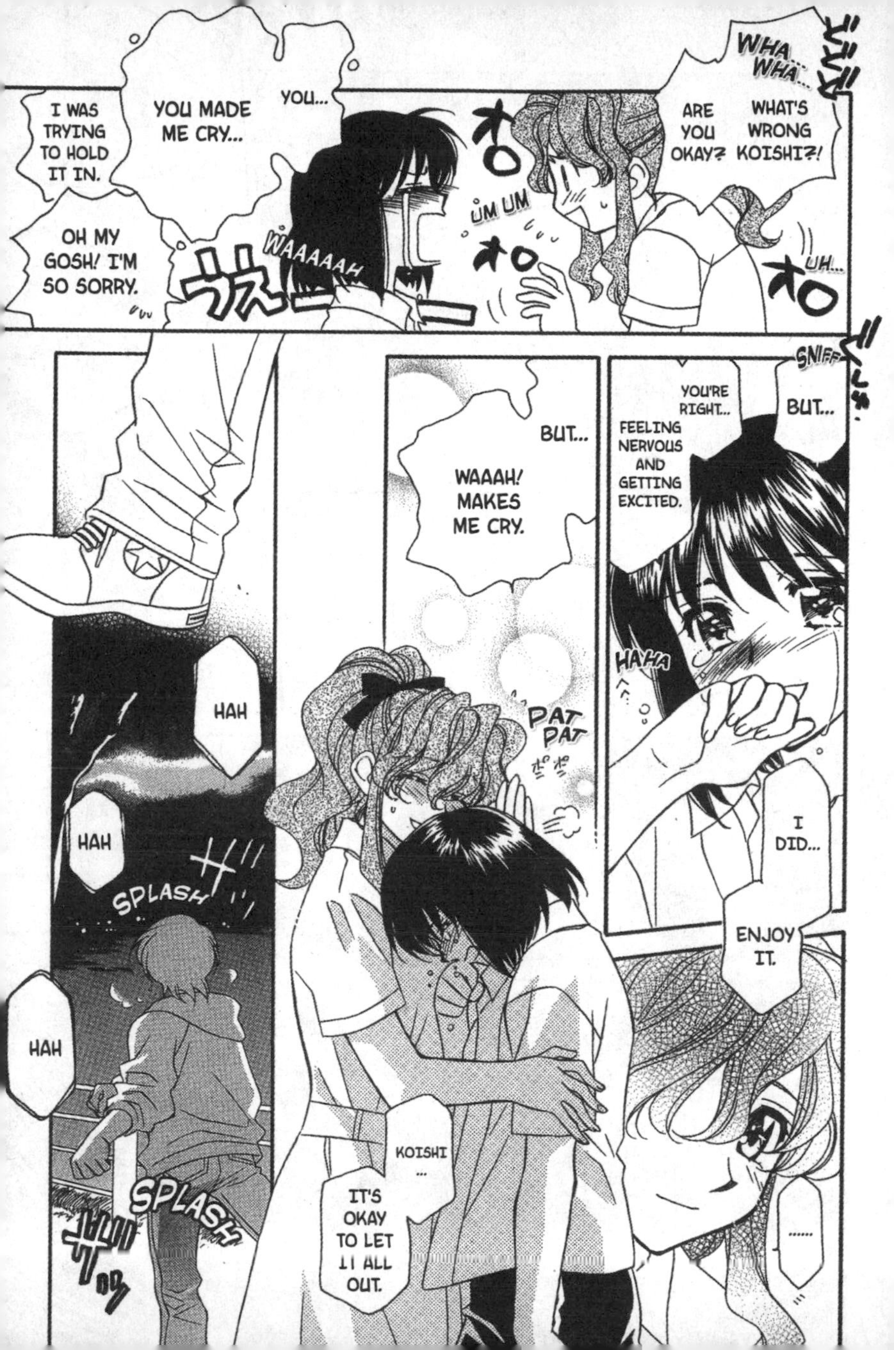
WHA... WHA...
WHAT'S WRONG KOISHI?!
ARE YOU OKAY?
UH...
UM UM
YOU...
YOU MADE ME CRY...
I WAS TRYING TO HOLD IT IN.
WAAAAAH
OH MY GOSH! I'M SO SORRY.
SNIFF
BUT...
YOU'RE RIGHT... FEELING NERVOUS AND GETTING EXCITED.
HAHA
I DID...
ENJOY IT.
BUT...
WAAAH! MAKES ME CRY.
PAT PAT
KOISHI...
IT'S OKAY TO LET IT ALL OUT.
......
HAH
HAH
SPLASH
SPLASH
HAH

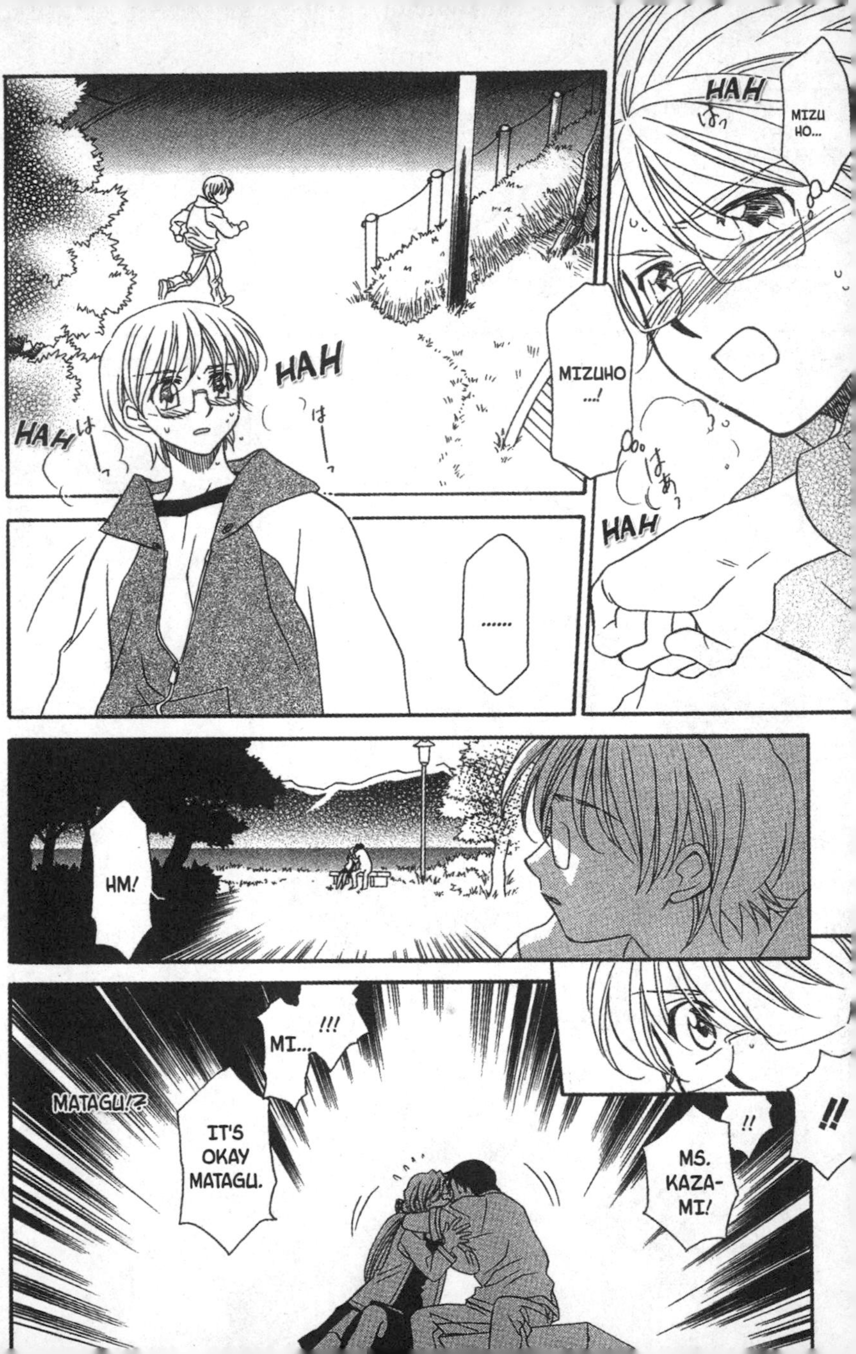
HAH
はっ
MIZU HO...
MIZUHO ...!
はあっ
HAH
HAH
はーっ
HAH
はーっ
......
HM!
!!
!!
MS. KAZA-MI!
MI... !!!
IT'S OKAY MATAGU.
MATAGU!?

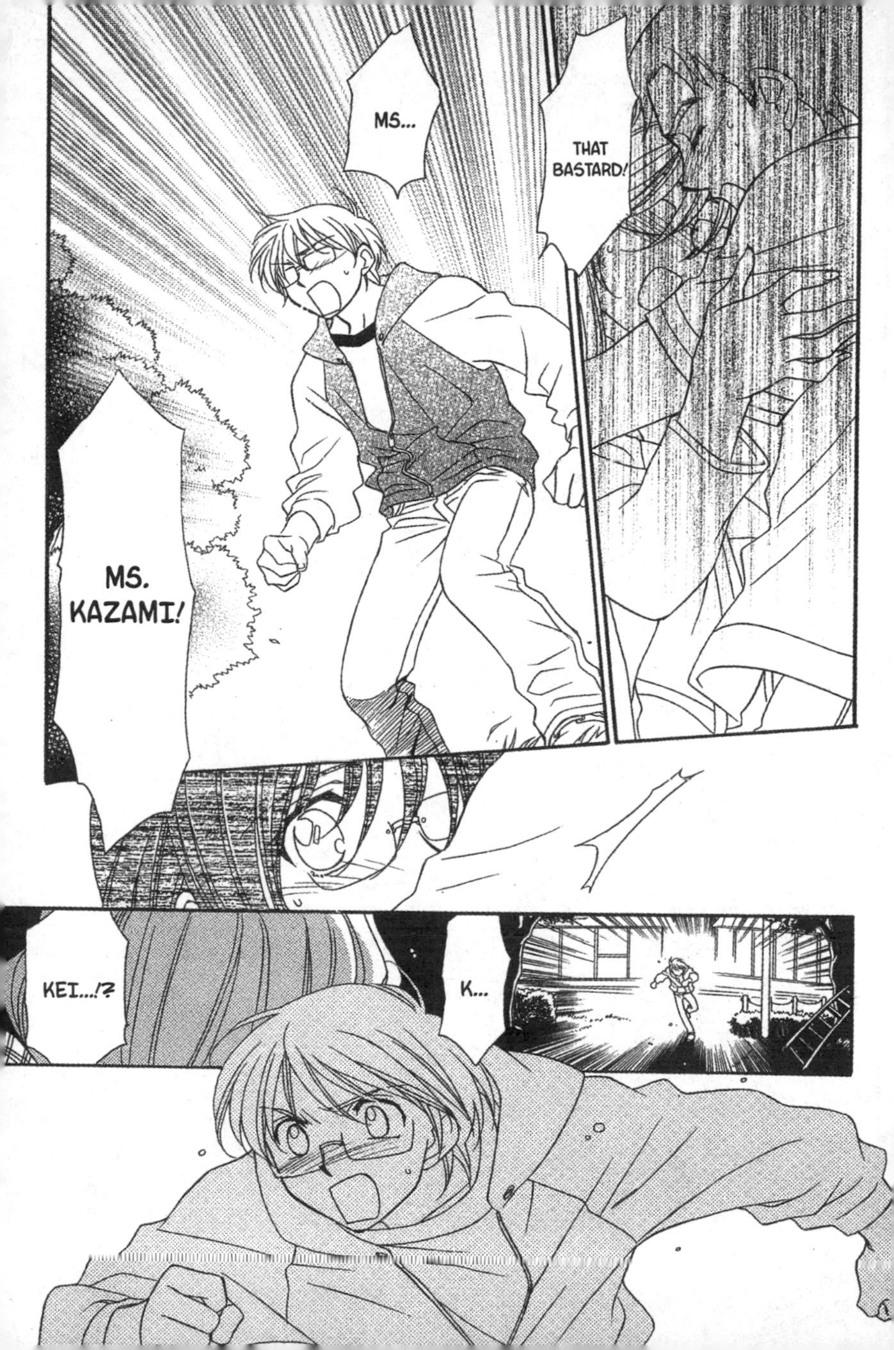

THAT BASTARD!
MS...
MS. KAZAMI!
K...
KEI...!?

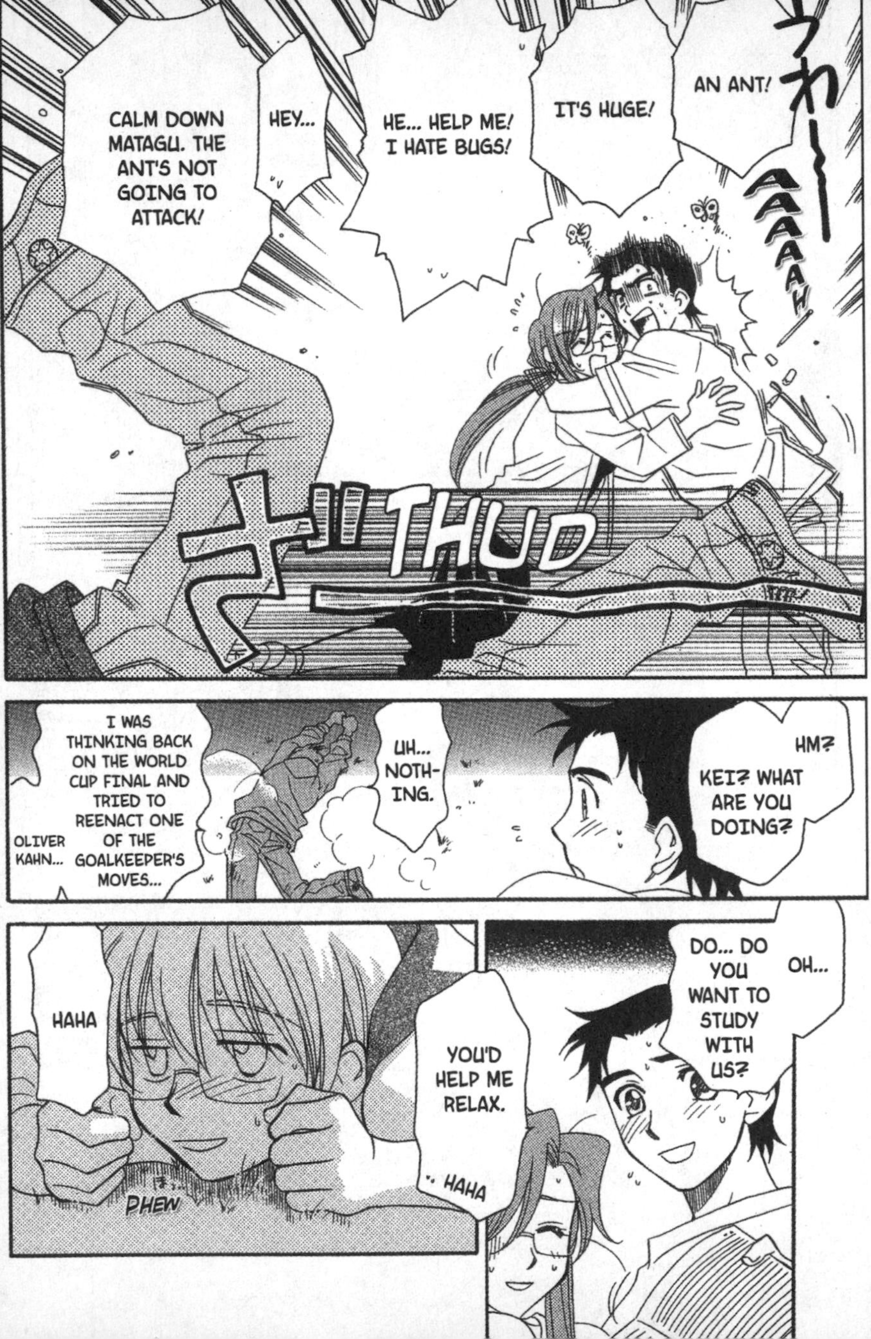

AAAAAH!
AN ANT!
IT'S HUGE!
HE... HELP ME! I HATE BUGS!
HEY...
CALM DOWN MATAGU. THE ANT'S NOT GOING TO ATTACK!
THUD
HM?
KEI? WHAT ARE YOU DOING?
UH... NOTHING.
I WAS THINKING BACK ON THE WORLD CUP FINAL AND TRIED TO REENACT ONE OF THE GOALKEEPER'S MOVES...
OLIVER KAHN...
OH...
DO... DO YOU WANT TO STUDY WITH US?
YOU'D HELP ME RELAX.
HAHA
HAHA
PHEW

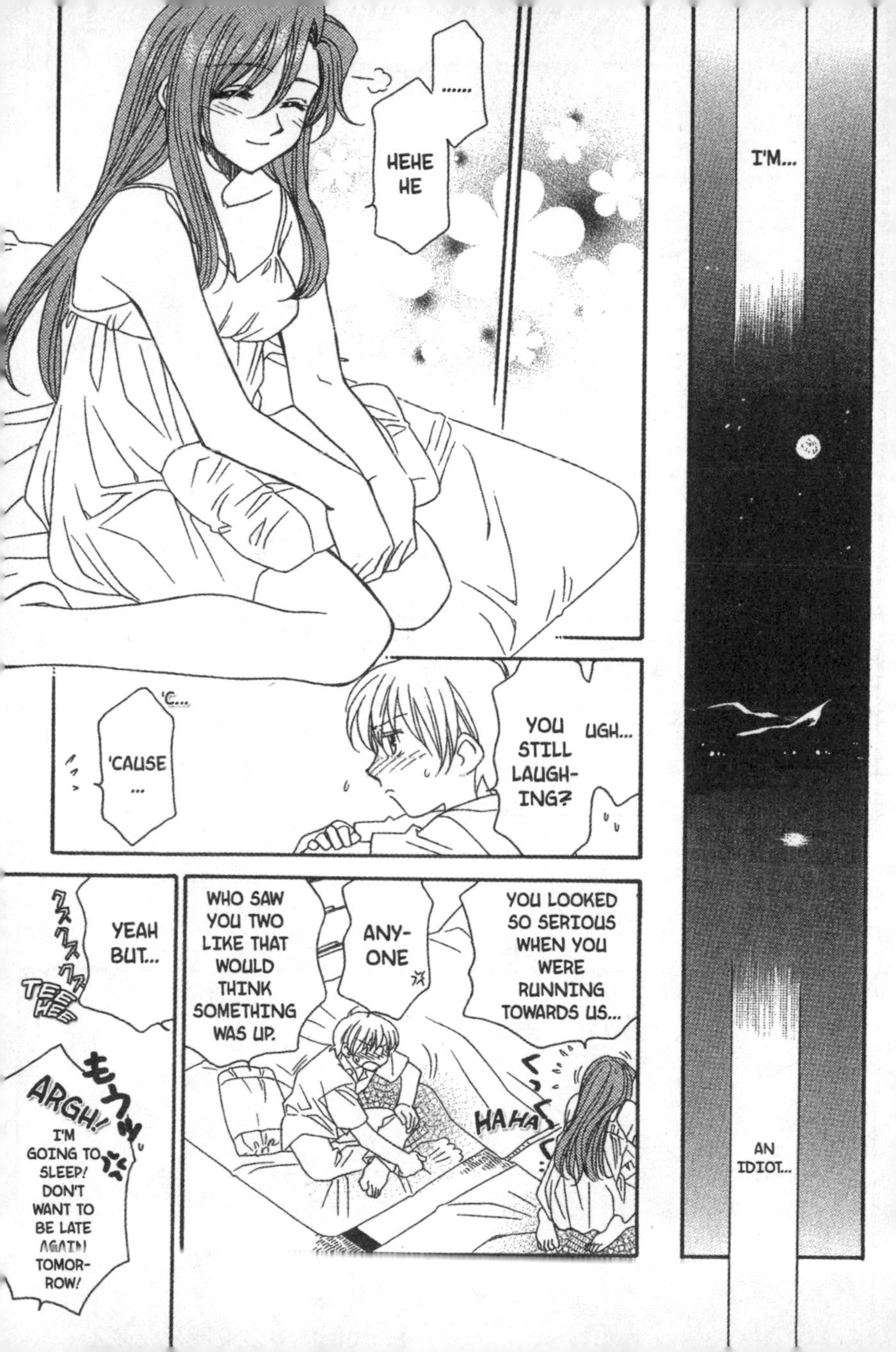

I'M...
AN IDIOT...
......
HEHE HE
UGH...
YOU STILL LAUGH-ING?
'C...
'CAUSE ...
YOU LOOKED SO SERIOUS WHEN YOU WERE RUNNING TOWARDS US...
ANY-ONE
WHO SAW YOU TWO LIKE THAT WOULD THINK SOMETHING WAS UP.
HAHA
YEAH BUT...
TEE HEE
ARGH!
I'M GOING TO SLEEP! DON'T WANT TO BE LATE AGAIN TOMOR-ROW!

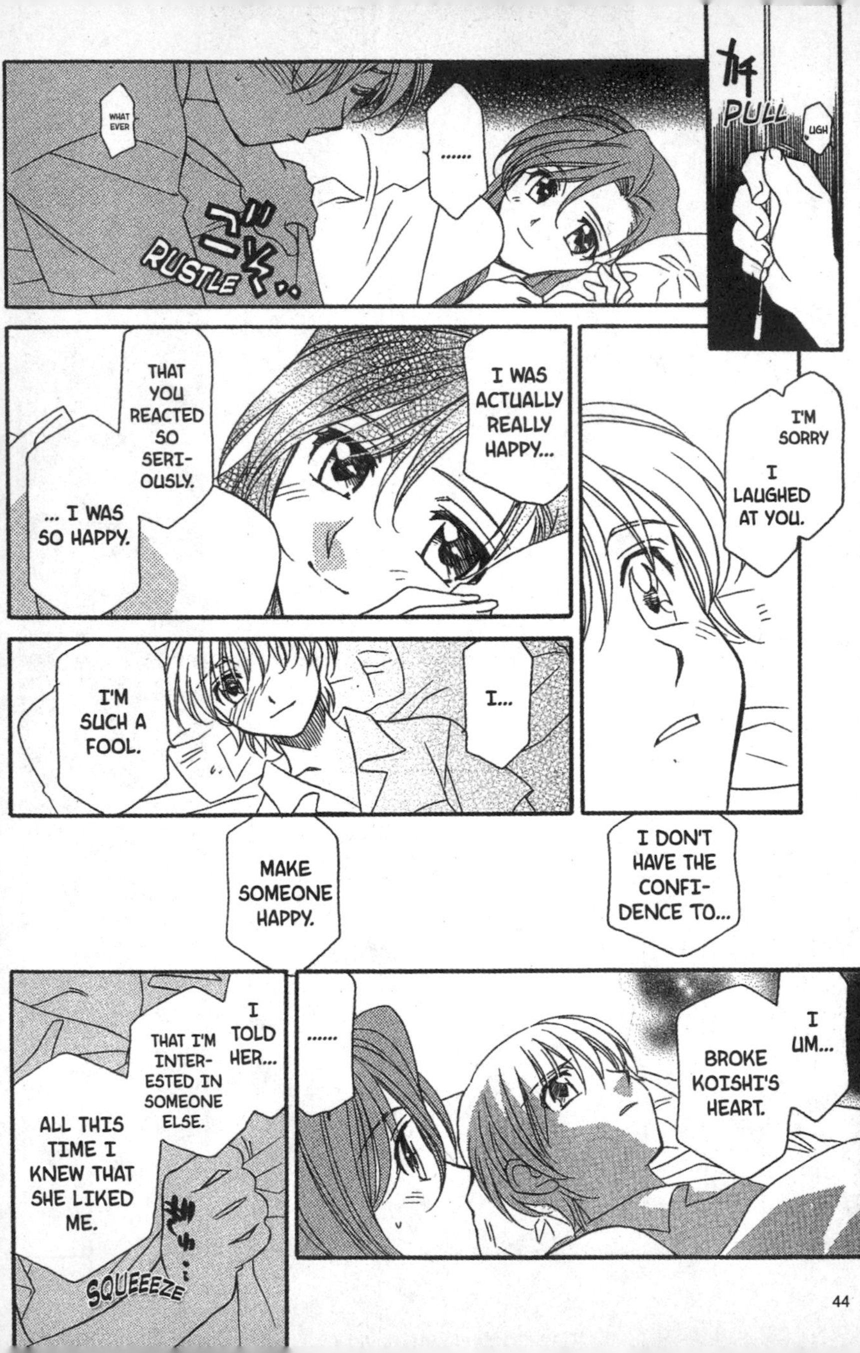
PULL
UGH
......
WHAT EVER
RUSTLE
I'M SORRY
I LAUGHED AT YOU.
I WAS ACTUALLY REALLY HAPPY...
THAT YOU REACTED SO SERI-OUSLY.
... I WAS SO HAPPY.
I...
I'M SUCH A FOOL.
I DON'T HAVE THE CONFI-DENCE TO...
MAKE SOMEONE HAPPY.
I UM...
BROKE KOISHI'S HEART.
......
I TOLD HER...
THAT I'M INTER-ESTED IN SOMEONE ELSE.
ALL THIS TIME I KNEW THAT SHE LIKED ME.
SQUEEEZE

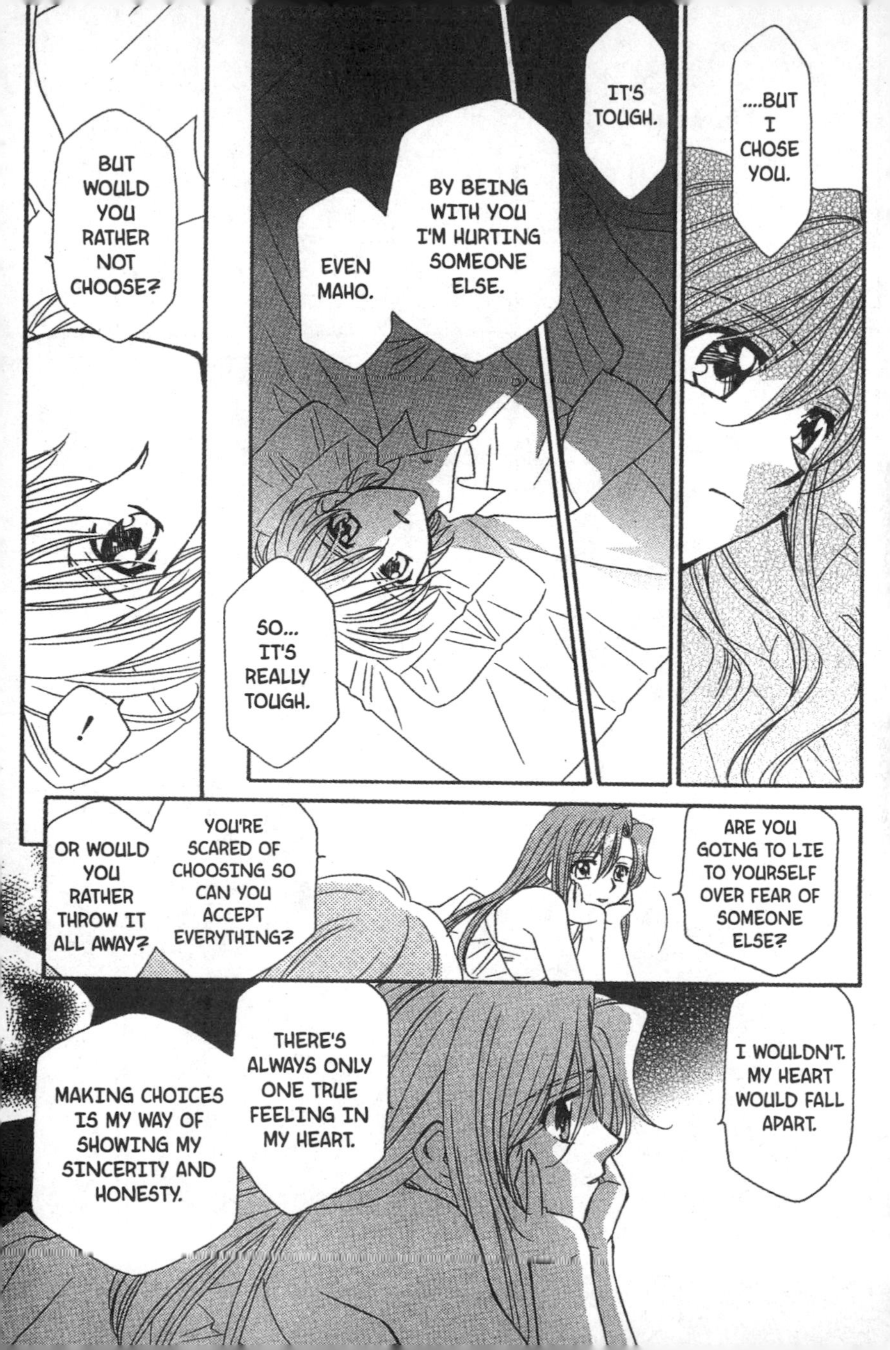
....BUT I CHOSE YOU.
IT'S TOUGH.
BY BEING WITH YOU I'M HURTING SOMEONE ELSE.
EVEN MAHO.
SO... IT'S REALLY TOUGH.
BUT WOULD YOU RATHER NOT CHOOSE?
!
ARE YOU GOING TO LIE TO YOURSELF OVER FEAR OF SOMEONE ELSE?
YOU'RE SCARED OF CHOOSING SO CAN YOU ACCEPT EVERYTHING?
OR WOULD YOU RATHER THROW IT ALL AWAY?
I WOULDN'T. MY HEART WOULD FALL APART.
THERE'S ALWAYS ONLY ONE TRUE FEELING IN MY HEART.
MAKING CHOICES IS MY WAY OF SHOWING MY SINCERITY AND HONESTY.

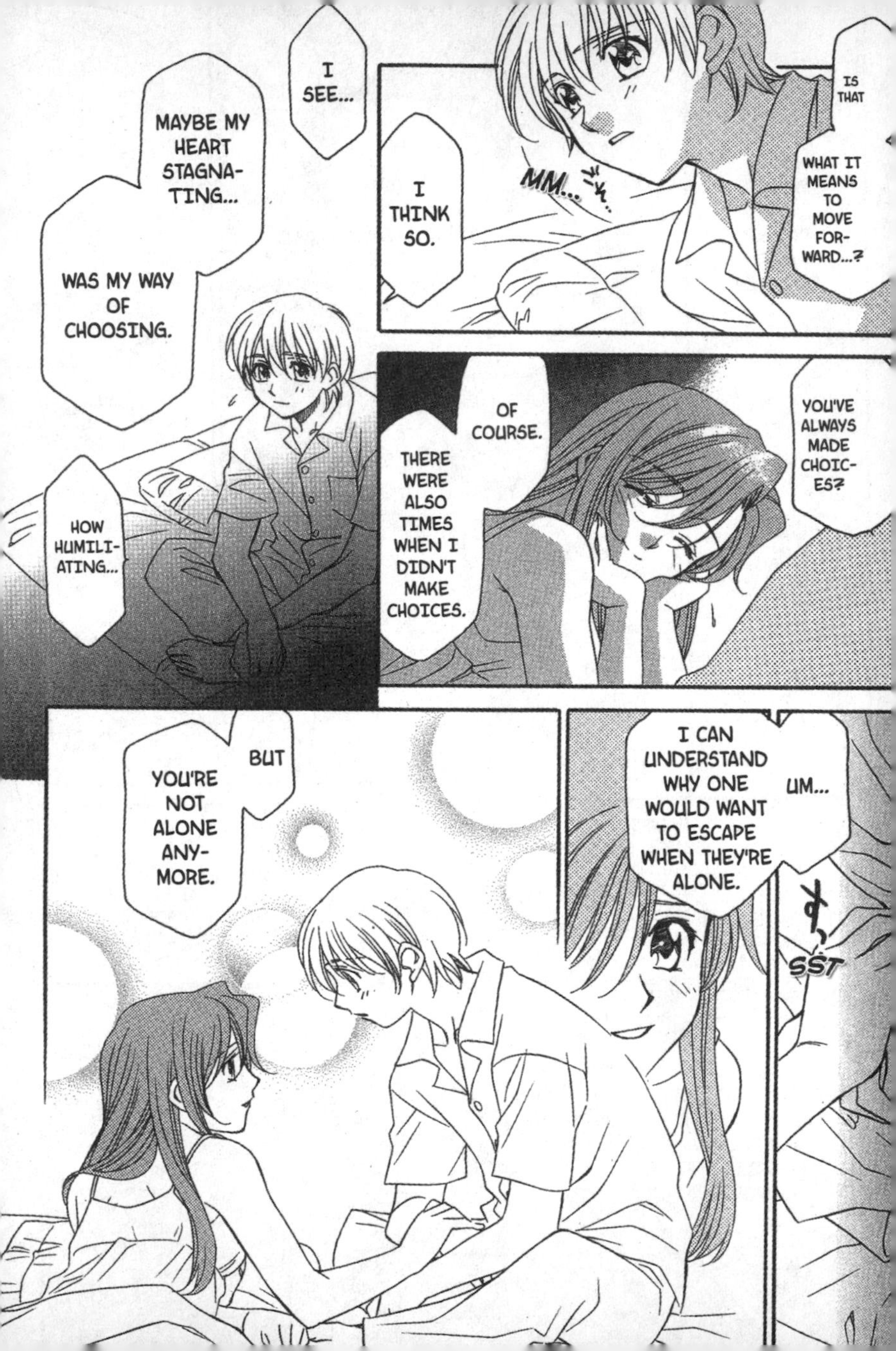

IS THAT
WHAT IT MEANS TO MOVE FOR-WARD...?
MM...
I THINK SO.
YOU'VE ALWAYS MADE CHOIC-ES?
OF COURSE.
THERE WERE ALSO TIMES WHEN I DIDN'T MAKE CHOICES.
I SEE...
MAYBE MY HEART STAGNA-TING...
WAS MY WAY OF CHOOSING.
HOW HUMILI-ATING...
UM...
SST
I CAN UNDERSTAND WHY ONE WOULD WANT TO ESCAPE WHEN THEY'RE ALONE.
BUT
YOU'RE NOT ALONE ANY-MORE.

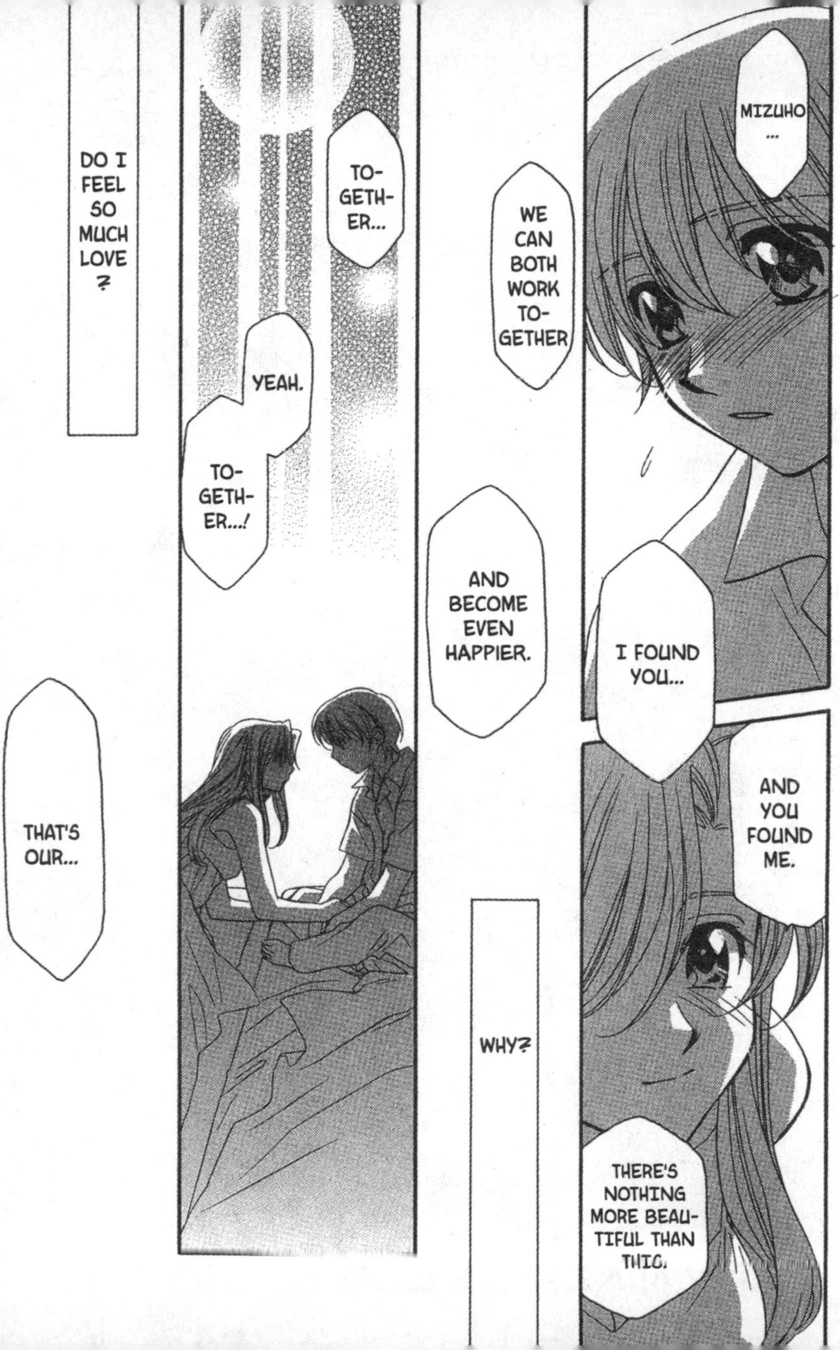
MIZUHO ...
WE CAN BOTH WORK TO-GETHER
AND BECOME EVEN HAPPIER.
I FOUND YOU...
AND YOU FOUND ME.
WHY?
THERE'S NOTHING MORE BEAU-TIFUL THAN THIS.
TO-GETH-ER...
YEAH.
TO-GETH-ER...!
DO I FEEL SO MUCH LOVE?
THAT'S OUR...

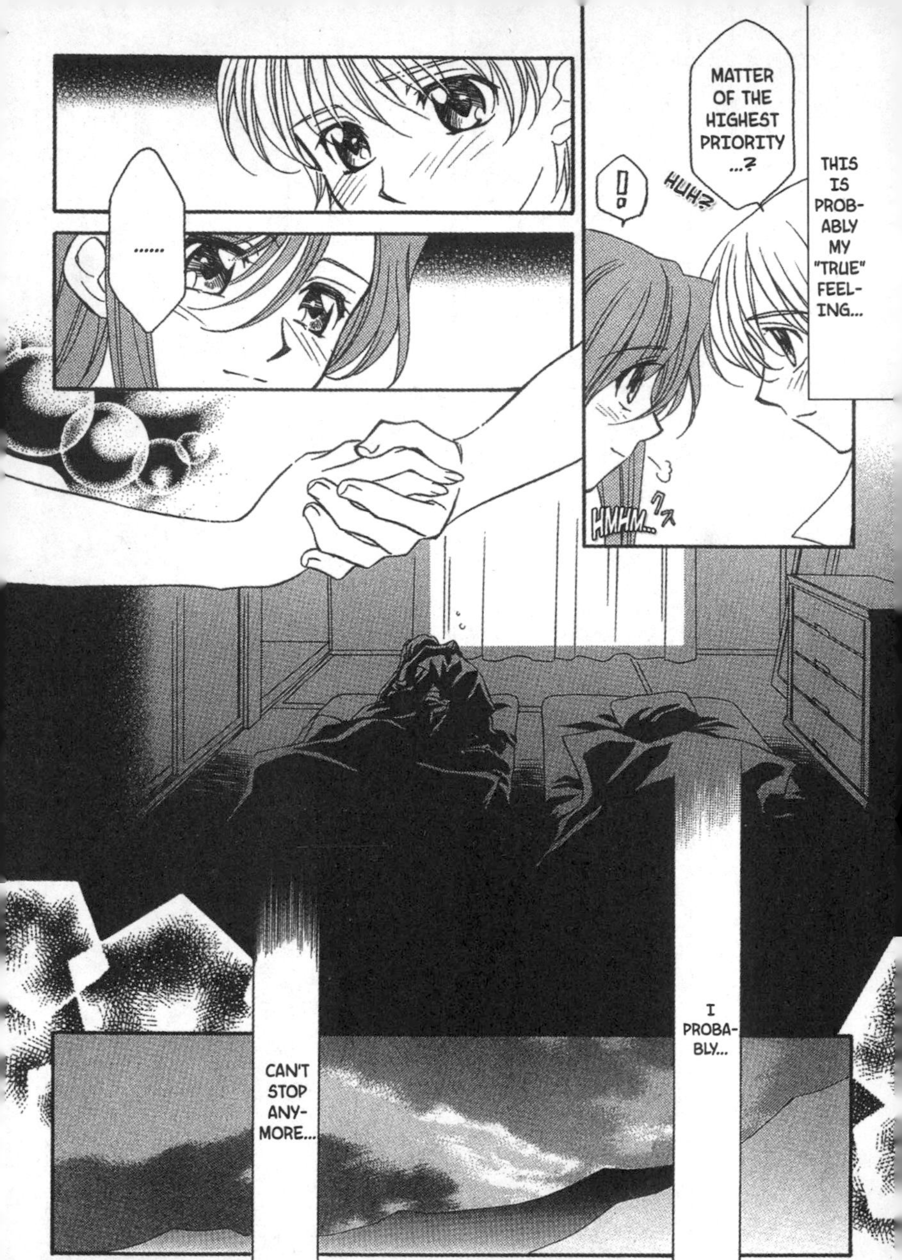
MATTER OF THE HIGHEST PRIORITY ...?
THIS IS PROBABLY MY "TRUE" FEELING...
HUH?
!
HMHM...
......
I PROBABLY...
CAN'T STOP ANYMORE...

STORY NINE - THE END

STORY TEN

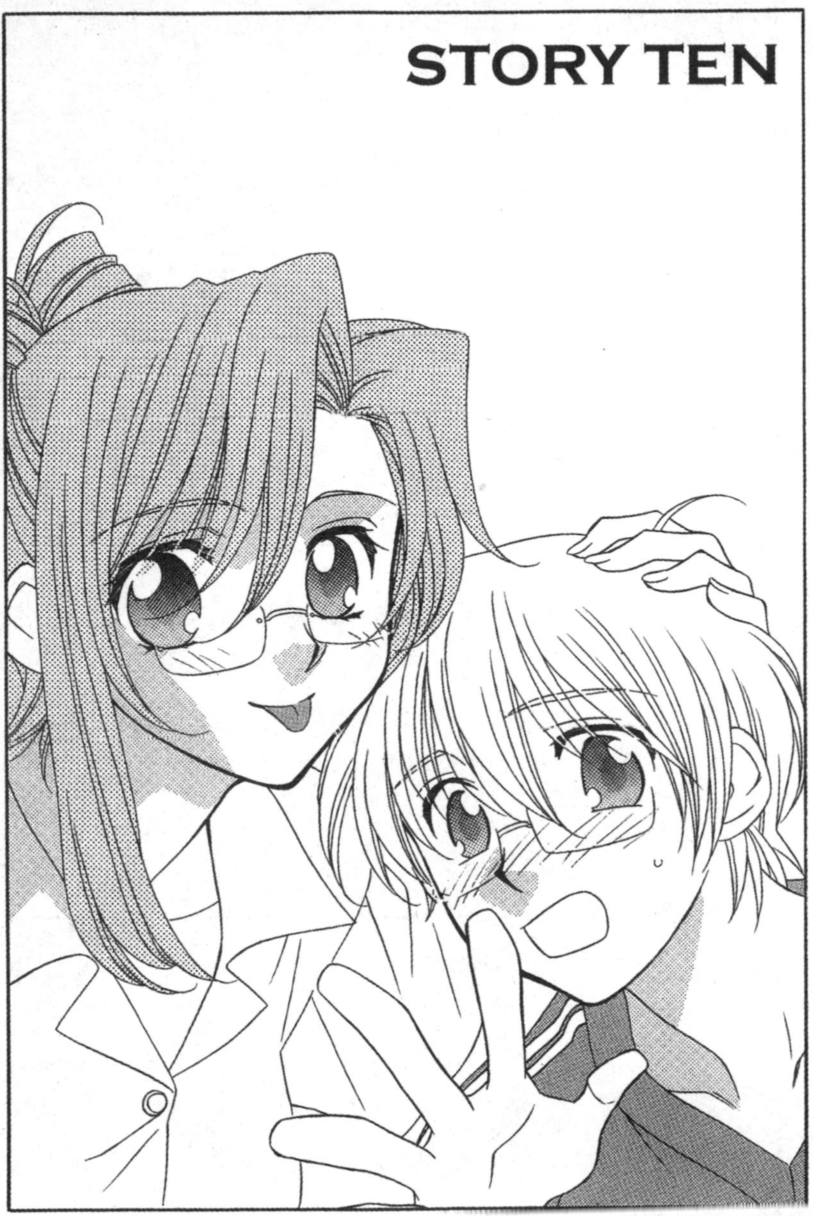

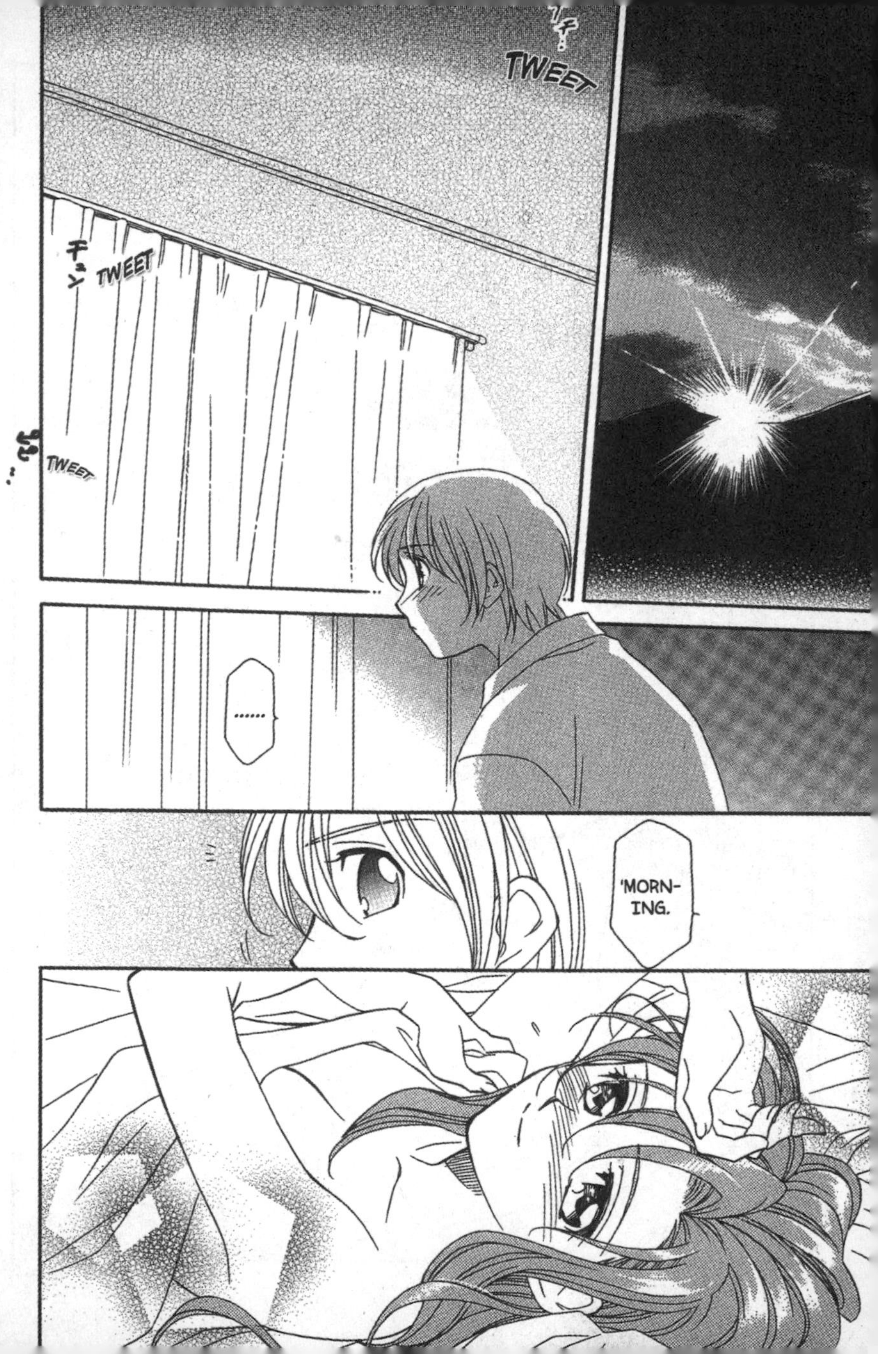
TWEET
TWEET
TWEET
......
'MORNING.

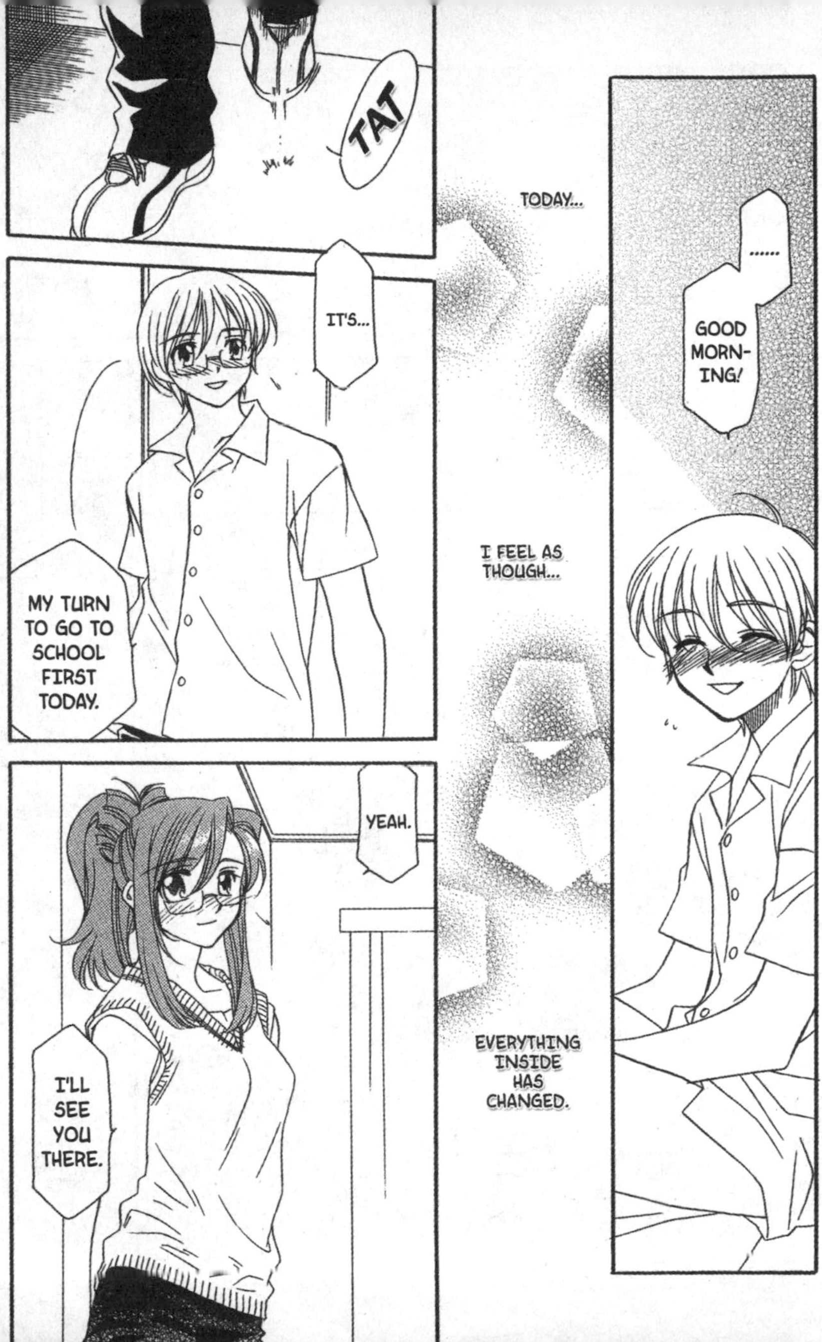
TODAY...
......
GOOD MORNING!
I FEEL AS THOUGH...
EVERYTHING INSIDE HAS CHANGED.
TAT
IT'S...
MY TURN TO GO TO SCHOOL FIRST TODAY.
YEAH.
I'LL SEE YOU THERE.

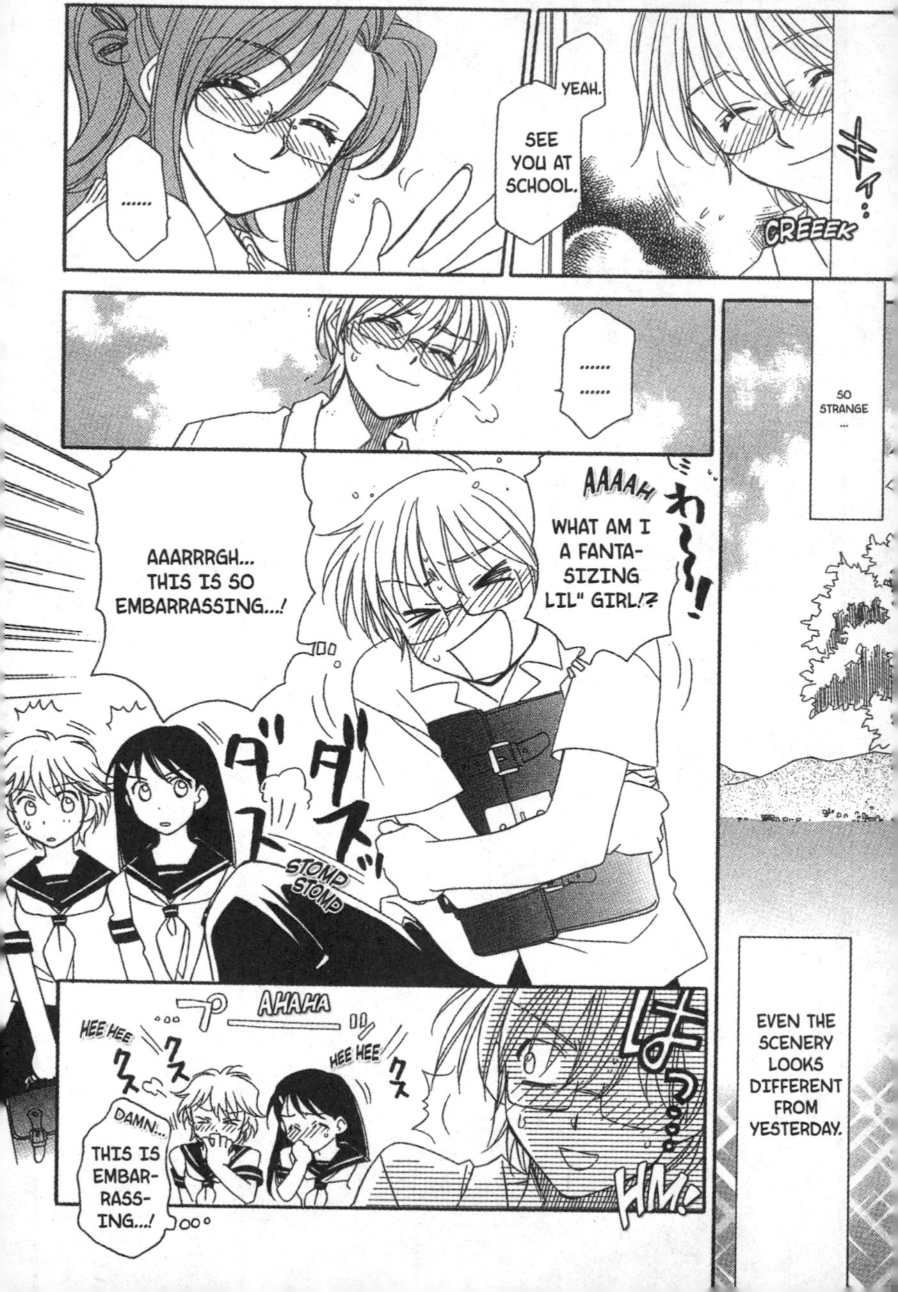
キィ・・
CREEEK
YEAH.
SEE YOU AT SCHOOL.
......
SO STRANGE ...
EVEN THE SCENERY LOOKS DIFFERENT FROM YESTERDAY.
......
......
AAAAH
わ〜〜!
WHAT AM I A FANTA-SIZING LIL" GIRL!?
AAARRRGH... THIS IS SO EMBARRASSING...!
ダスッ
ダス
STOMP STOMP
はっ
HM!
AHAHA
プーーッ
HEE HEE
クス
HEE HEE
クス
クス
DAMN...
THIS IS EMBAR-RASS-ING...!

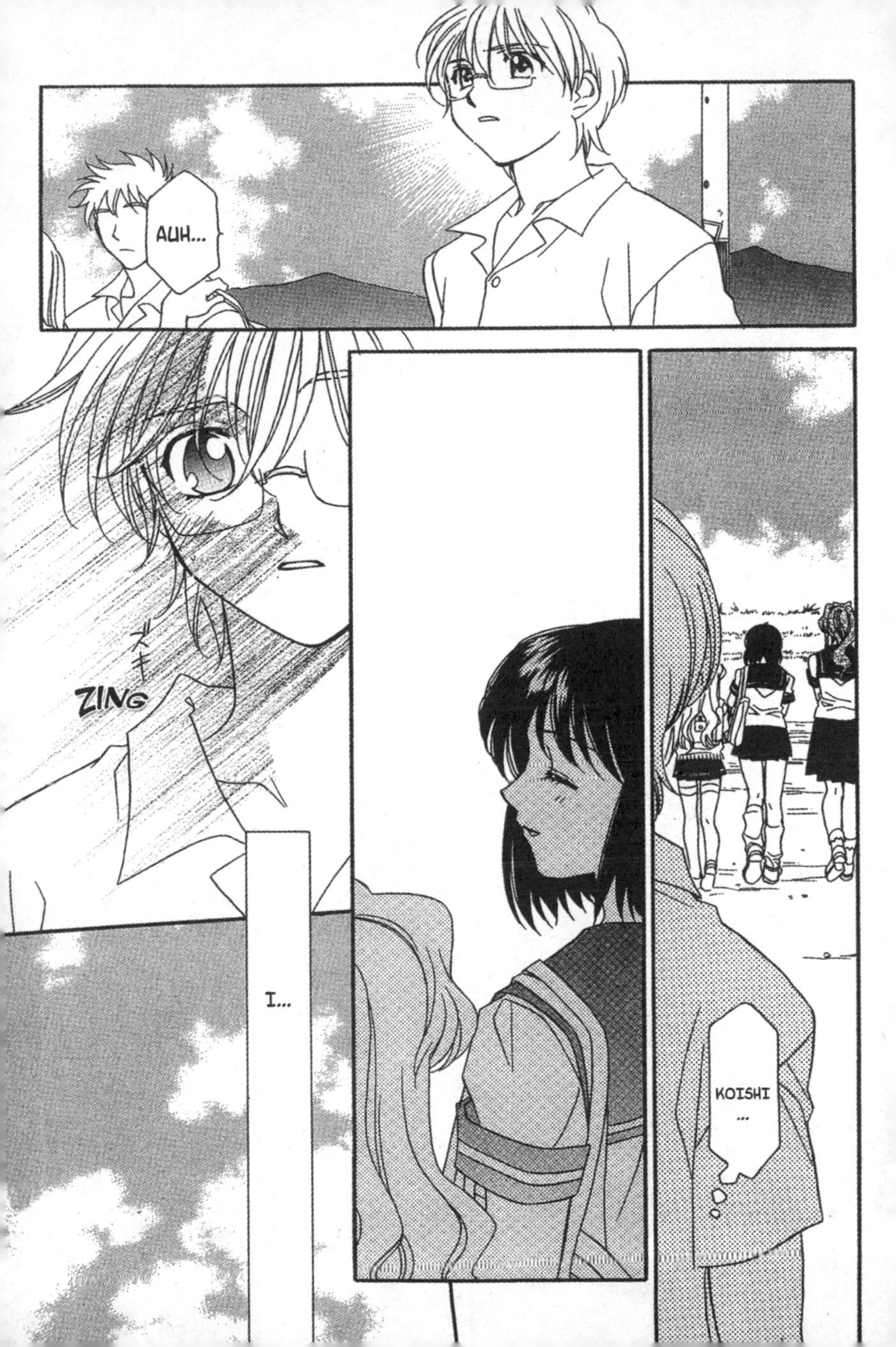
AUH...
KOISHI ...
ズキ
ZING
I...

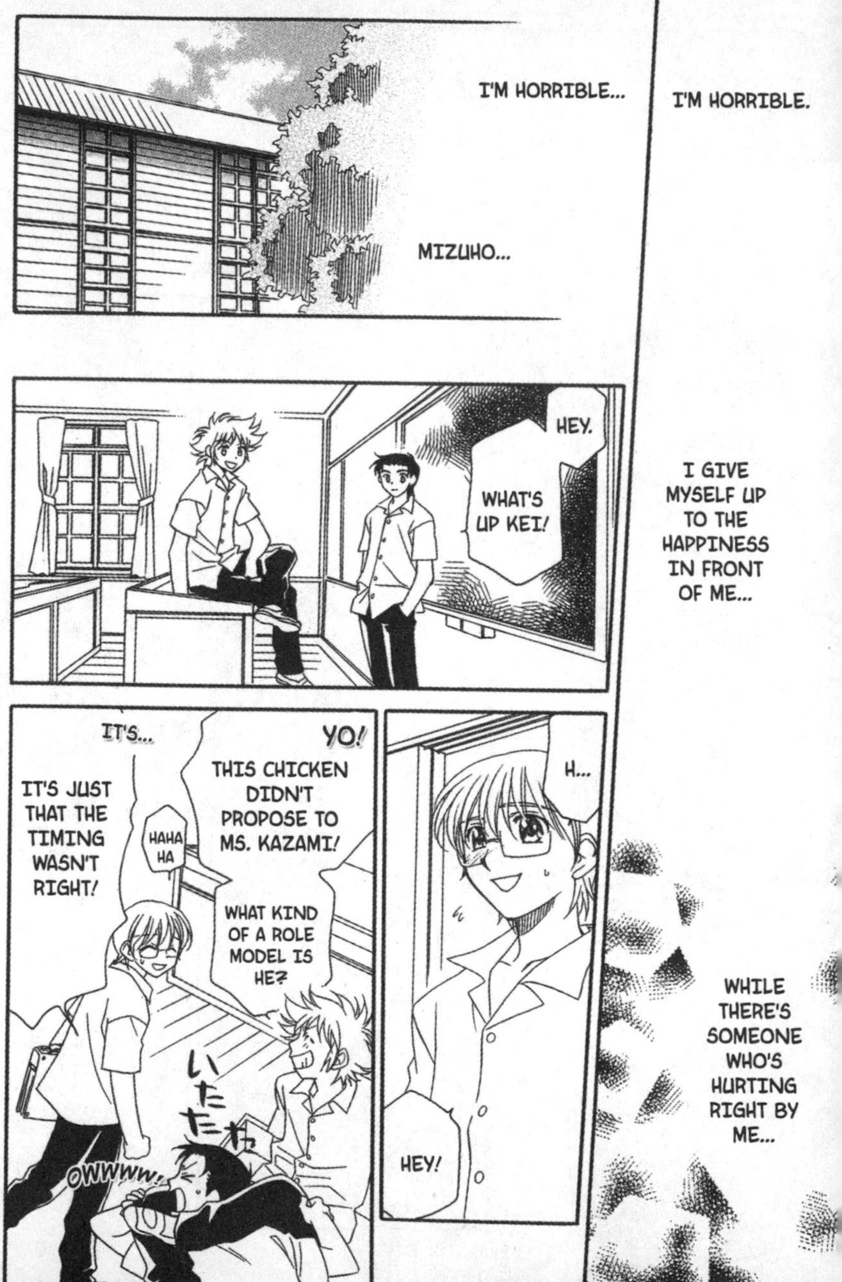
I'M HORRIBLE.
I'M HORRIBLE...
MIZUHO...
I GIVE MYSELF UP TO THE HAPPINESS IN FRONT OF ME...
HEY.
WHAT'S UP KEI!
WHILE THERE'S SOMEONE WHO'S HURTING RIGHT BY ME...
H...
HEY!
YO!
THIS CHICKEN DIDN'T PROPOSE TO MS. KAZAMI!
IT'S...
IT'S JUST THAT THE TIMING WASN'T RIGHT!
HAHA HA
WHAT KIND OF A ROLE MODEL IS HE?
いたたた
OWWWW!

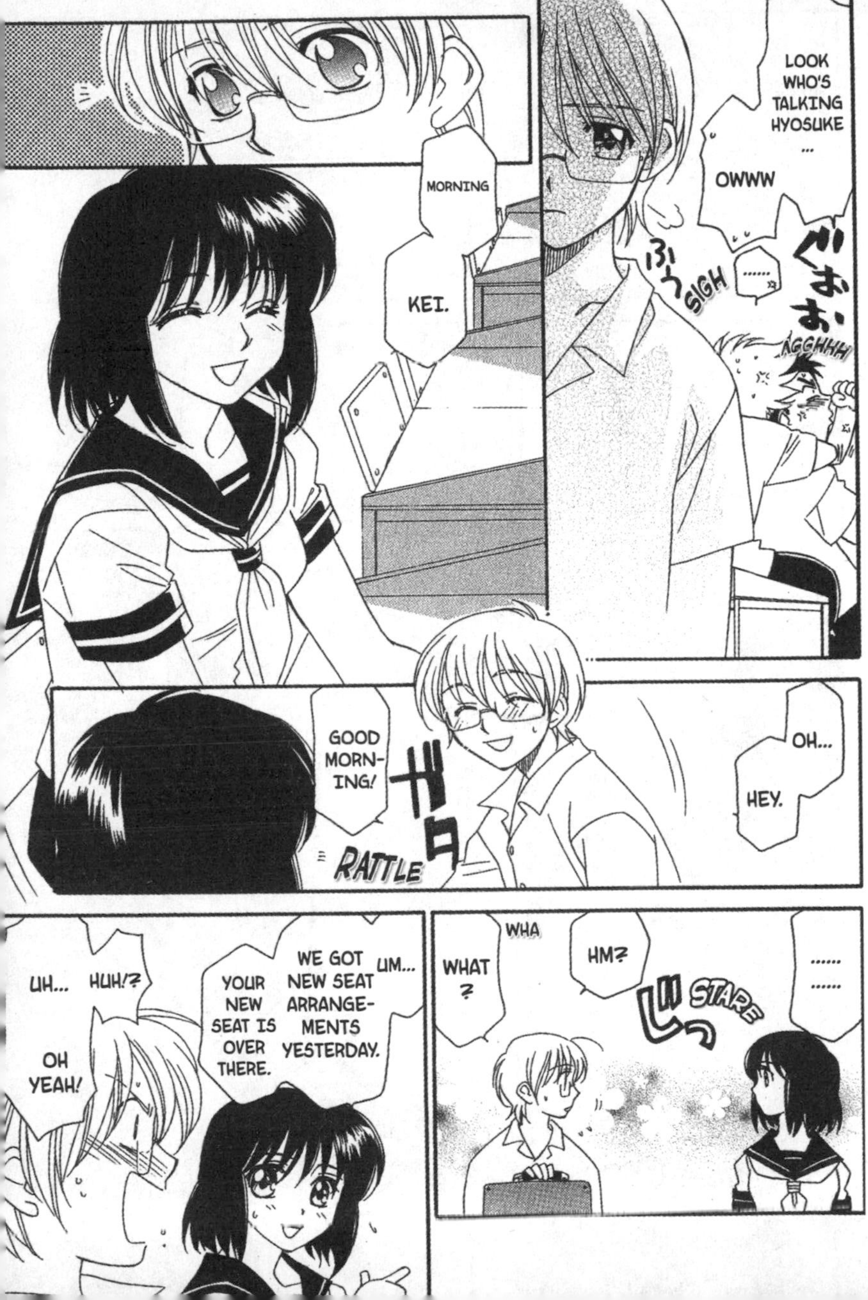
LOOK WHO'S TALKING HYOSUKE ...
OWWW
ぐおお AGGHHH
......
ふう SIGH
MORNING
KEI.
OH... HEY.
GOOD MORN-ING!
ガタ RATTLE
....
じっ STARE
HM?
WHA
WHAT?
UM...
WE GOT NEW SEAT ARRANGE-MENTS YESTERDAY.
YOUR NEW SEAT IS OVER THERE.
UH... HUH!?
OH YEAH!

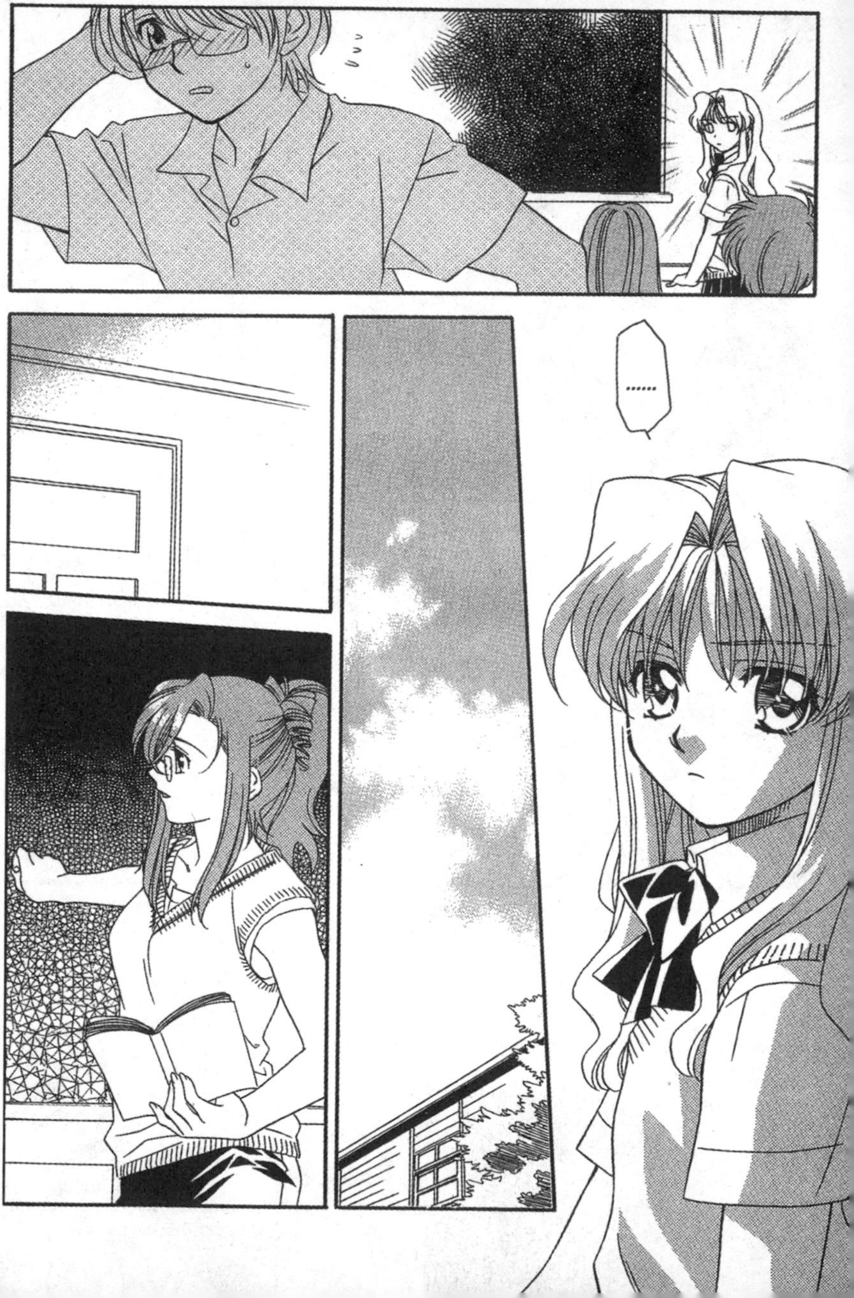
……

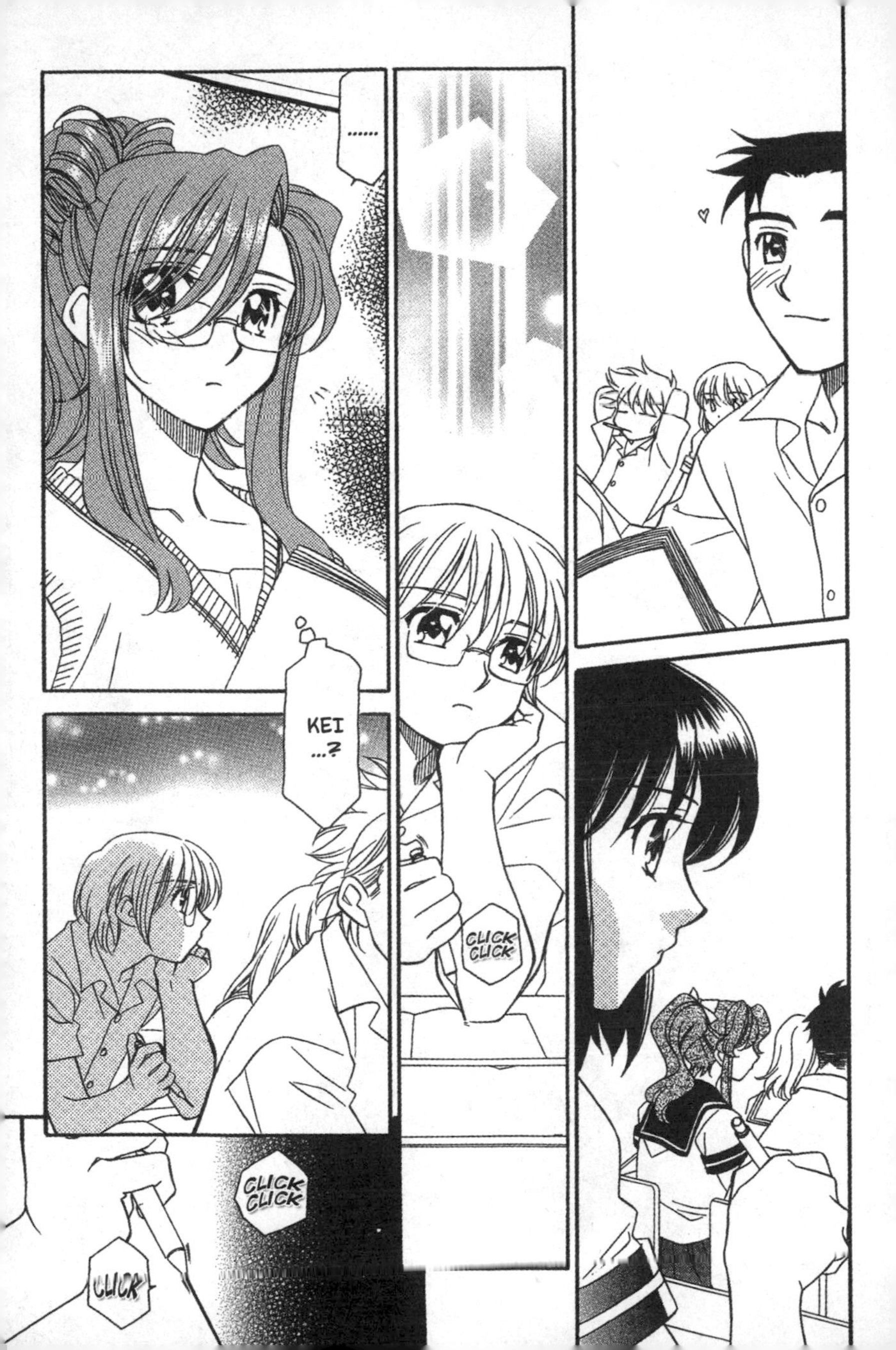

KEI ...?
CLICK CLICK
......
CLICK CLICK
CLICK

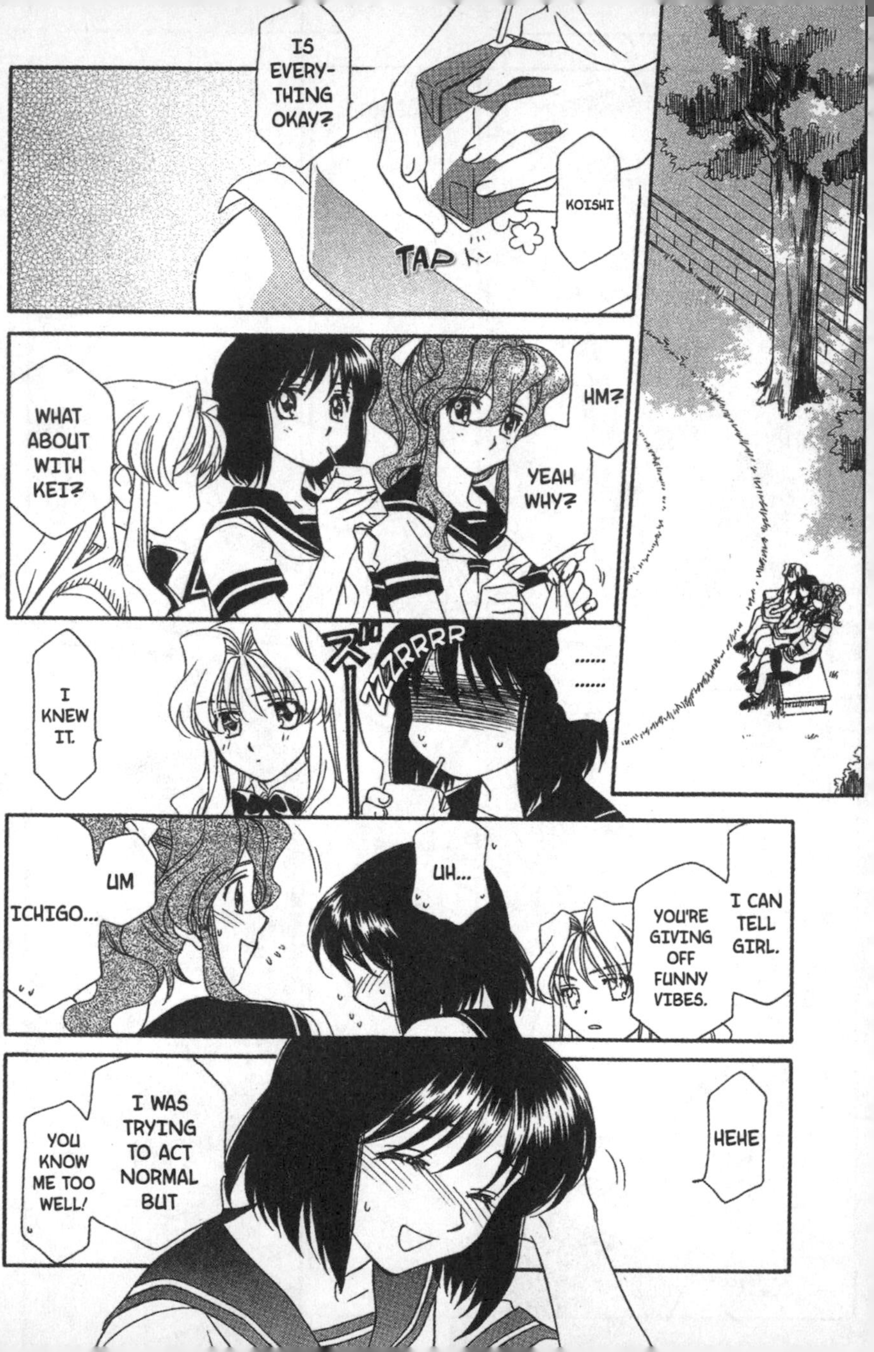
KOISHI
IS EVERY-THING OKAY?
TAP
HM?
YEAH WHY?
WHAT ABOUT WITH KEI?
ZZZRRRR
......
......
I KNEW IT.
I CAN TELL GIRL.
YOU'RE GIVING OFF FUNNY VIBES.
UH...
UM
ICHIGO...
HEHE
I WAS TRYING TO ACT NORMAL BUT
YOU KNOW ME TOO WELL!

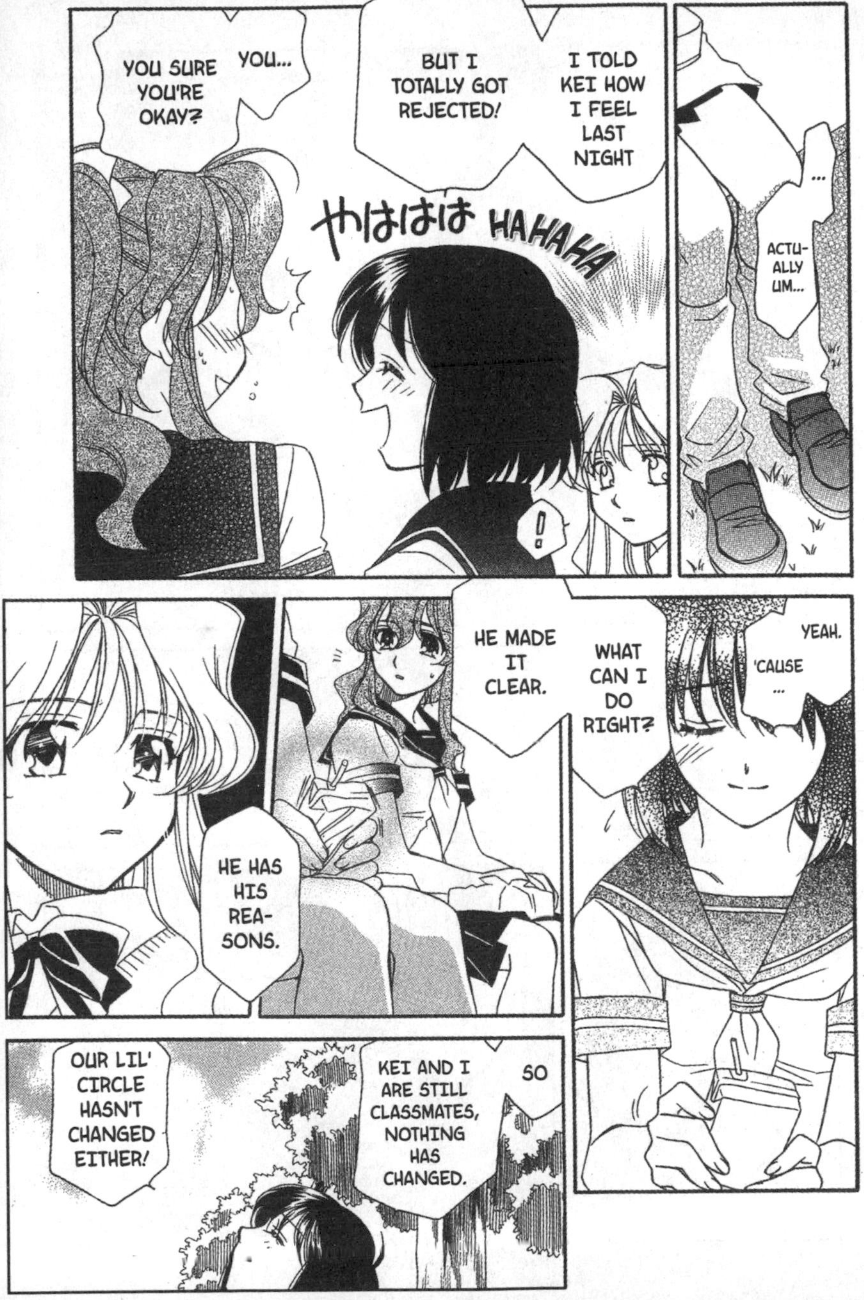
...
ACTU-ALLY UM...
I TOLD KEI HOW I FEEL LAST NIGHT
BUT I TOTALLY GOT REJECTED!
やははは HAHAHA
YOU...
YOU SURE YOU'RE OKAY?
!
YEAH.
'CAUSE ...
WHAT CAN I DO RIGHT?
HE MADE IT CLEAR.
HE HAS HIS REA-SONS.
SO
KEI AND I ARE STILL CLASSMATES, NOTHING HAS CHANGED.
OUR LIL' CIRCLE HASN'T CHANGED EITHER!

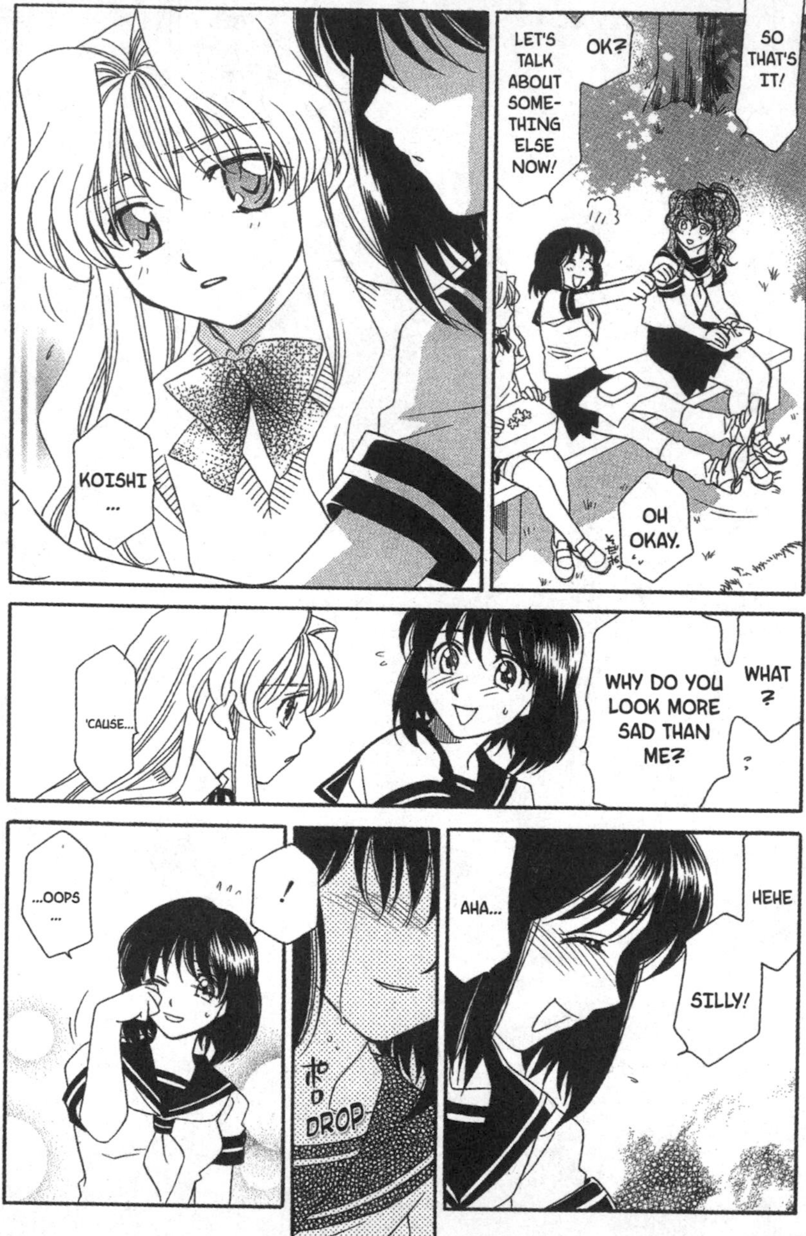
SO THAT'S IT!
OK?
LET'S TALK ABOUT SOME-THING ELSE NOW!
OH OKAY.
KOISHI ...
WHAT?
WHY DO YOU LOOK MORE SAD THAN ME?
'CAUSE...
HEHE
SILLY!
AHA...
!
ポロ
DROP
...OOPS ...

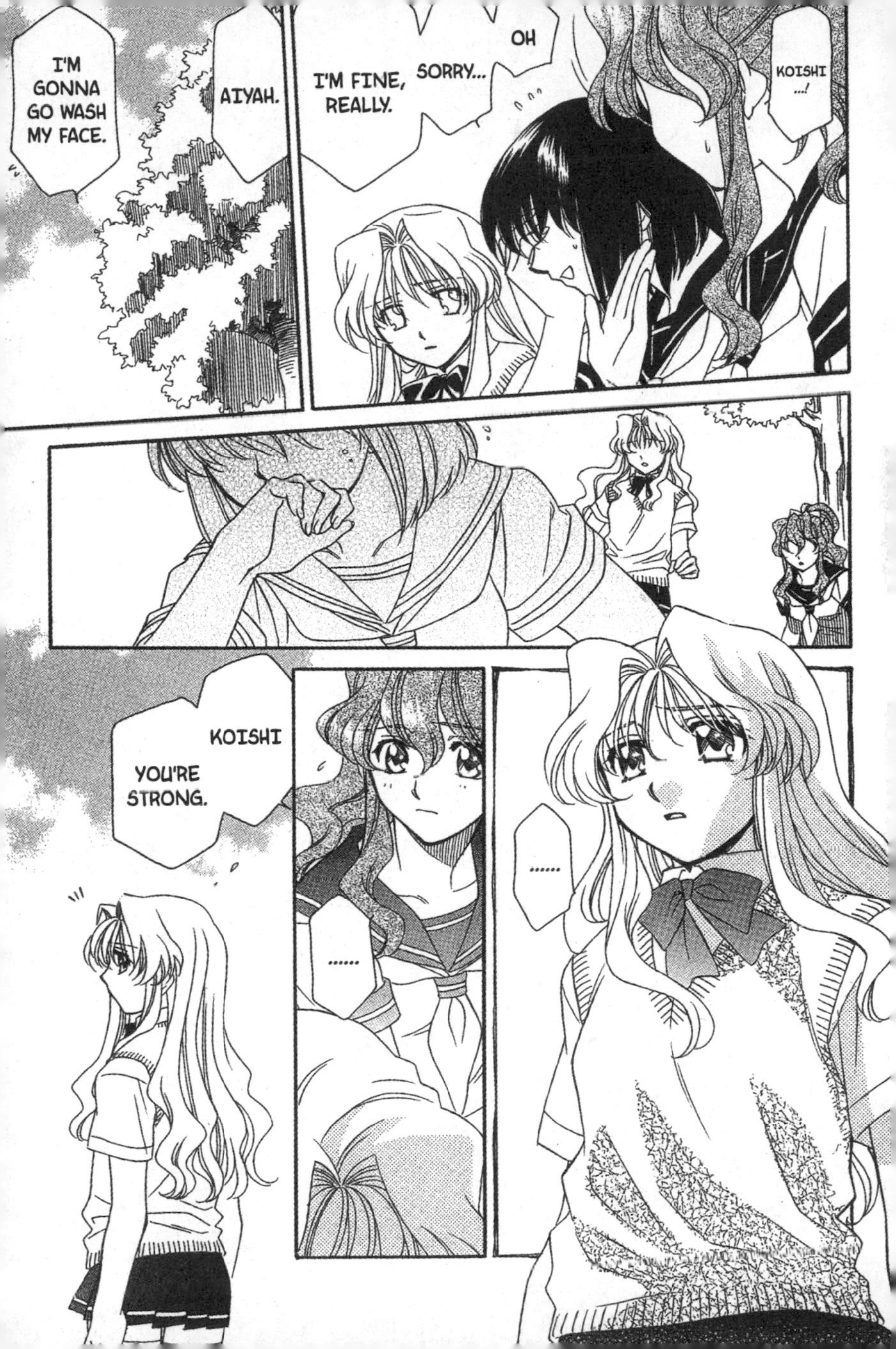
KOISHI ...!
OH
SORRY...
I'M FINE, REALLY.
AIYAH.
I'M GONNA GO WASH MY FACE.
......
......
KOISHI
YOU'RE STRONG.

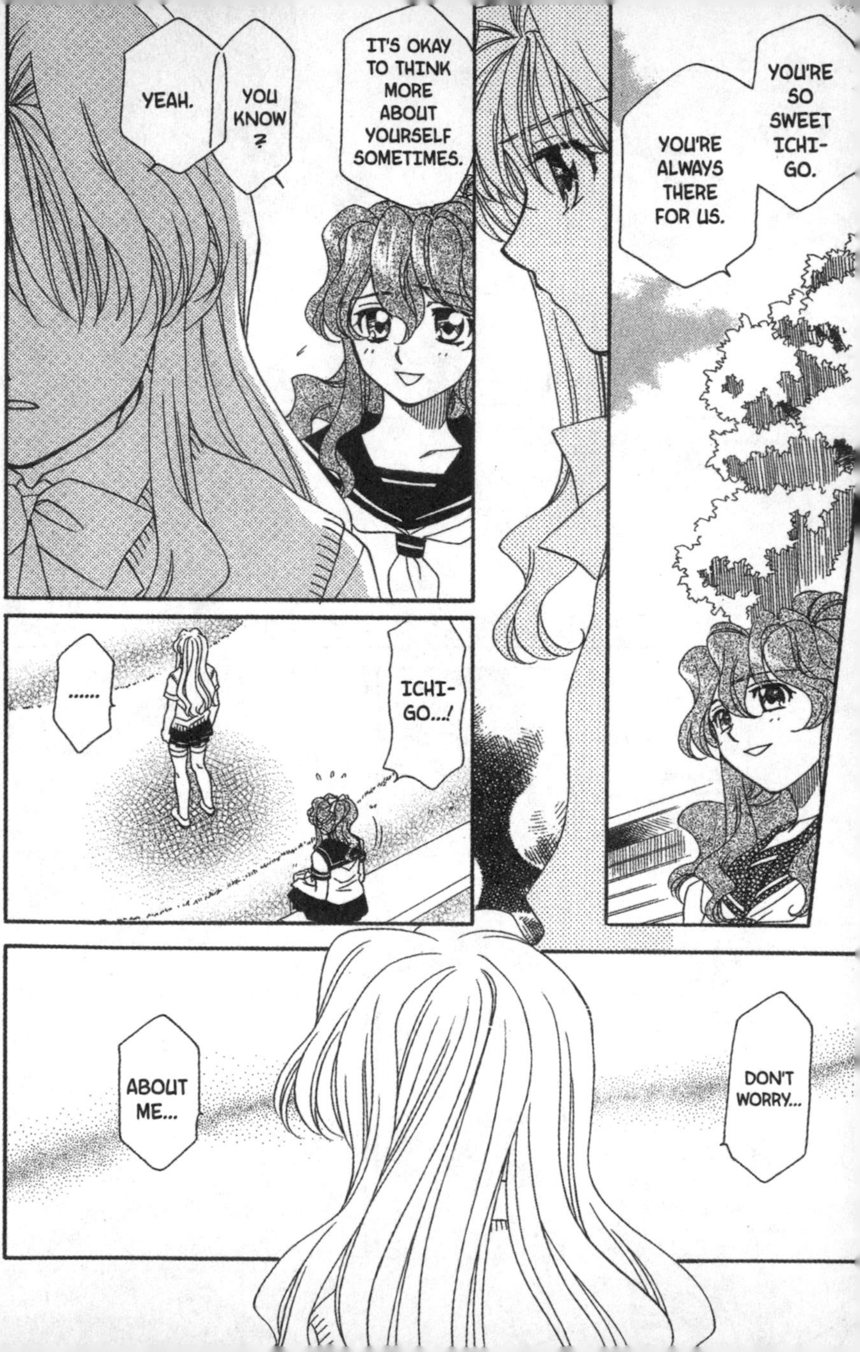
YOU'RE SO SWEET ICHI-GO.
YOU'RE ALWAYS THERE FOR US.
IT'S OKAY TO THINK MORE ABOUT YOURSELF SOMETIMES.
YOU KNOW?
YEAH.
ICHI-GO...!
......
DON'T WORRY...
ABOUT ME...

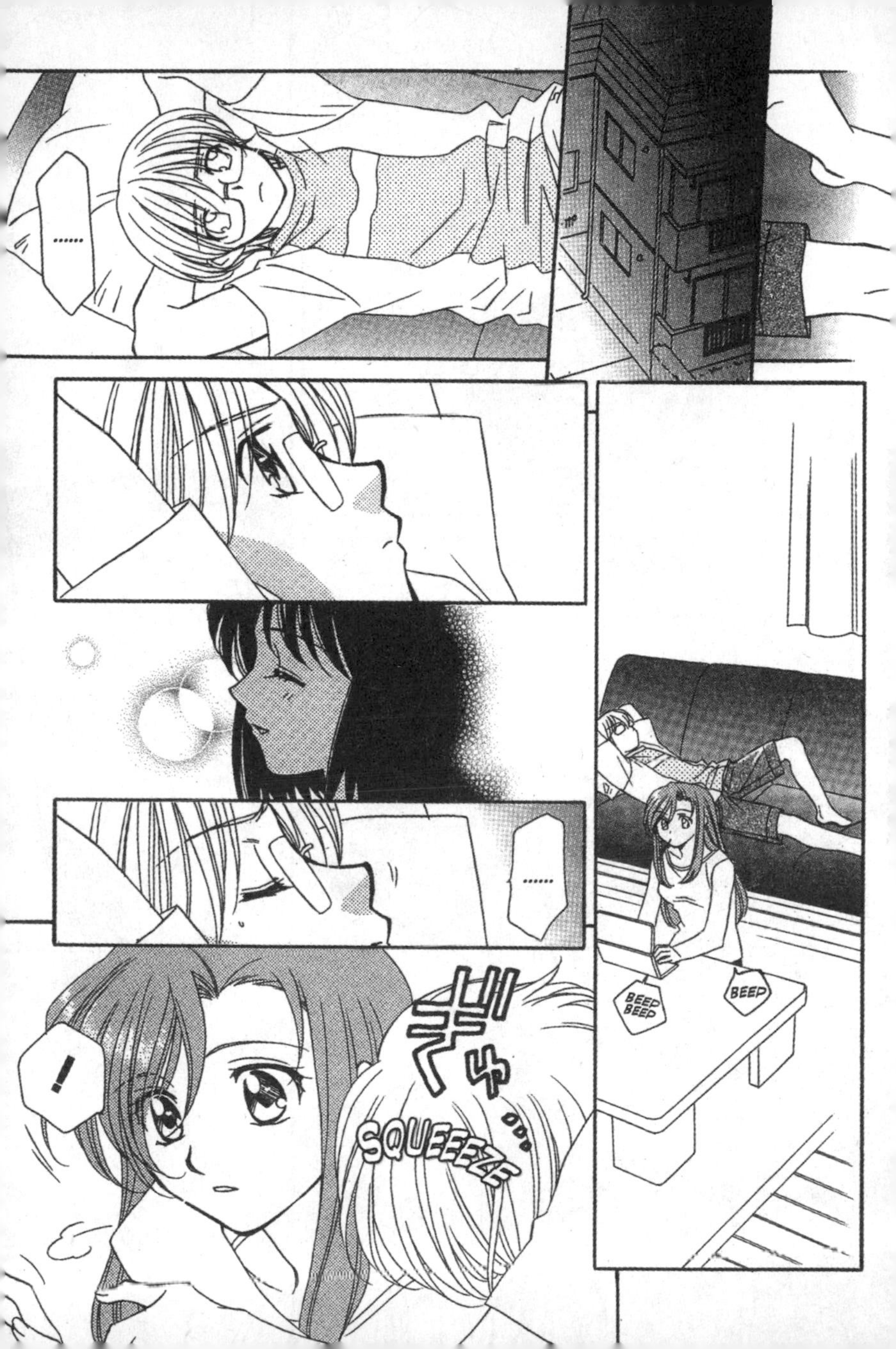

......
BEEP
BEEP BEEP
......
ぎゅ...
SQUEEEZE
!

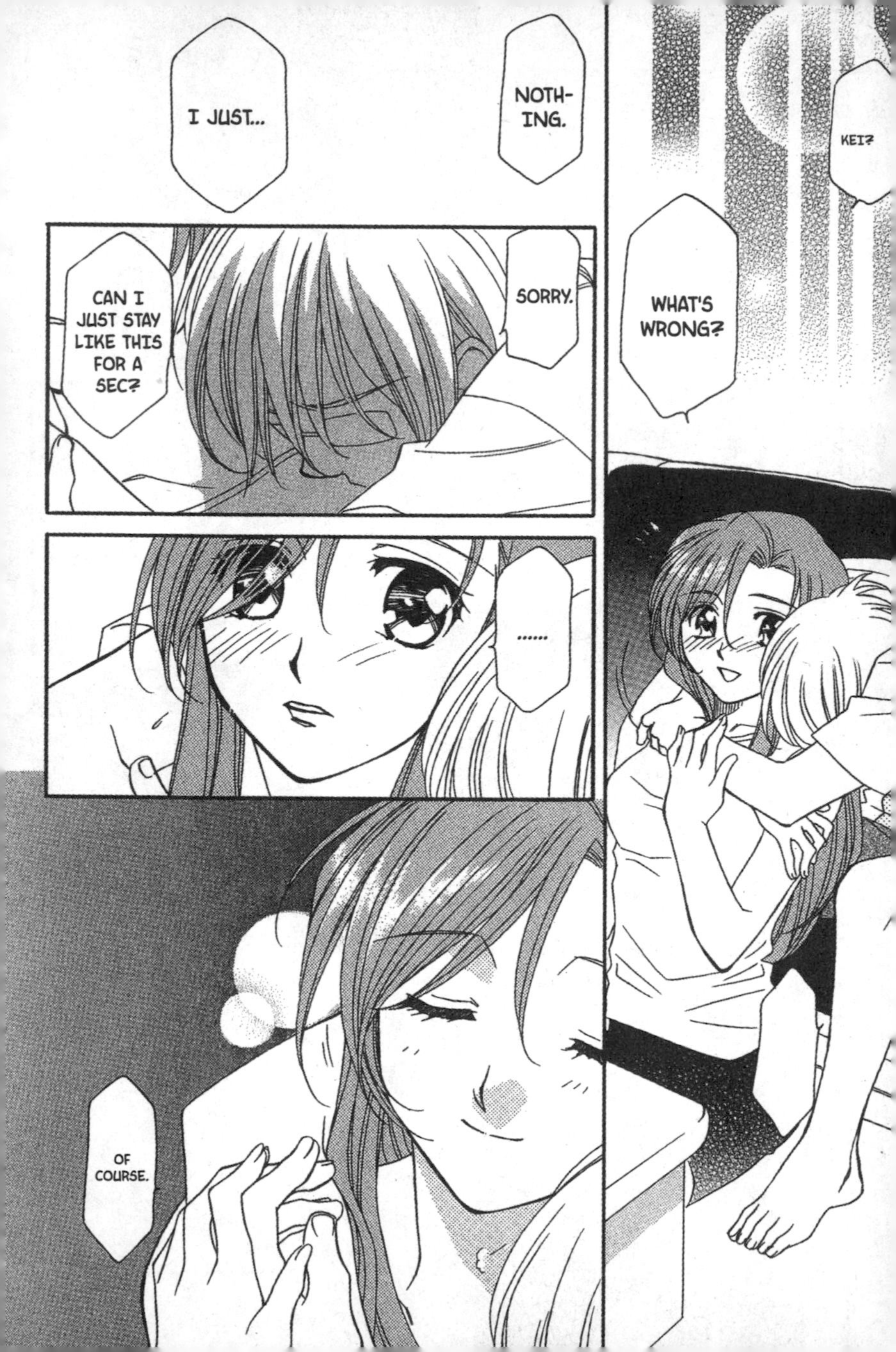
KEI?
WHAT'S WRONG?
NOTH-ING.
I JUST...
SORRY.
CAN I JUST STAY LIKE THIS FOR A SEC?
......
OF COURSE.

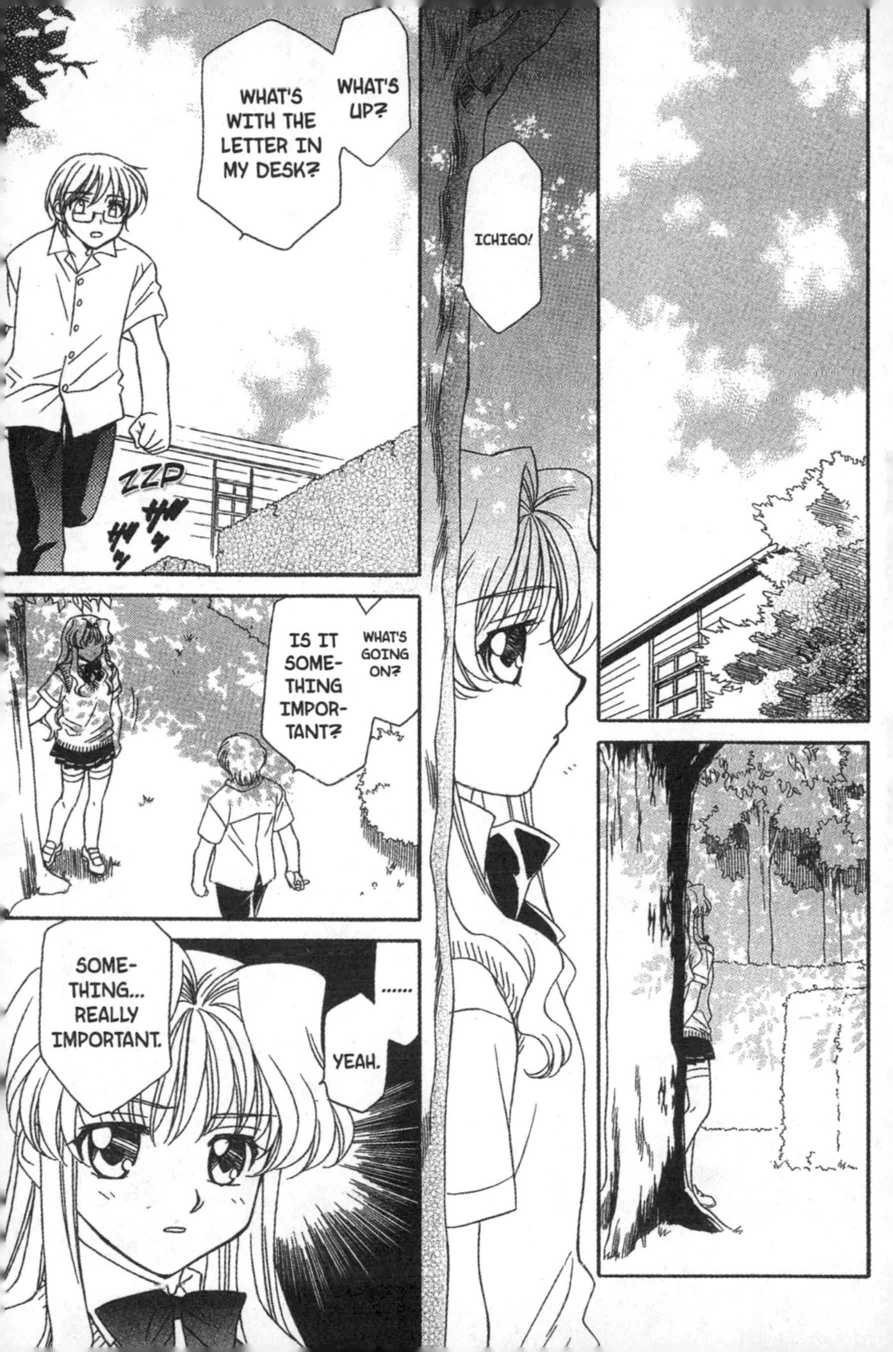
ICHIGO!
WHAT'S UP?
WHAT'S WITH THE LETTER IN MY DESK?
ZZP
WHAT'S GOING ON?
IS IT SOME-THING IMPOR-TANT?
......
YEAH.
SOME-THING... REALLY IMPORTANT.

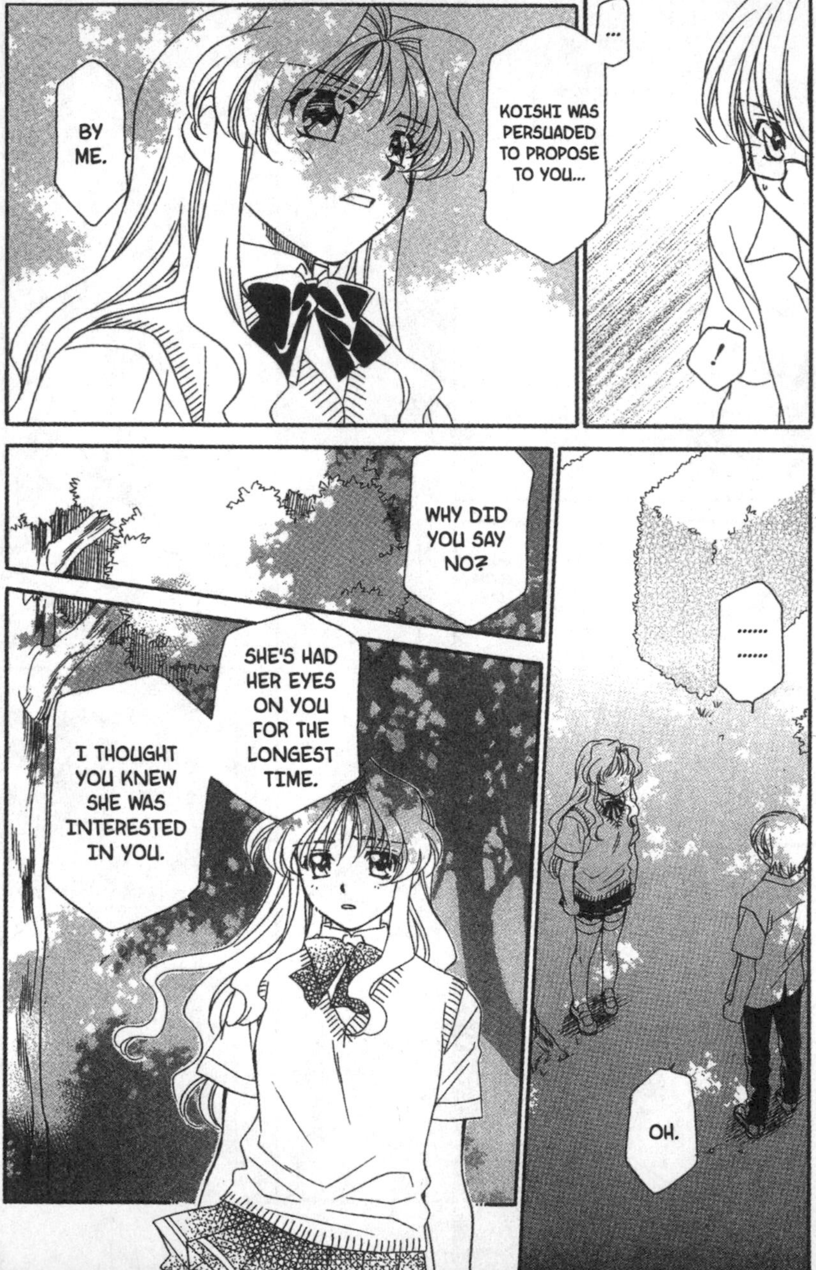
...
!
KOISHI WAS PERSUADED TO PROPOSE TO YOU...
BY ME.
......
......
OH.
WHY DID YOU SAY NO?
SHE'S HAD HER EYES ON YOU FOR THE LONGEST TIME.
I THOUGHT YOU KNEW SHE WAS INTERESTED IN YOU.

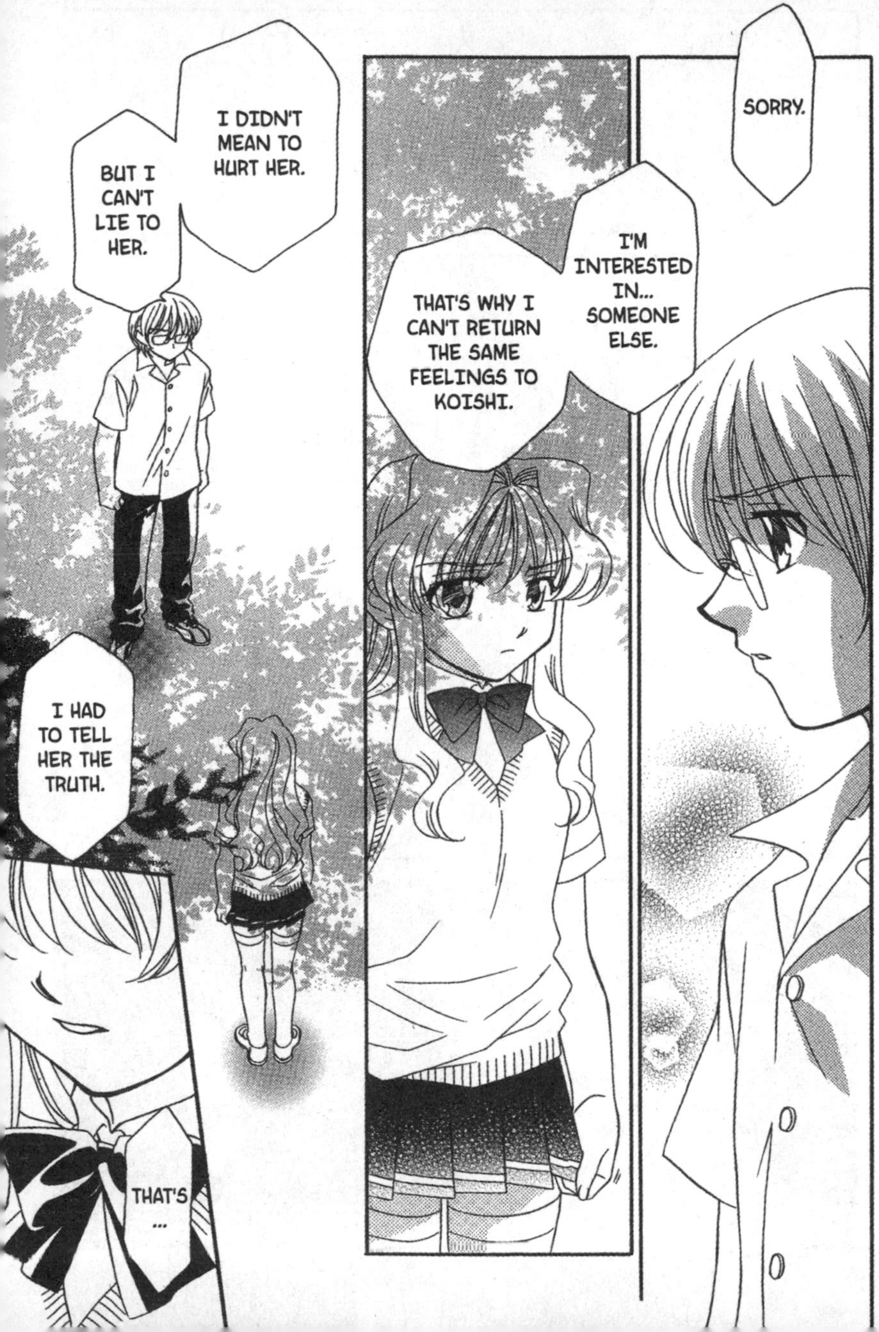
SORRY.
I'M INTERESTED IN... SOMEONE ELSE.
THAT'S WHY I CAN'T RETURN THE SAME FEELINGS TO KOISHI.
I DIDN'T MEAN TO HURT HER.
BUT I CAN'T LIE TO HER.
I HAD TO TELL HER THE TRUTH.
THAT'S ...

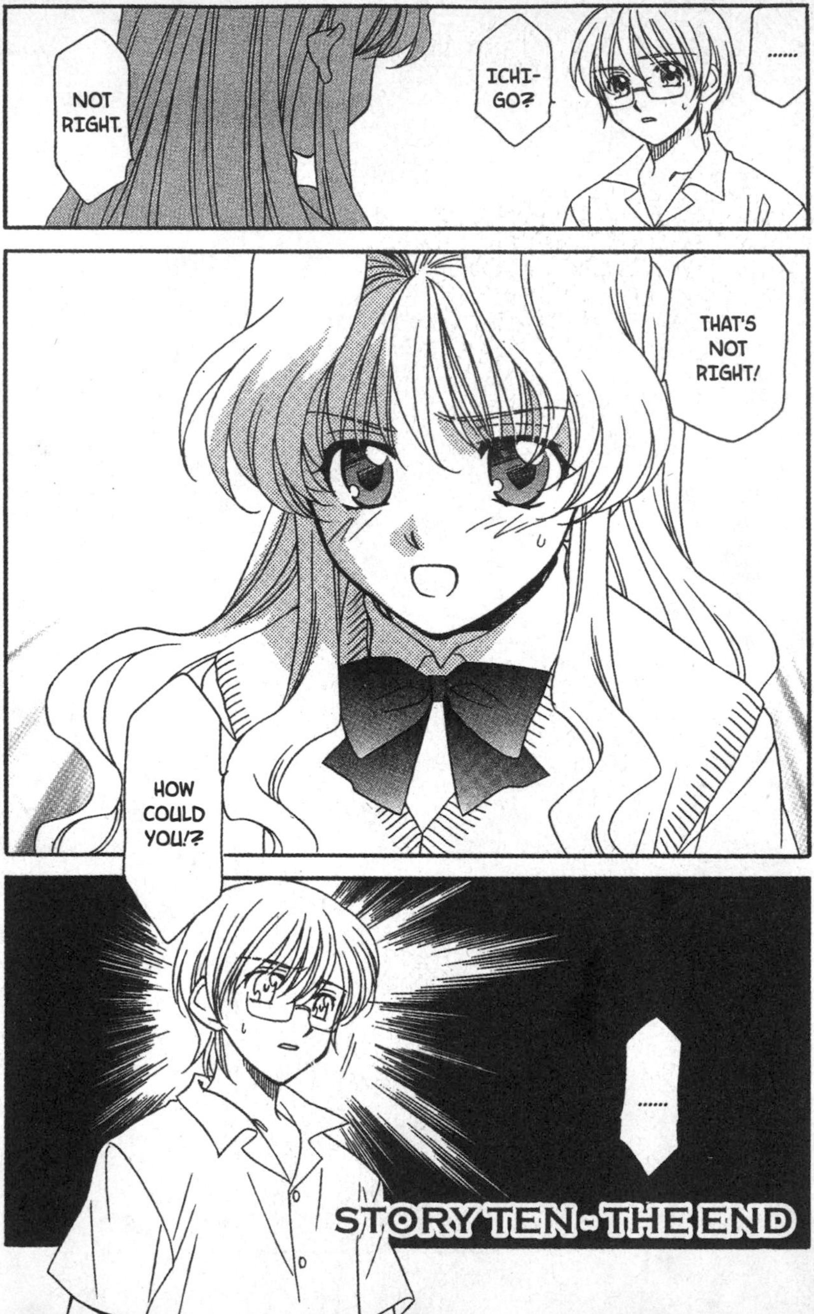
......
ICHI-GO?
NOT RIGHT.
THAT'S NOT RIGHT!
HOW COULD YOU!?
......
STORY TEN - THE END

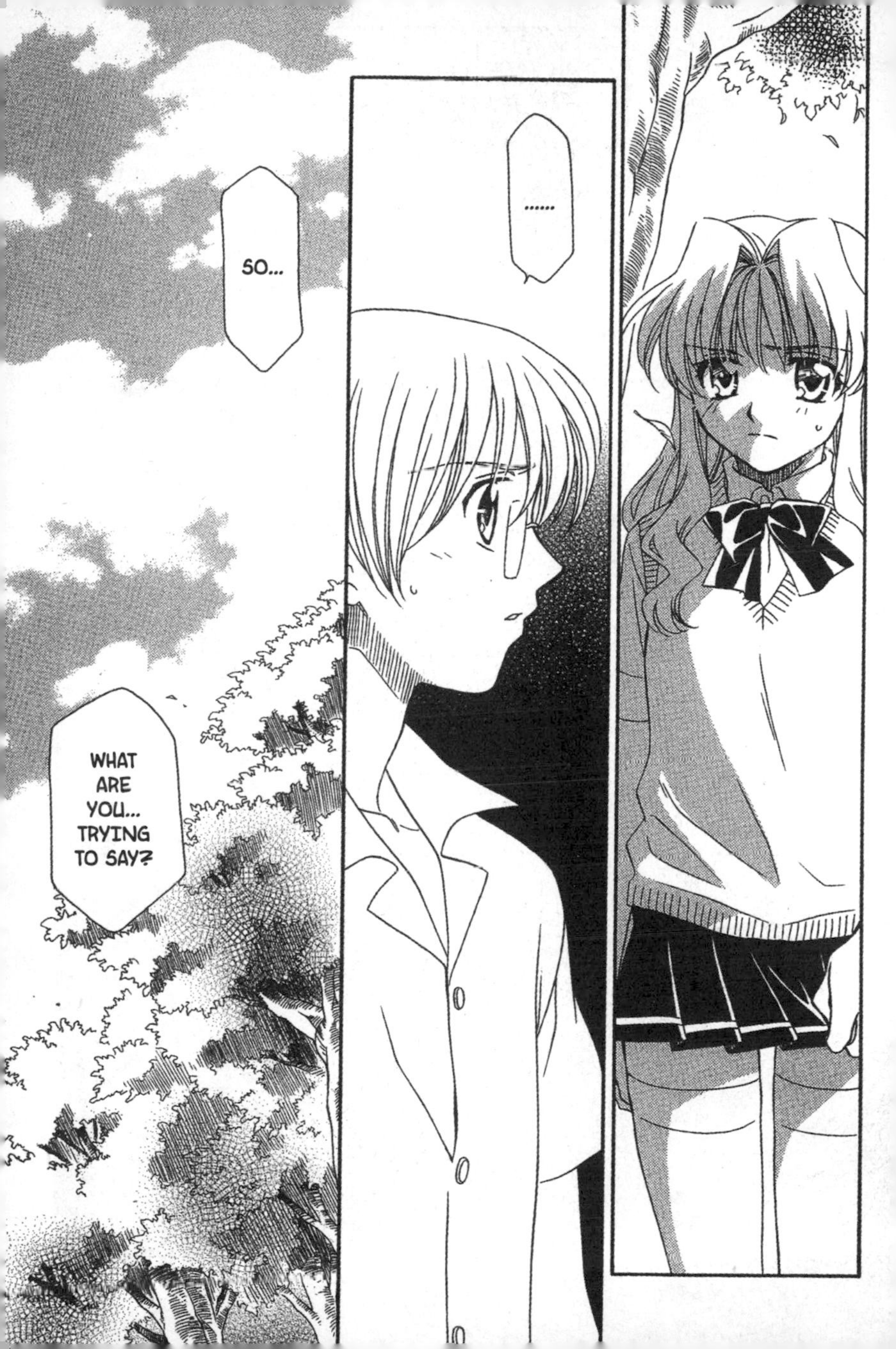
......
SO...
WHAT ARE YOU... TRYING TO SAY?

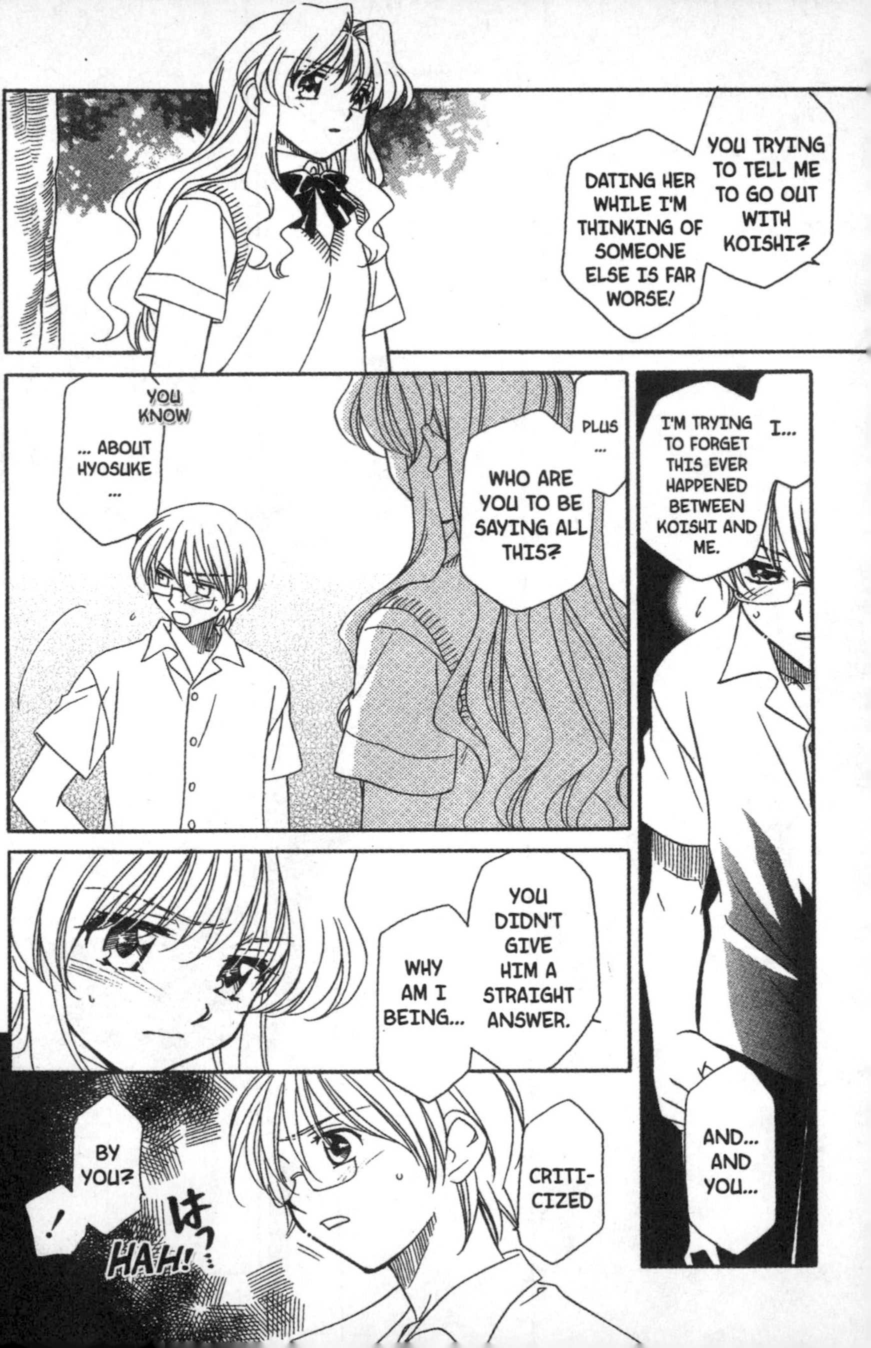
YOU TRYING TO TELL ME TO GO OUT WITH KOISHI?
DATING HER WHILE I'M THINKING OF SOMEONE ELSE IS FAR WORSE!
I...
I'M TRYING TO FORGET THIS EVER HAPPENED BETWEEN KOISHI AND ME.
AND... AND YOU...
PLUS ...
WHO ARE YOU TO BE SAYING ALL THIS?
YOU KNOW
... ABOUT HYOSUKE ...
YOU DIDN'T GIVE HIM A STRAIGHT ANSWER.
WHY AM I BEING...
CRITICIZED
BY YOU?
!
はっ
HAH!

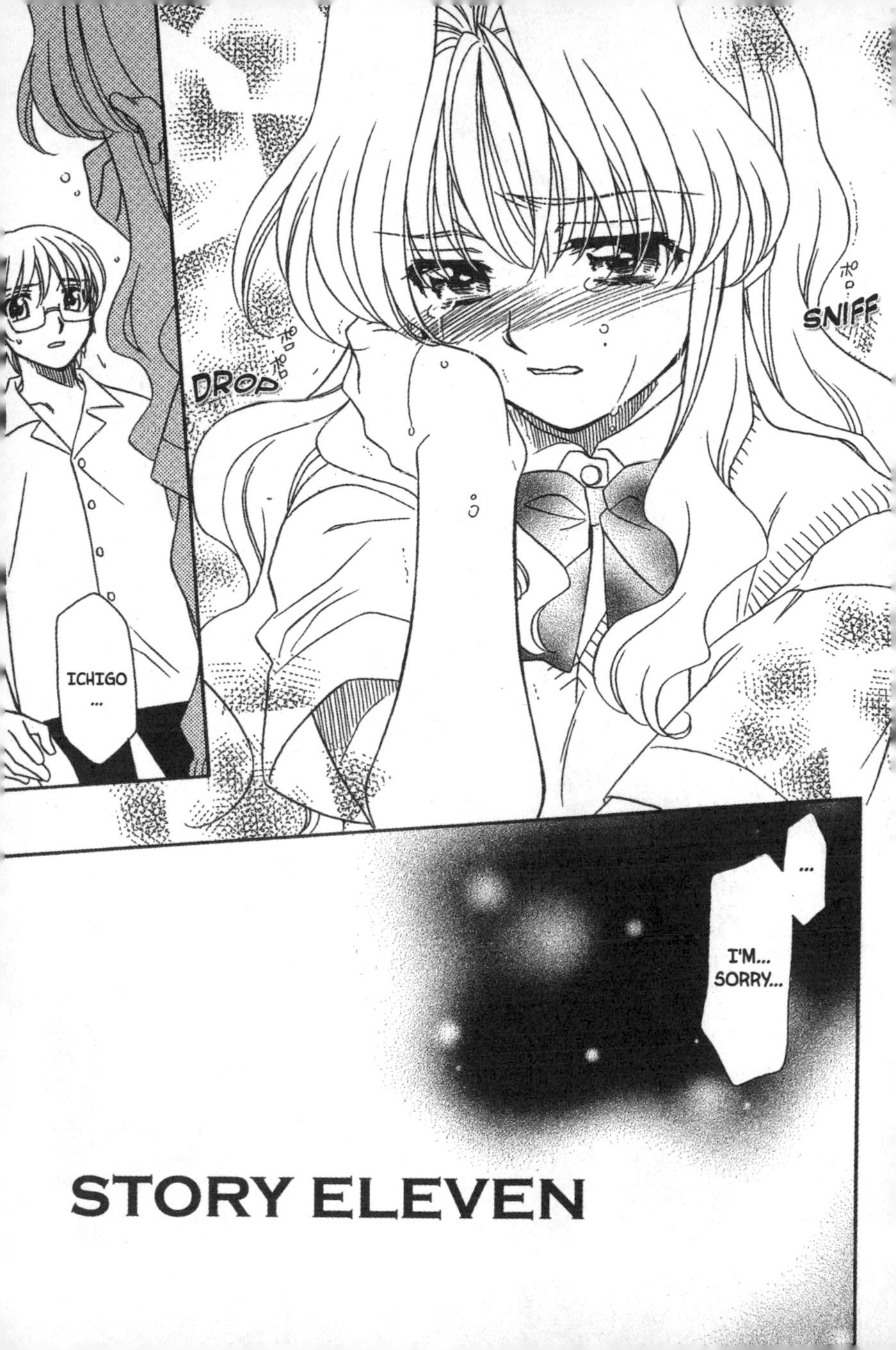
ポロ
SNIFF
ポロポロ
DROP
ICHIGO ...
...
I'M... SORRY...

STORY ELEVEN

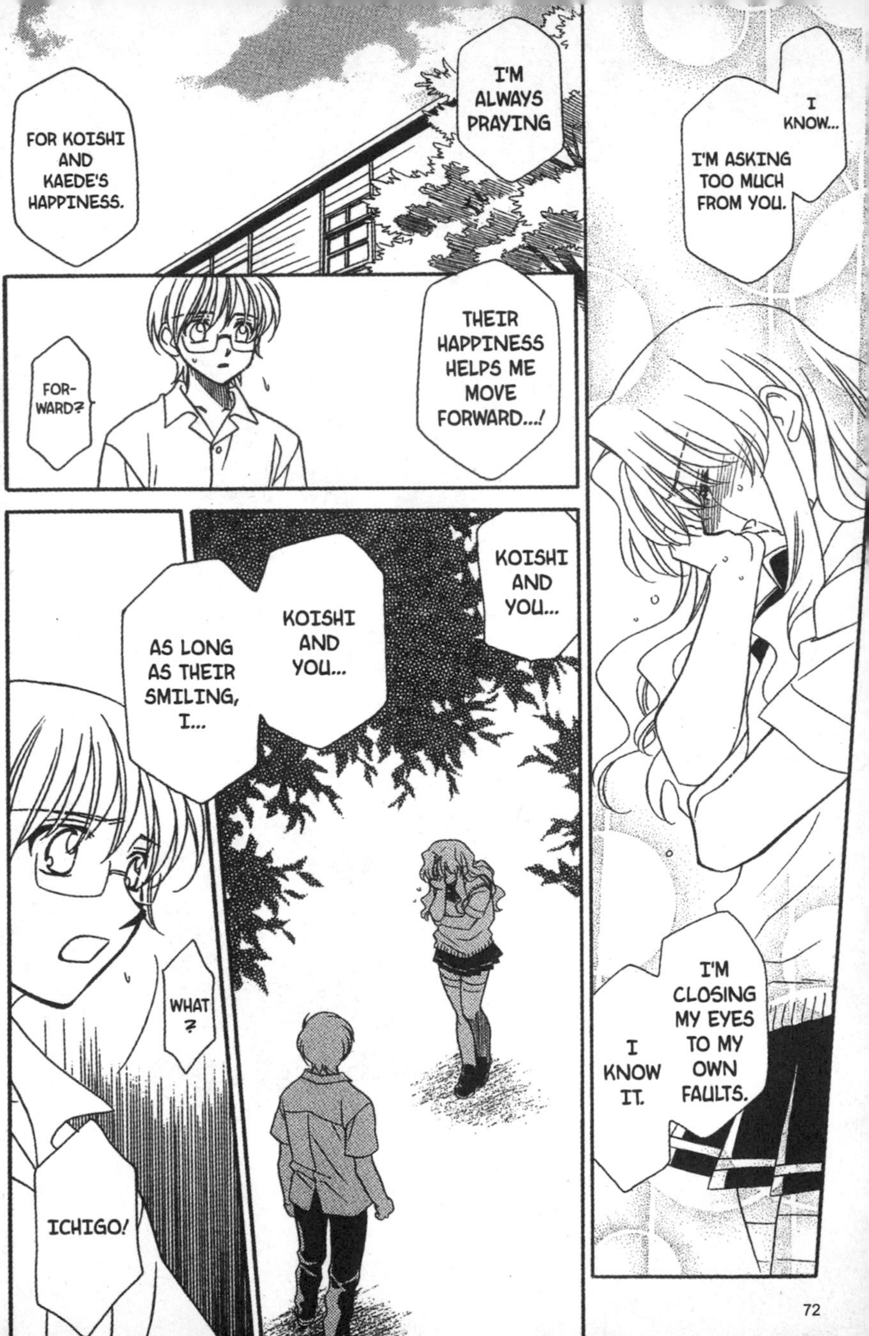
I KNOW...
I'M ASKING TOO MUCH FROM YOU.
I'M CLOSING MY EYES TO MY OWN FAULTS.
I KNOW IT.
I'M ALWAYS PRAYING
FOR KOISHI AND KAEDE'S HAPPINESS.
THEIR HAPPINESS HELPS ME MOVE FORWARD...!
FOR-WARD?
KOISHI AND YOU...
KOISHI AND YOU...
AS LONG AS THEIR SMILING, I...
WHAT?
ICHIGO!

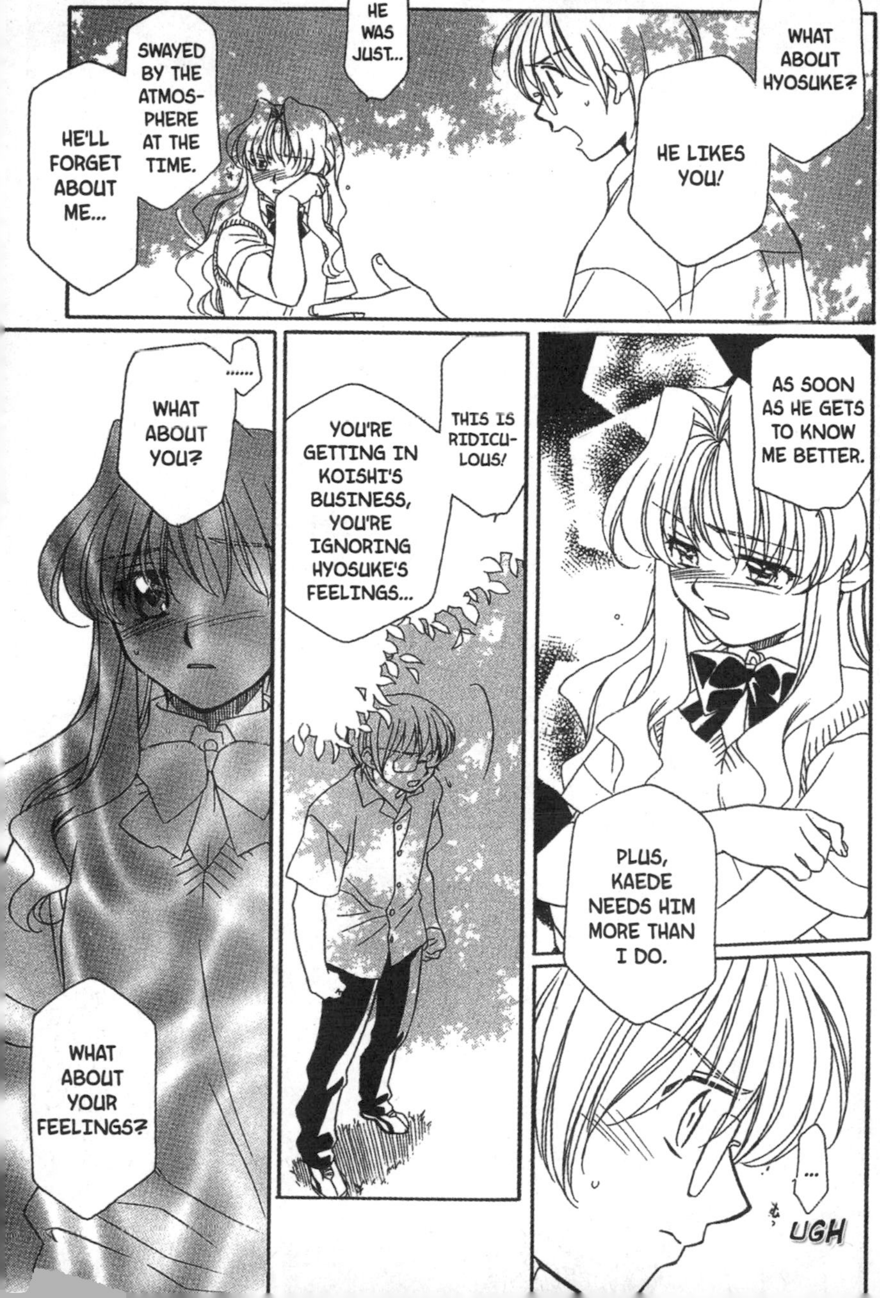

WHAT ABOUT HYOSUKE?
HE LIKES YOU!
HE WAS JUST...
SWAYED BY THE ATMOS-PHERE AT THE TIME.
HE'LL FORGET ABOUT ME...
AS SOON AS HE GETS TO KNOW ME BETTER.
PLUS, KAEDE NEEDS HIM MORE THAN I DO.
...
UGH
THIS IS RIDICU-LOUS!
YOU'RE GETTING IN KOISHI'S BUSINESS, YOU'RE IGNORING HYOSUKE'S FEELINGS...
......
WHAT ABOUT YOU?
WHAT ABOUT YOUR FEELINGS?

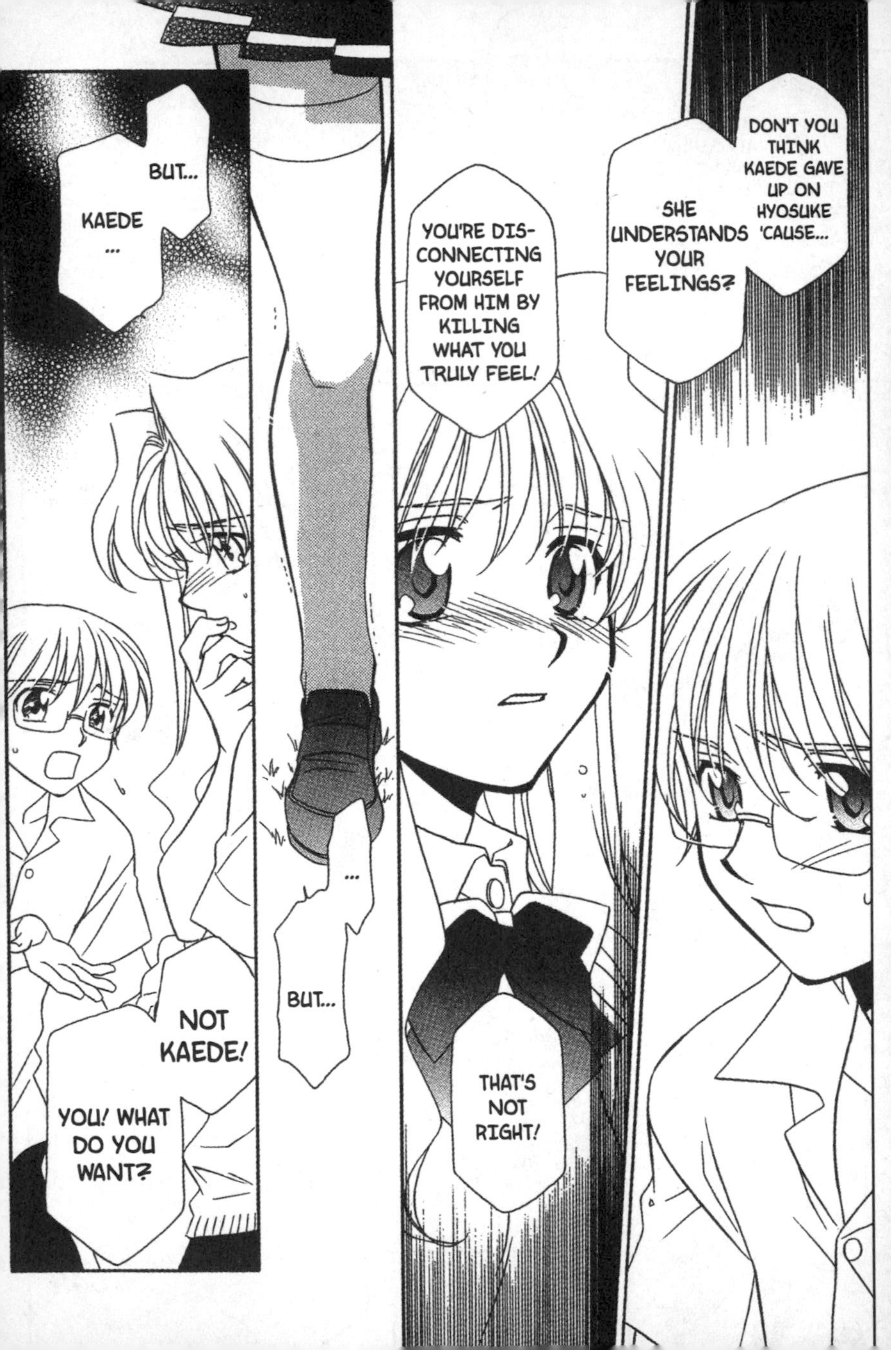
DON'T YOU THINK KAEDE GAVE UP ON HYOSUKE 'CAUSE...
SHE UNDERSTANDS YOUR FEELINGS?
YOU'RE DIS-CONNECTING YOURSELF FROM HIM BY KILLING WHAT YOU TRULY FEEL!
THAT'S NOT RIGHT!
...
BUT...
BUT...
KAEDE ...
NOT KAEDE!
YOU! WHAT DO YOU WANT?

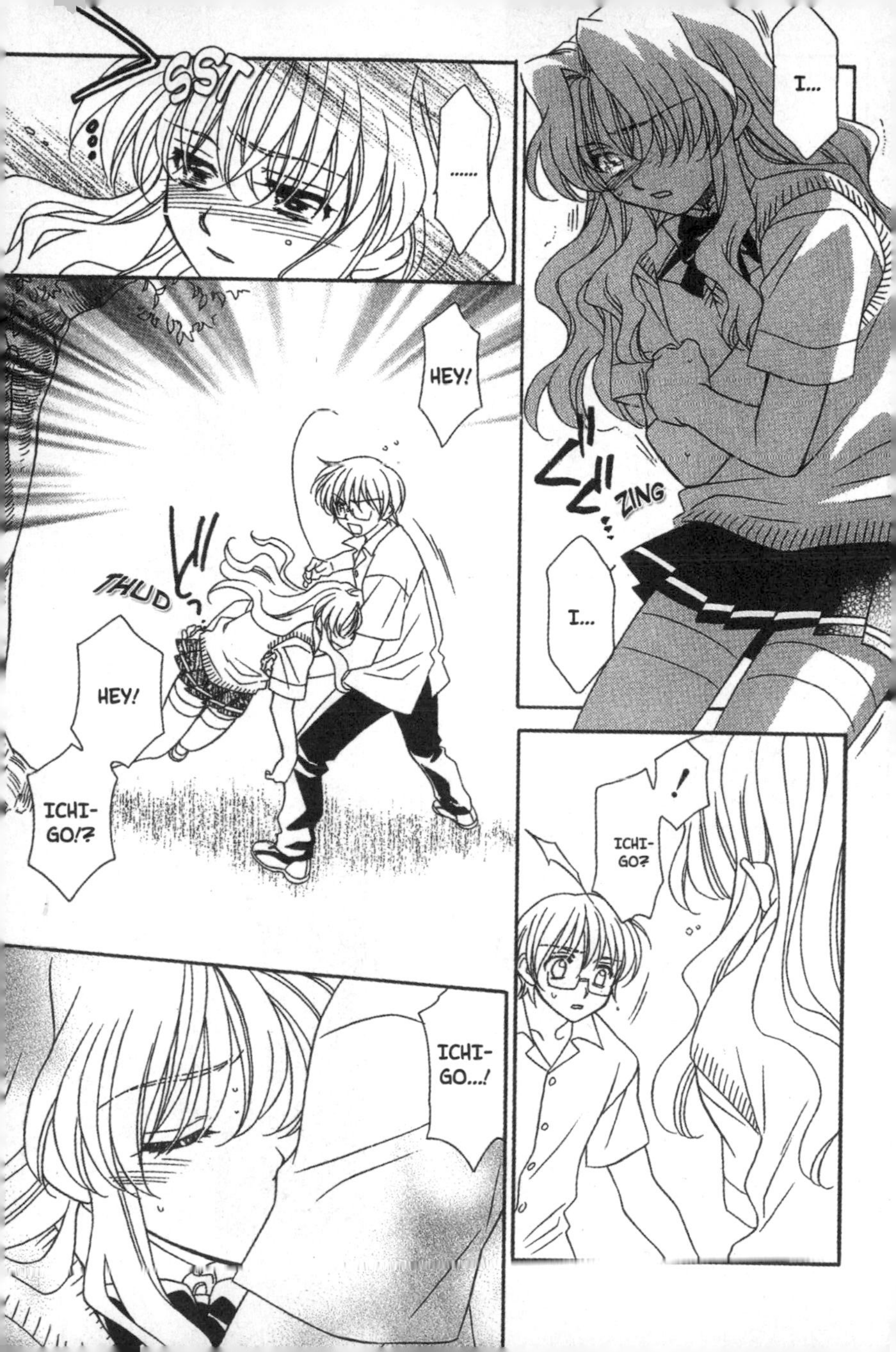

I...
ZING
I...
SST
......
HEY!
THUD
HEY!
ICHI-GO!?
!
ICHI-GO?
ICHI-GO...!

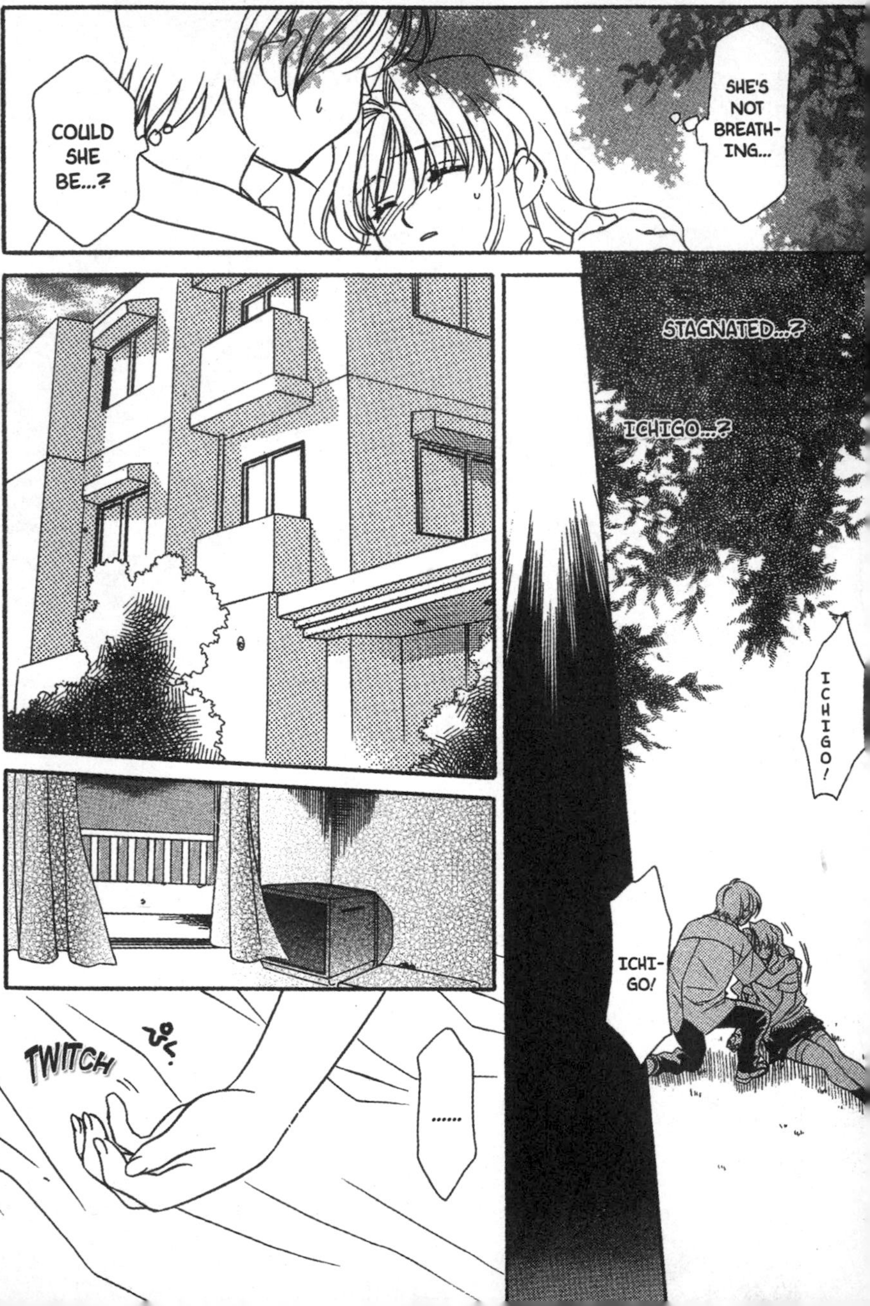
SHE'S NOT BREATHING...
COULD SHE BE...?
STAGNATED...?
ICHIGO...?
ICHIGO!
ICHI-GO!
TWITCH
......

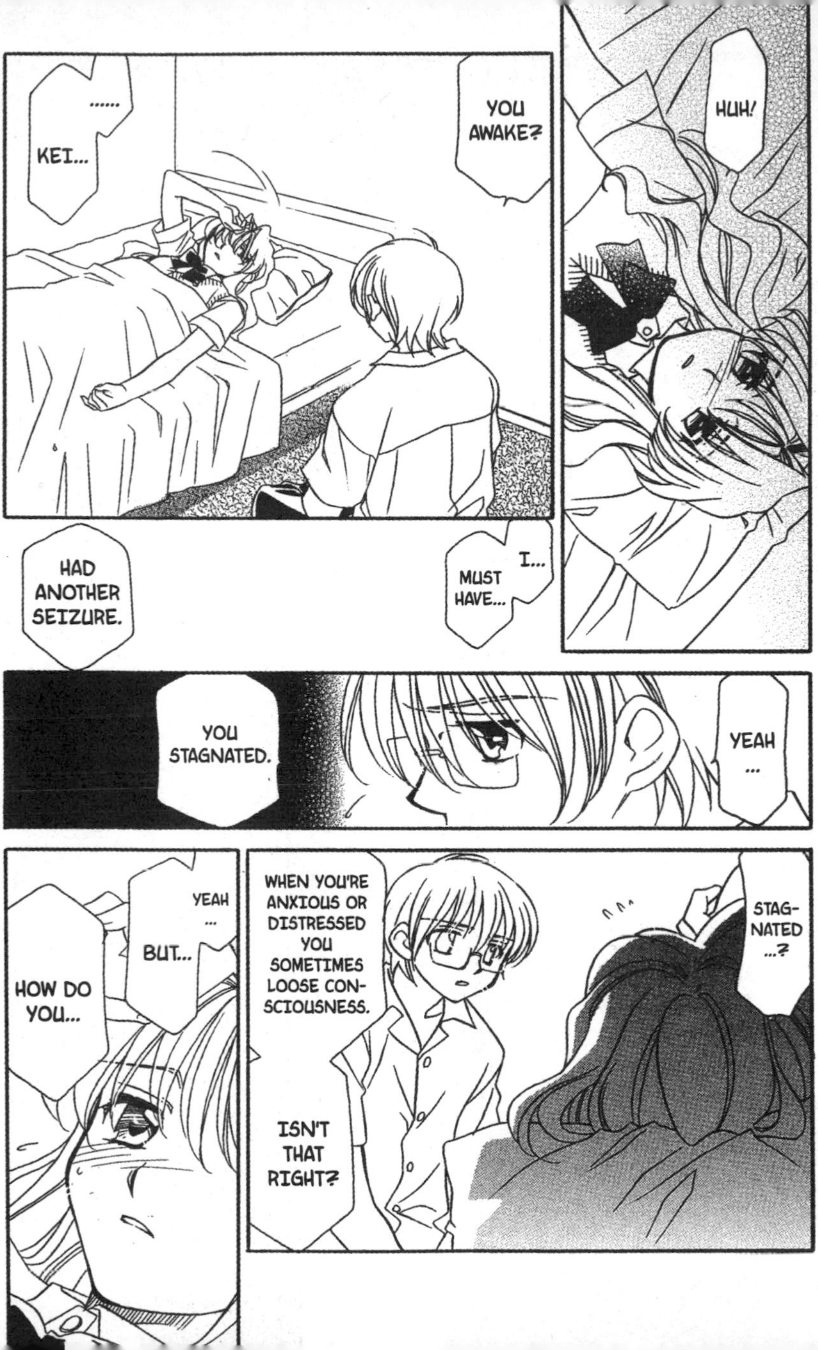
HUH!
YOU AWAKE?
......
KEI...
I... MUST HAVE...
HAD ANOTHER SEIZURE.
YEAH ...
YOU STAGNATED.
STAG-NATED ...?
WHEN YOU'RE ANXIOUS OR DISTRESSED YOU SOMETIMES LOOSE CON-SCIOUSNESS.
ISN'T THAT RIGHT?
YEAH ...
BUT...
HOW DO YOU...

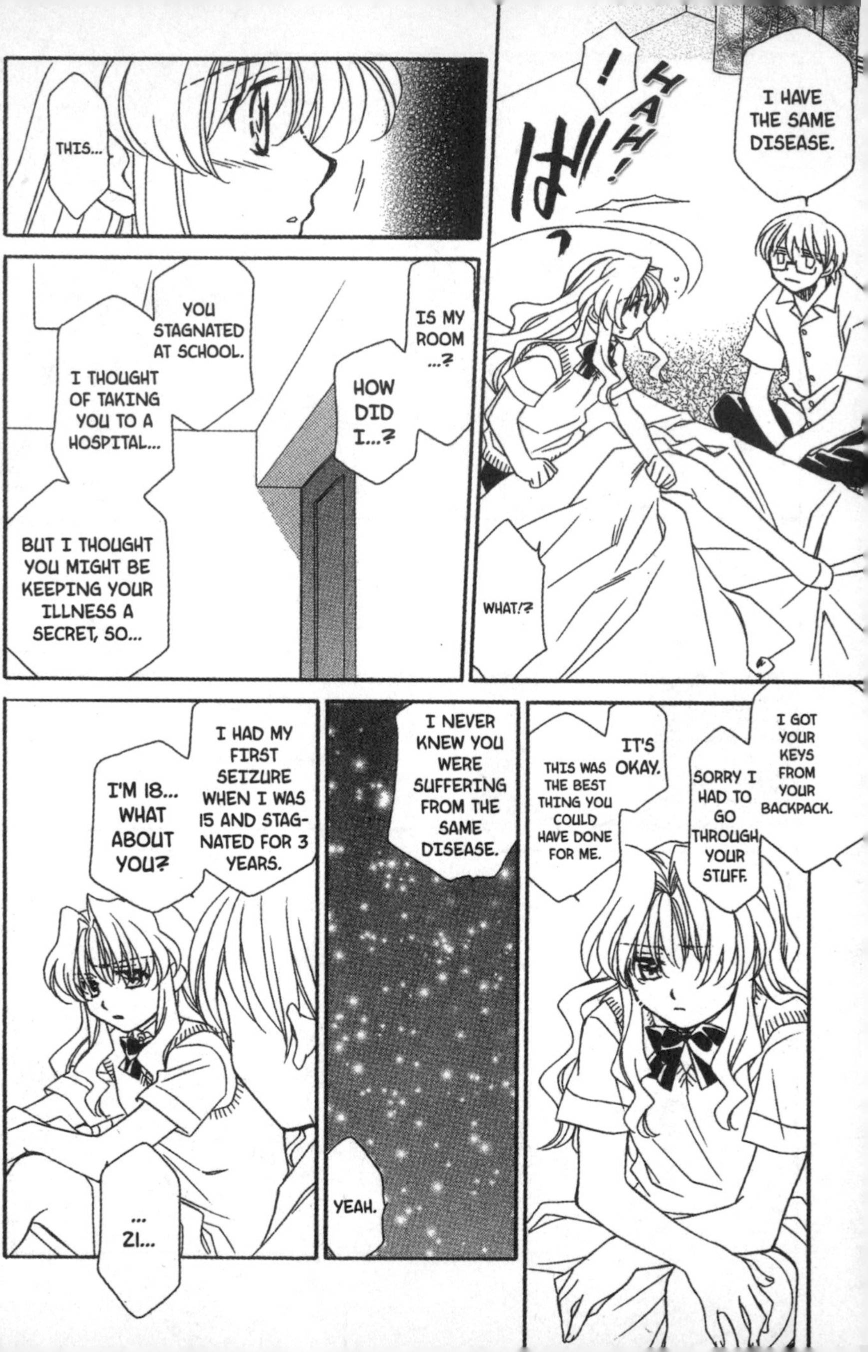
I HAVE THE SAME DISEASE.
HAH!
!
ば
WHAT!?
THIS...
IS MY ROOM ...?
HOW DID I...?
YOU STAGNATED AT SCHOOL.
I THOUGHT OF TAKING YOU TO A HOSPITAL...
BUT I THOUGHT YOU MIGHT BE KEEPING YOUR ILLNESS A SECRET, SO...
I GOT YOUR KEYS FROM YOUR BACKPACK.
SORRY I HAD TO GO THROUGH YOUR STUFF.
IT'S OKAY.
THIS WAS THE BEST THING YOU COULD HAVE DONE FOR ME.
I NEVER KNEW YOU WERE SUFFERING FROM THE SAME DISEASE.
YEAH.
I HAD MY FIRST SEIZURE WHEN I WAS 15 AND STAGNATED FOR 3 YEARS.
I'M 18... WHAT ABOUT YOU?
... 21...

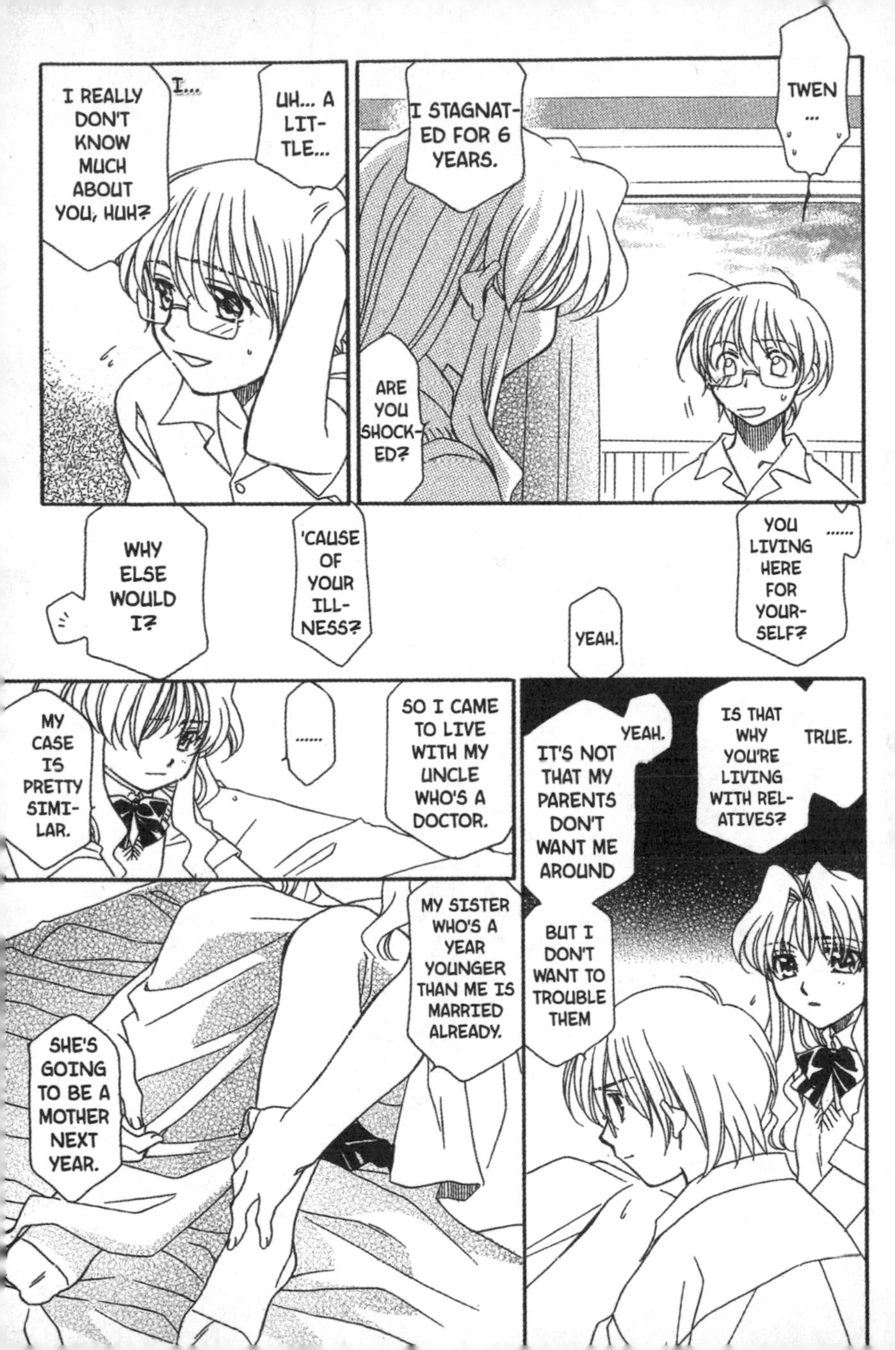
TWEN ...
I STAGNATED FOR 6 YEARS.
ARE YOU SHOCKED?
UH... A LITTLE...
I...
I REALLY DON'T KNOW MUCH ABOUT YOU, HUH?
......
YOU LIVING HERE FOR YOURSELF?
YEAH.
'CAUSE OF YOUR ILLNESS?
WHY ELSE WOULD I?
TRUE.
IS THAT WHY YOU'RE LIVING WITH RELATIVES?
YEAH.
IT'S NOT THAT MY PARENTS DON'T WANT ME AROUND
BUT I DON'T WANT TO TROUBLE THEM
SO I CAME TO LIVE WITH MY UNCLE WHO'S A DOCTOR.
......
MY CASE IS PRETTY SIMILAR.
MY SISTER WHO'S A YEAR YOUNGER THAN ME IS MARRIED ALREADY.
SHE'S GOING TO BE A MOTHER NEXT YEAR.

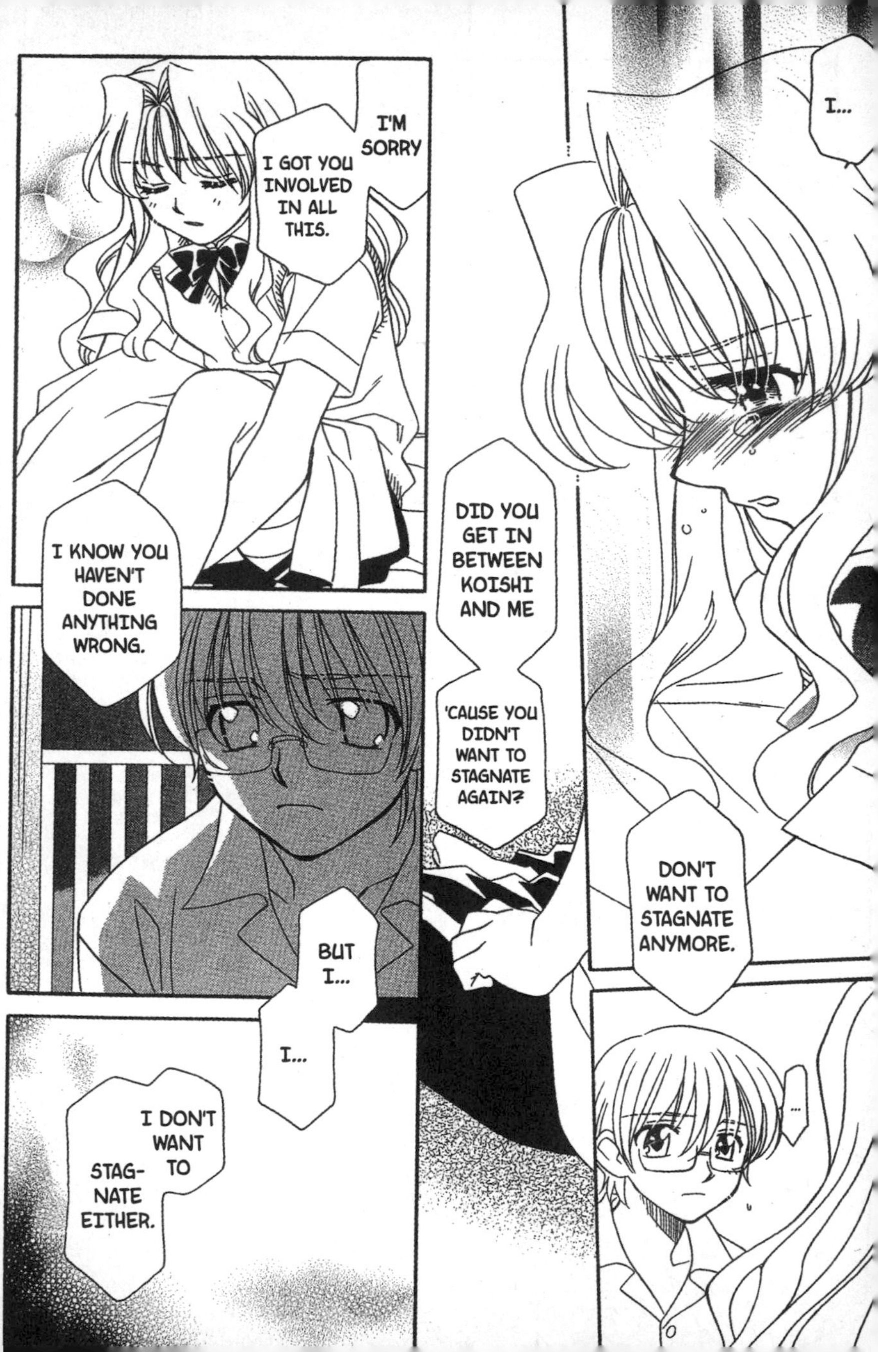
I...
DON'T WANT TO STAGNATE ANYMORE.
I'M SORRY
I GOT YOU INVOLVED IN ALL THIS.
I KNOW YOU HAVEN'T DONE ANYTHING WRONG.
DID YOU GET IN BETWEEN KOISHI AND ME
'CAUSE YOU DIDN'T WANT TO STAGNATE AGAIN?
...
BUT I...
I...
I DON'T WANT TO STAGNATE EITHER.

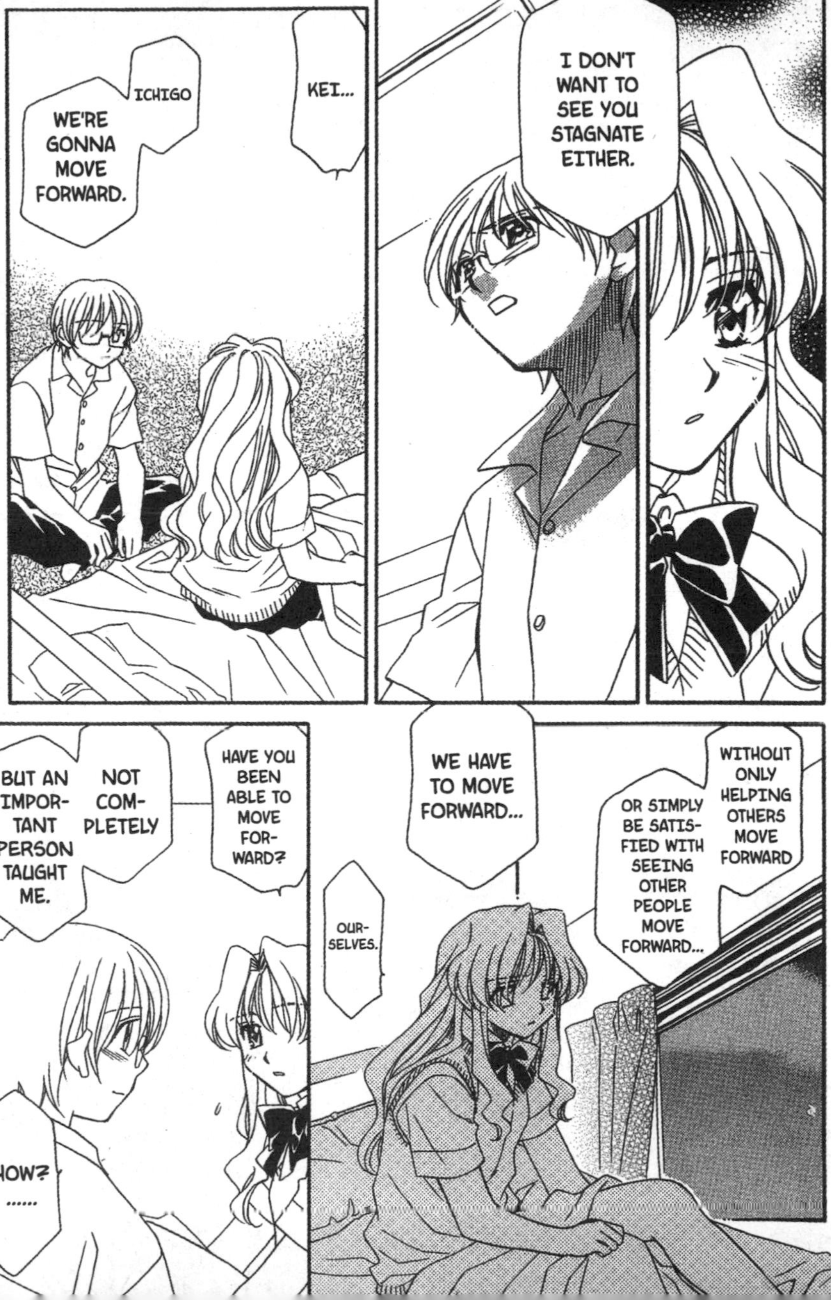
I DON'T WANT TO SEE YOU STAGNATE EITHER.
KEI...
ICHIGO
WE'RE GONNA MOVE FORWARD.
WITHOUT ONLY HELPING OTHERS MOVE FORWARD
OR SIMPLY BE SATISFIED WITH SEEING OTHER PEOPLE MOVE FORWARD...
WE HAVE TO MOVE FORWARD...
OURSELVES.
HAVE YOU BEEN ABLE TO MOVE FORWARD?
NOT COMPLETELY
BUT AN IMPORTANT PERSON TAUGHT ME.
HOW?
....

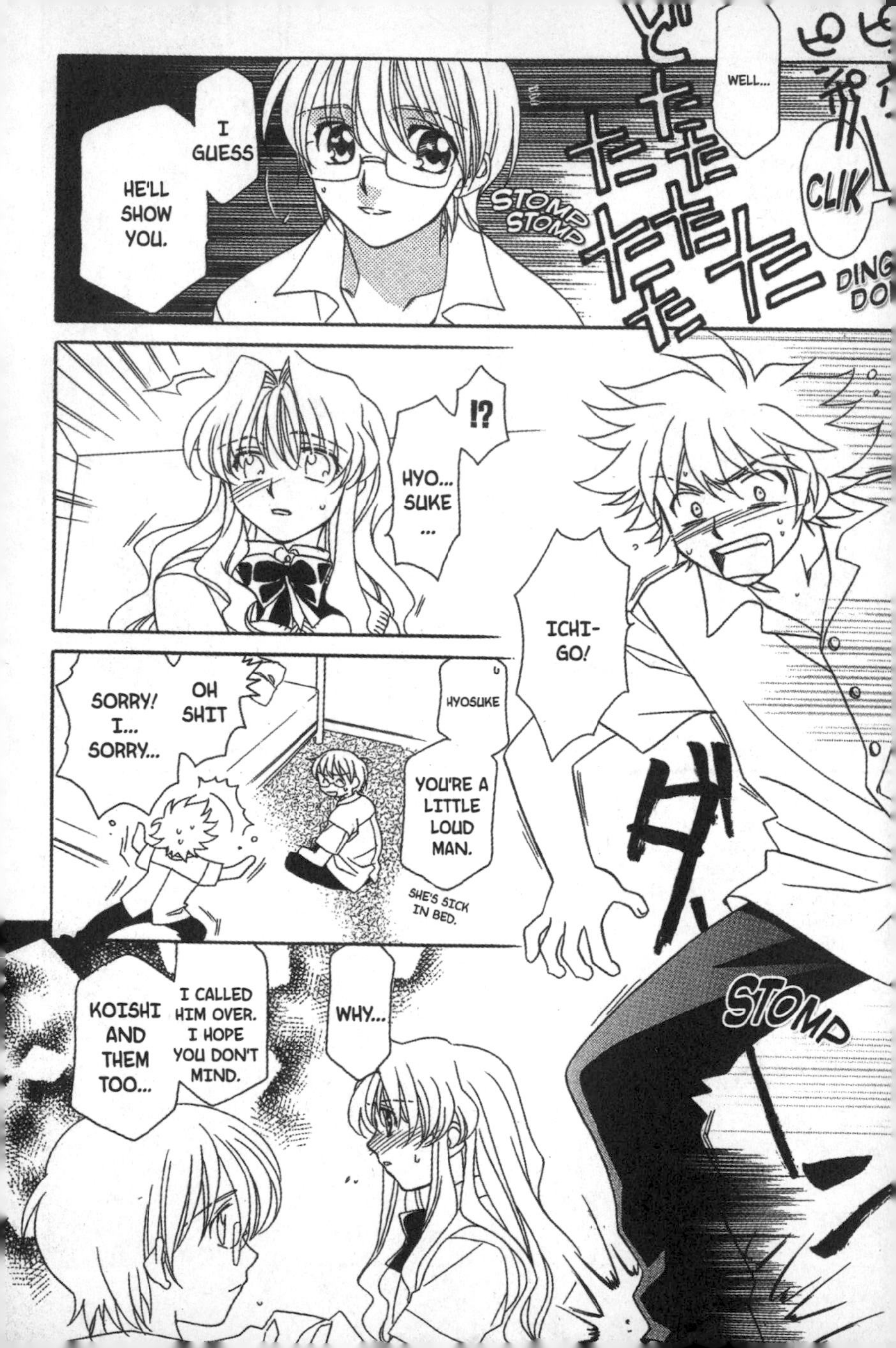
WELL...
CLIK
DING DO
STOMP STOMP
I GUESS HE'LL SHOW YOU.
ICHI-GO!
STOMP
!?
HYO... SUKE ...
HYOSUKE YOU'RE A LITTLE LOUD MAN.
SHE'S SICK IN BED.
OH SHIT
SORRY! I... SORRY...
WHY...
I CALLED HIM OVER. I HOPE YOU DON'T MIND.
KOISHI AND THEM TOO...

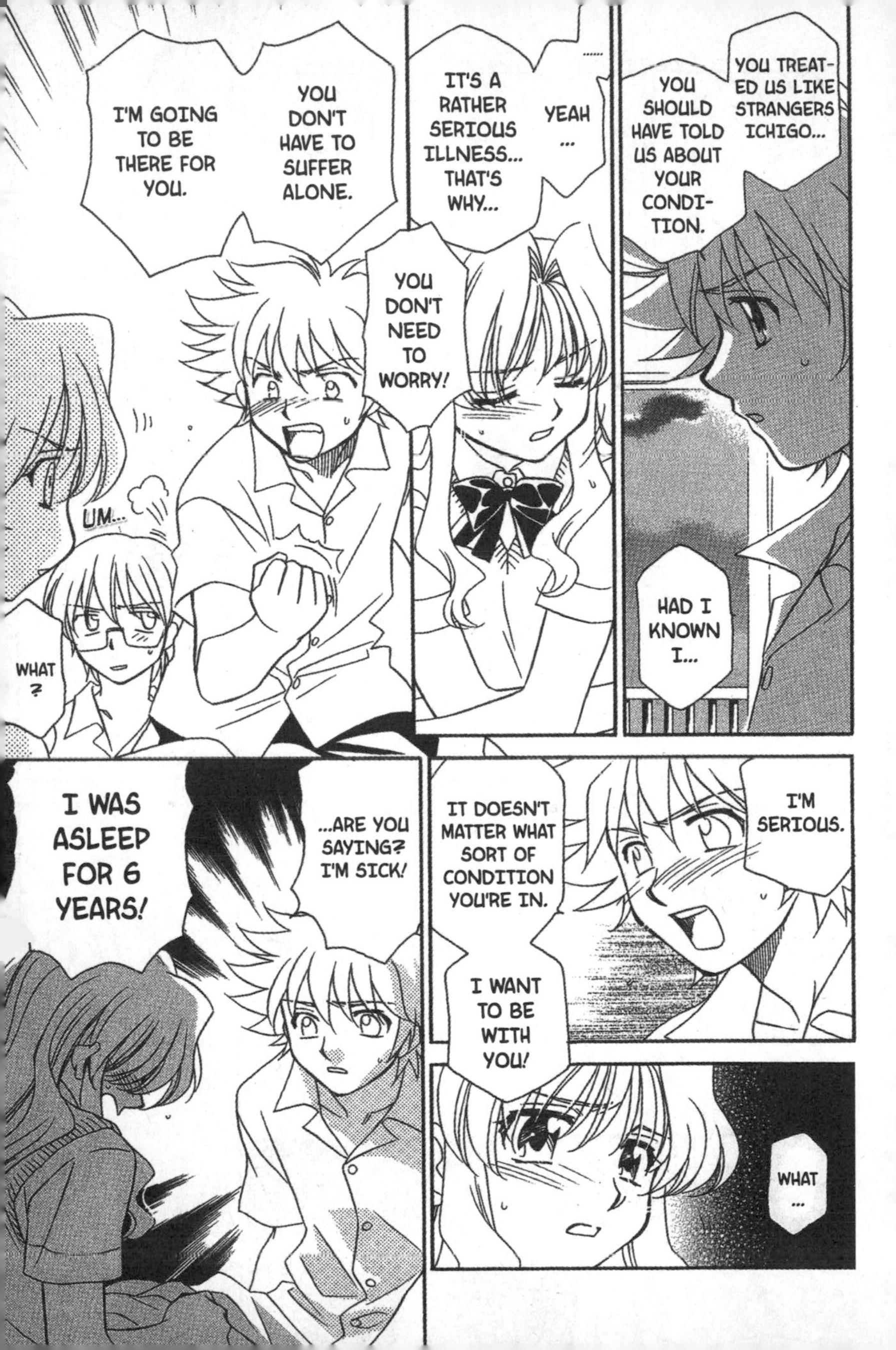

YOU TREAT-ED US LIKE STRANGERS ICHIGO...
YOU SHOULD HAVE TOLD US ABOUT YOUR CONDI-TION.
HAD I KNOWN I...
......
YEAH ...
IT'S A RATHER SERIOUS ILLNESS... THAT'S WHY...
YOU DON'T NEED TO WORRY!
YOU DON'T HAVE TO SUFFER ALONE.
I'M GOING TO BE THERE FOR YOU.
UM...
WHAT ?
I'M SERIOUS.
IT DOESN'T MATTER WHAT SORT OF CONDITION YOU'RE IN.
I WANT TO BE WITH YOU!
WHAT ...
...ARE YOU SAYING? I'M SICK!
I WAS ASLEEP FOR 6 YEARS!

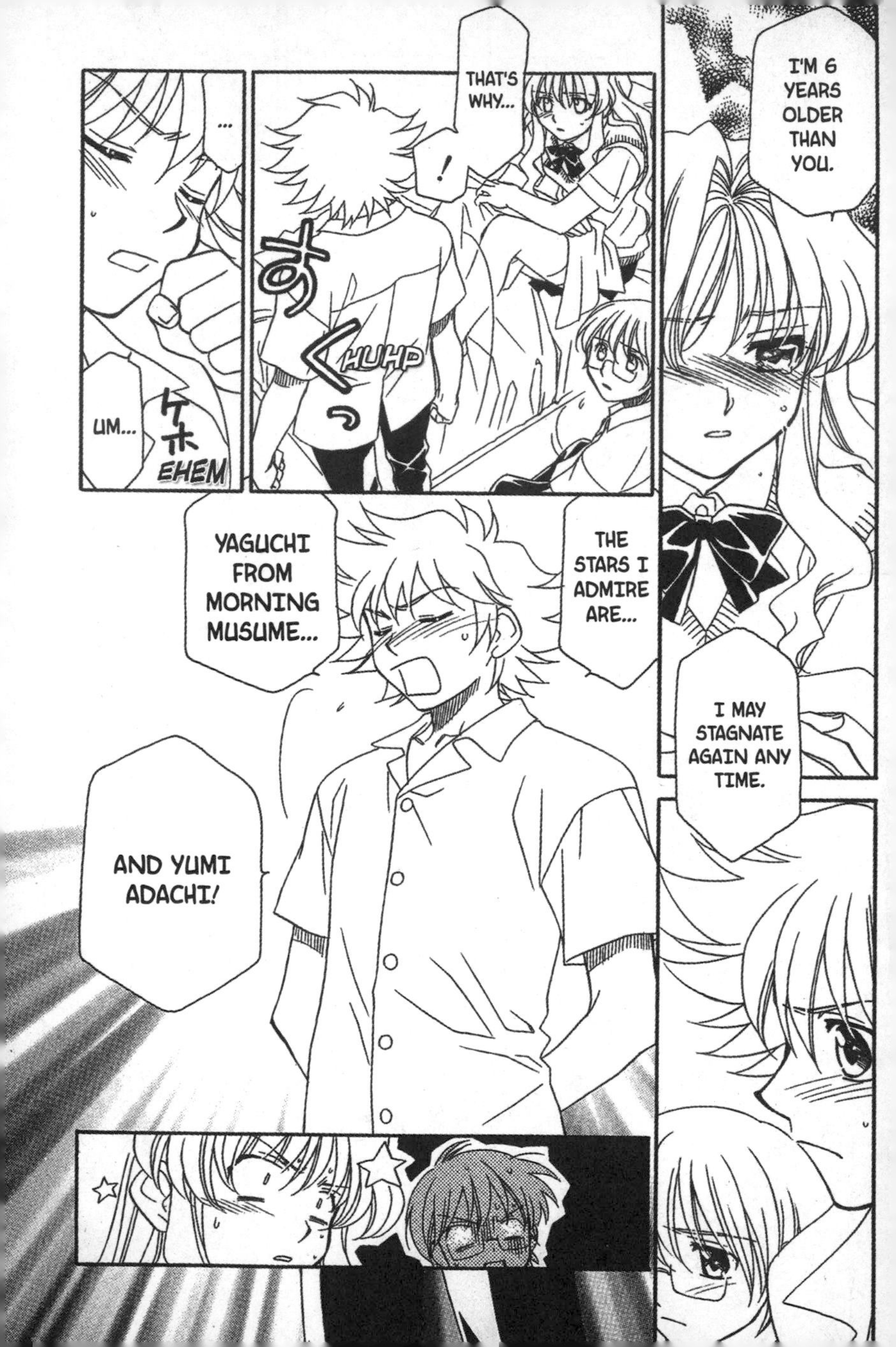

I'M 6 YEARS OLDER THAN YOU.
I MAY STAGNATE AGAIN ANY TIME.
THAT'S WHY...
!
あっく
HUHP
...
UM...
ケホ
EHEM
THE STARS I ADMIRE ARE...
YAGUCHI FROM MORNING MUSUME...
AND YUMI ADACHI!

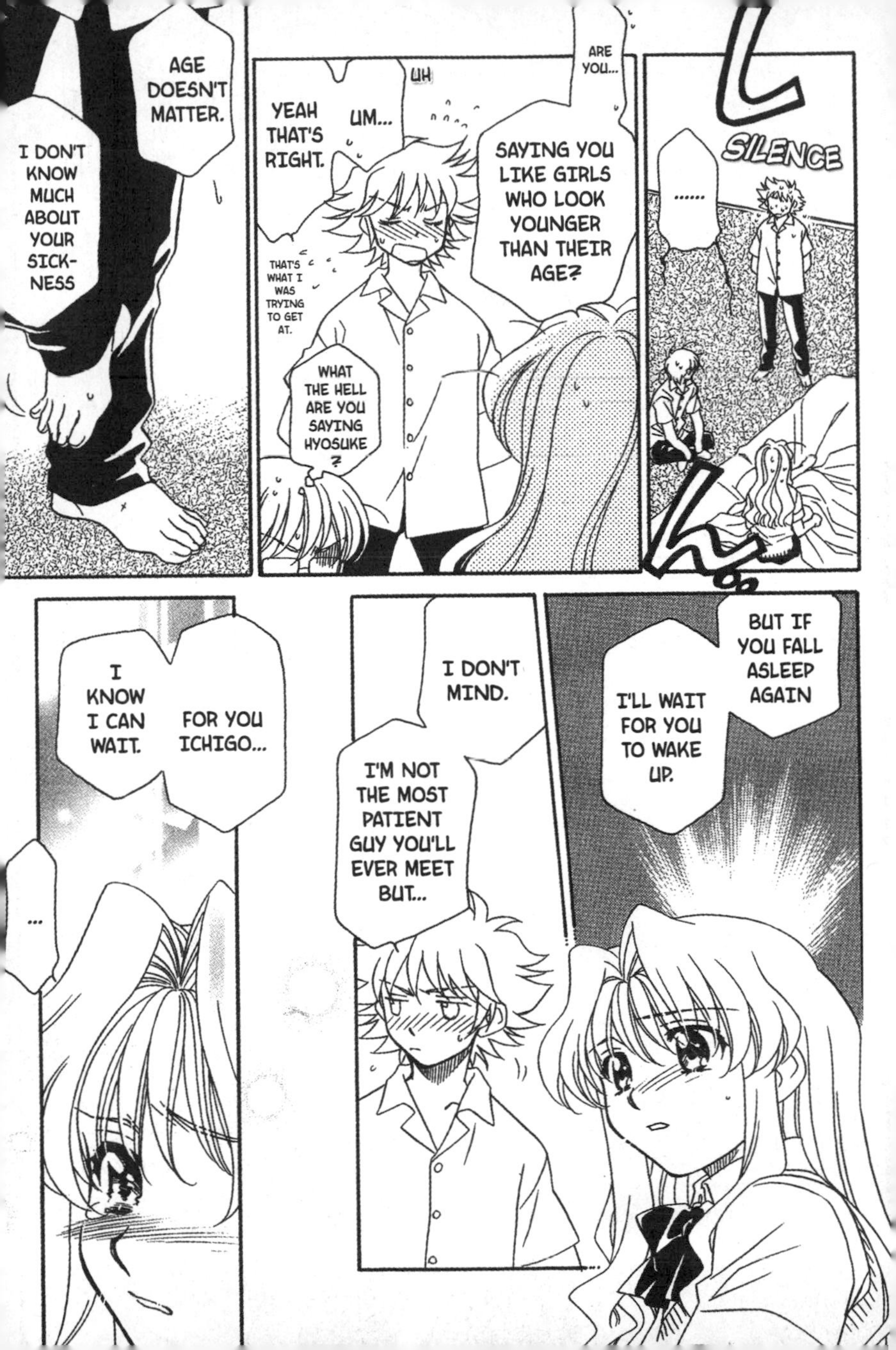
SILENCE
......
ARE YOU...
SAYING YOU LIKE GIRLS WHO LOOK YOUNGER THAN THEIR AGE?
UH
UM...
YEAH THAT'S RIGHT.
THAT'S WHAT I WAS TRYING TO GET AT.
WHAT THE HELL ARE YOU SAYING HYOSUKE?
AGE DOESN'T MATTER.
I DON'T KNOW MUCH ABOUT YOUR SICK-NESS
BUT IF YOU FALL ASLEEP AGAIN
I'LL WAIT FOR YOU TO WAKE UP.
I DON'T MIND.
I'M NOT THE MOST PATIENT GUY YOU'LL EVER MEET BUT...
I KNOW I CAN WAIT.
FOR YOU ICHIGO...
...

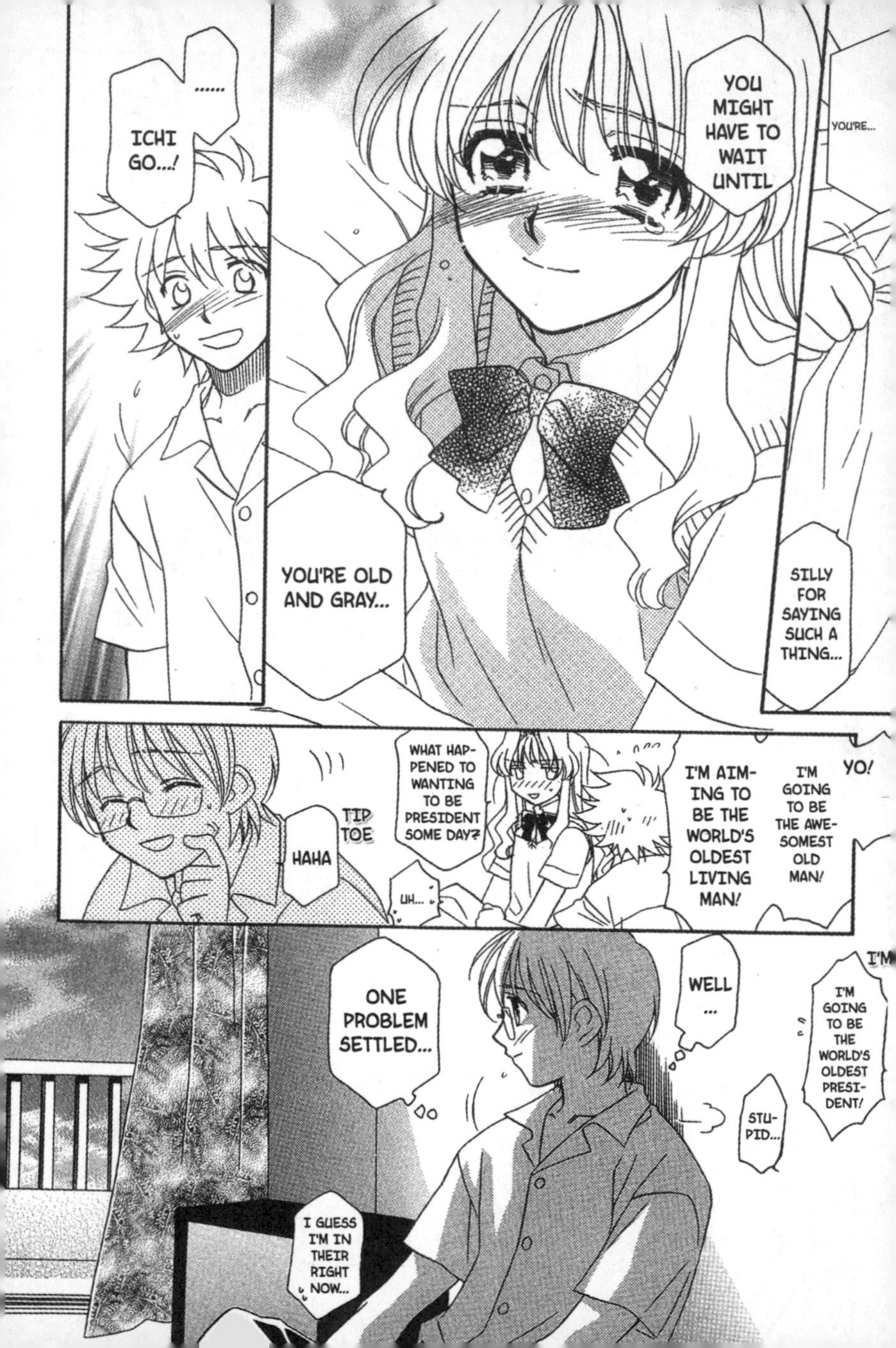
YOU'RE...
SILLY FOR SAYING SUCH A THING...
YOU MIGHT HAVE TO WAIT UNTIL
YOU'RE OLD AND GRAY...
......
ICHI GO...!
YO!
I'M GOING TO BE THE AWE-SOMEST OLD MAN!
I'M AIM-ING TO BE THE WORLD'S OLDEST LIVING MAN!
WHAT HAP-PENED TO WANTING TO BE PRESIDENT SOME DAY?
UH...
TIP TOE
HAHA
I'M
I'M GOING TO BE THE WORLD'S OLDEST PRESI-DENT!
STU-PID...
WELL ...
ONE PROBLEM SETTLED...
I GUESS I'M IN THEIR RIGHT NOW...

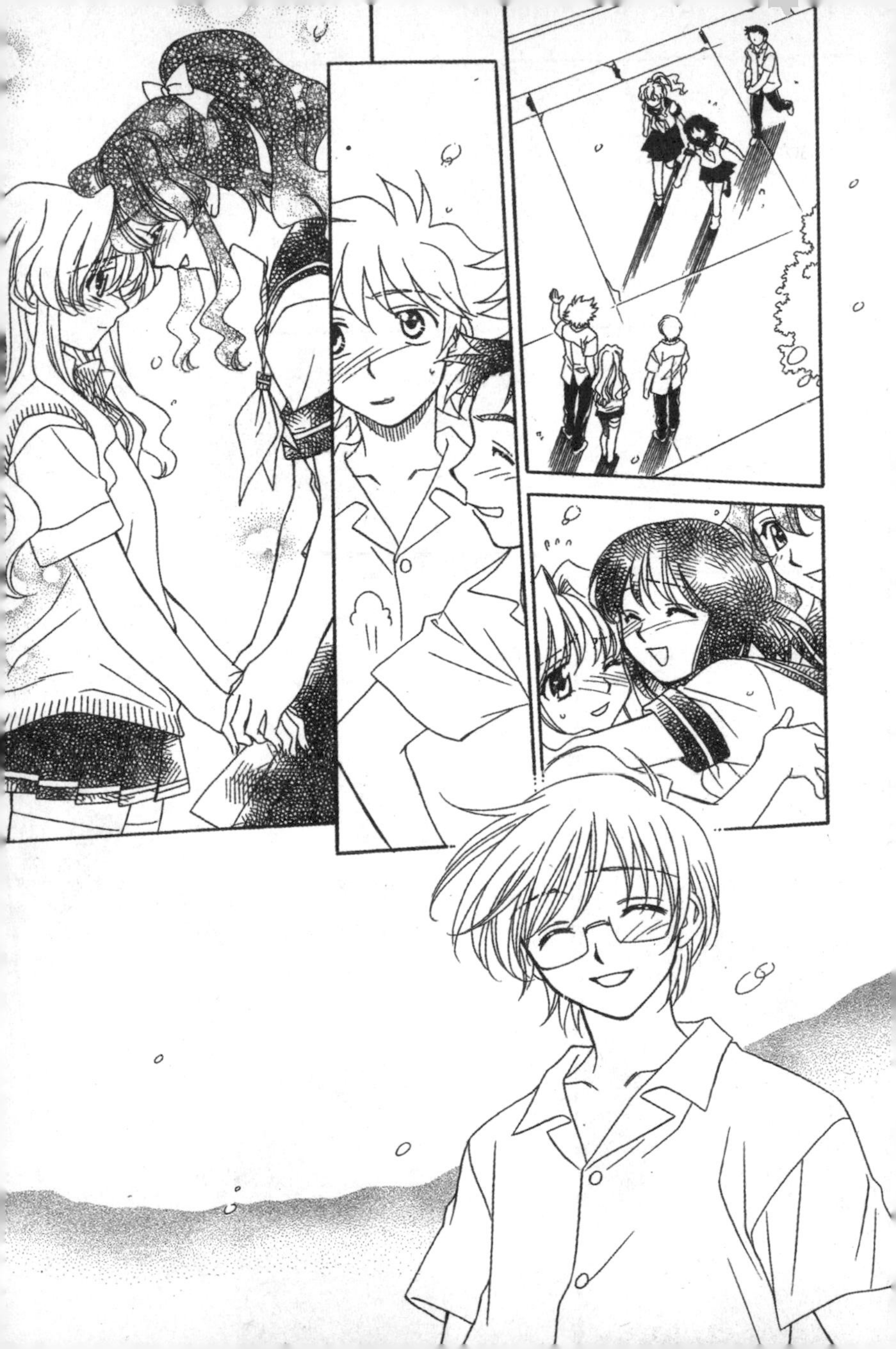

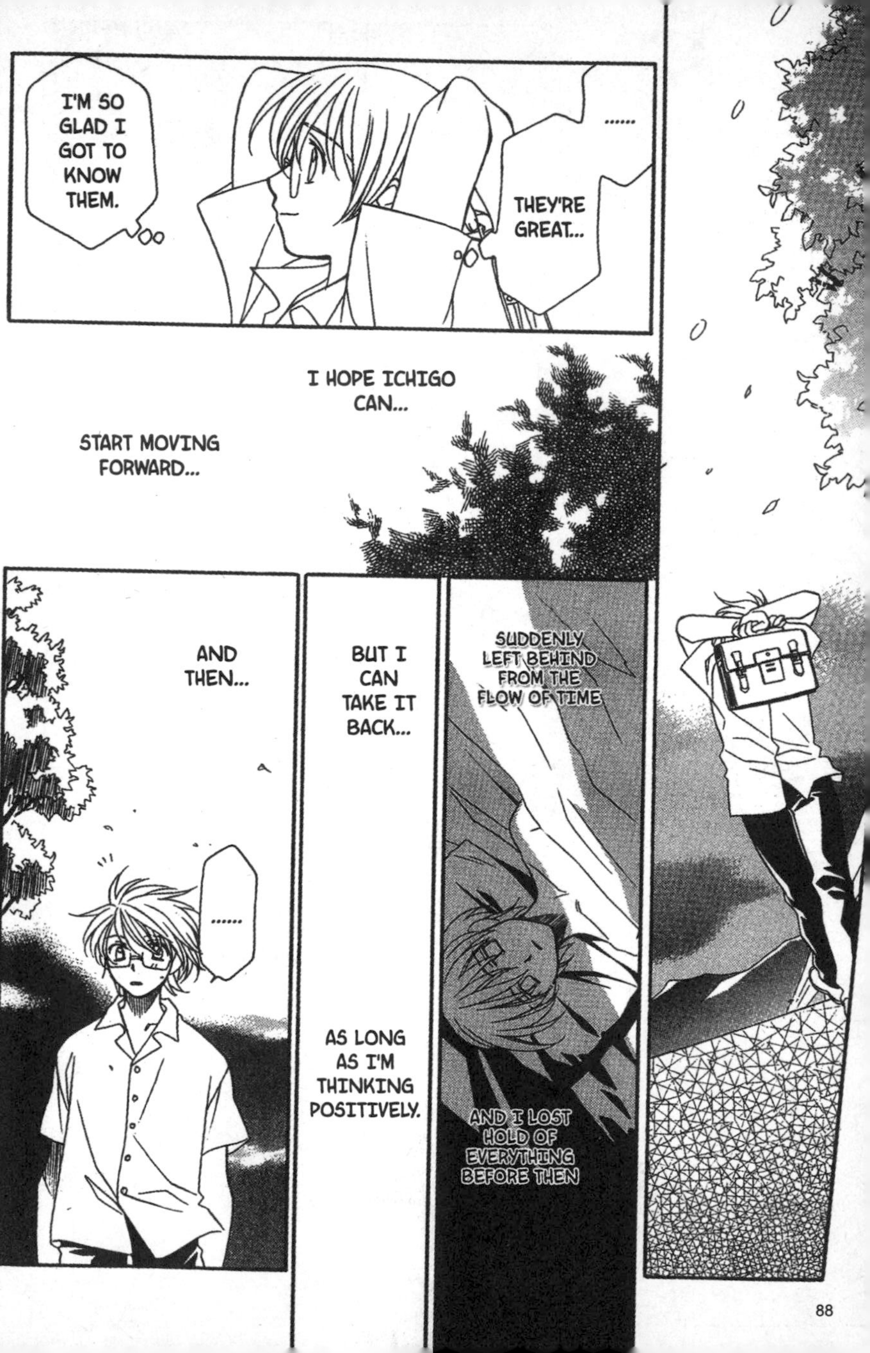
......
THEY'RE GREAT...
I'M SO GLAD I GOT TO KNOW THEM.
I HOPE ICHIGO CAN...
START MOVING FORWARD...
SUDDENLY LEFT BEHIND FROM THE FLOW OF TIME
AND I LOST HOLD OF EVERYTHING BEFORE THEN
BUT I CAN TAKE IT BACK...
AS LONG AS I'M THINKING POSITIVELY.
AND THEN...
......

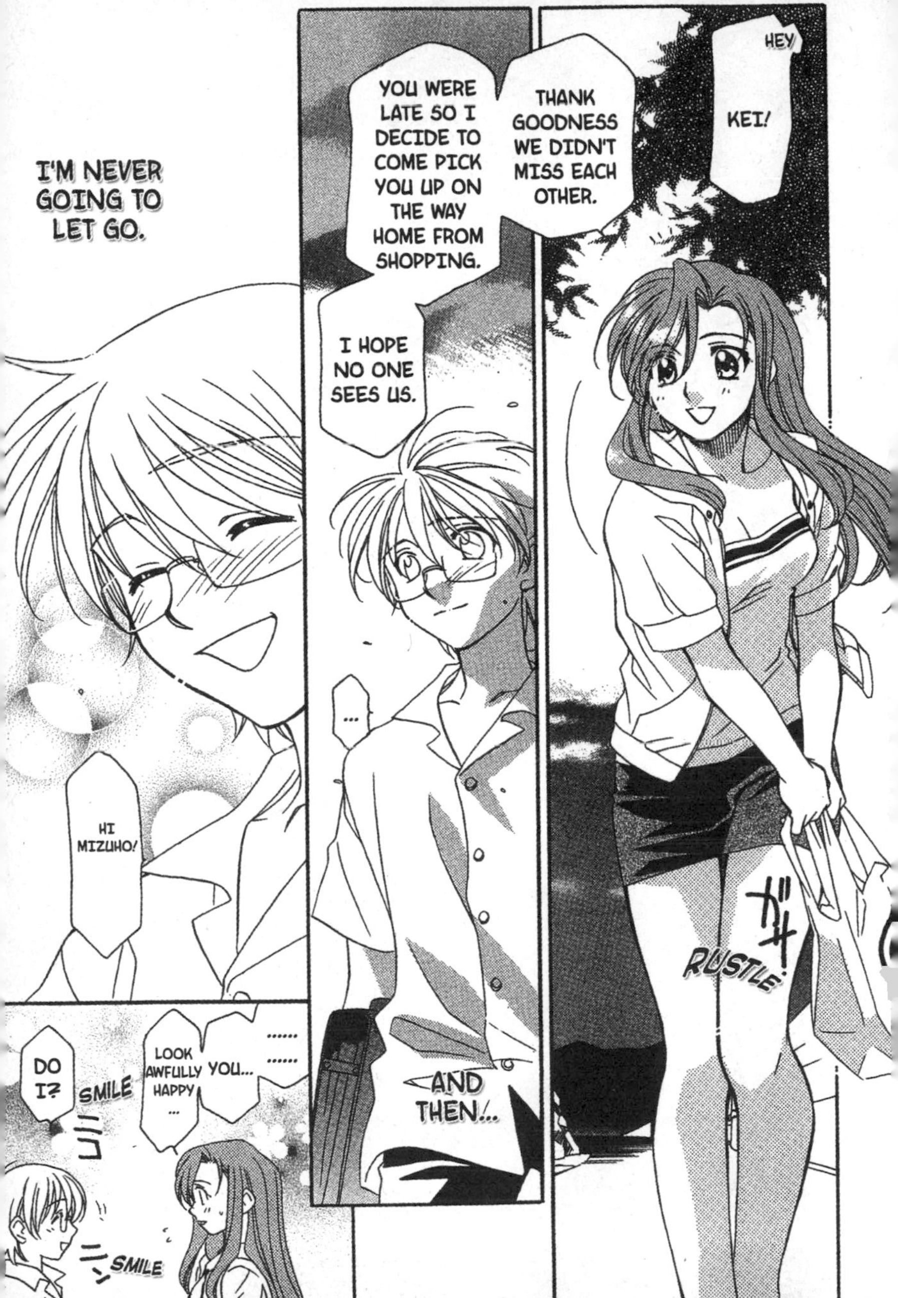

HEY KEI!
THANK GOODNESS WE DIDN'T MISS EACH OTHER.
YOU WERE LATE SO I DECIDE TO COME PICK YOU UP ON THE WAY HOME FROM SHOPPING.
ガサ
RUSTLE!
I HOPE NO ONE SEES US.
...
AND THEN...
I'M NEVER GOING TO LET GO.
HI MIZUHO!
......
......
YOU...
LOOK AWFULLY HAPPY ...
DO I?
ニコ
SMILE
ニコ
SMILE

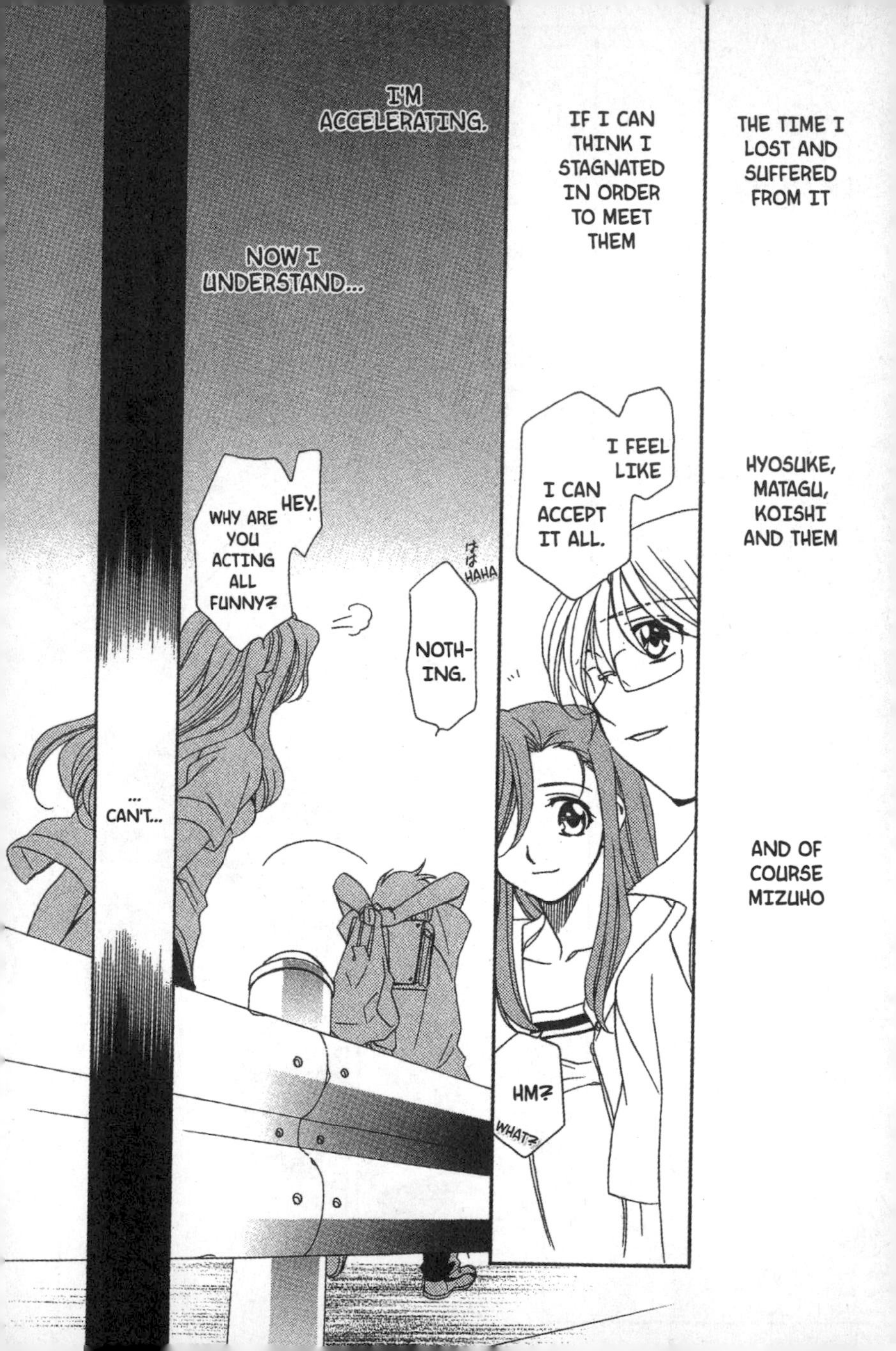
THE TIME I LOST AND SUFFERED FROM IT
HYOSUKE, MATAGU, KOISHI AND THEM
AND OF COURSE MIZUHO
IF I CAN THINK I STAGNATED IN ORDER TO MEET THEM
I FEEL LIKE I CAN ACCEPT IT ALL.
HM?
WHAT?
I'M ACCELERATING.
NOW I UNDERSTAND...
HEY. WHY ARE YOU ACTING ALL FUNNY?
はは HAHA
NOTH-ING.
... CAN'T...

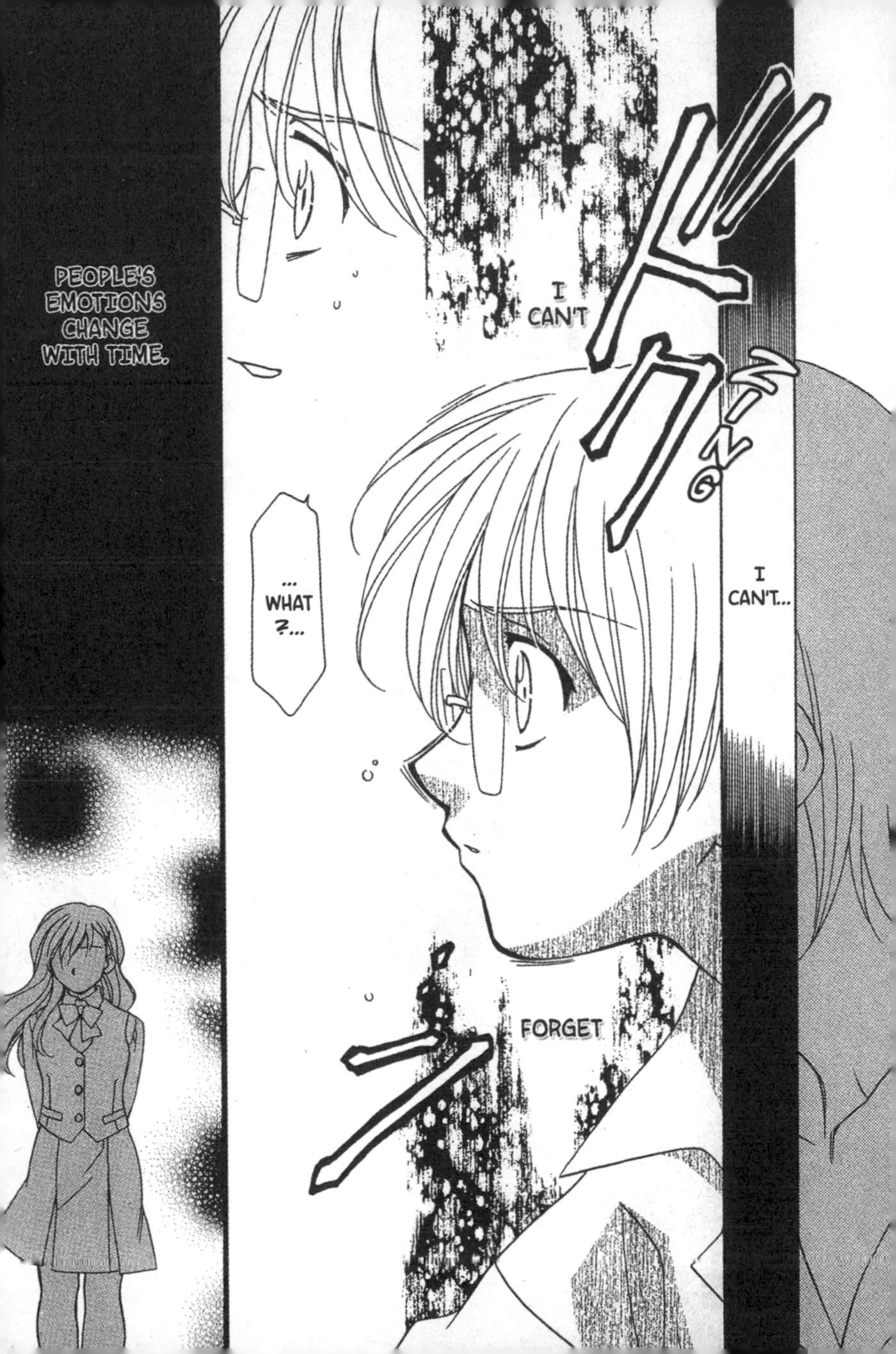

I CAN'T...
I CAN'T
ドクン
ZING
...WHAT?...
FORGET
PEOPLE'S EMOTIONS CHANGE WITH TIME.

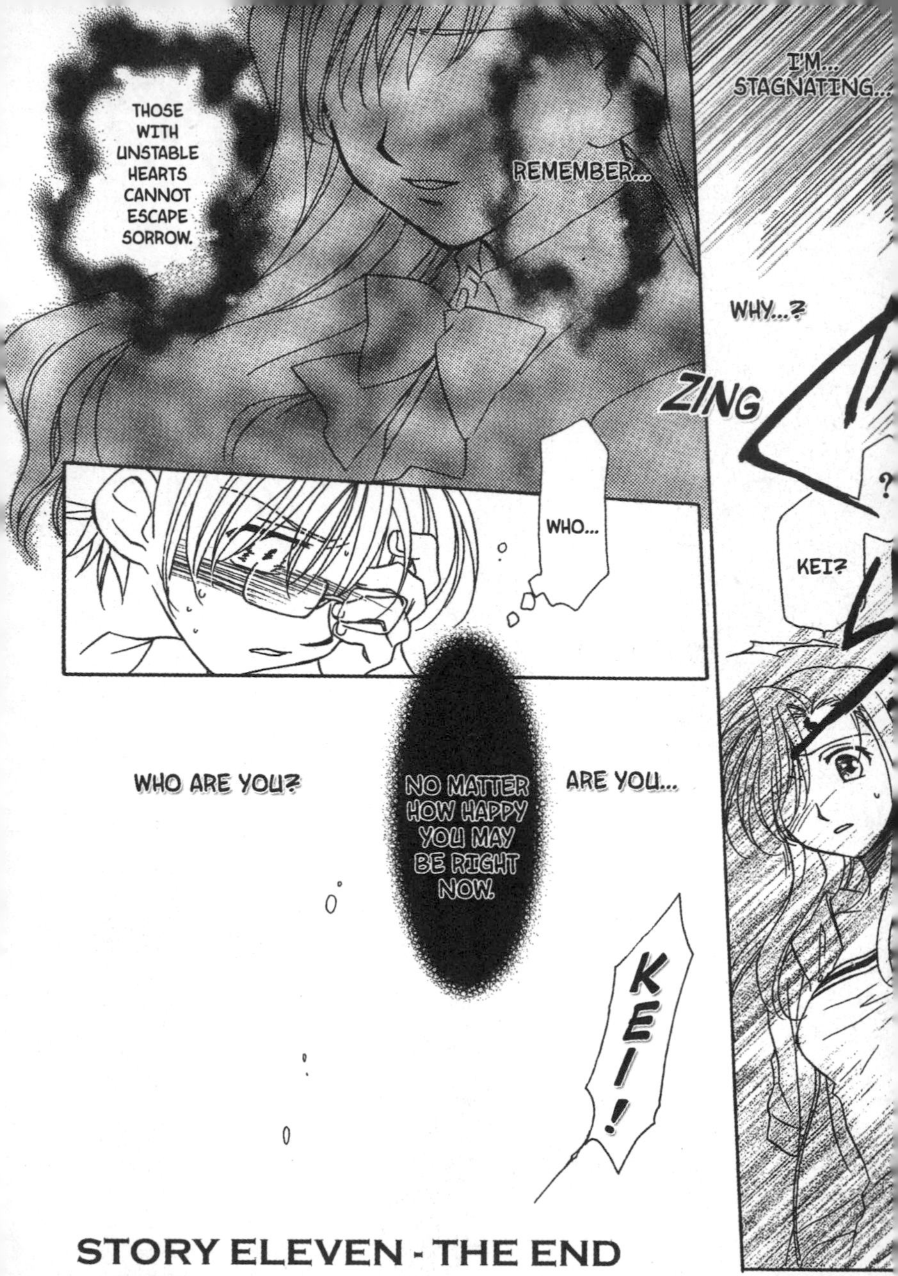
I'M... STAGNATING...
WHY...?
ZING
?
KEI?
REMEMBER...
THOSE WITH UNSTABLE HEARTS CANNOT ESCAPE SORROW.
WHO...
ARE YOU...
NO MATTER HOW HAPPY YOU MAY BE RIGHT NOW.
WHO ARE YOU?
KEI!!

STORY ELEVEN - THE END

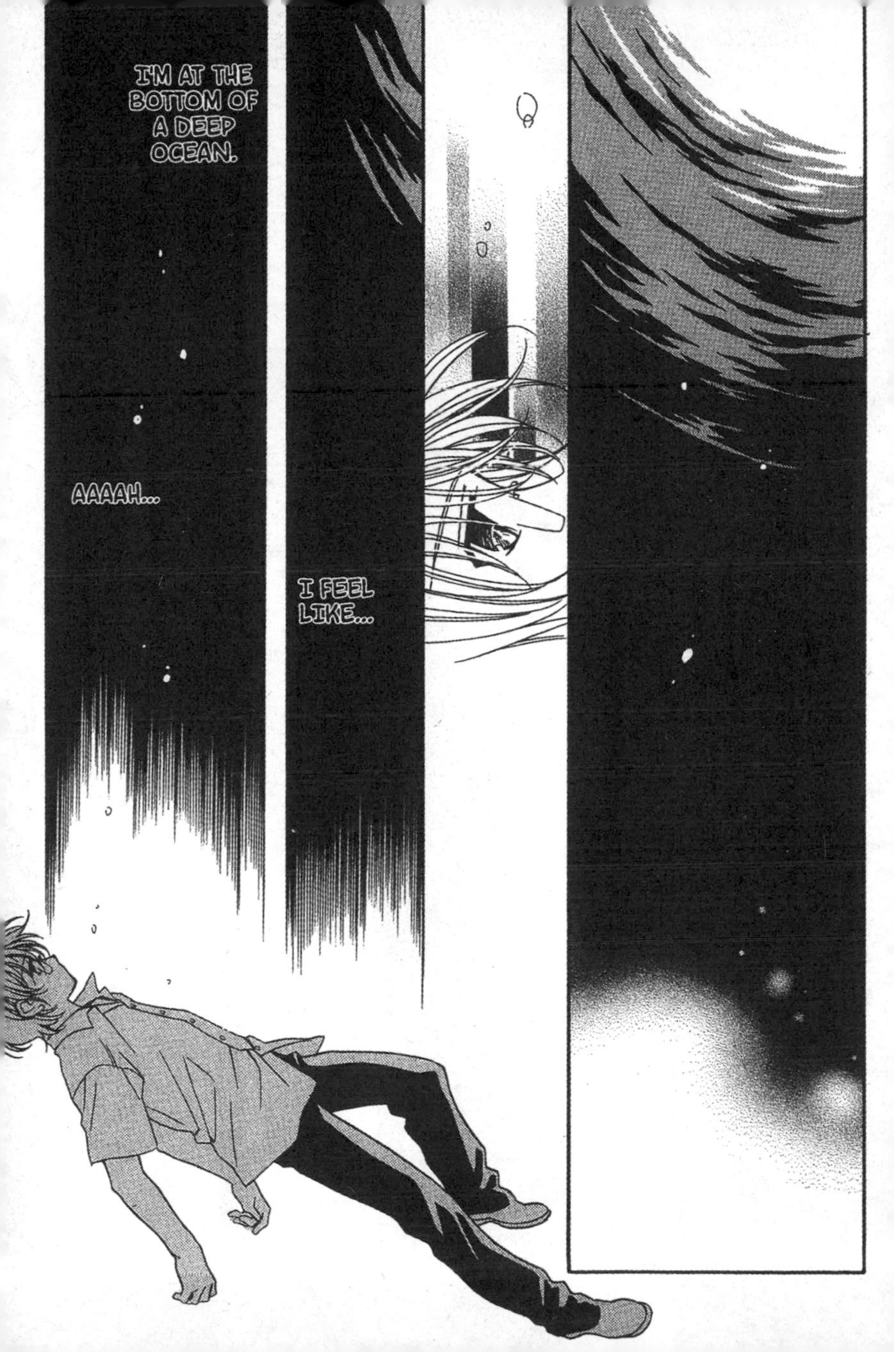
I FEEL LIKE...
I'M AT THE BOTTOM OF A DEEP OCEAN.
AAAAH...

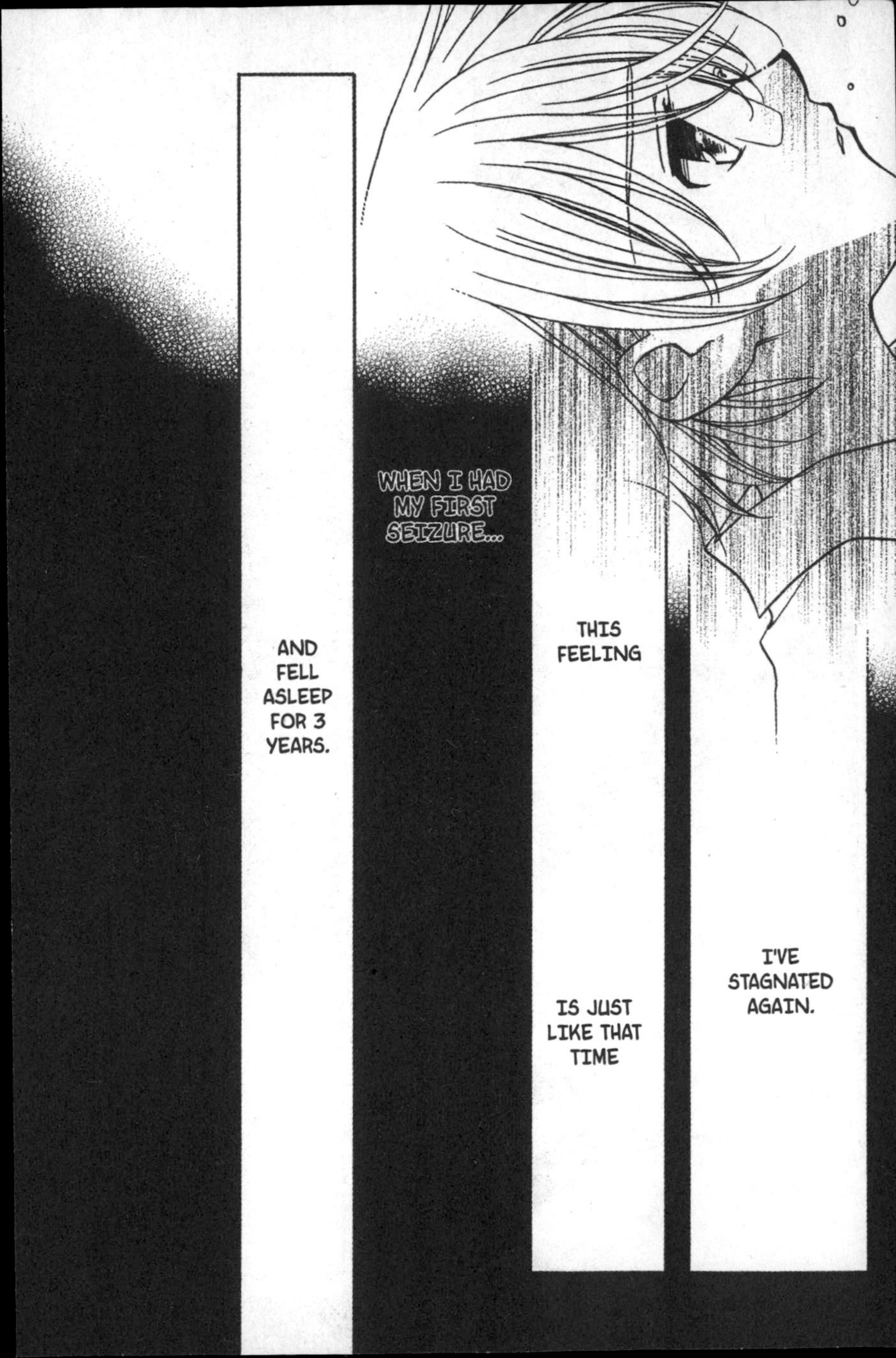
I'VE STAGNATED AGAIN.
THIS FEELING
IS JUST LIKE THAT TIME
WHEN I HAD MY FIRST SEIZURE...
AND FELL ASLEEP FOR 3 YEARS.

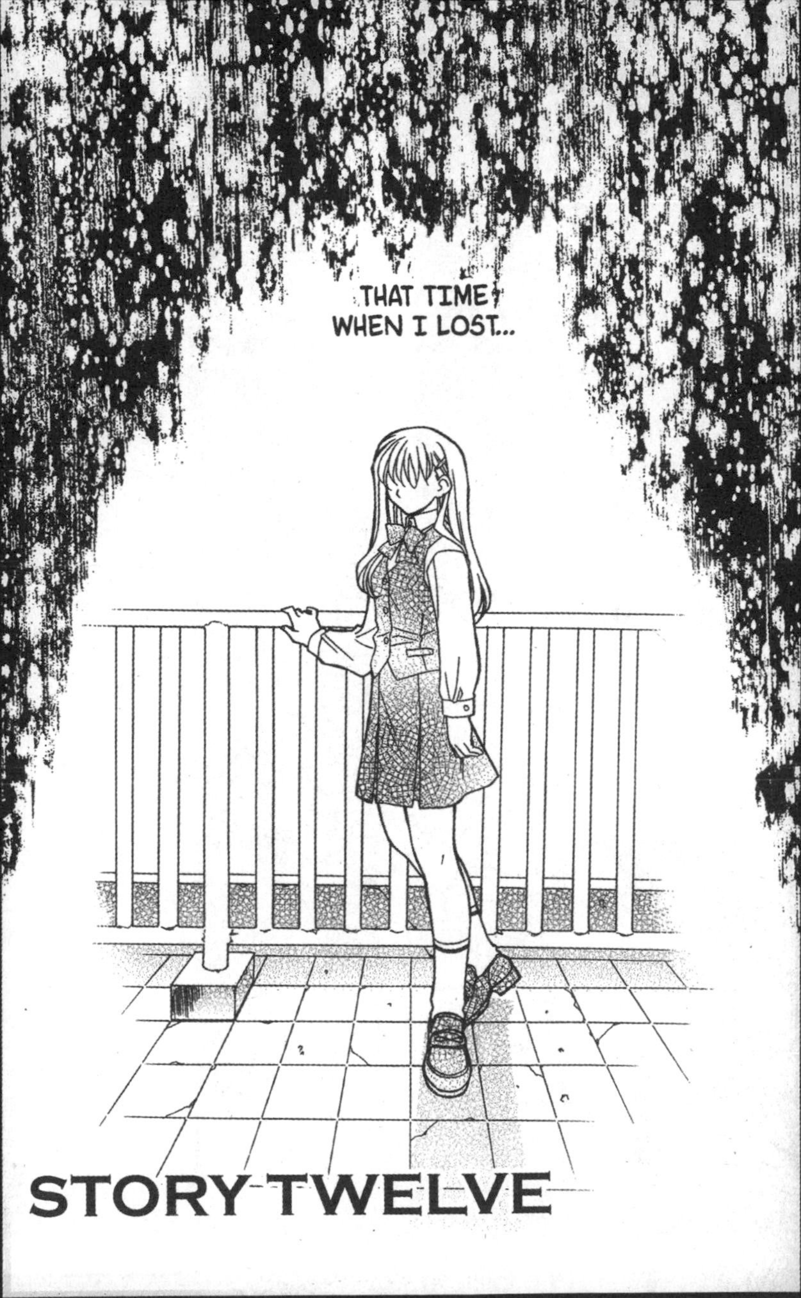
THAT TIME WHEN I LOST...
STORY TWELVE

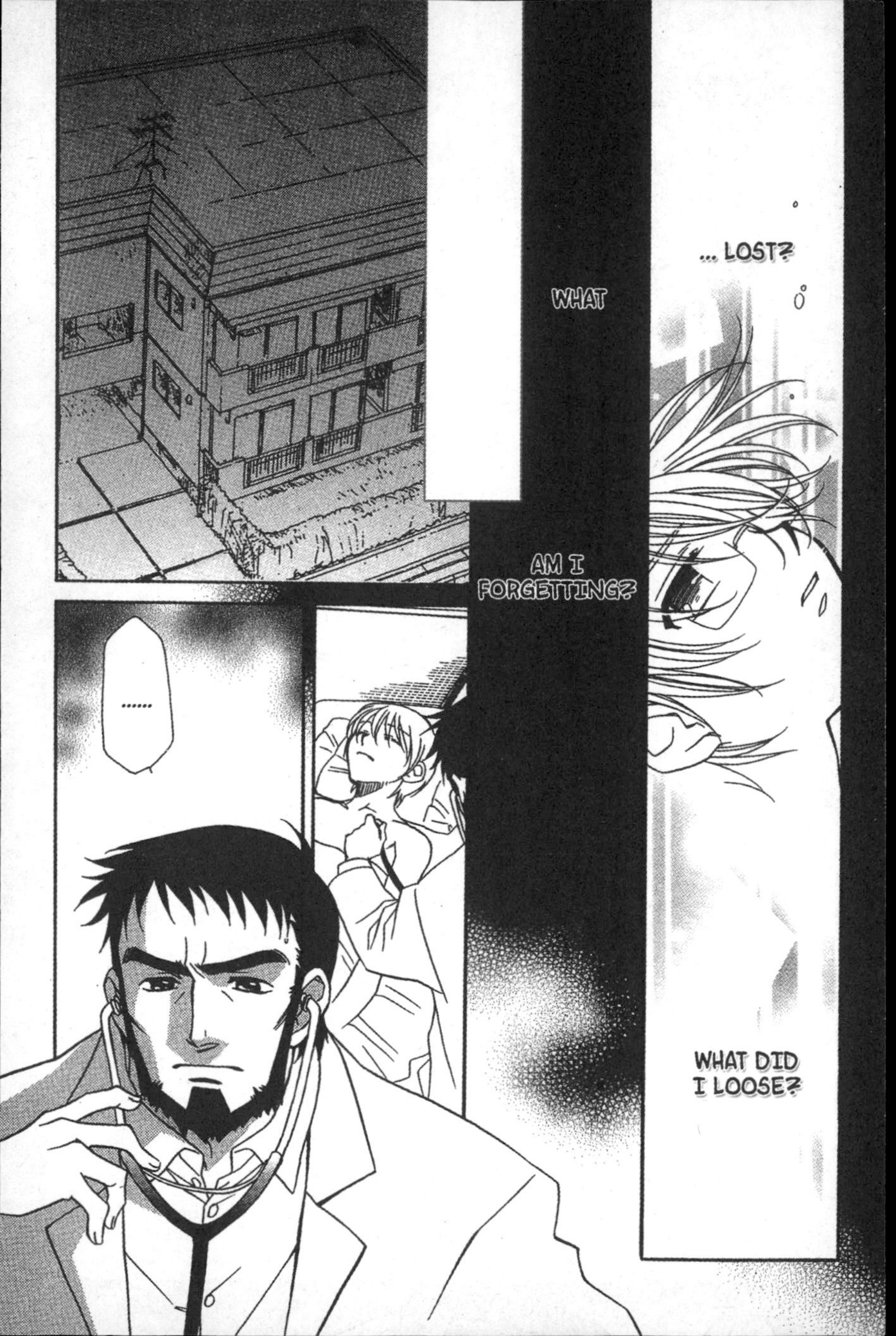

... LOST?
WHAT
AM I FORGETTING?
WHAT DID I LOOSE?
......

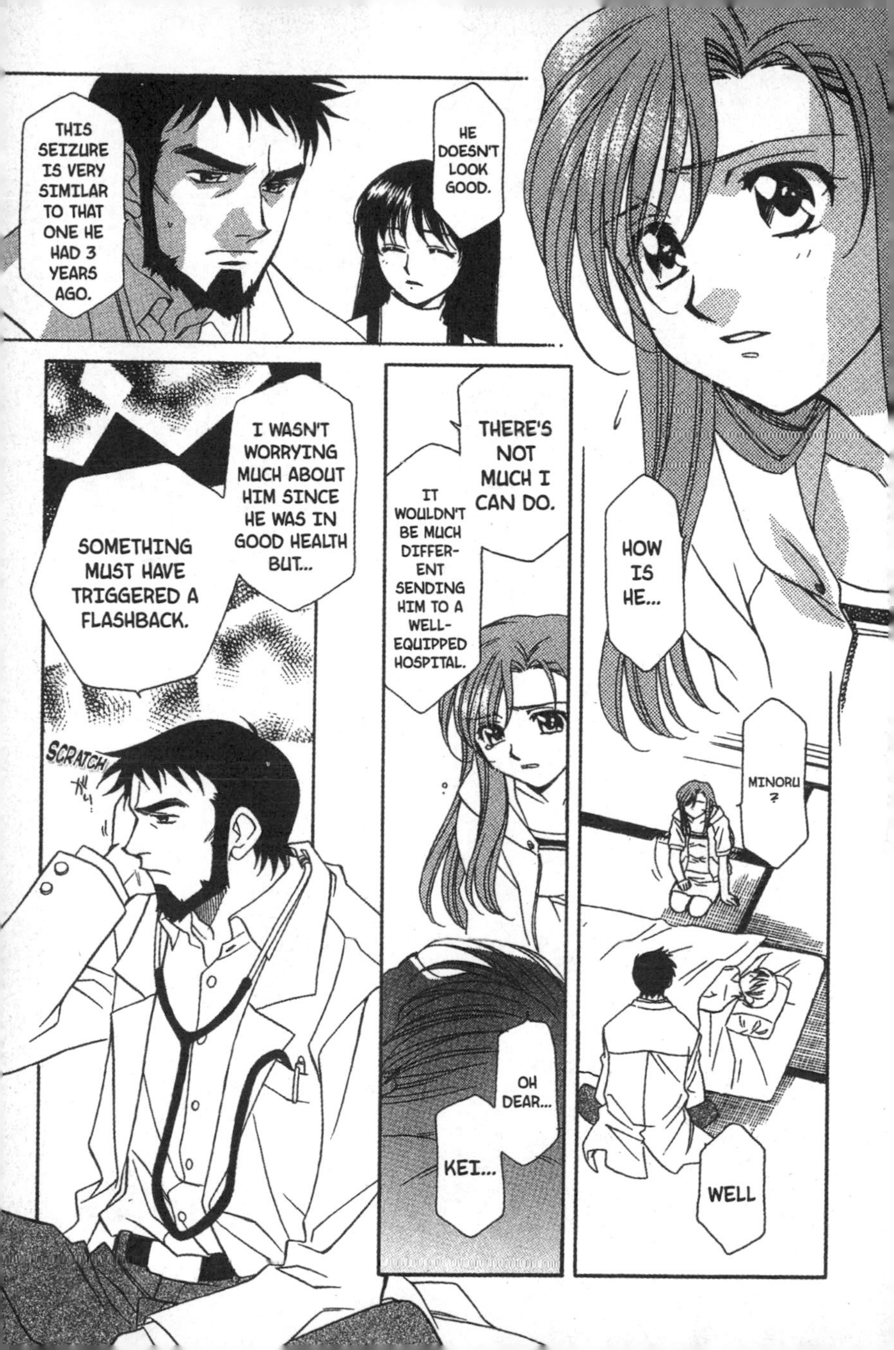
HOW IS HE...
MINORU?
WELL
HE DOESN'T LOOK GOOD.
THIS SEIZURE IS VERY SIMILAR TO THAT ONE HE HAD 3 YEARS AGO.
THERE'S NOT MUCH I CAN DO.
IT WOULDN'T BE MUCH DIFFER-ENT SENDING HIM TO A WELL-EQUIPPED HOSPITAL.
OH DEAR...
KEI...
I WASN'T WORRYING MUCH ABOUT HIM SINCE HE WAS IN GOOD HEALTH BUT...
SOMETHING MUST HAVE TRIGGERED A FLASHBACK.
SCRATCH

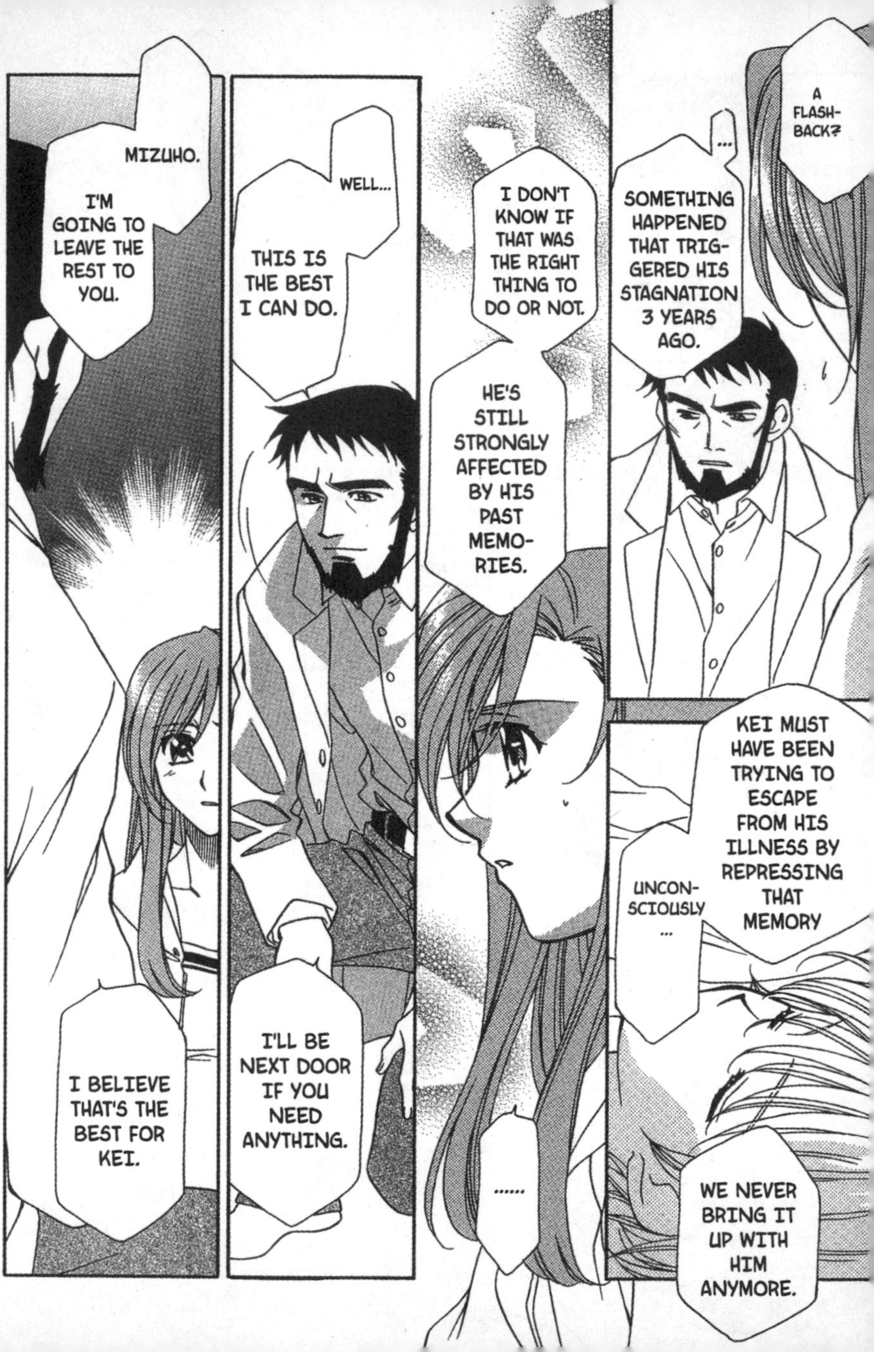
A FLASHBACK?
...
SOMETHING HAPPENED THAT TRIGGERED HIS STAGNATION 3 YEARS AGO.
KEI MUST HAVE BEEN TRYING TO ESCAPE FROM HIS ILLNESS BY REPRESSING THAT MEMORY
UNCONSCIOUSLY...
WE NEVER BRING IT UP WITH HIM ANYMORE.
I DON'T KNOW IF THAT WAS THE RIGHT THING TO DO OR NOT.
HE'S STILL STRONGLY AFFECTED BY HIS PAST MEMORIES.
......
WELL...
THIS IS THE BEST I CAN DO.
I'LL BE NEXT DOOR IF YOU NEED ANYTHING.
MIZUHO.
I'M GOING TO LEAVE THE REST TO YOU.
I BELIEVE THAT'S THE BEST FOR KEI.

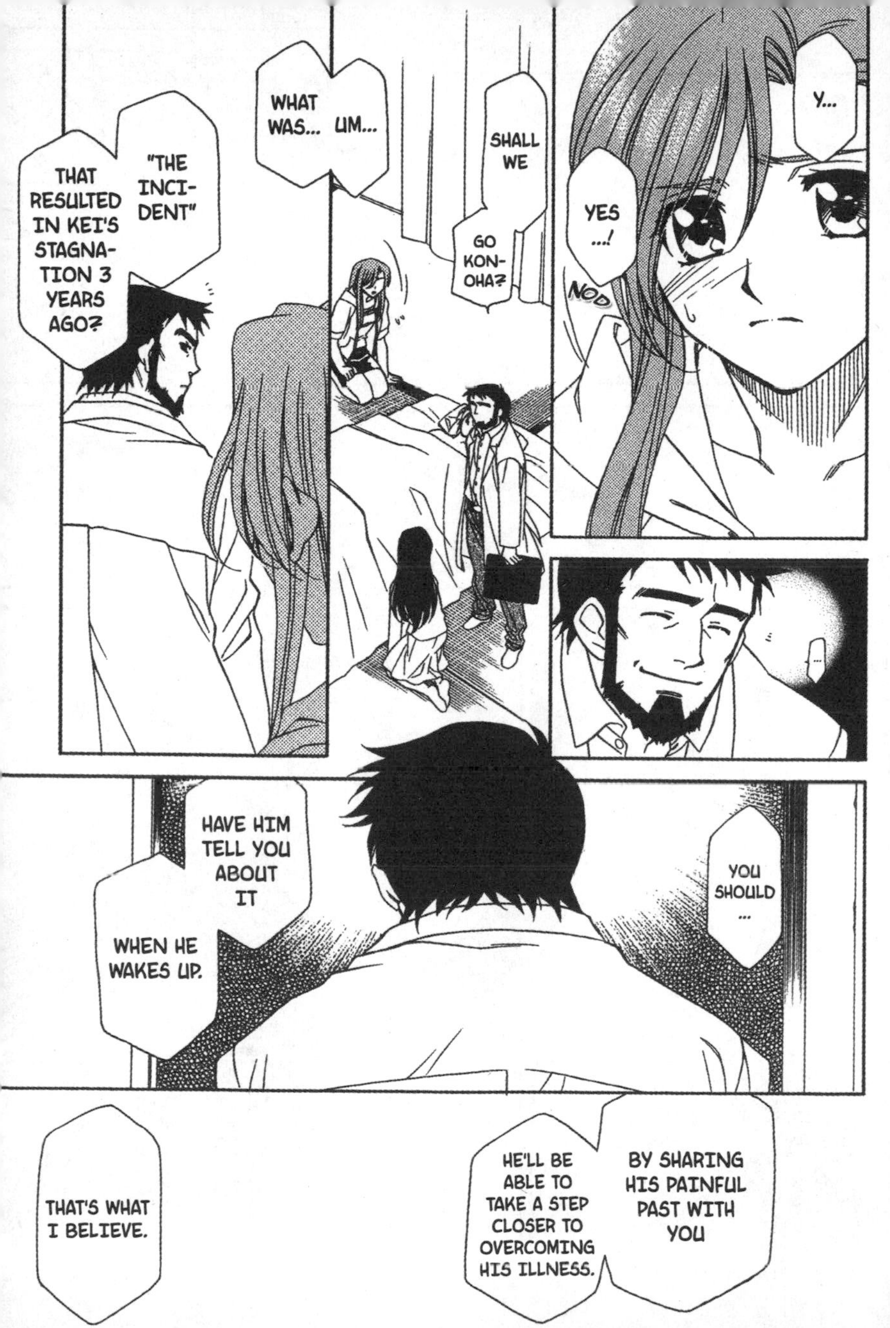
Y...
YES ...!
NOD
...
SHALL WE GO KONOHA?
WHAT WAS... UM...
"THE INCIDENT"
THAT RESULTED IN KEI'S STAGNATION 3 YEARS AGO?
YOU SHOULD ...
HAVE HIM TELL YOU ABOUT IT
WHEN HE WAKES UP.
BY SHARING HIS PAINFUL PAST WITH YOU
HE'LL BE ABLE TO TAKE A STEP CLOSER TO OVERCOMING HIS ILLNESS.
THAT'S WHAT I BELIEVE.

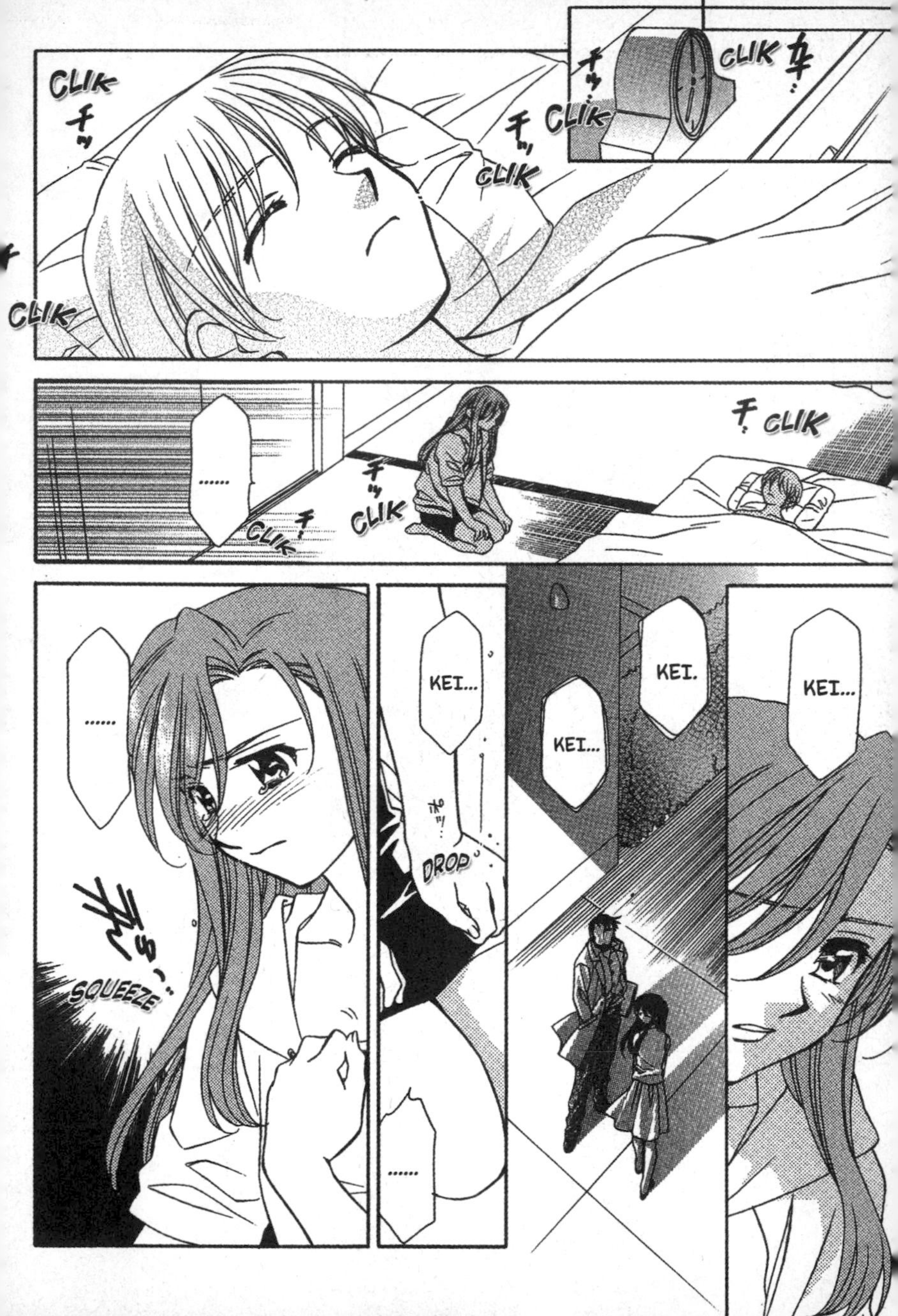

CLIK
チッ
CLIK
CLIK
チッ
CLIK
チッ
CLIK
CLIK
CLIK
......
チッ
CLIK
CLIK
KEI...
KEI.
KEI...
KEI...
DROP
......
......
SQUEEZE

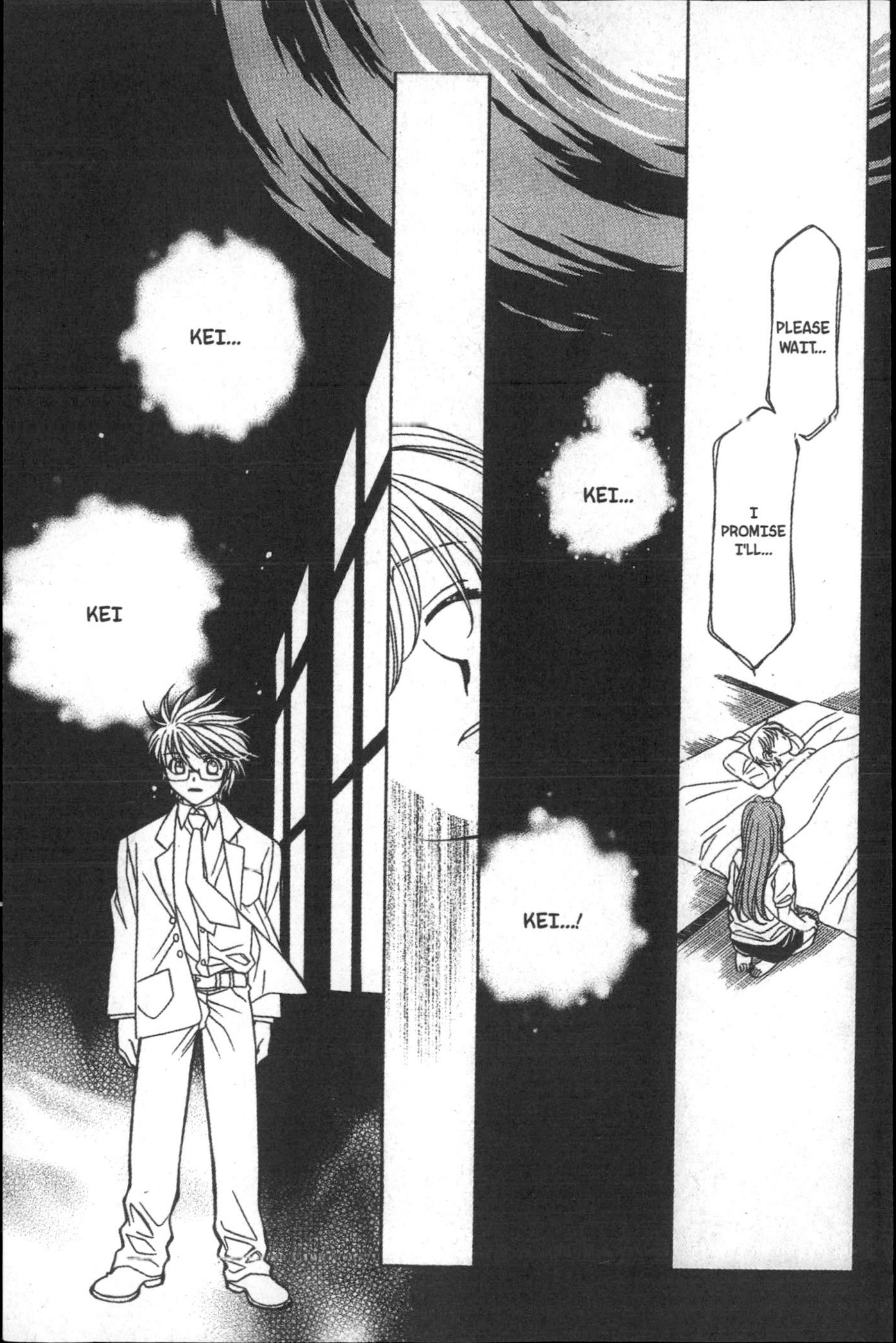
PLEASE WAIT...
I PROMISE I'LL...
KEI...
KEI...!
KEI...
KEI

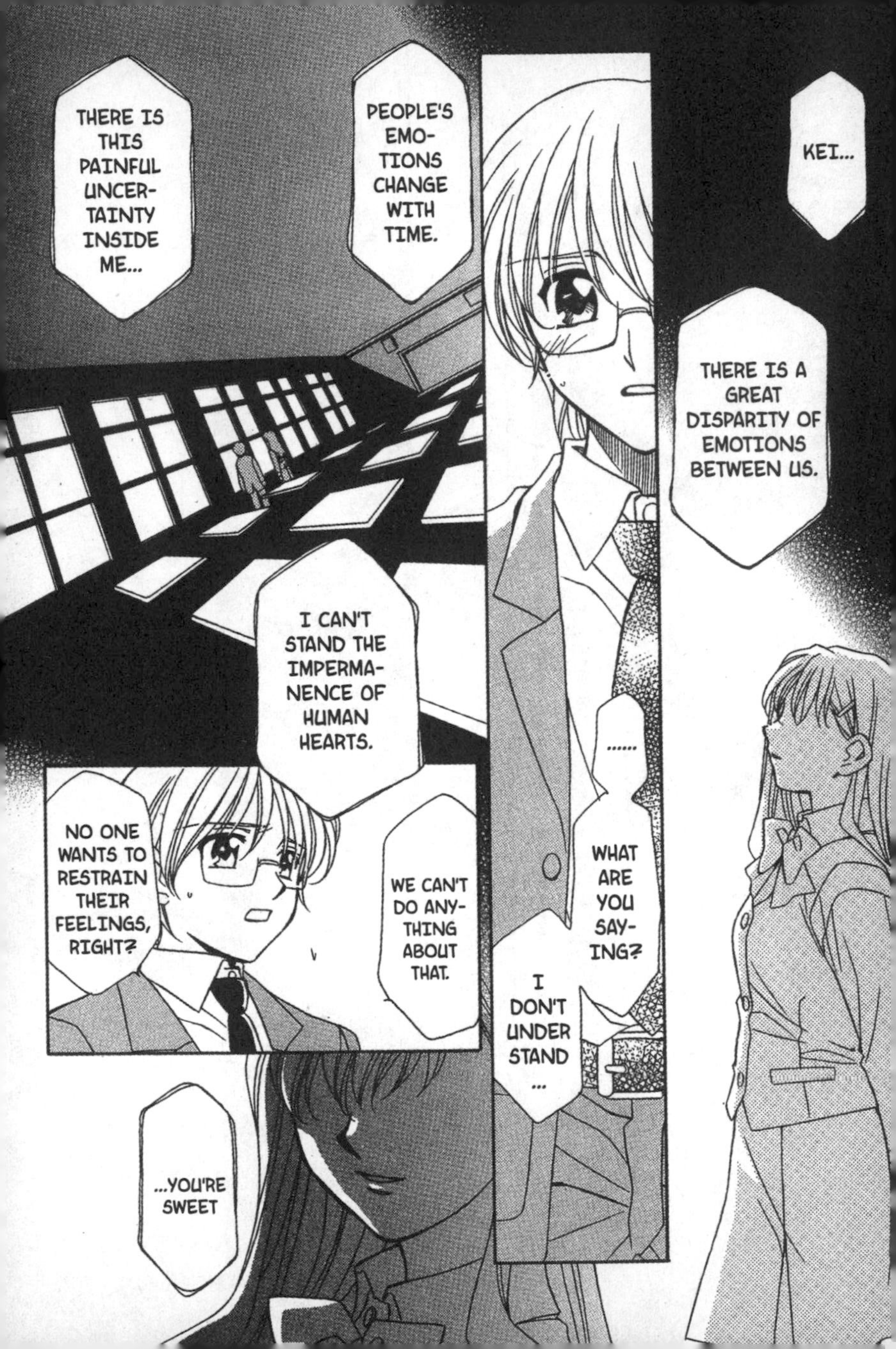
KEI...
THERE IS A GREAT DISPARITY OF EMOTIONS BETWEEN US.
......
WHAT ARE YOU SAYING?
I DON'T UNDER STAND ...
PEOPLE'S EMO-TIONS CHANGE WITH TIME.
THERE IS THIS PAINFUL UNCER-TAINTY INSIDE ME...
I CAN'T STAND THE IMPERMA-NENCE OF HUMAN HEARTS.
WE CAN'T DO ANY-THING ABOUT THAT.
NO ONE WANTS TO RESTRAIN THEIR FEELINGS, RIGHT?
...YOU'RE SWEET

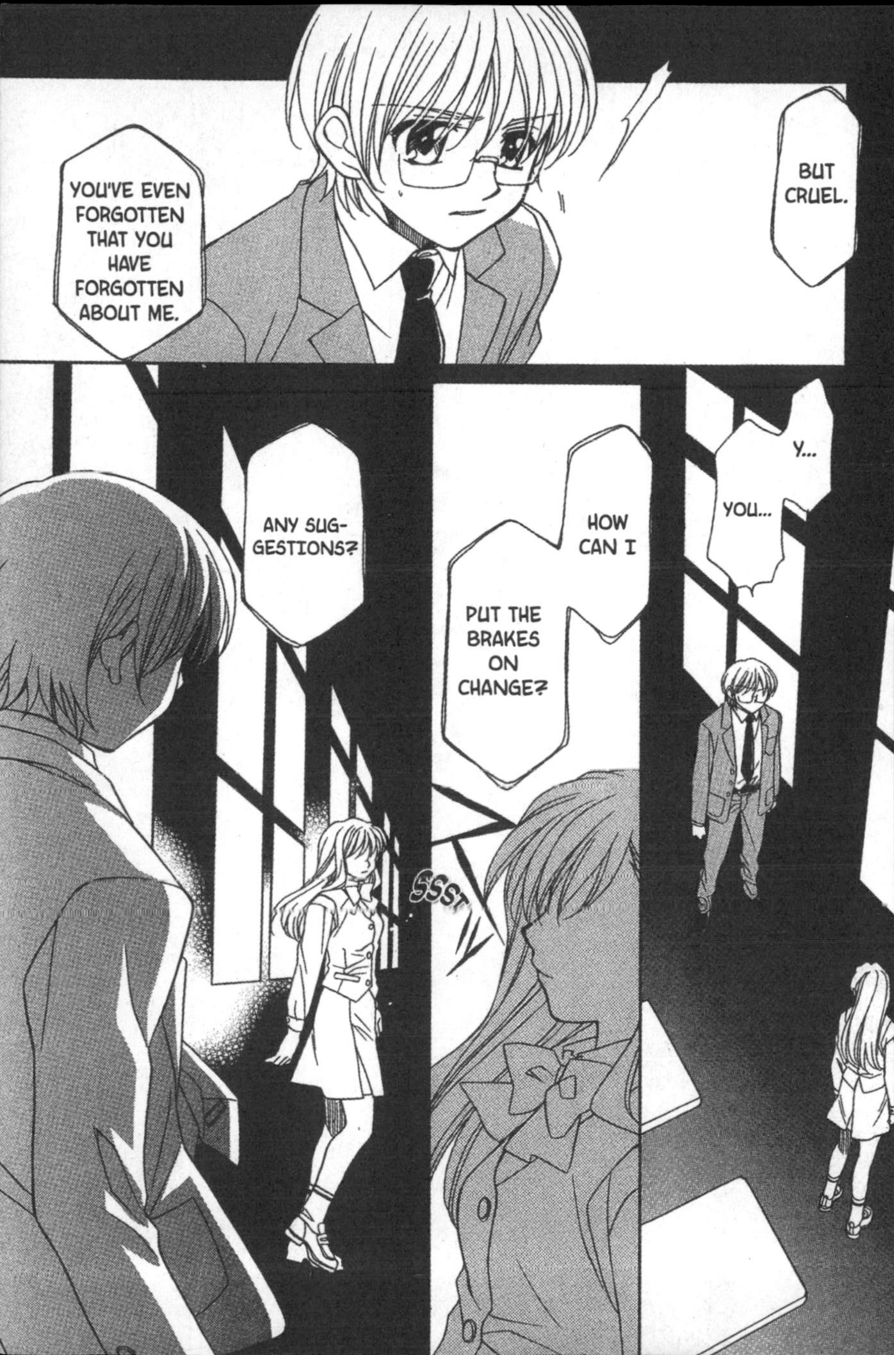
BUT CRUEL.
YOU'VE EVEN FORGOTTEN THAT YOU HAVE FORGOTTEN ABOUT ME.
Y...
YOU...
HOW CAN I
PUT THE BRAKES ON CHANGE?
SSST
ANY SUG-GESTIONS?

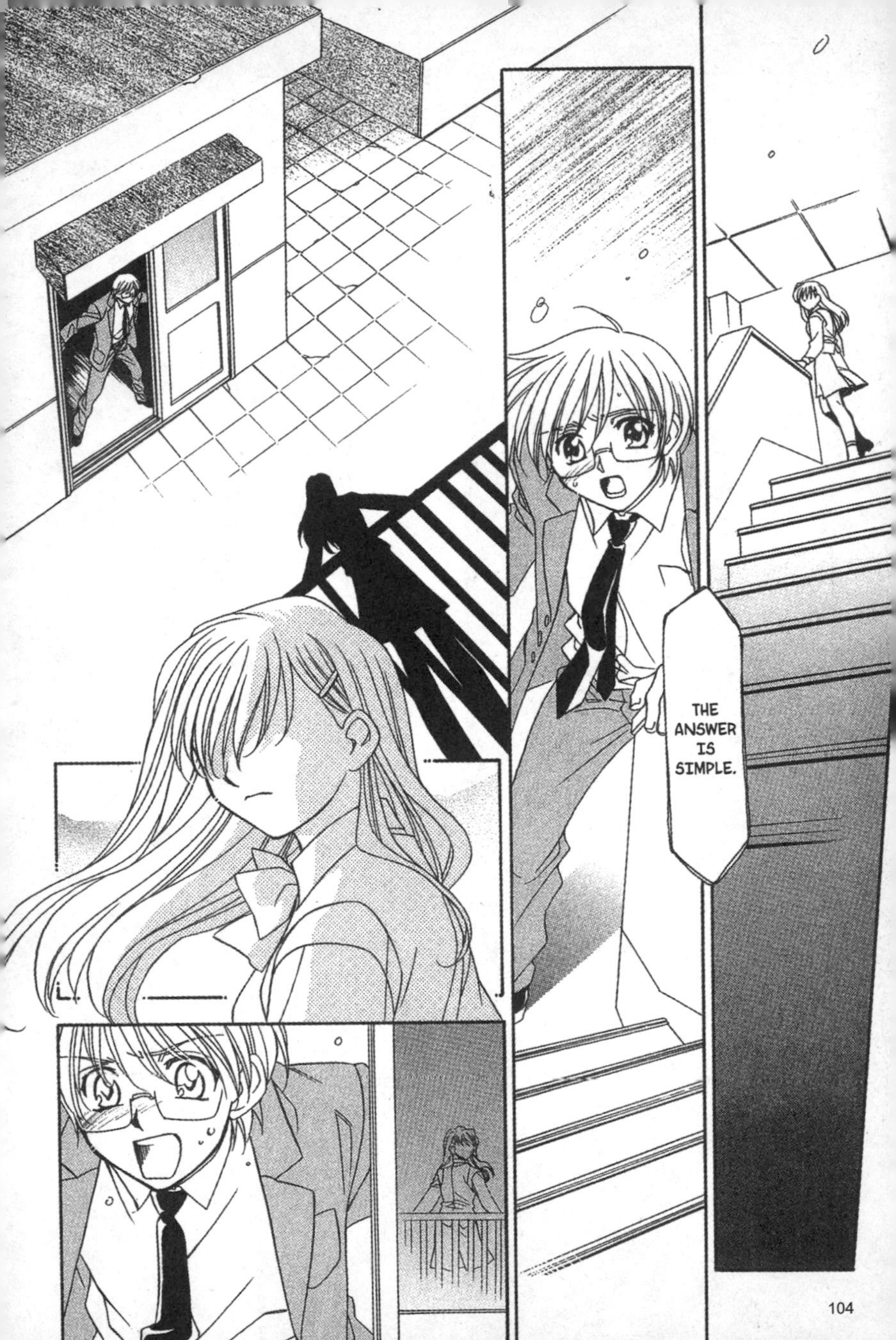
THE ANSWER IS SIMPLE.

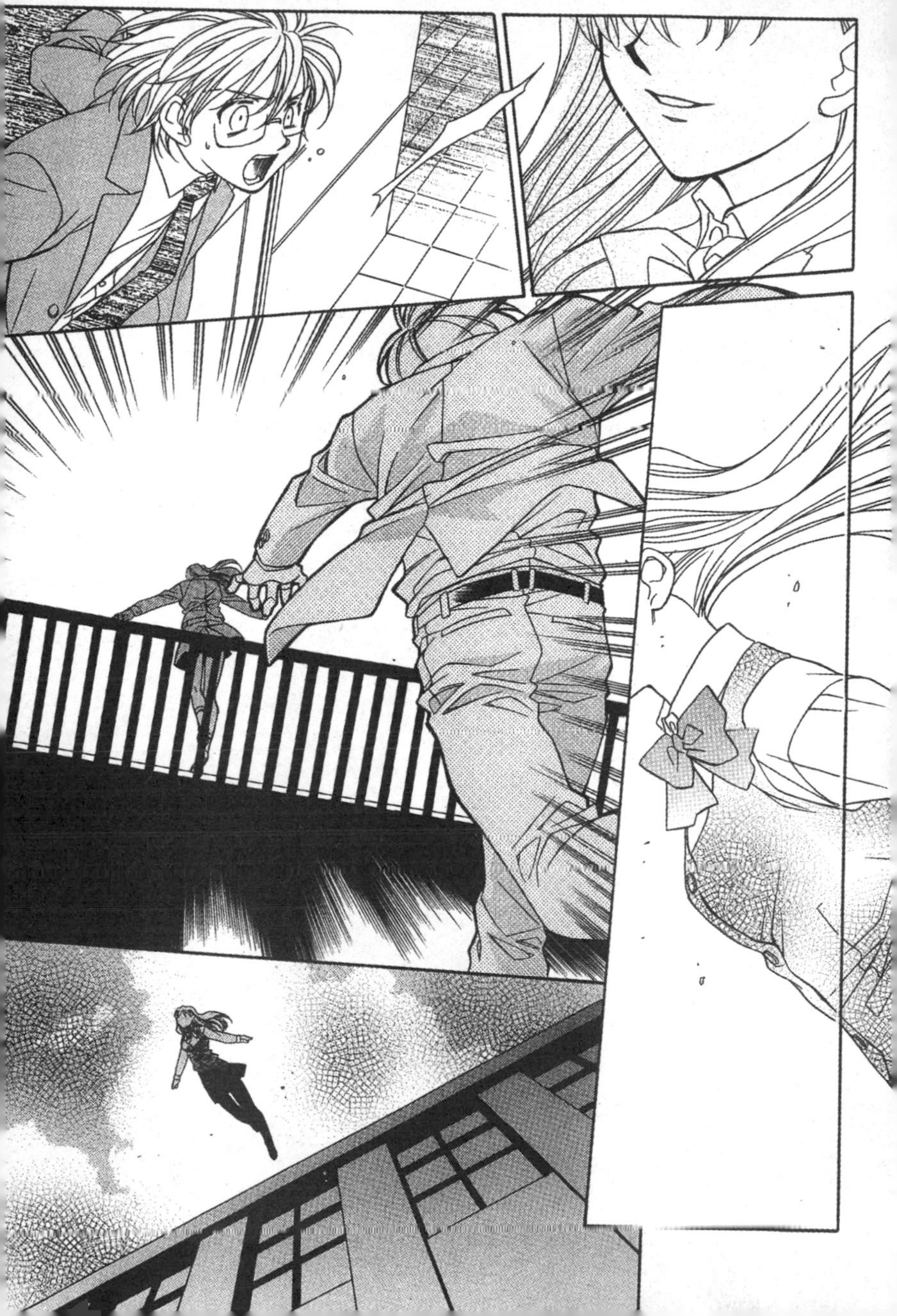

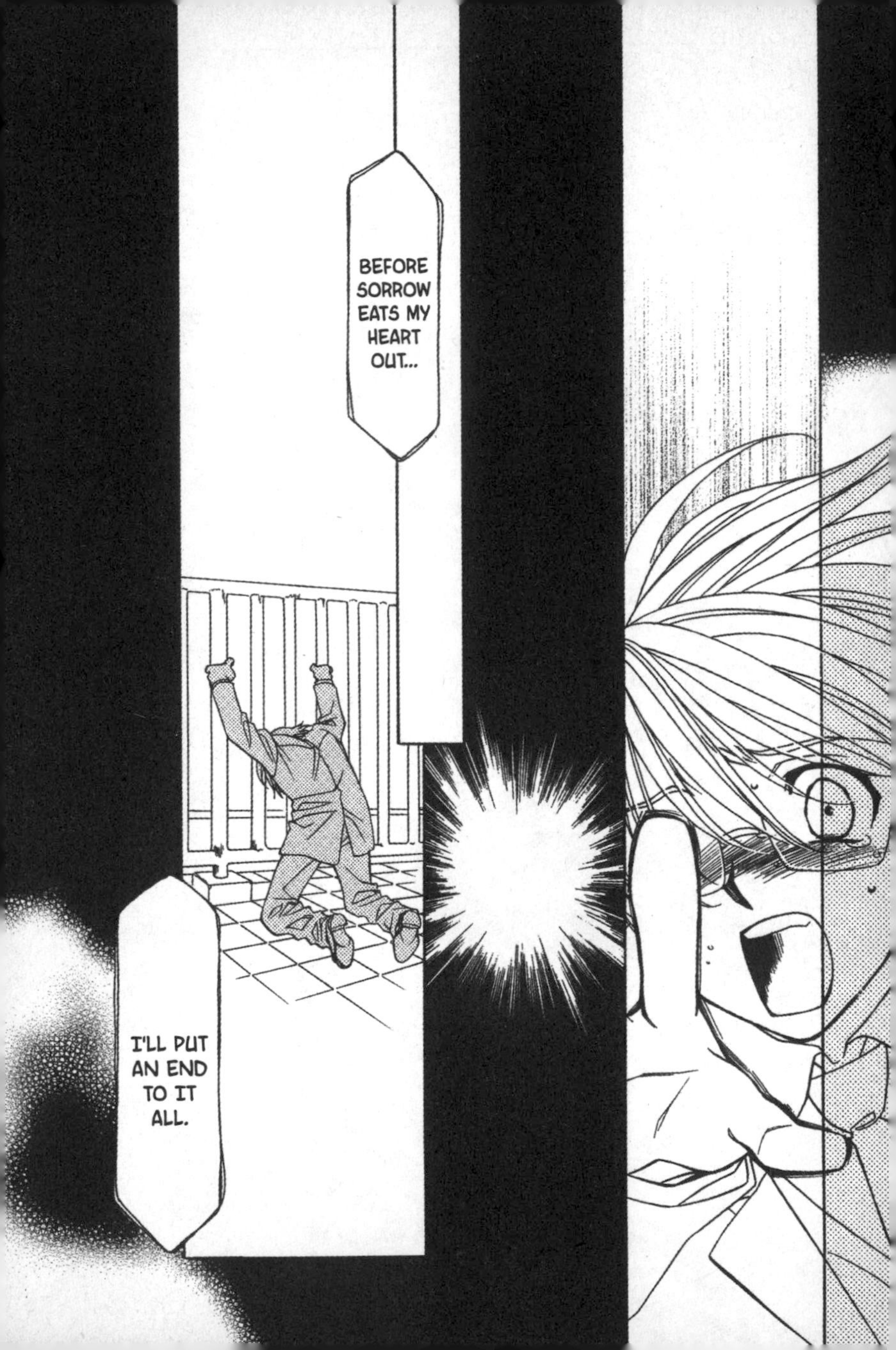
BEFORE SORROW EATS MY HEART OUT...
I'LL PUT AN END TO IT ALL.

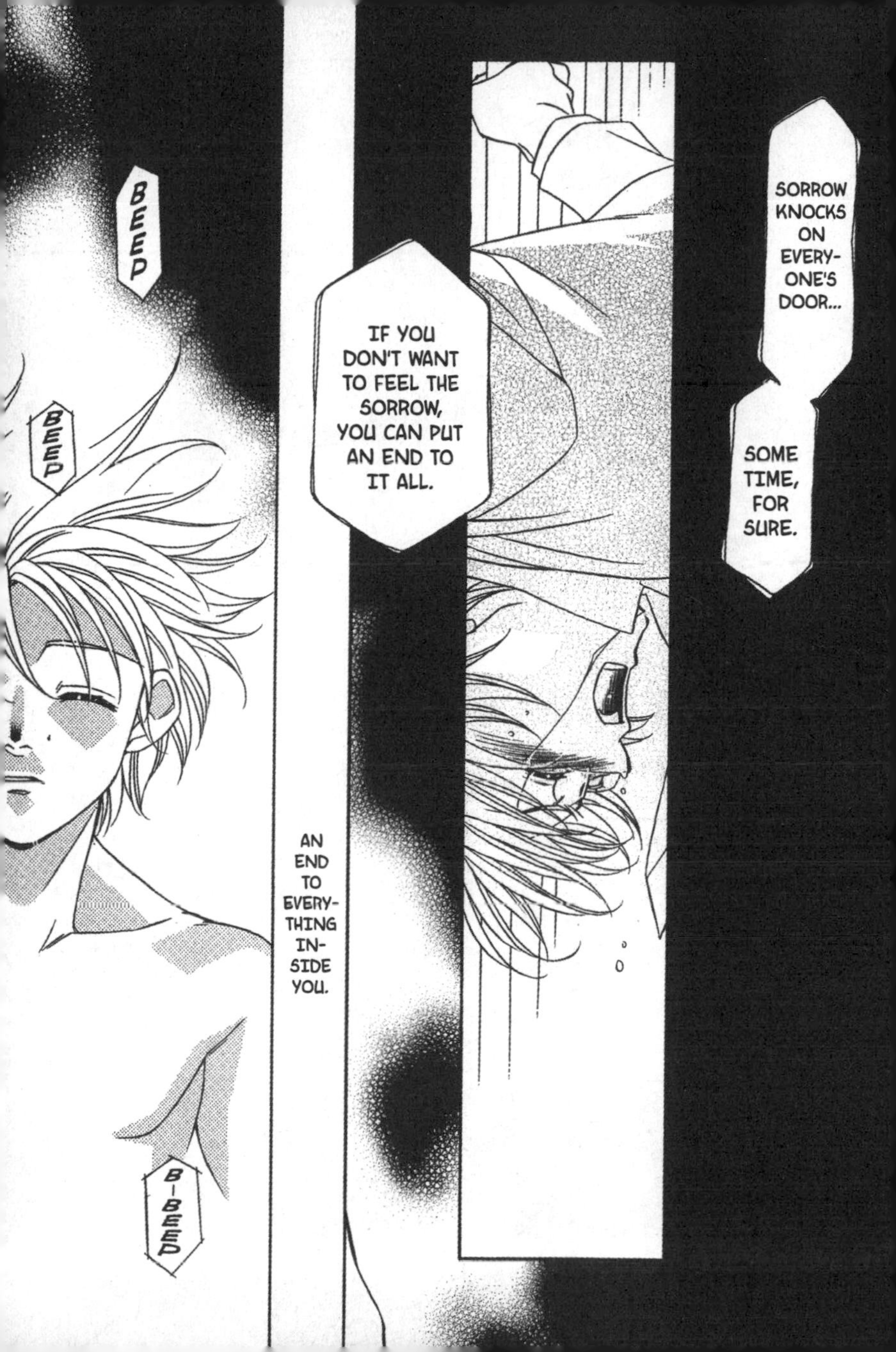
SORROW KNOCKS ON EVERY-ONE'S DOOR...
SOME TIME, FOR SURE.
IF YOU DON'T WANT TO FEEL THE SORROW, YOU CAN PUT AN END TO IT ALL.
AN END TO EVERY-THING IN-SIDE YOU.
BEEP
BEEP
B-BEEP

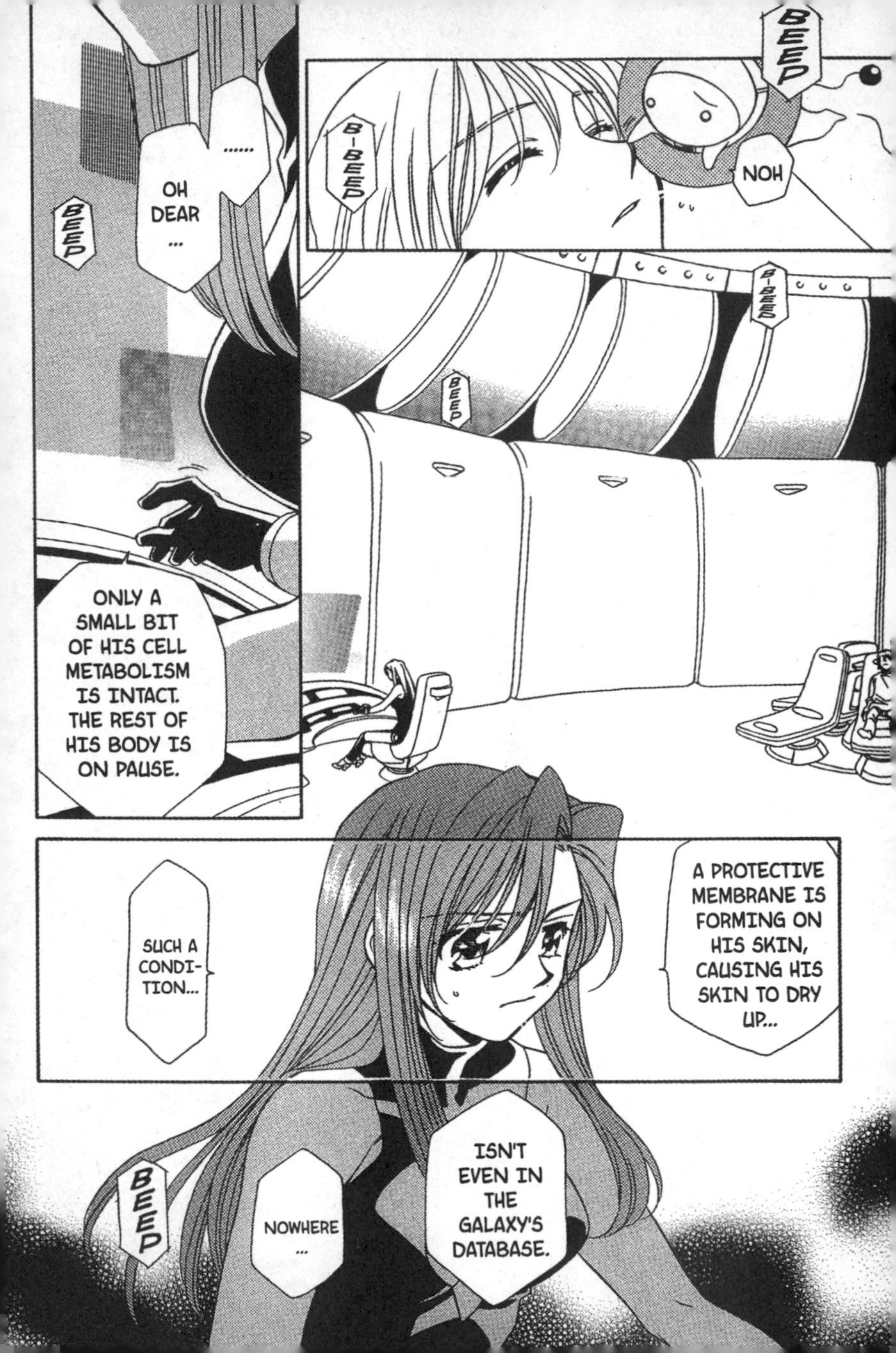
BEEP
NOH
B-BEEP
B-BEEP
BEEP
......
OH DEAR ...
BEEP
ONLY A SMALL BIT OF HIS CELL METABOLISM IS INTACT. THE REST OF HIS BODY IS ON PAUSE.
A PROTECTIVE MEMBRANE IS FORMING ON HIS SKIN, CAUSING HIS SKIN TO DRY UP...
SUCH A CONDITION...
ISN'T EVEN IN THE GALAXY'S DATABASE.
NOWHERE ...
BEEP

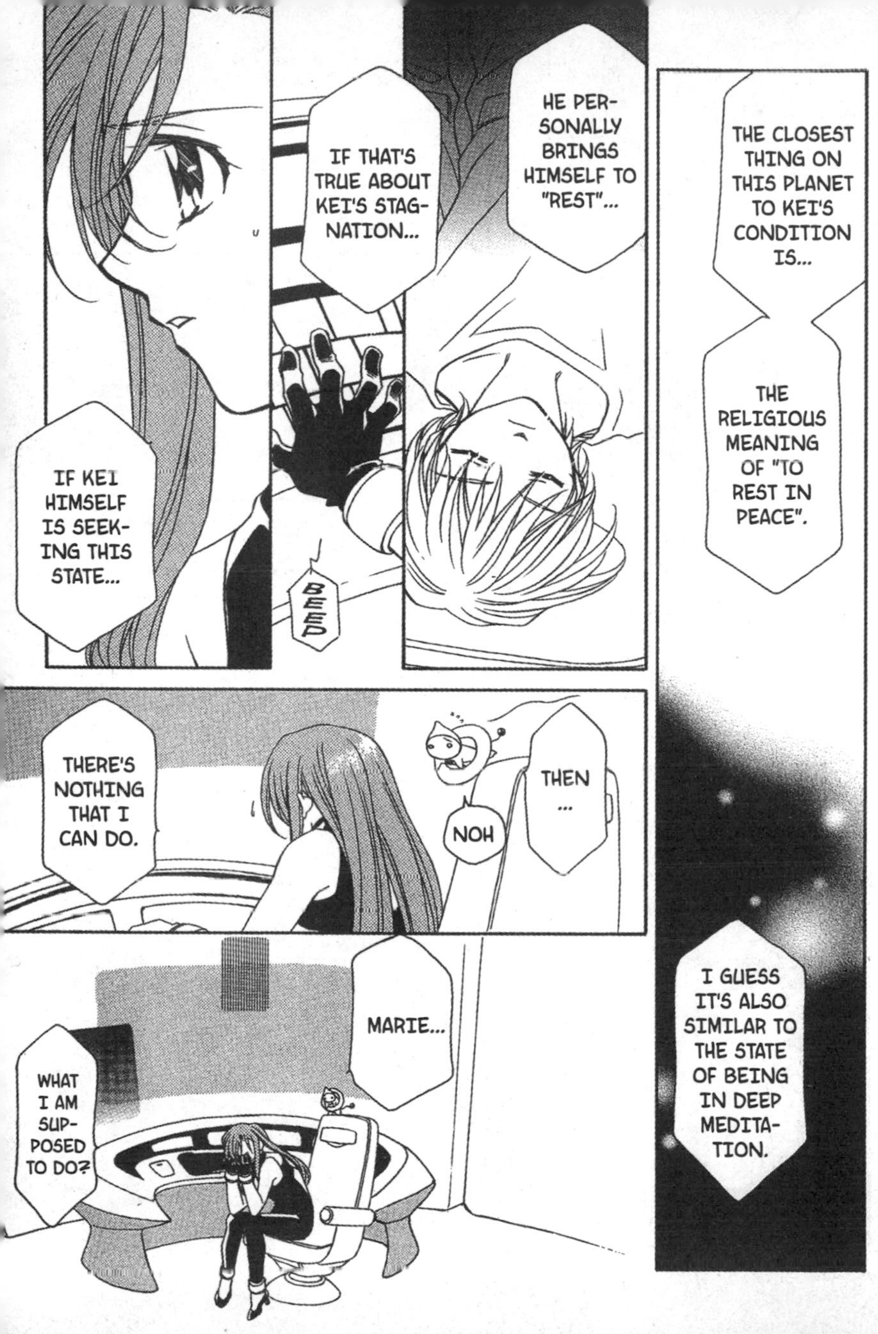
THE CLOSEST THING ON THIS PLANET TO KEI'S CONDITION IS...
THE RELIGIOUS MEANING OF "TO REST IN PEACE".
I GUESS IT'S ALSO SIMILAR TO THE STATE OF BEING IN DEEP MEDITATION.
HE PERSONALLY BRINGS HIMSELF TO "REST"...
IF THAT'S TRUE ABOUT KEI'S STAGNATION...
IF KEI HIMSELF IS SEEKING THIS STATE...
BEEP
THEN ...
NOH
THERE'S NOTHING THAT I CAN DO.
MARIE...
WHAT I AM SUPPOSED TO DO?

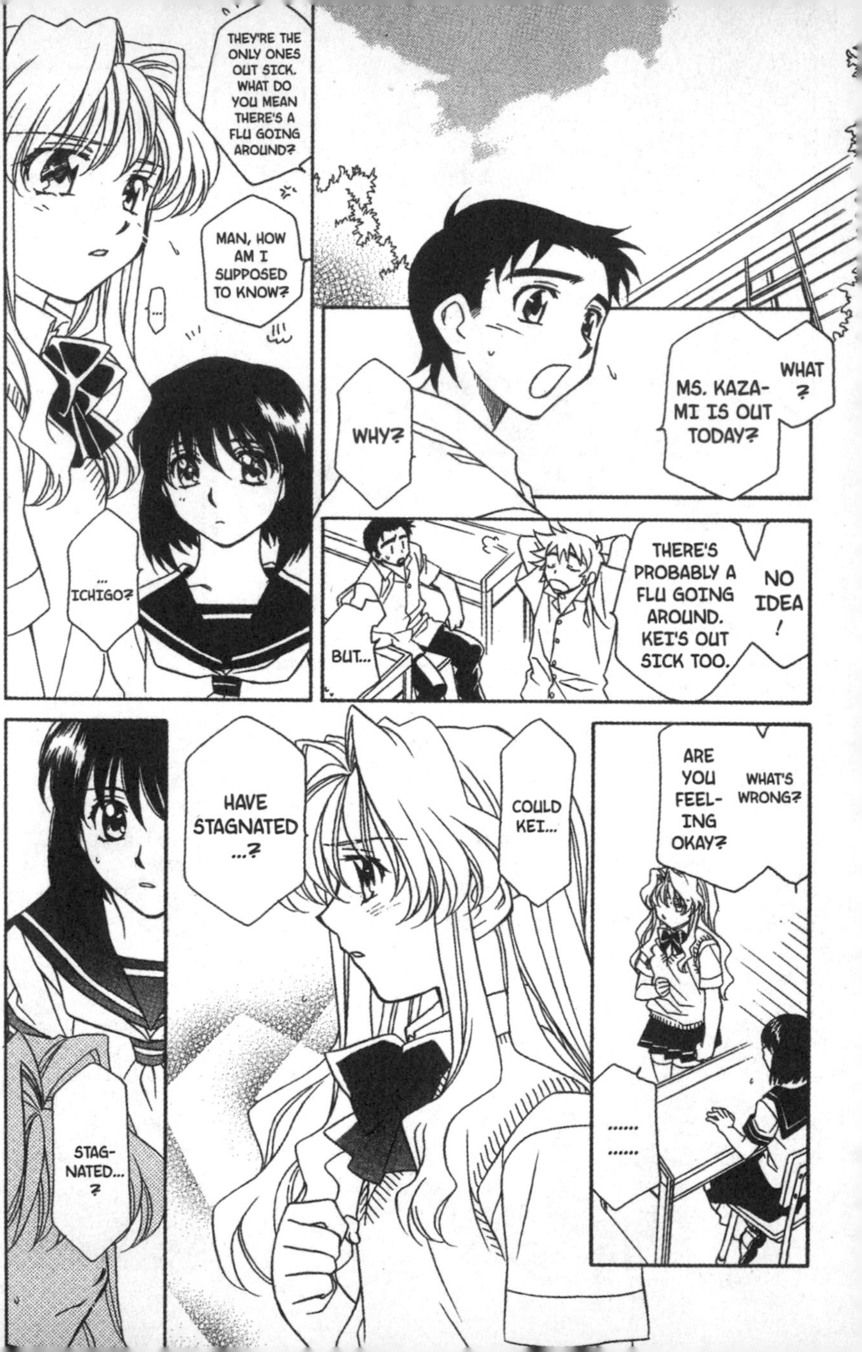
WHAT?
MS. KAZAMI IS OUT TODAY?
WHY?
NO IDEA!
THERE'S PROBABLY A FLU GOING AROUND. KEI'S OUT SICK TOO.
BUT...
THEY'RE THE ONLY ONES OUT SICK. WHAT DO YOU MEAN THERE'S A FLU GOING AROUND?
MAN, HOW AM I SUPPOSED TO KNOW?
...
...ICHIGO?
WHAT'S WRONG?
ARE YOU FEELING OKAY?
......
......
COULD KEI...
HAVE STAGNATED...?
STAGNATED...?

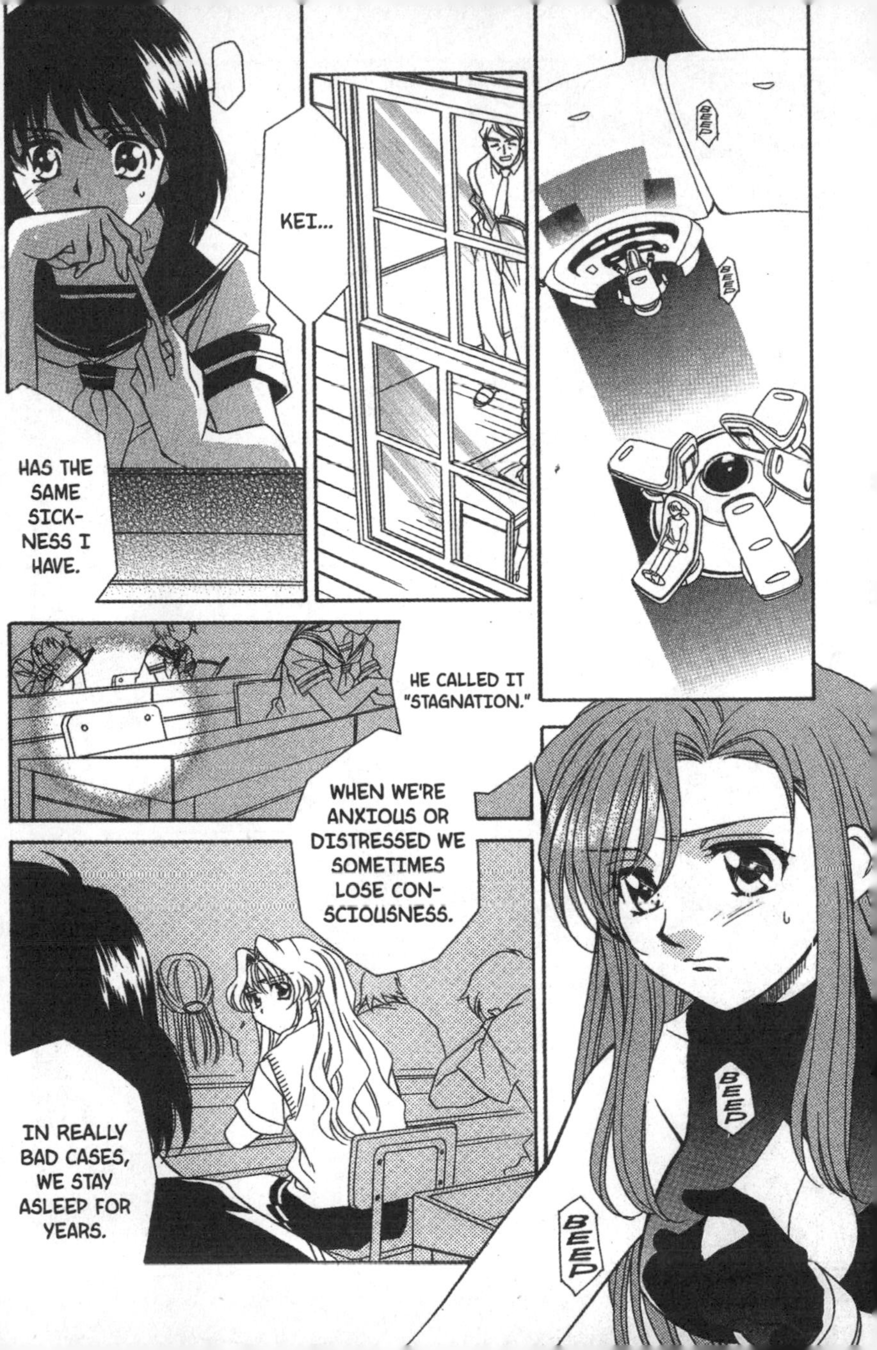
BEEP
BEEP
KEI...
HAS THE SAME SICKNESS I HAVE.
BEEP
BEEP
HE CALLED IT "STAGNATION."
WHEN WE'RE ANXIOUS OR DISTRESSED WE SOMETIMES LOSE CONSCIOUSNESS.
IN REALLY BAD CASES, WE STAY ASLEEP FOR YEARS.

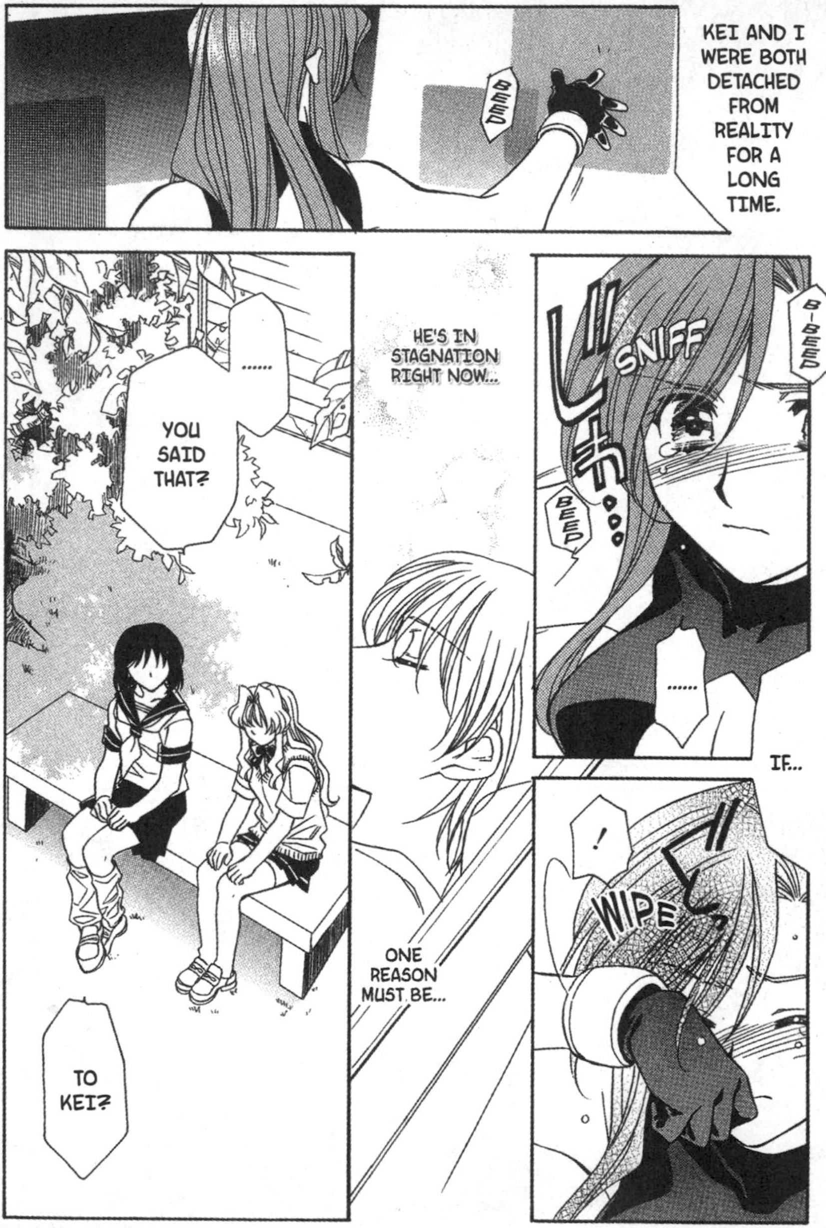

KEI AND I WERE BOTH DETACHED FROM REALITY FOR A LONG TIME.
BEEP
B-BEEP
SNIFF
BEEP
......
HE'S IN STAGNATION RIGHT NOW...
IF...
!
WIPE
ONE REASON MUST BE...
......
YOU SAID THAT?
TO KEI?

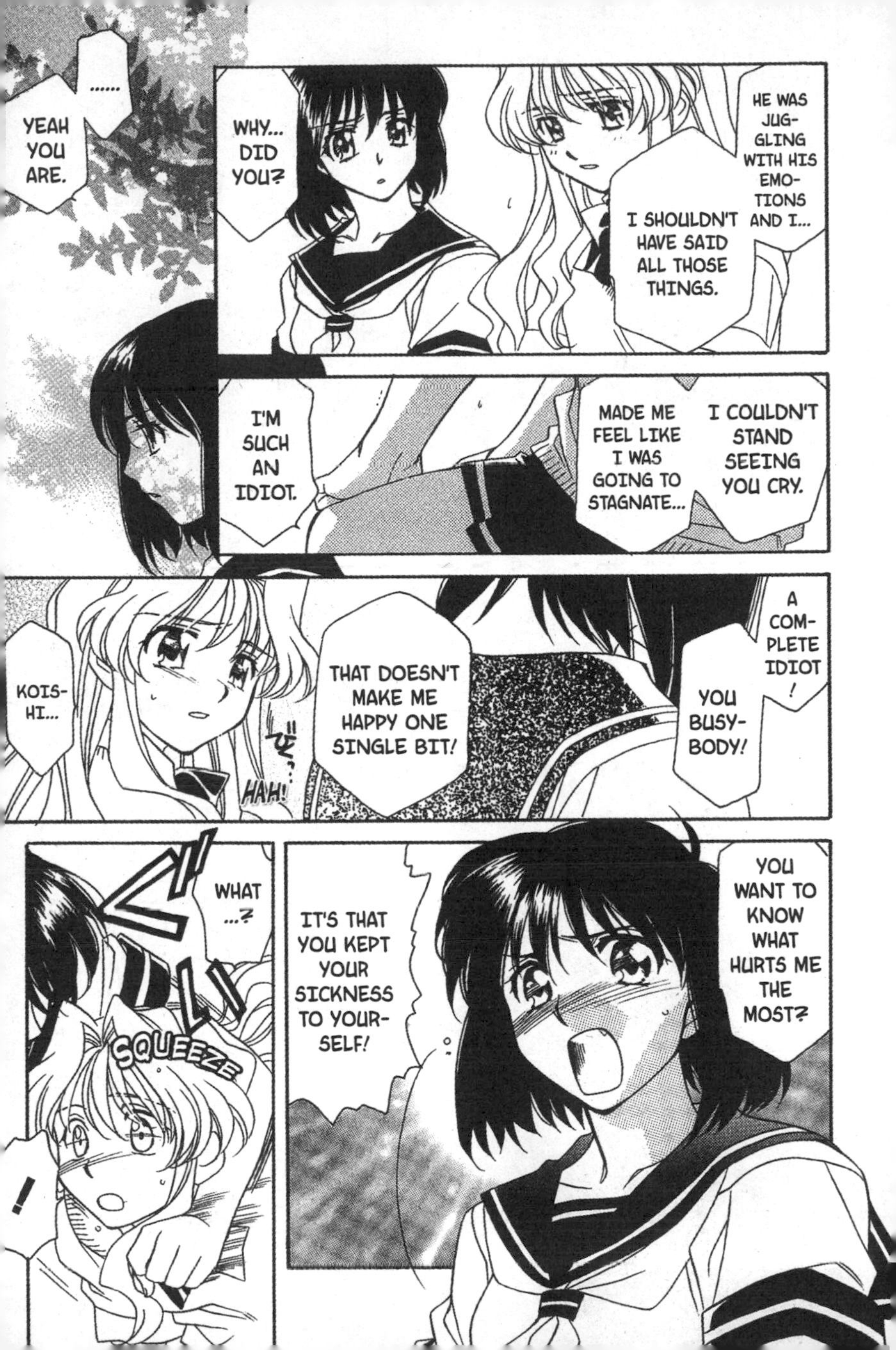
HE WAS JUG-GLING WITH HIS EMO-TIONS AND I...
I SHOULDN'T HAVE SAID ALL THOSE THINGS.
WHY... DID YOU?
I COULDN'T STAND SEEING YOU CRY.
MADE ME FEEL LIKE I WAS GOING TO STAGNATE...
I'M SUCH AN IDIOT.
......
YEAH YOU ARE.
A COM-PLETE IDIOT!
YOU BUSY-BODY!
THAT DOESN'T MAKE ME HAPPY ONE SINGLE BIT!
HAH!
KOIS-HI...
YOU WANT TO KNOW WHAT HURTS ME THE MOST?
IT'S THAT YOU KEPT YOUR SICKNESS TO YOUR-SELF!
WHAT ...?
SQUEEZE
!

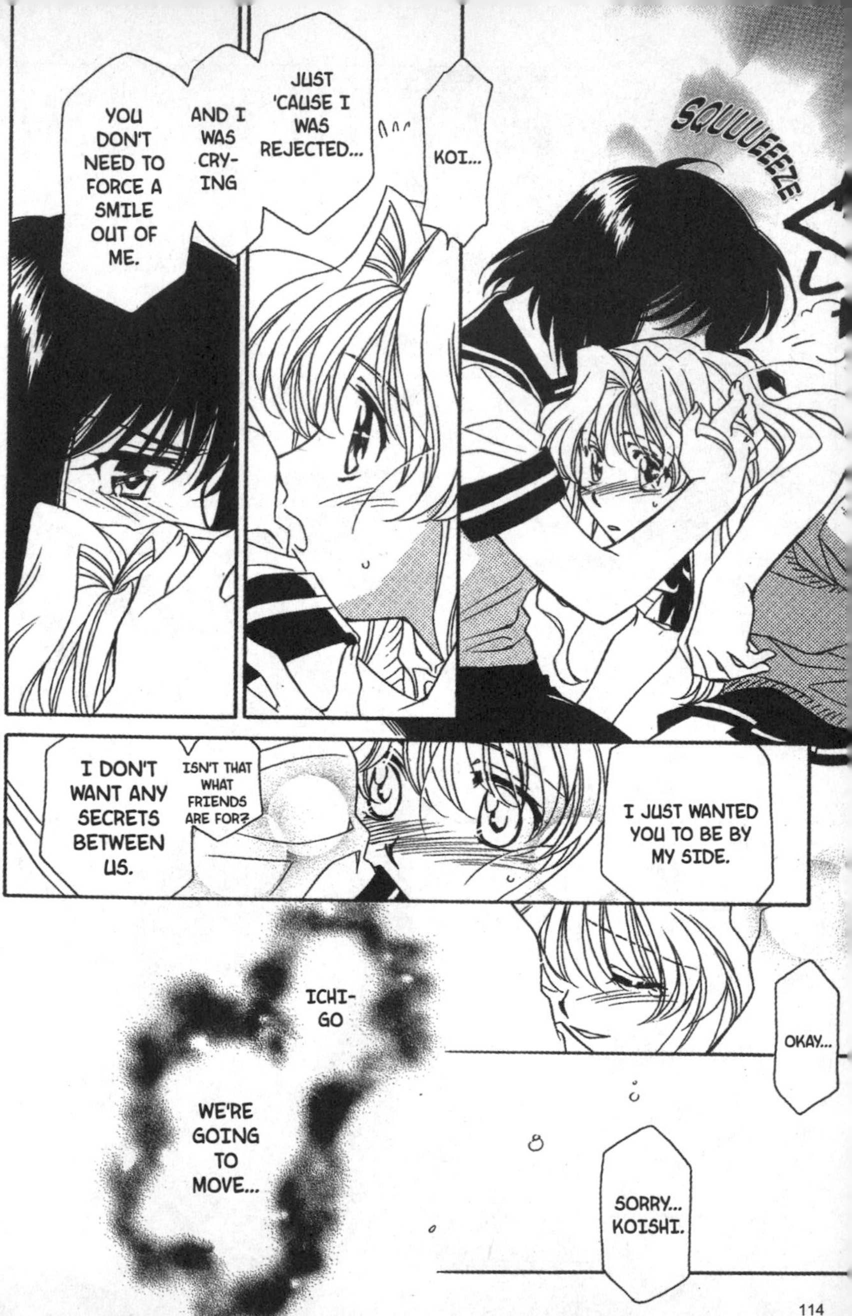
SQUUUEEZE
KOI...
JUST 'CAUSE I WAS REJECTED...
AND I WAS CRY-ING
YOU DON'T NEED TO FORCE A SMILE OUT OF ME.
I JUST WANTED YOU TO BE BY MY SIDE.
ISN'T THAT WHAT FRIENDS ARE FOR?
I DON'T WANT ANY SECRETS BETWEEN US.
OKAY...
SORRY... KOISHI.
ICHI-GO
WE'RE GOING TO MOVE...

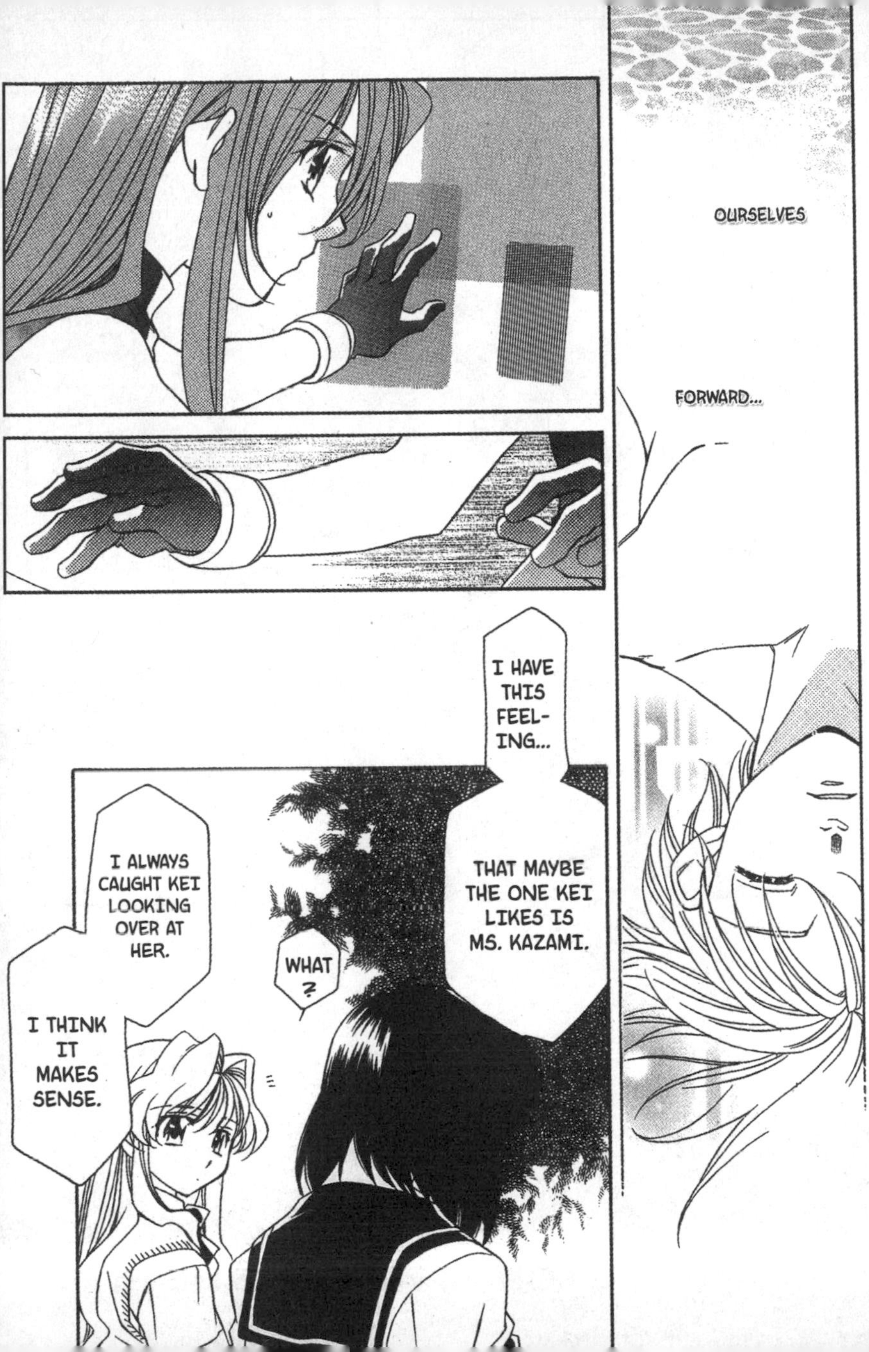
OURSELVES
FORWARD...
I HAVE THIS FEEL-ING...
THAT MAYBE THE ONE KEI LIKES IS MS. KAZAMI.
WHAT?
I ALWAYS CAUGHT KEI LOOKING OVER AT HER.
I THINK IT MAKES SENSE.

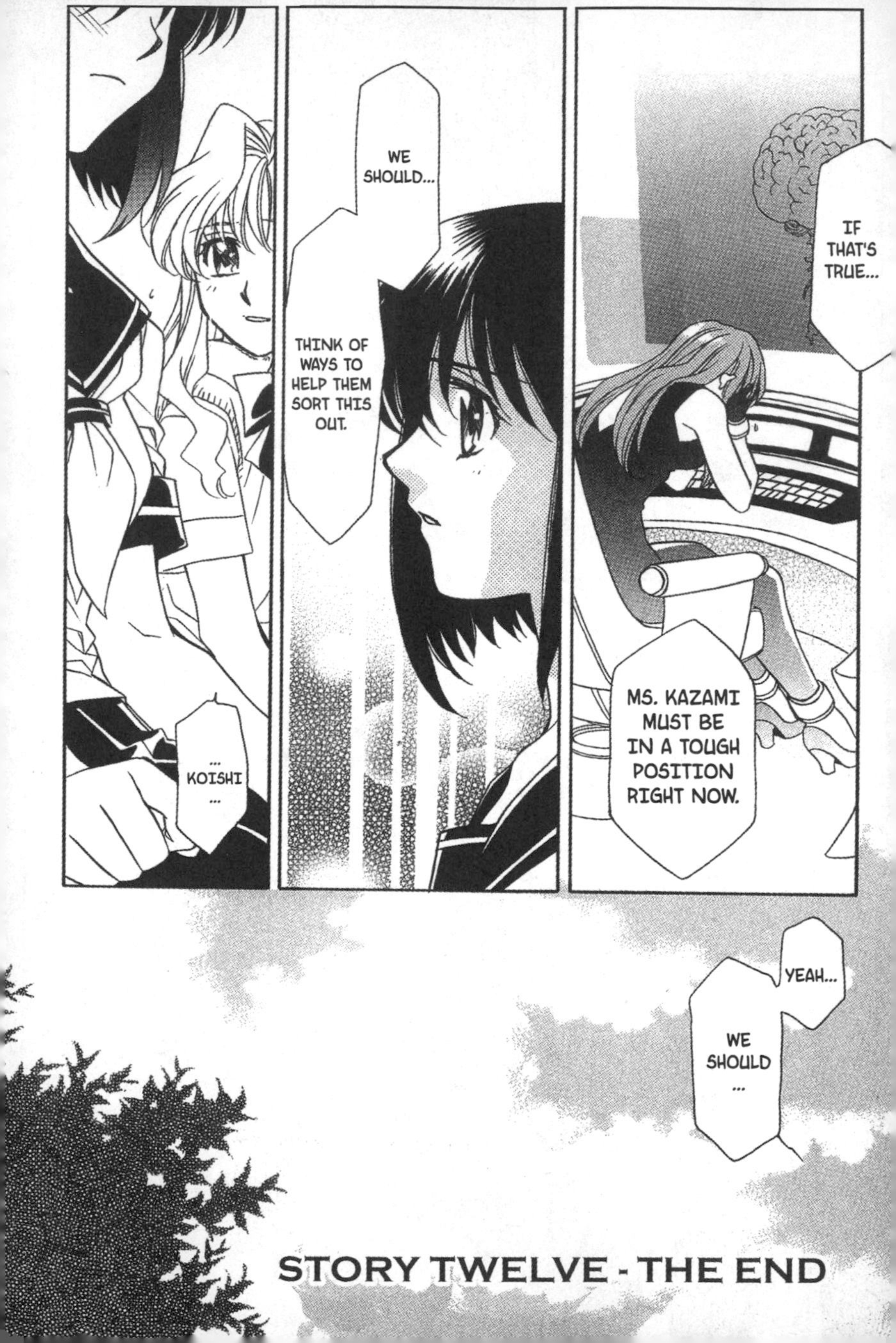
IF THAT'S TRUE...
MS. KAZAMI MUST BE IN A TOUGH POSITION RIGHT NOW.
WE SHOULD...
THINK OF WAYS TO HELP THEM SORT THIS OUT.
...KOISHI...
YEAH...
WE SHOULD...
STORY TWELVE - THE END

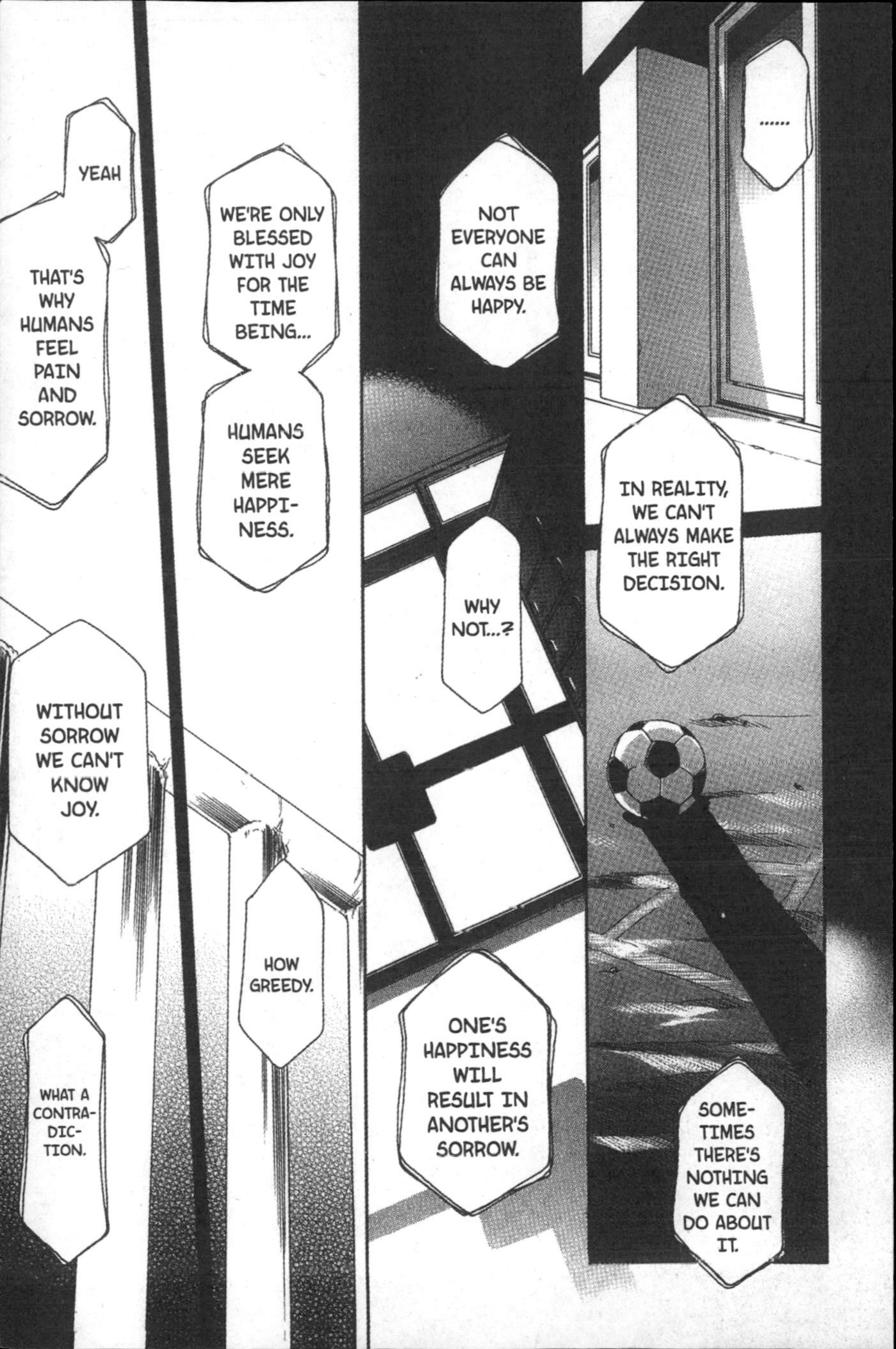
......
NOT EVERYONE CAN ALWAYS BE HAPPY.
IN REALITY, WE CAN'T ALWAYS MAKE THE RIGHT DECISION.
WHY NOT...?
ONE'S HAPPINESS WILL RESULT IN ANOTHER'S SORROW.
SOME-TIMES THERE'S NOTHING WE CAN DO ABOUT IT.
WE'RE ONLY BLESSED WITH JOY FOR THE TIME BEING...
HUMANS SEEK MERE HAPPI-NESS.
HOW GREEDY.
YEAH
THAT'S WHY HUMANS FEEL PAIN AND SORROW.
WITHOUT SORROW WE CAN'T KNOW JOY.
WHAT A CONTRA-DIC-TION.

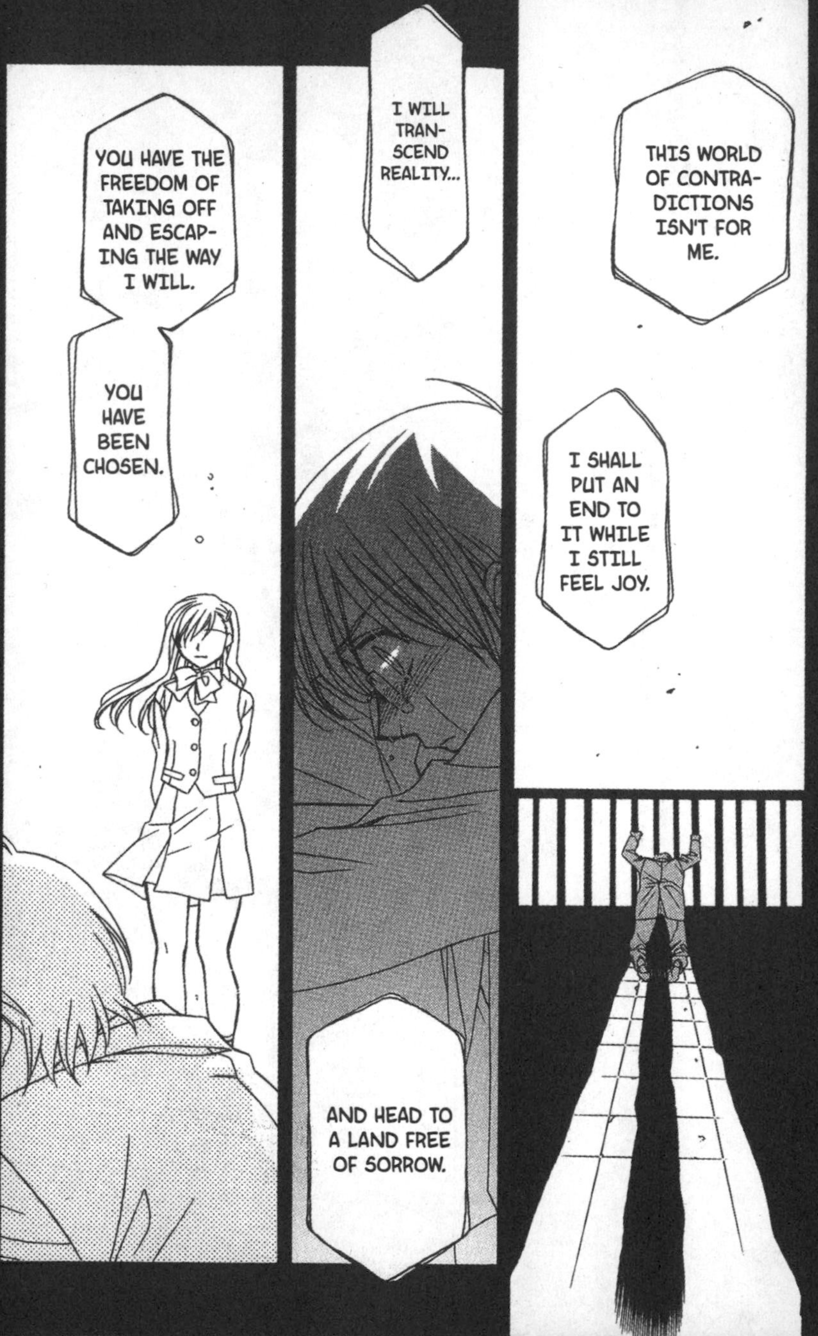
THIS WORLD OF CONTRA-DICTIONS ISN'T FOR ME.
I SHALL PUT AN END TO IT WHILE I STILL FEEL JOY.
I WILL TRAN-SCEND REALITY...
AND HEAD TO A LAND FREE OF SORROW.
YOU HAVE THE FREEDOM OF TAKING OFF AND ESCAP-ING THE WAY I WILL.
YOU HAVE BEEN CHOSEN.

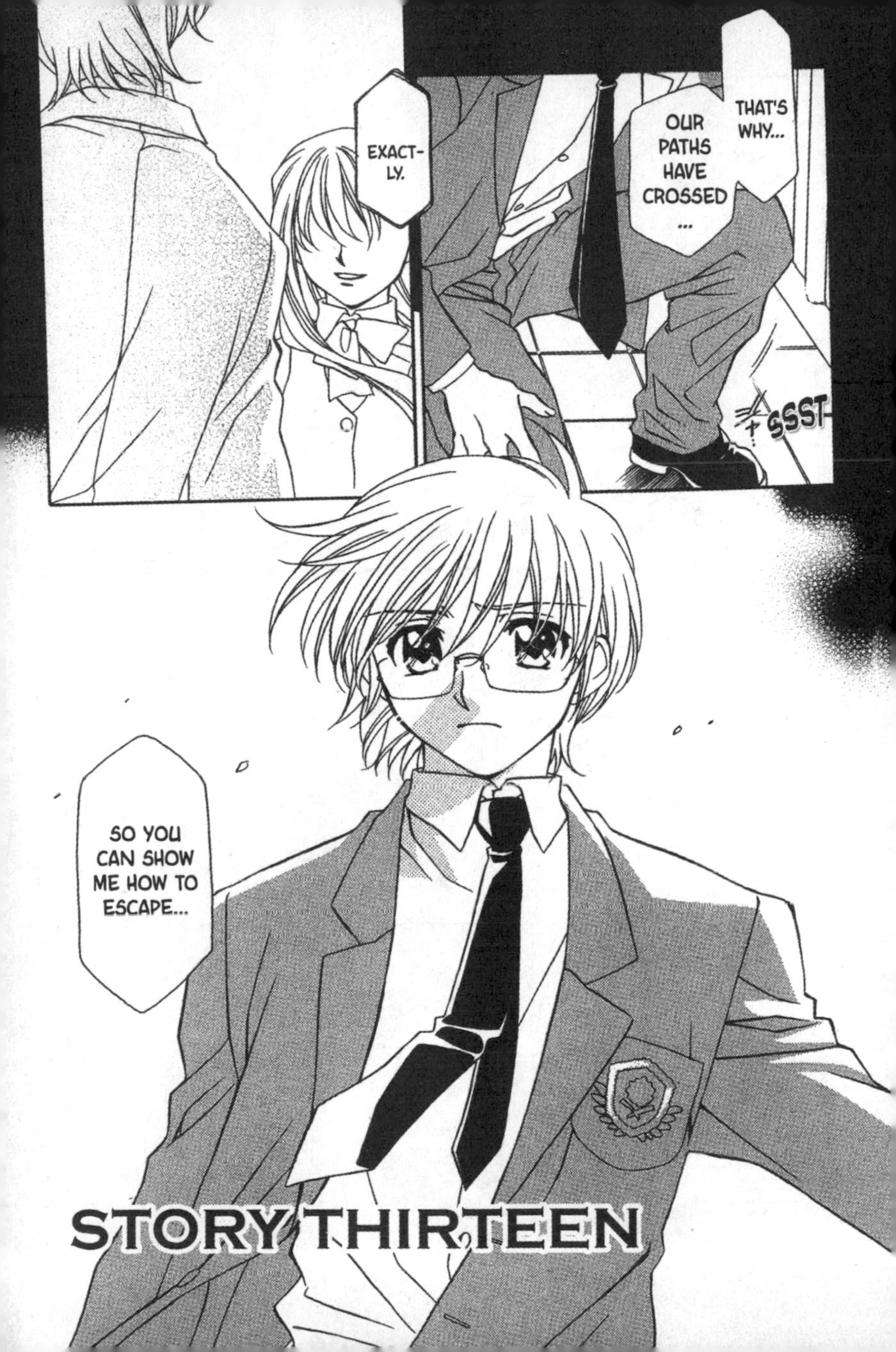
THAT'S WHY...
OUR PATHS HAVE CROSSED...
SSST
EXACT-LY.
SO YOU CAN SHOW ME HOW TO ESCAPE...

STORY THIRTEEN

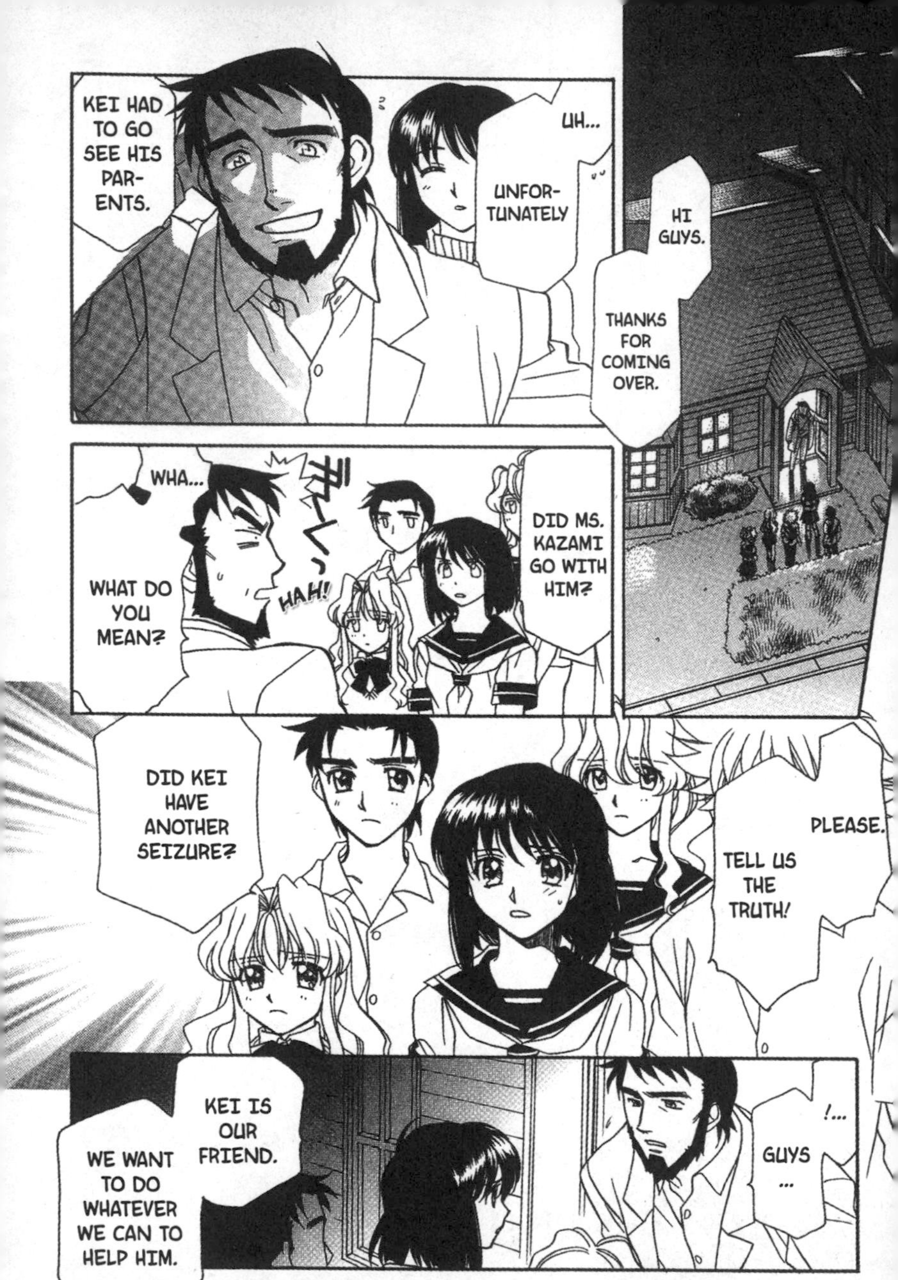
HI GUYS.
THANKS FOR COMING OVER.
UH...
UNFORTUNATELY
KEI HAD TO GO SEE HIS PARENTS.
DID MS. KAZAMI GO WITH HIM?
HAH!
WHA...
WHAT DO YOU MEAN?
PLEASE.
TELL US THE TRUTH!
DID KEI HAVE ANOTHER SEIZURE?
!...
GUYS ...
KEI IS OUR FRIEND.
WE WANT TO DO WHATEVER WE CAN TO HELP HIM.

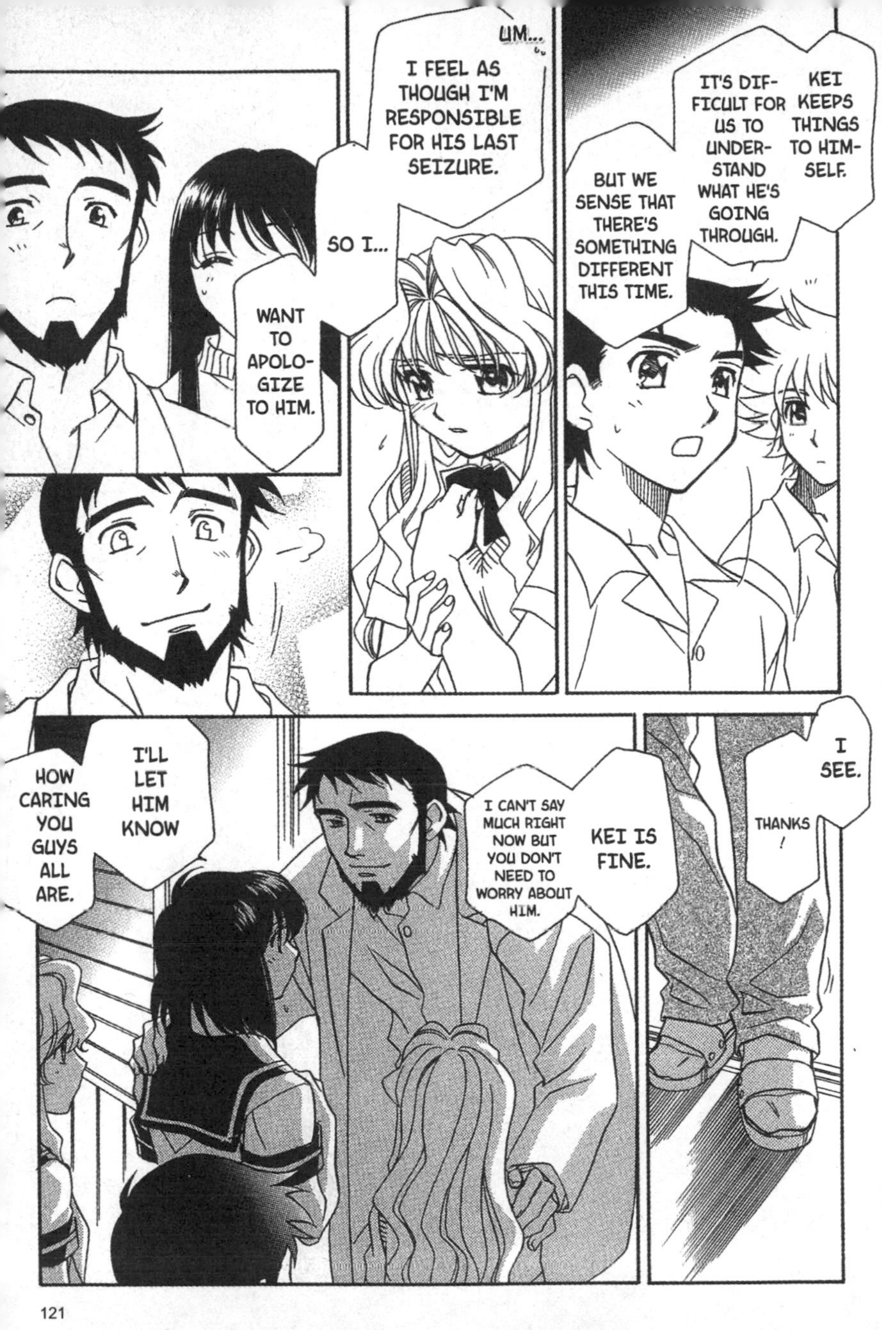
KEI KEEPS THINGS TO HIMSELF.
IT'S DIFFICULT FOR US TO UNDERSTAND WHAT HE'S GOING THROUGH.
BUT WE SENSE THAT THERE'S SOMETHING DIFFERENT THIS TIME.
UM...
I FEEL AS THOUGH I'M RESPONSIBLE FOR HIS LAST SEIZURE.
SO I...
WANT TO APOLOGIZE TO HIM.
I SEE.
THANKS!
KEI IS FINE.
I CAN'T SAY MUCH RIGHT NOW BUT YOU DON'T NEED TO WORRY ABOUT HIM.
I'LL LET HIM KNOW
HOW CARING YOU GUYS ALL ARE.

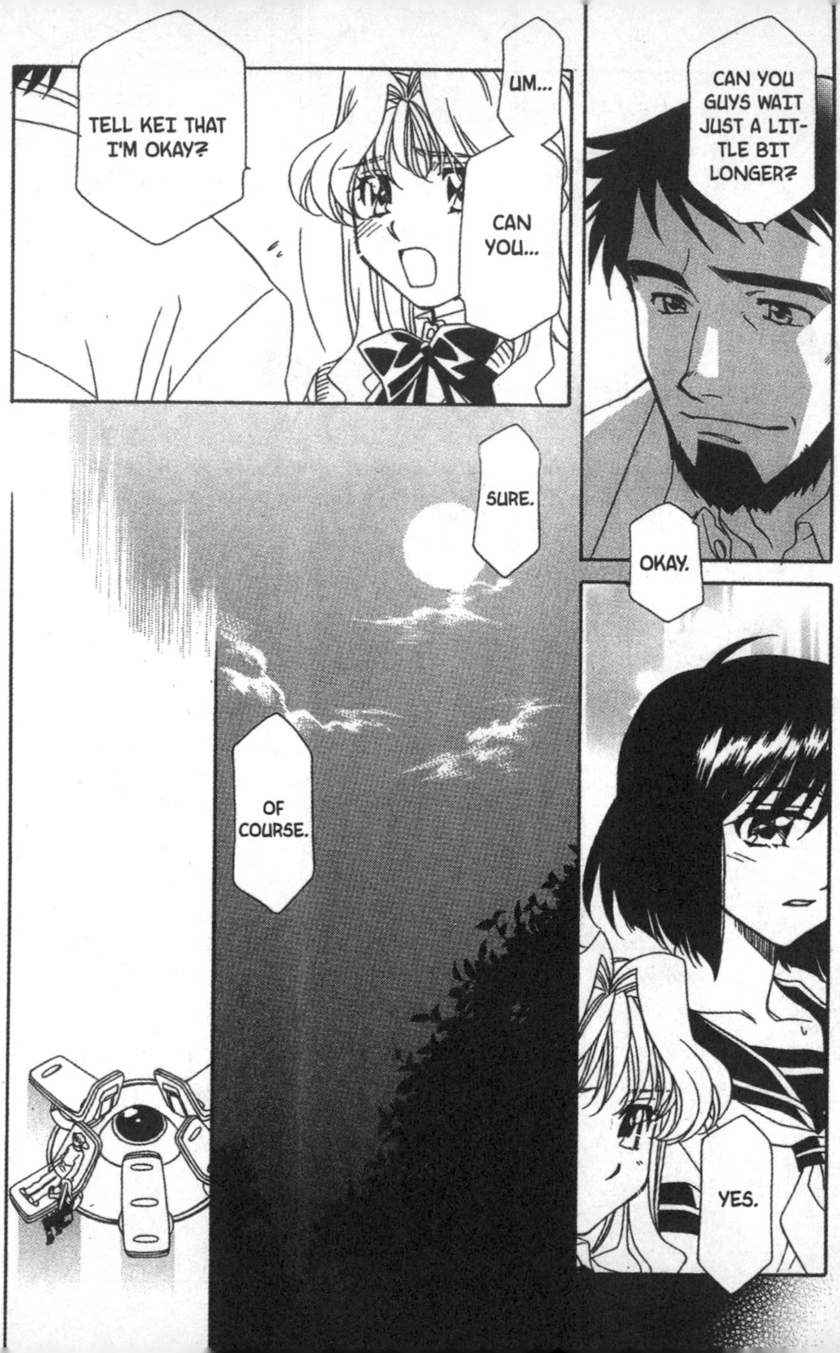
CAN YOU GUYS WAIT JUST A LIT-TLE BIT LONGER?
UM...
CAN YOU...
TELL KEI THAT I'M OKAY?
OKAY.
YES.
SURE.
OF COURSE.

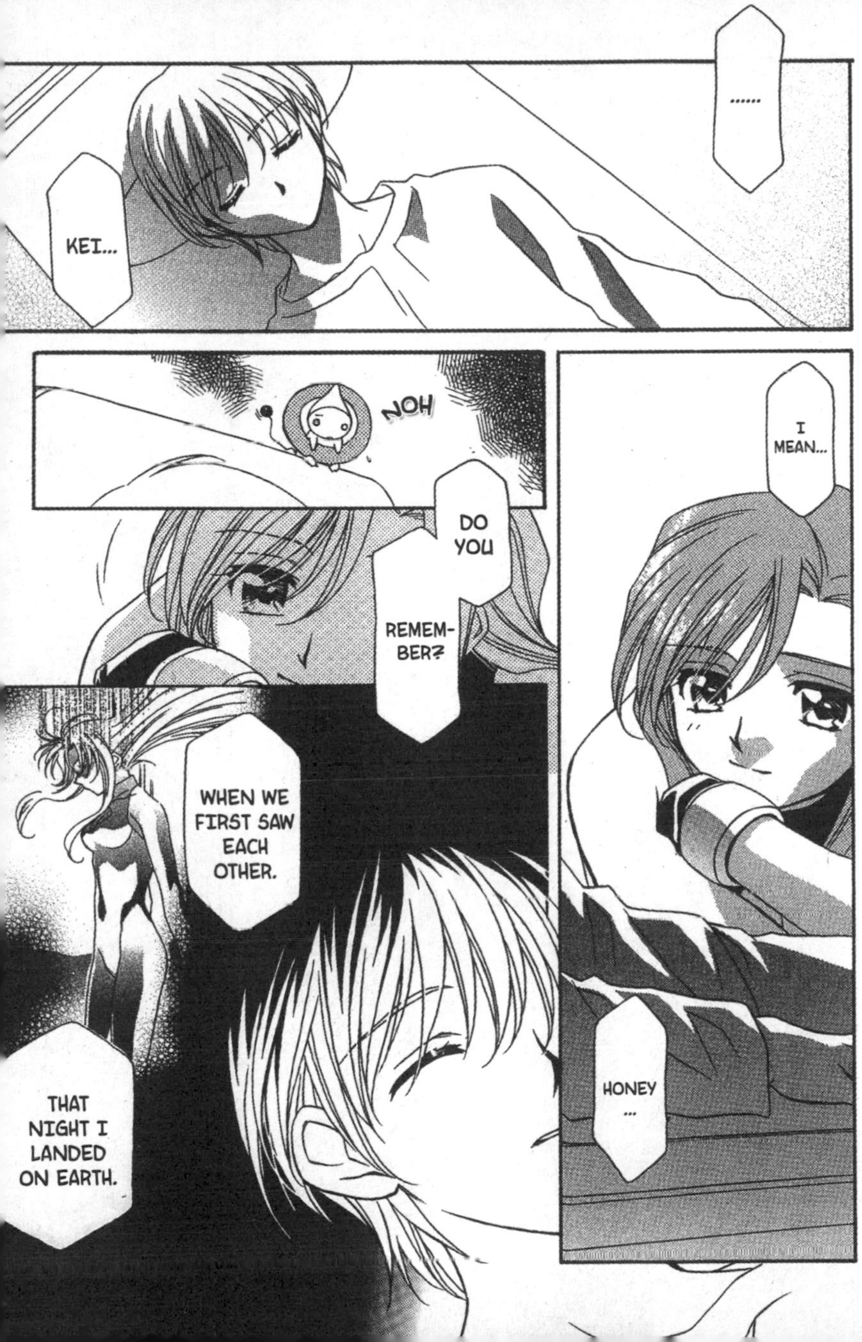
......
KEI...
I MEAN...
HONEY ...
NOH
DO YOU REMEMBER?
WHEN WE FIRST SAW EACH OTHER.
THAT NIGHT I LANDED ON EARTH.

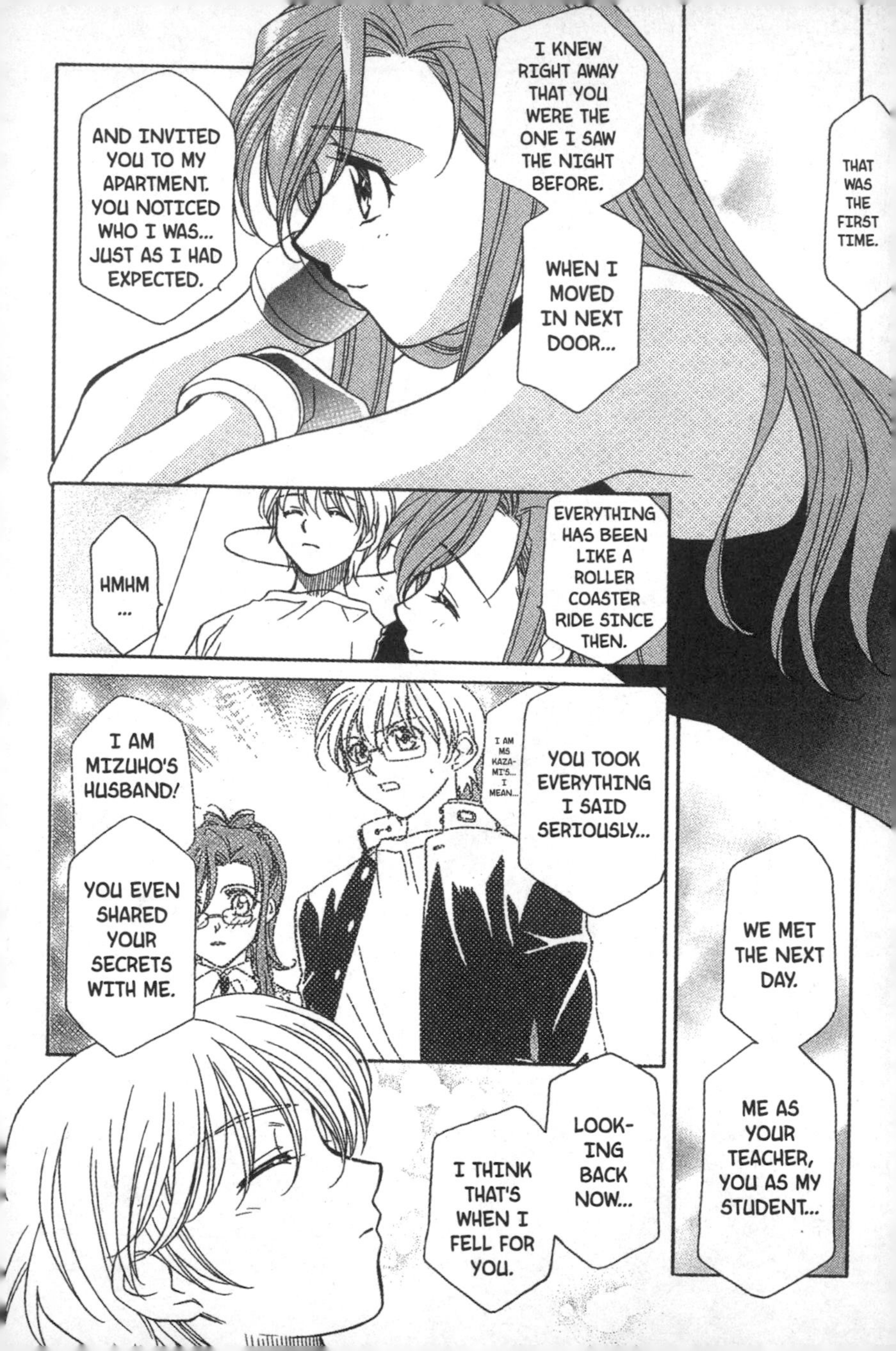
THAT WAS THE FIRST TIME.
I KNEW RIGHT AWAY THAT YOU WERE THE ONE I SAW THE NIGHT BEFORE.
WHEN I MOVED IN NEXT DOOR...
AND INVITED YOU TO MY APARTMENT. YOU NOTICED WHO I WAS... JUST AS I HAD EXPECTED.
EVERYTHING HAS BEEN LIKE A ROLLER COASTER RIDE SINCE THEN.
HMHM ...
WE MET THE NEXT DAY.
ME AS YOUR TEACHER, YOU AS MY STUDENT...
YOU TOOK EVERYTHING I SAID SERIOUSLY...
I AM MS KAZA-MI'S... I MEAN...
I AM MIZUHO'S HUSBAND!
YOU EVEN SHARED YOUR SECRETS WITH ME.
LOOK-ING BACK NOW...
I THINK THAT'S WHEN I FELL FOR YOU.

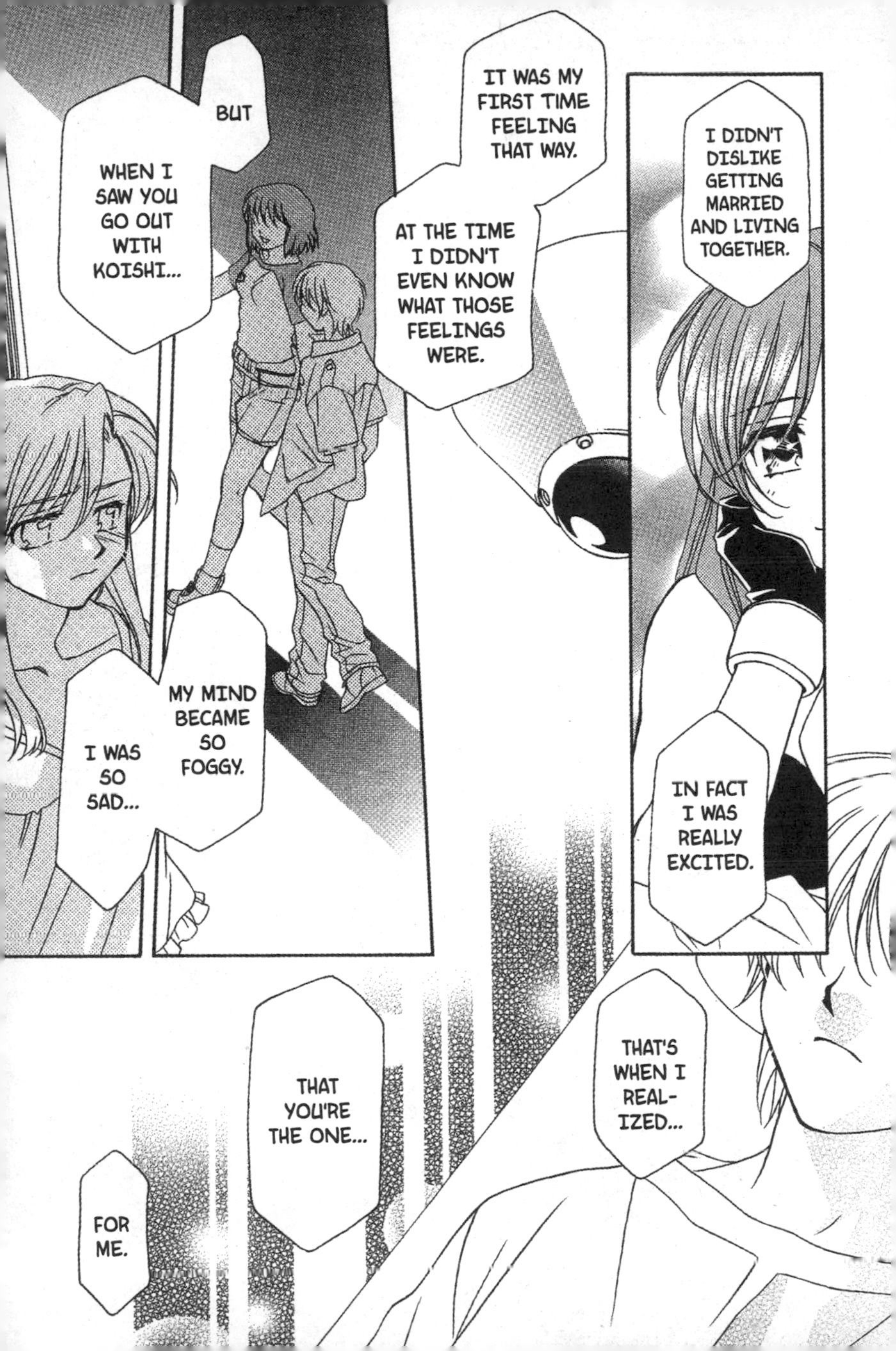

I DIDN'T DISLIKE GETTING MARRIED AND LIVING TOGETHER.
IN FACT I WAS REALLY EXCITED.
IT WAS MY FIRST TIME FEELING THAT WAY.
AT THE TIME I DIDN'T EVEN KNOW WHAT THOSE FEELINGS WERE.
BUT
WHEN I SAW YOU GO OUT WITH KOISHI...
MY MIND BECAME SO FOGGY.
I WAS SO SAD...
THAT'S WHEN I REAL-IZED...
THAT YOU'RE THE ONE...
FOR ME.

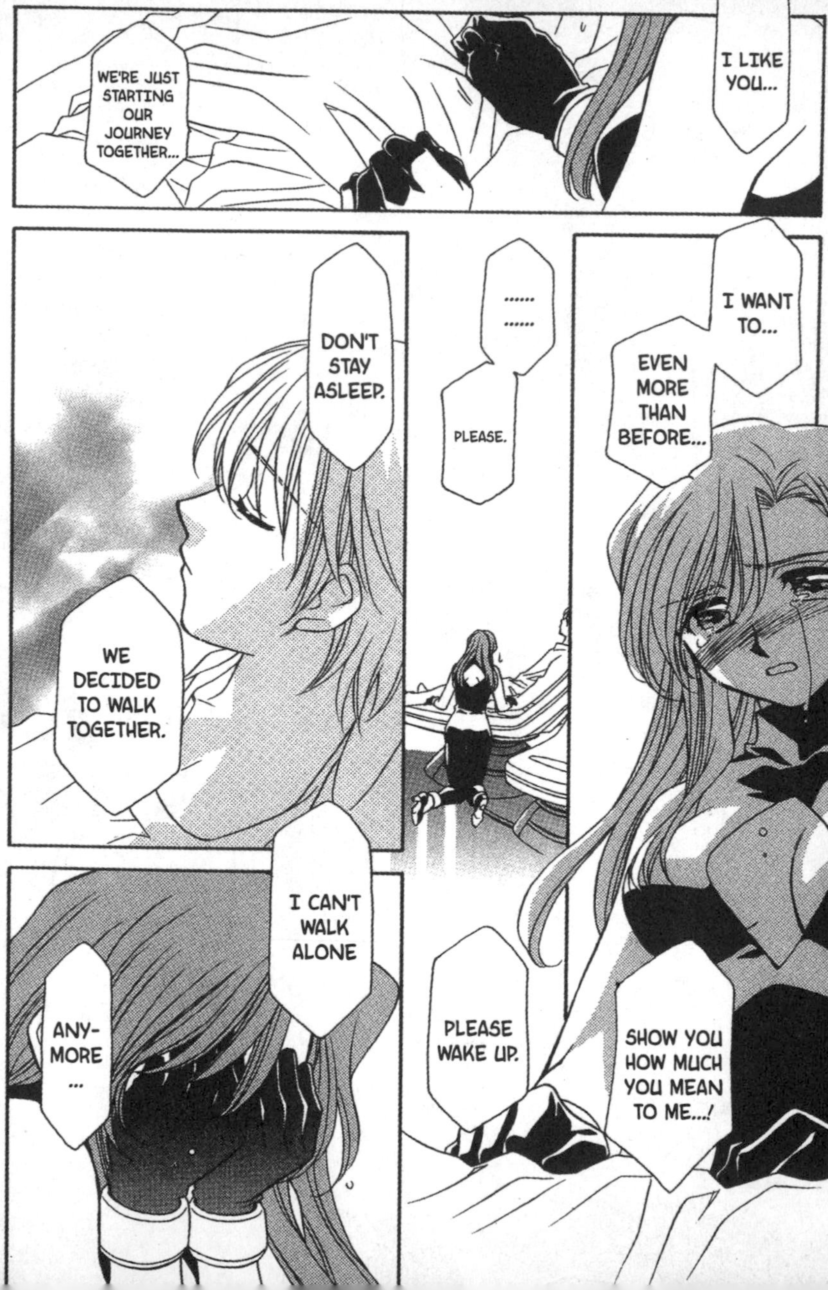
I LIKE YOU...
WE'RE JUST STARTING OUR JOURNEY TOGETHER...
I WANT TO...
EVEN MORE THAN BEFORE...
SHOW YOU HOW MUCH YOU MEAN TO ME...!
PLEASE WAKE UP.
......
......
PLEASE.
DON'T STAY ASLEEP.
WE DECIDED TO WALK TOGETHER.
I CAN'T WALK ALONE
ANY-MORE
...

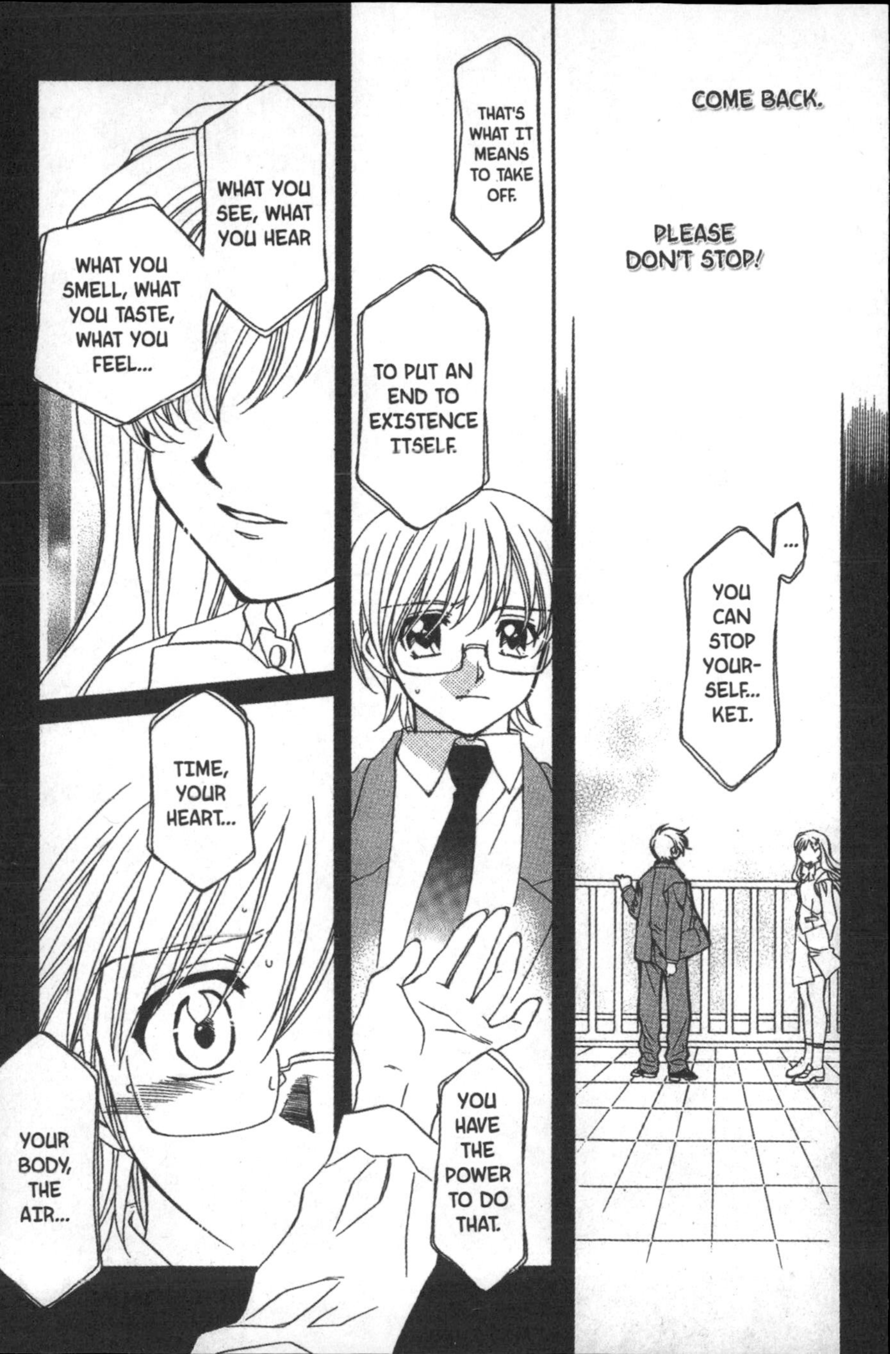
COME BACK.
PLEASE DON'T STOP!
...
YOU CAN STOP YOUR-SELF... KEI.
THAT'S WHAT IT MEANS TO TAKE OFF.
TO PUT AN END TO EXISTENCE ITSELF.
YOU HAVE THE POWER TO DO THAT.
WHAT YOU SEE, WHAT YOU HEAR
WHAT YOU SMELL, WHAT YOU TASTE, WHAT YOU FEEL...
TIME, YOUR HEART...
YOUR BODY, THE AIR...

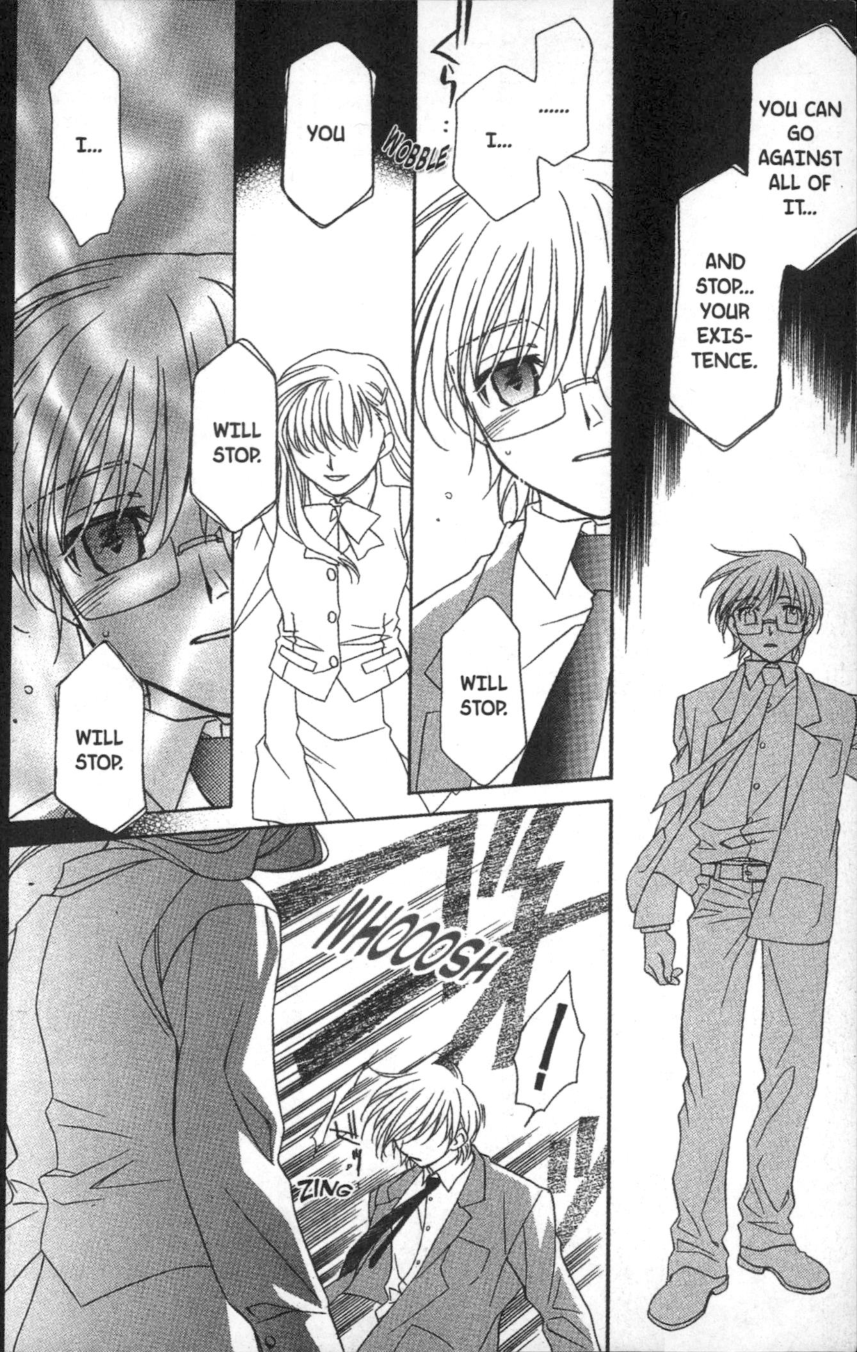
YOU CAN GO AGAINST ALL OF IT...
AND STOP... YOUR EXISTENCE.
......
I...
WILL STOP.
YOU
WOBBLE
WILL STOP.
I...
WILL STOP.
WHOOOSH
!
ZING

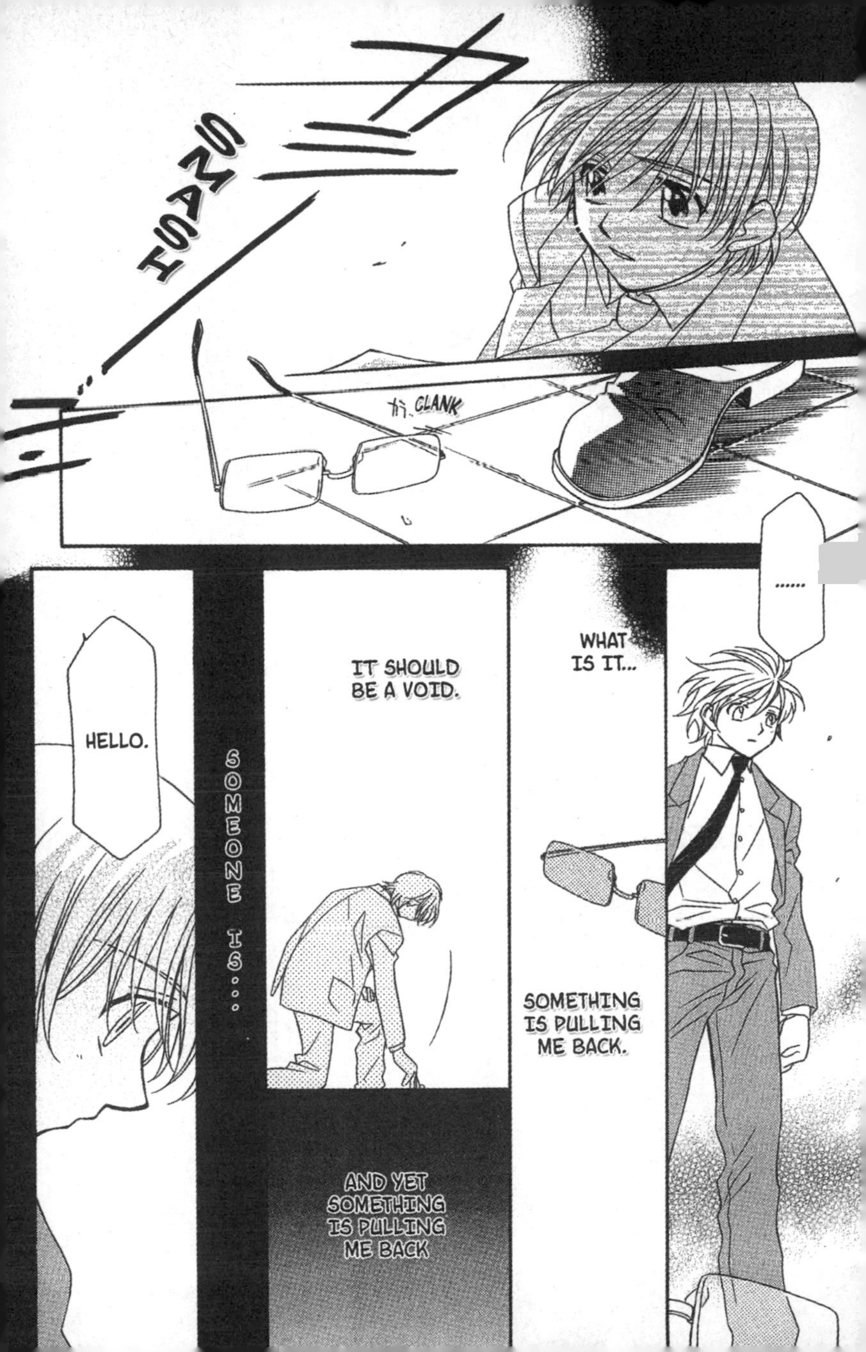
SMASH
CLANK
......
WHAT IS IT...
SOMETHING IS PULLING ME BACK.
IT SHOULD BE A VOID.
AND YET SOMETHING IS PULLING ME BACK
SOMEONE IS...
HELLO.

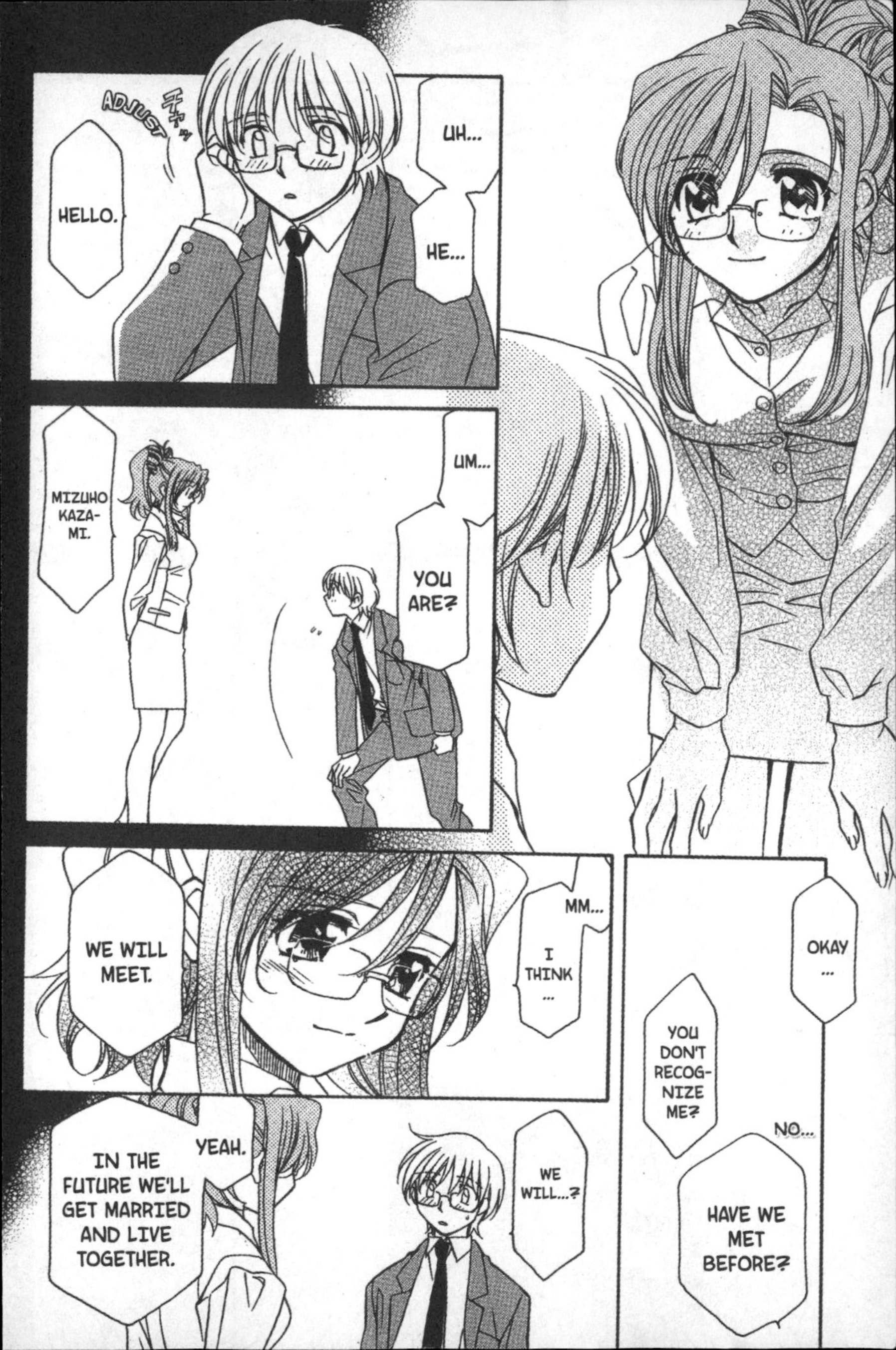
UH...
HE...
ADJUST
HELLO.
UM...
YOU ARE?
MIZUHO KAZAMI.
OKAY...
YOU DON'T RECOGNIZE ME?
NO...
HAVE WE MET BEFORE?
MM... I THINK...
WE WILL MEET.
WE WILL...?
YEAH.
IN THE FUTURE WE'LL GET MARRIED AND LIVE TOGETHER.

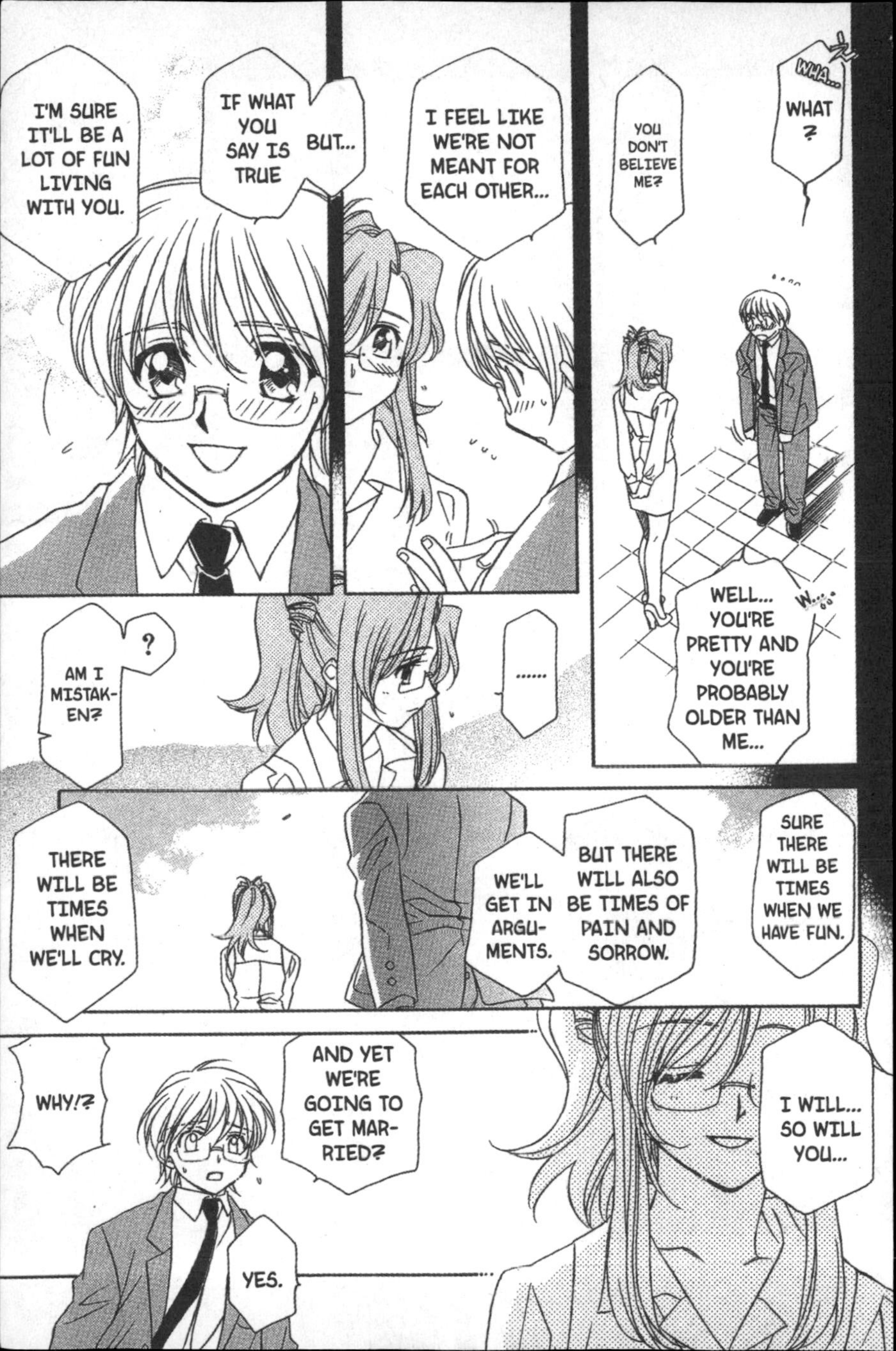
WHA...
WHAT?
YOU DON'T BELIEVE ME?
W...
WELL... YOU'RE PRETTY AND YOU'RE PROBABLY OLDER THAN ME...
I FEEL LIKE WE'RE NOT MEANT FOR EACH OTHER...
BUT...
IF WHAT YOU SAY IS TRUE
I'M SURE IT'LL BE A LOT OF FUN LIVING WITH YOU.
......
?
AM I MISTAKEN?
SURE THERE WILL BE TIMES WHEN WE HAVE FUN.
BUT THERE WILL ALSO BE TIMES OF PAIN AND SORROW.
WE'LL GET IN ARGUMENTS.
THERE WILL BE TIMES WHEN WE'LL CRY.
I WILL... SO WILL YOU...
AND YET WE'RE GOING TO GET MARRIED?
WHY!?
YES.

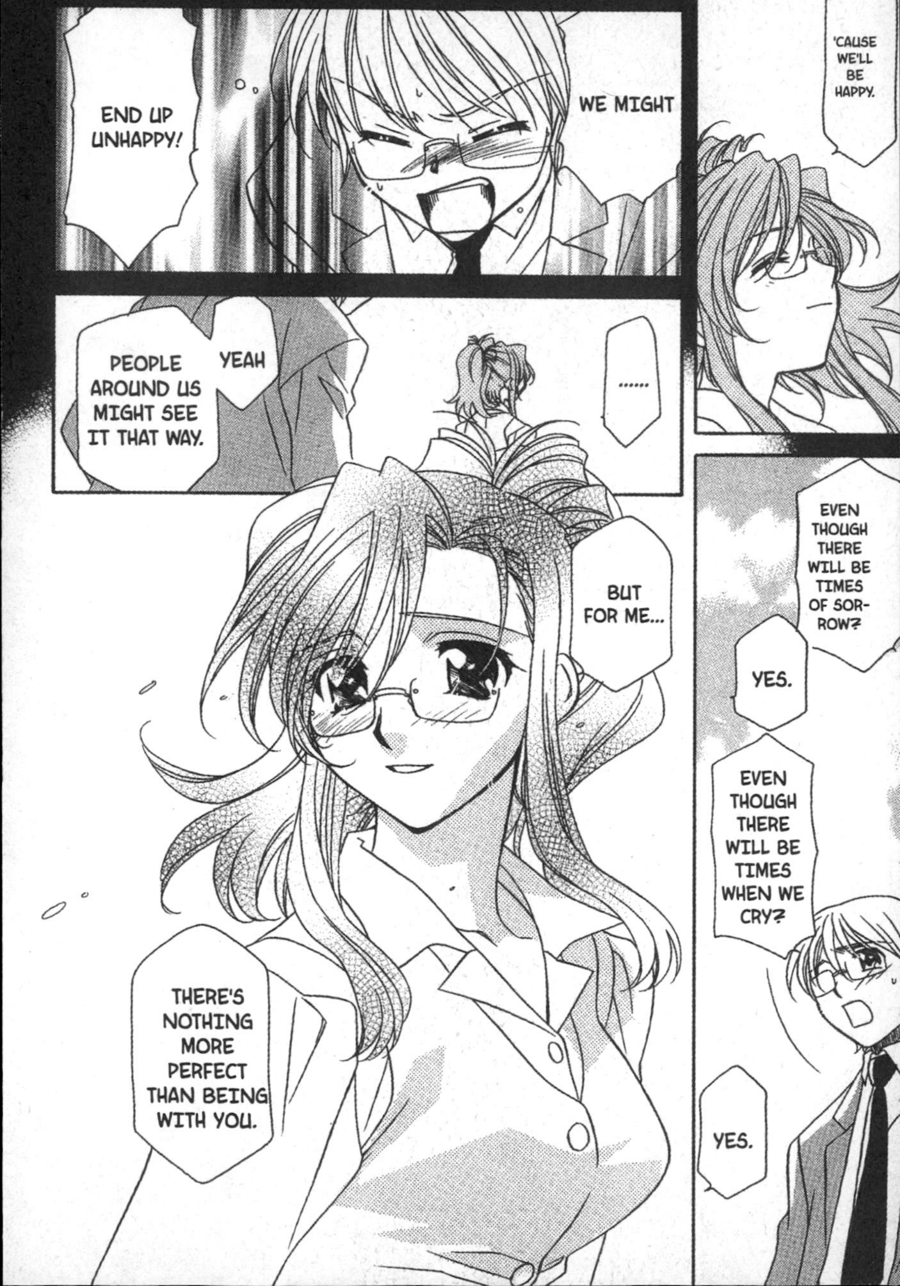
'CAUSE WE'LL BE HAPPY.
EVEN THOUGH THERE WILL BE TIMES OF SOR-ROW?
YES.
EVEN THOUGH THERE WILL BE TIMES WHEN WE CRY?
YES.
WE MIGHT
END UP UNHAPPY!
YEAH
PEOPLE AROUND US MIGHT SEE IT THAT WAY.
......
BUT FOR ME...
THERE'S NOTHING MORE PERFECT THAN BEING WITH YOU.

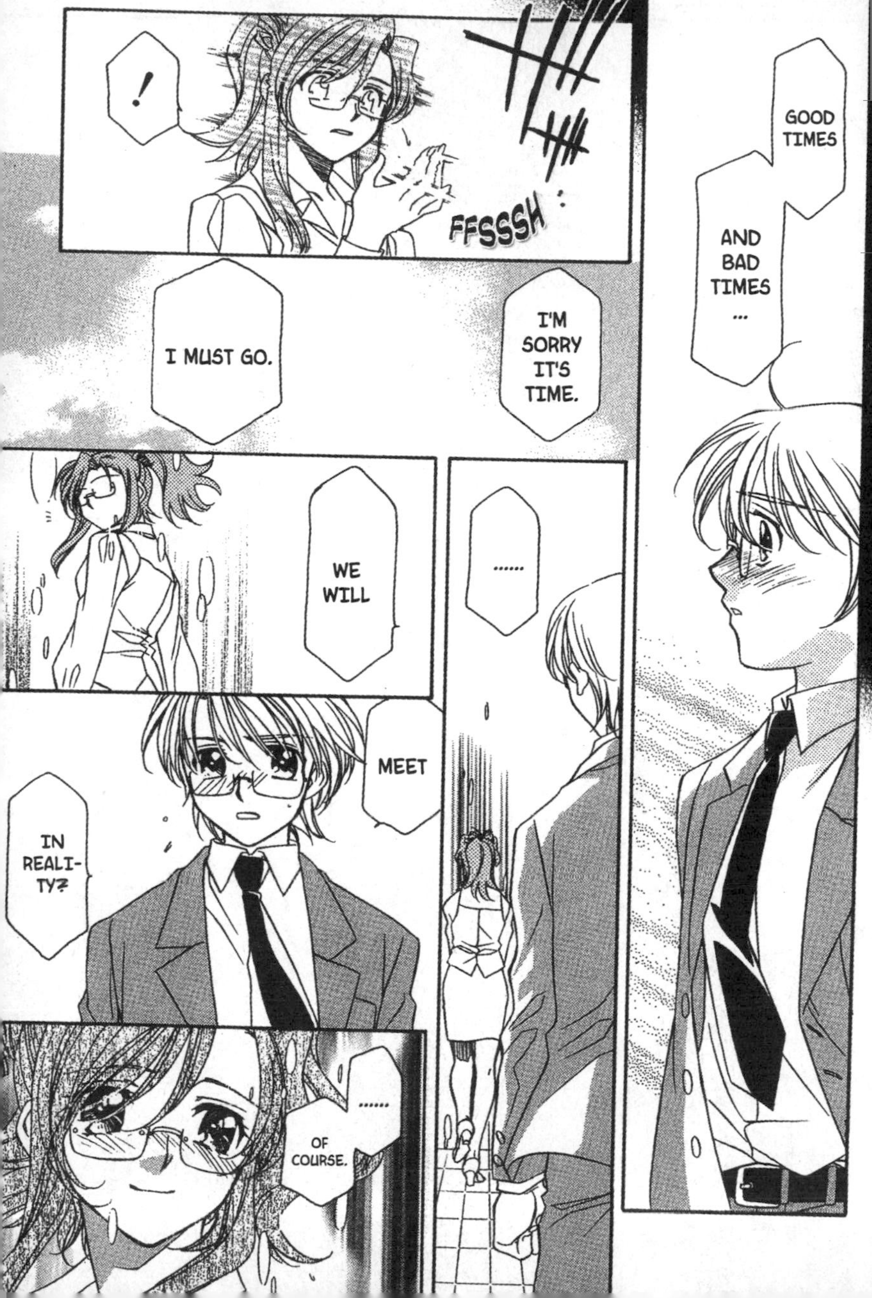
GOOD TIMES
AND BAD TIMES ...
!
FFSSSH
I'M SORRY IT'S TIME.
I MUST GO.
......
WE WILL
MEET
IN REALITY?
......
OF COURSE.

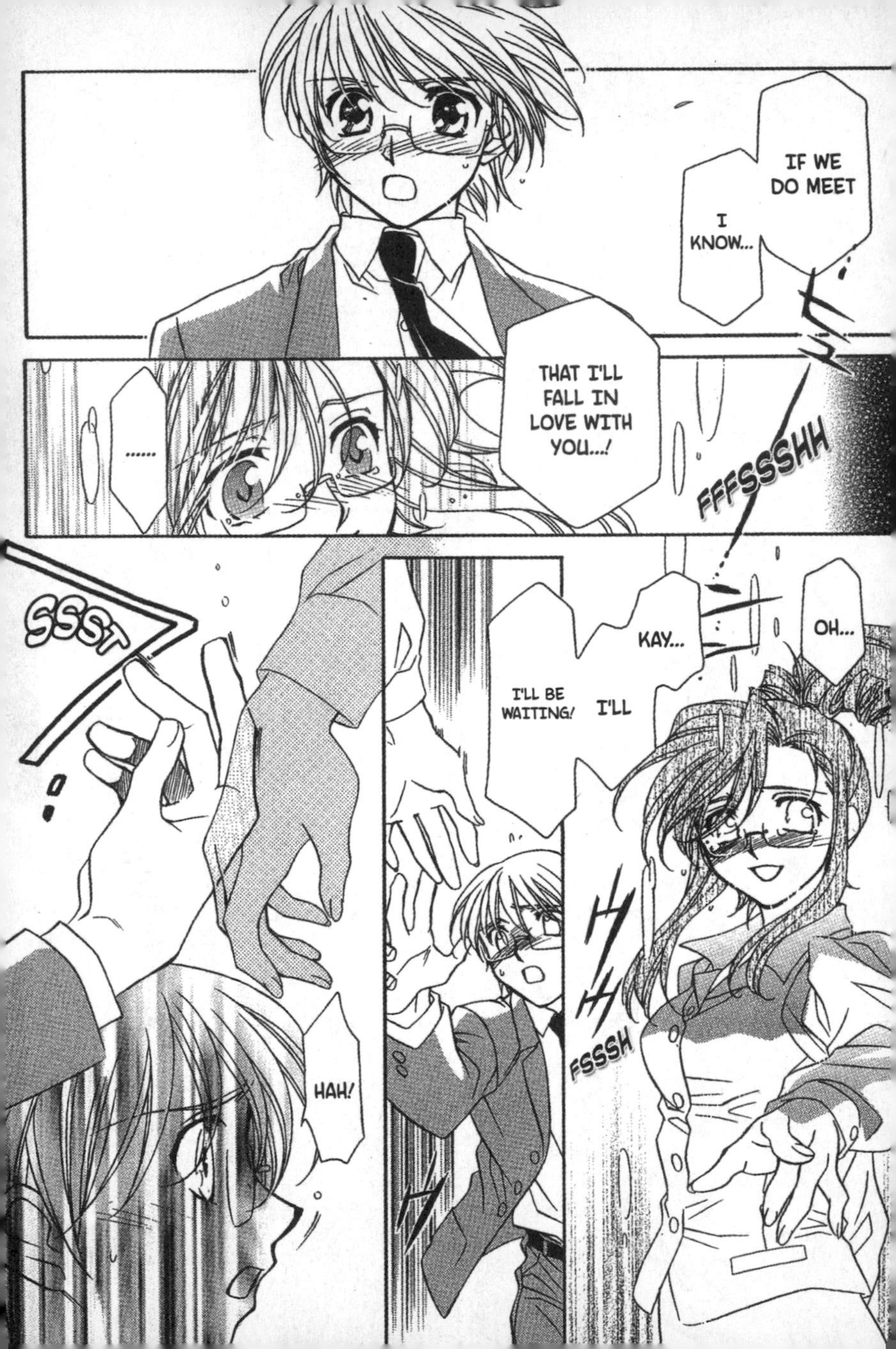
IF WE DO MEET
I KNOW...
THAT I'LL FALL IN LOVE WITH YOU...!
......
FFFSSSHH
OH...
KAY...
I'LL
I'LL BE WAITING!
FSSSH
SSST
HAH!

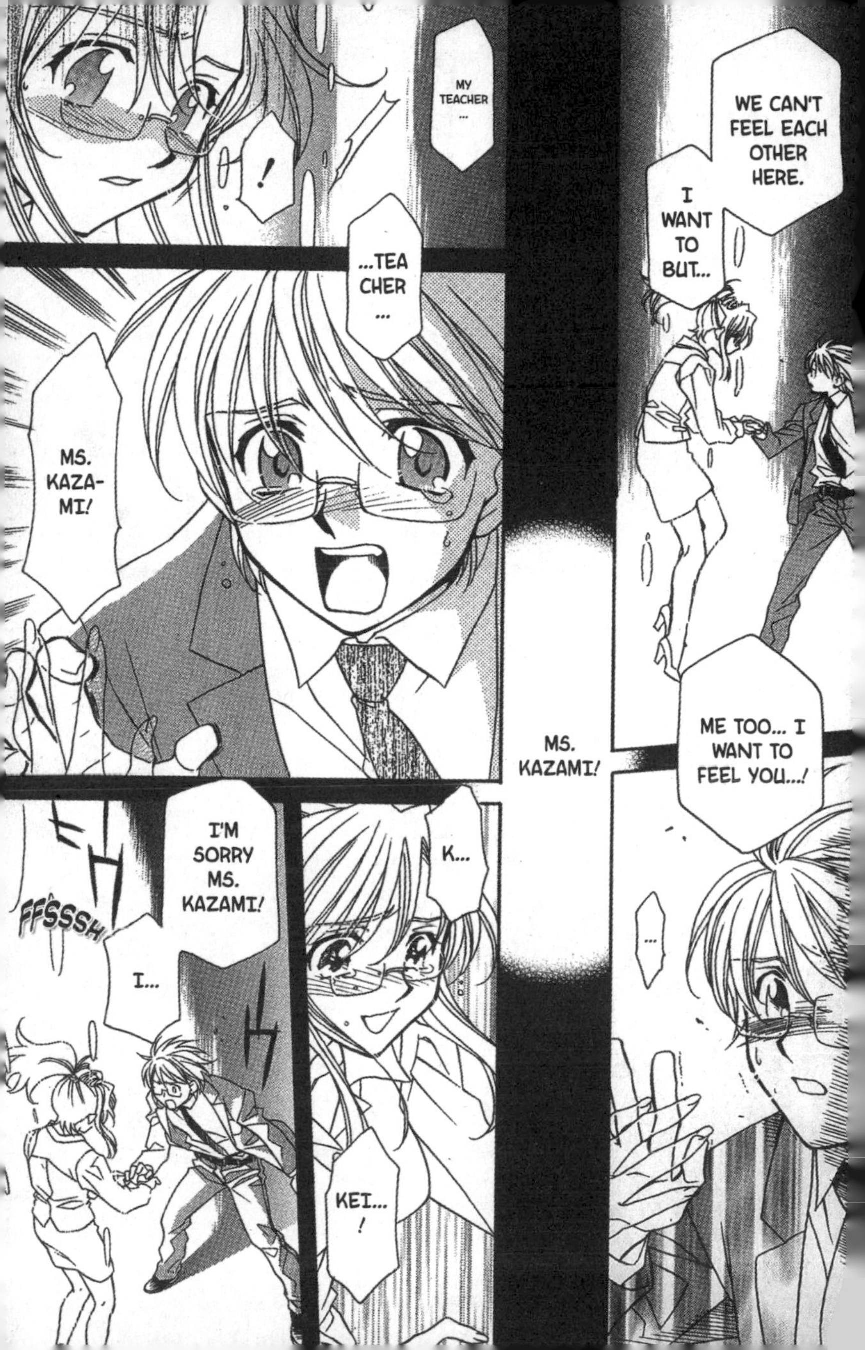
WE CAN'T FEEL EACH OTHER HERE.
I WANT TO BUT...
ME TOO... I WANT TO FEEL YOU...!
...
MS. KAZAMI!
MY TEACHER ...
!
...TEA CHER ...
MS. KAZA-MI!
K...
KEI... !
I'M SORRY MS. KAZAMI!
I...
FFSSSH

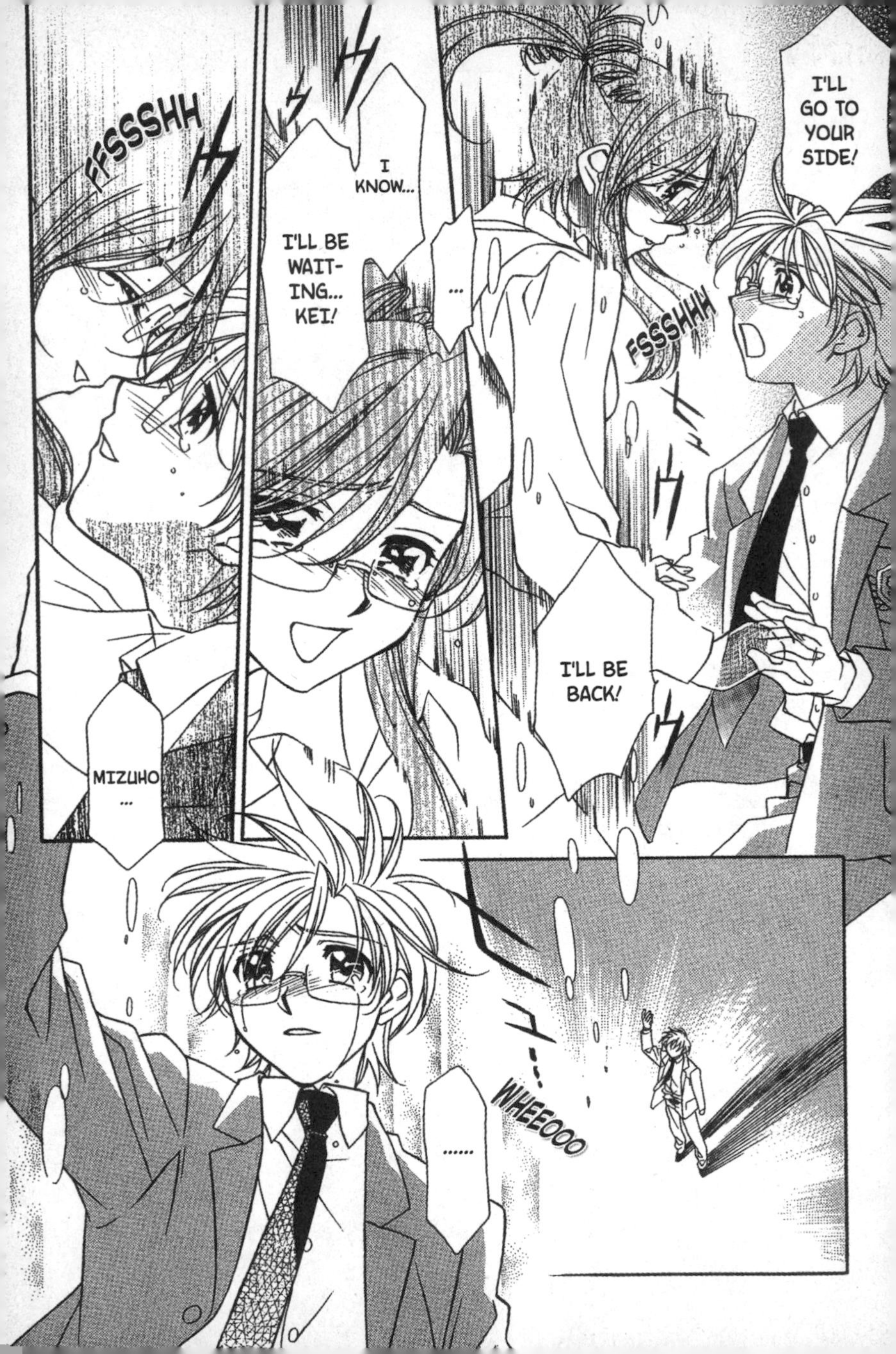
I'LL GO TO YOUR SIDE!
FSSSHH
...
I'LL BE BACK!
I KNOW...
I'LL BE WAITING... KEI!
FFSSSHH
MIZUHO ...
WHEEOOO
......

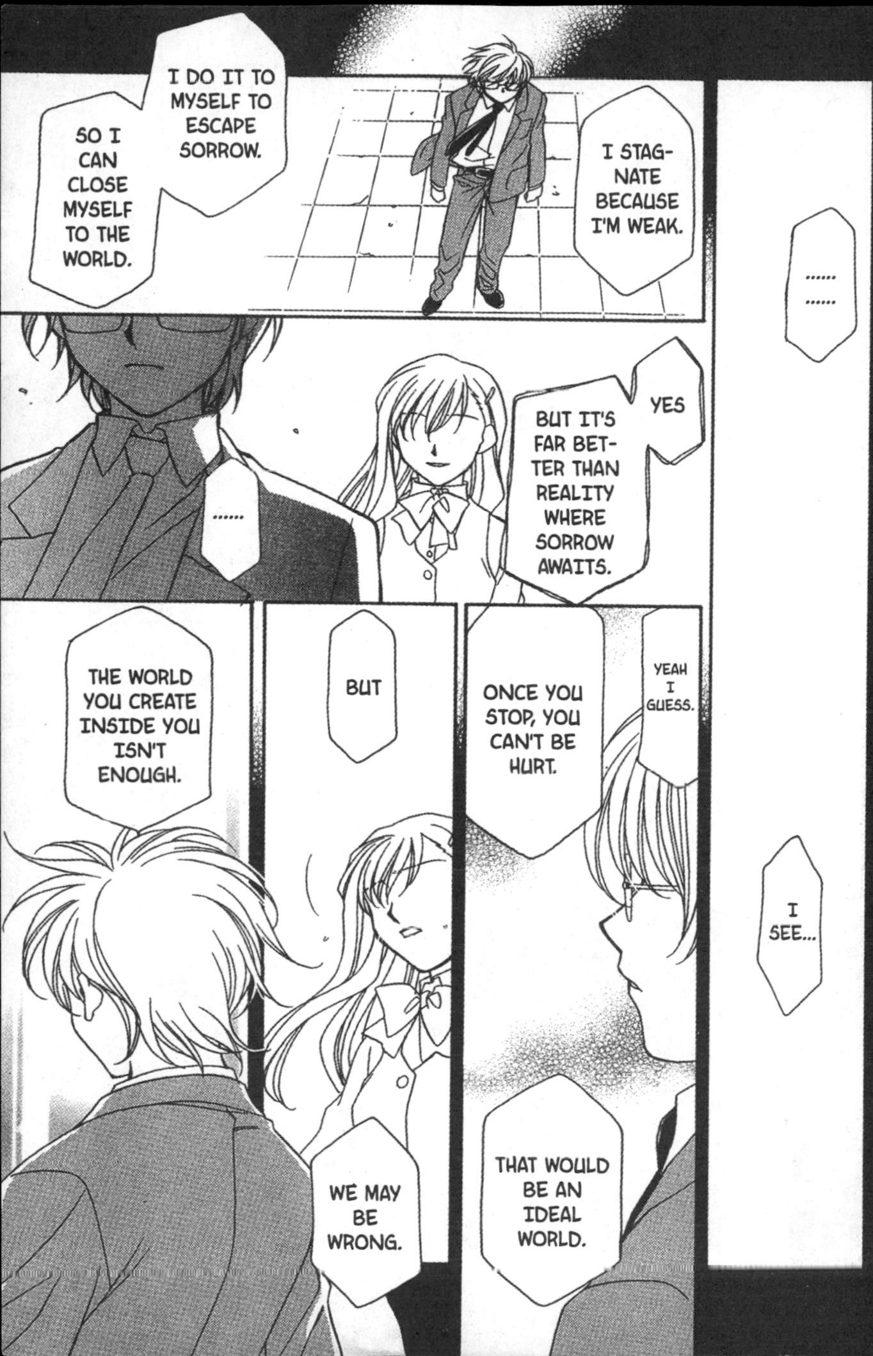
......
......
I SEE...
I STAG-NATE BECAUSE I'M WEAK.
I DO IT TO MYSELF TO ESCAPE SORROW.
SO I CAN CLOSE MYSELF TO THE WORLD.
YES
BUT IT'S FAR BET-TER THAN REALITY WHERE SORROW AWAITS.
......
YEAH I GUESS.
ONCE YOU STOP, YOU CAN'T BE HURT.
THAT WOULD BE AN IDEAL WORLD.
BUT
WE MAY BE WRONG.
THE WORLD YOU CREATE INSIDE YOU ISN'T ENOUGH.

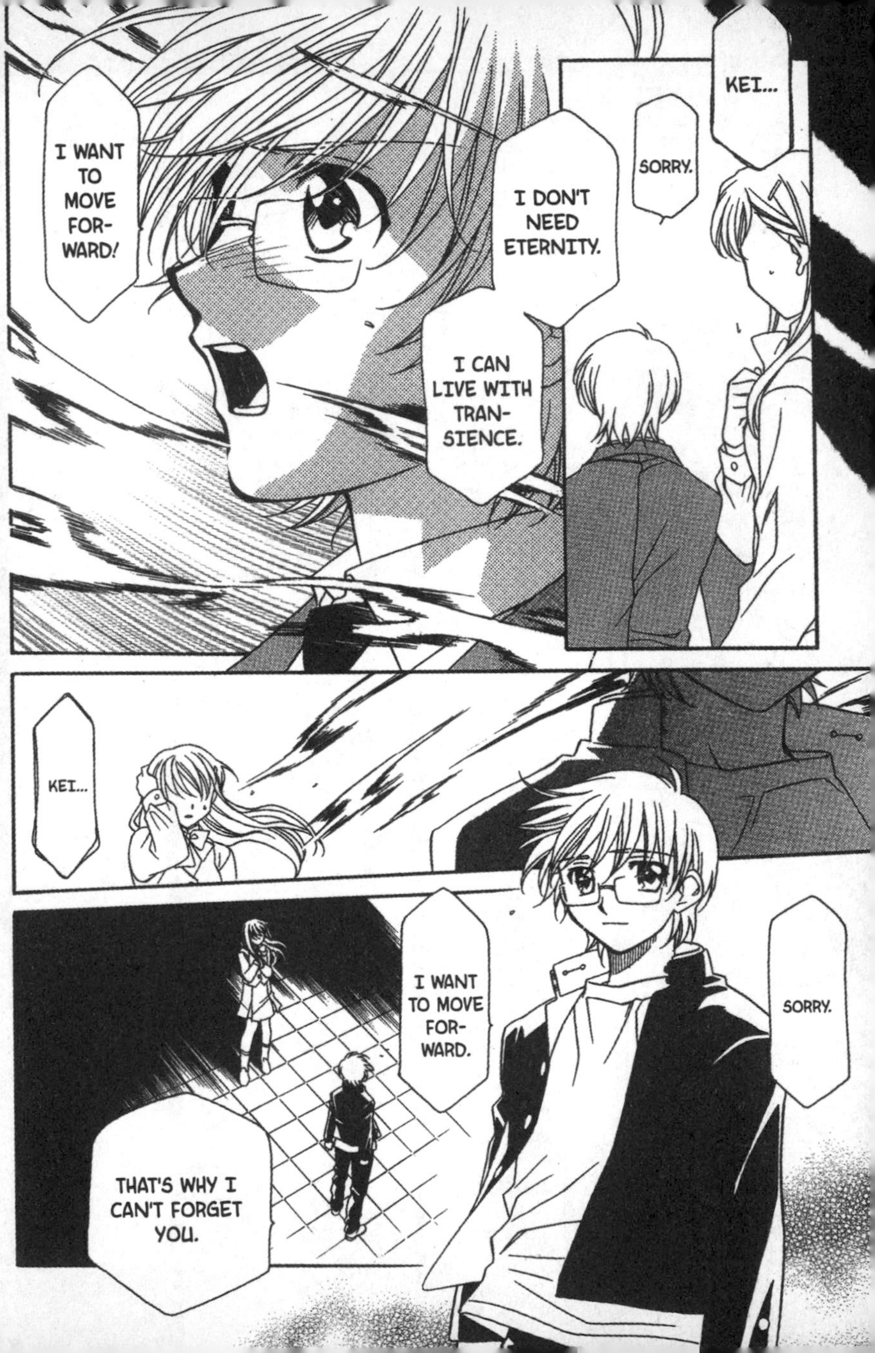
KEI...
SORRY.
I DON'T NEED ETERNITY.
I CAN LIVE WITH TRANSIENCE.
I WANT TO MOVE FORWARD!
KEI...
SORRY.
I WANT TO MOVE FORWARD.
THAT'S WHY I CAN'T FORGET YOU.

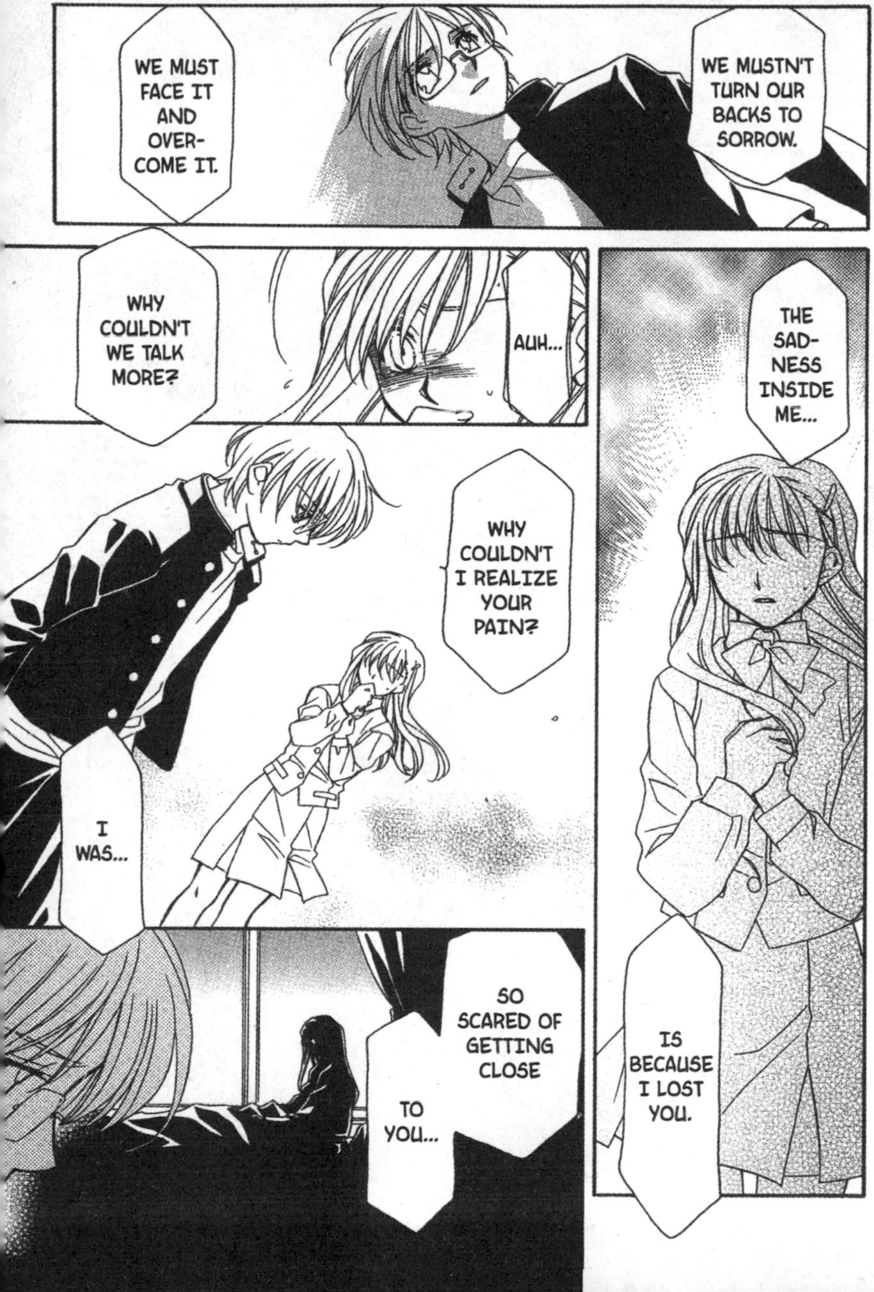
WE MUSTN'T TURN OUR BACKS TO SORROW.
WE MUST FACE IT AND OVER-COME IT.
THE SAD-NESS INSIDE ME...
IS BECAUSE I LOST YOU.
AUH...
WHY COULDN'T WE TALK MORE?
WHY COULDN'T I REALIZE YOUR PAIN?
I WAS...
SO SCARED OF GETTING CLOSE
TO YOU...

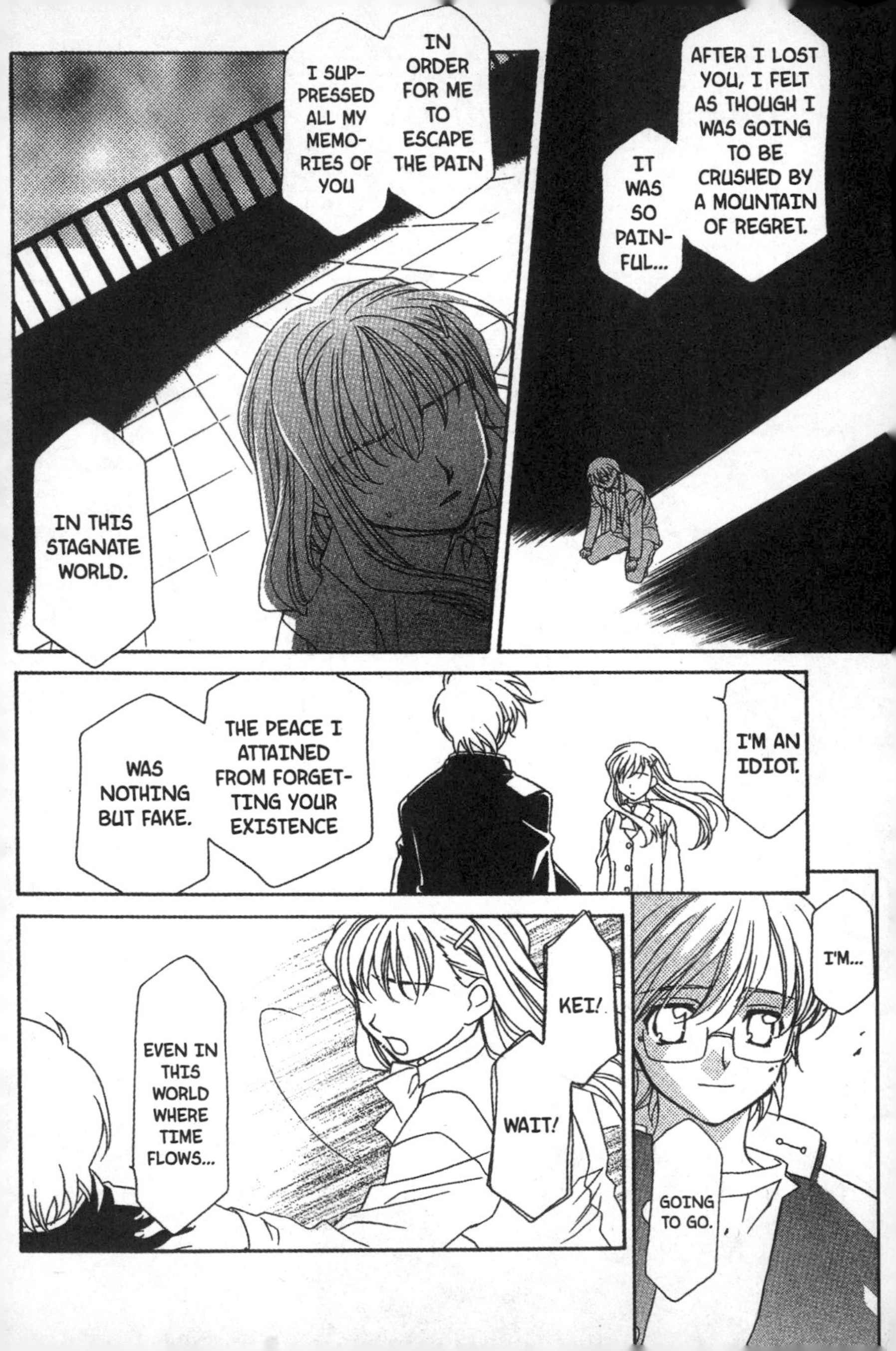
AFTER I LOST YOU, I FELT AS THOUGH I WAS GOING TO BE CRUSHED BY A MOUNTAIN OF REGRET.
IT WAS SO PAINFUL...
IN ORDER FOR ME TO ESCAPE THE PAIN
I SUPPRESSED ALL MY MEMORIES OF YOU
IN THIS STAGNATE WORLD.
I'M AN IDIOT.
THE PEACE I ATTAINED FROM FORGETTING YOUR EXISTENCE
WAS NOTHING BUT FAKE.
I'M...
GOING TO GO.
KEI!
WAIT!
EVEN IN THIS WORLD WHERE TIME FLOWS...

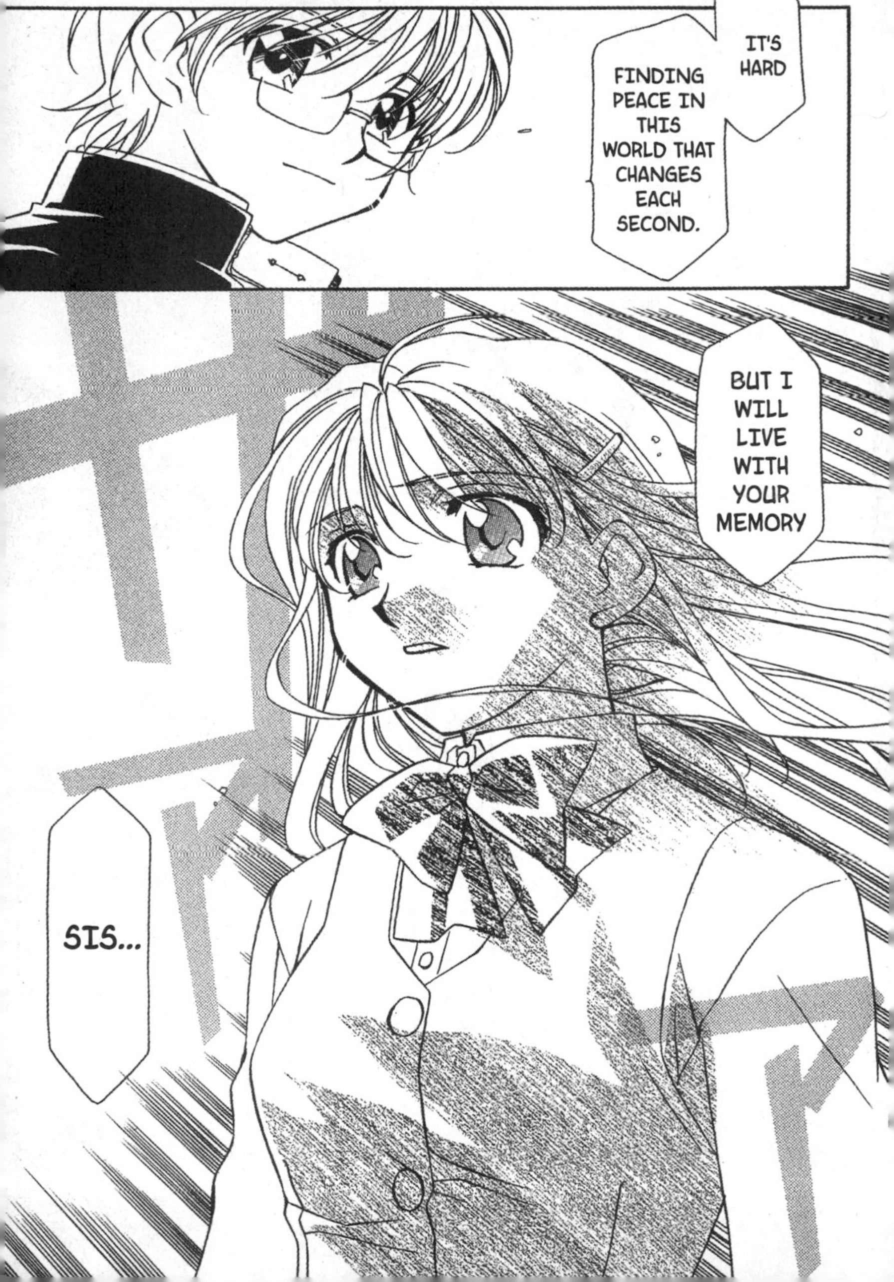
IT'S HARD
FINDING PEACE IN THIS WORLD THAT CHANGES EACH SECOND.
BUT I WILL LIVE WITH YOUR MEMORY
SIS...

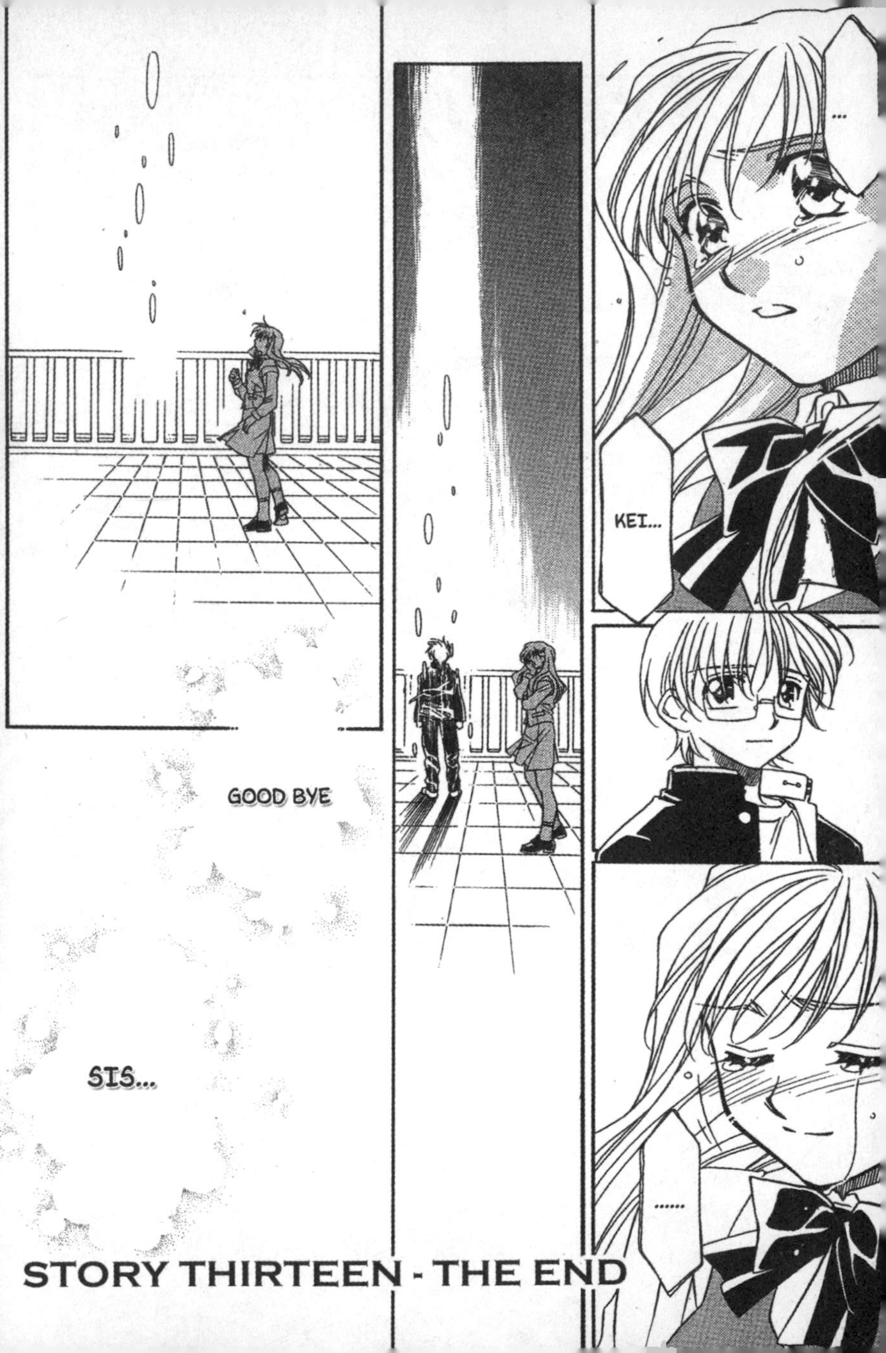
...
KEI...
......
GOOD BYE
SIS...

STORY THIRTEEN - THE END

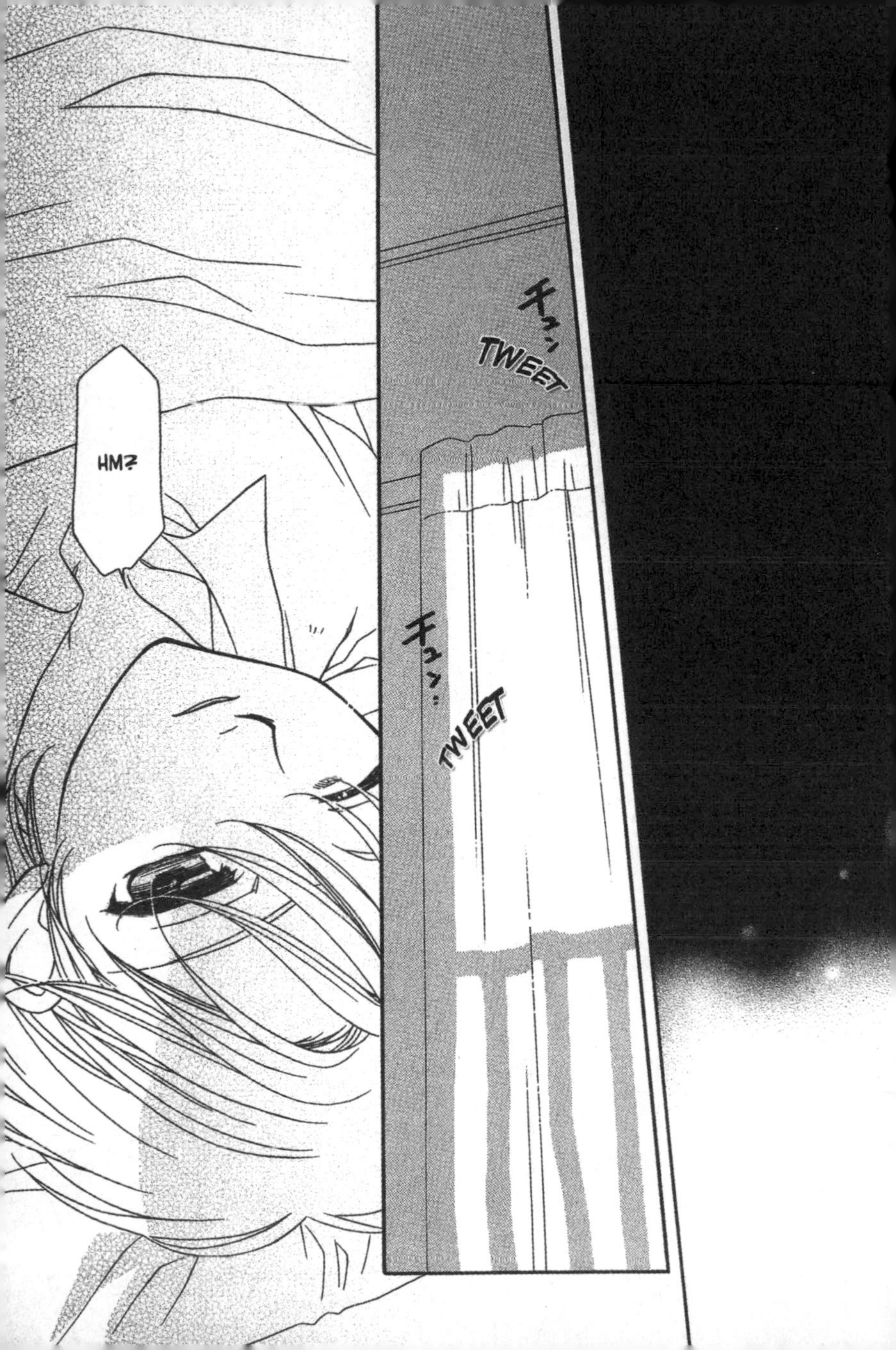

チュン
TWEET
チュン‥
TWEET
HM?

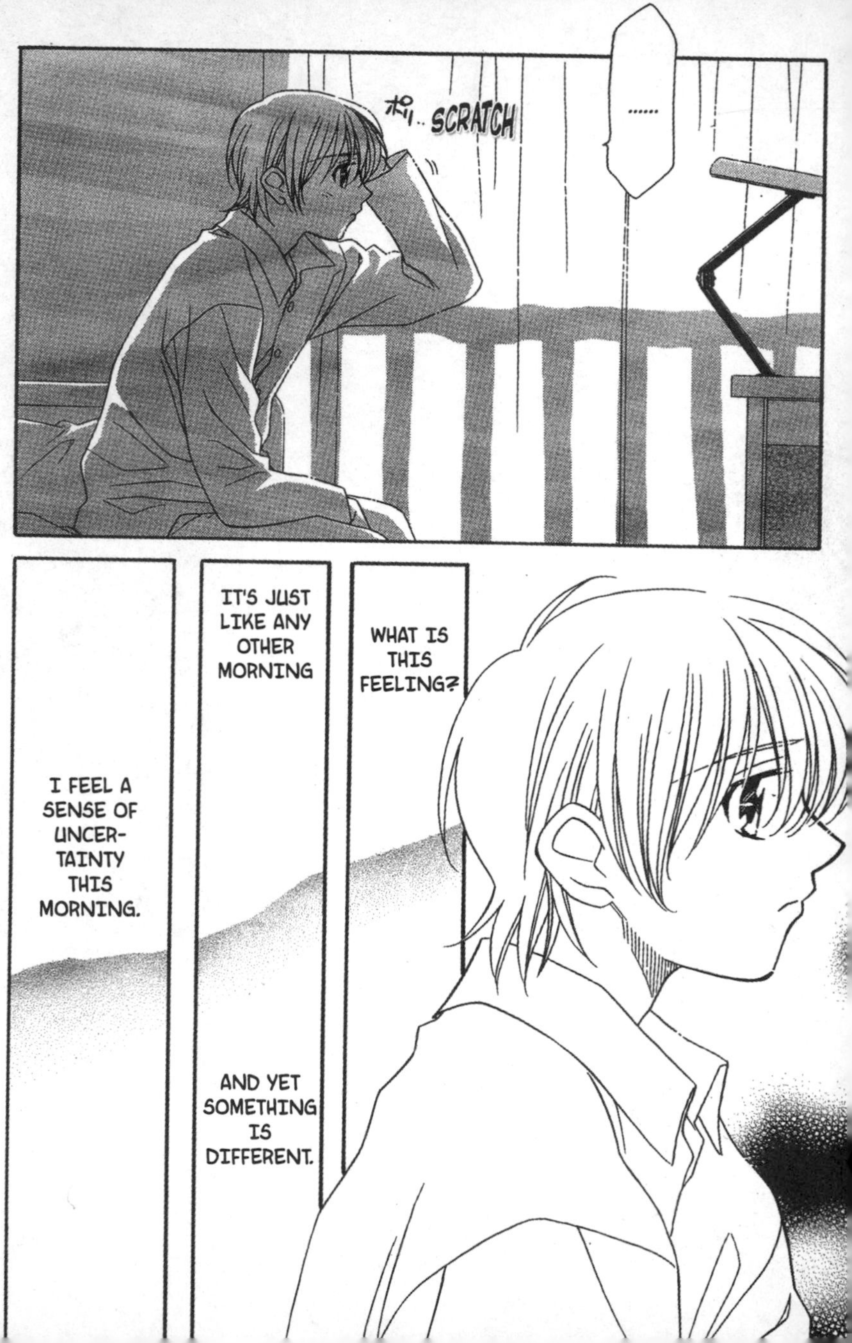

......
ポリ.. SCRATCH
WHAT IS THIS FEELING?
IT'S JUST LIKE ANY OTHER MORNING
AND YET SOMETHING IS DIFFERENT.
I FEEL A SENSE OF UNCER-TAINTY THIS MORNING.

FINAL STORY

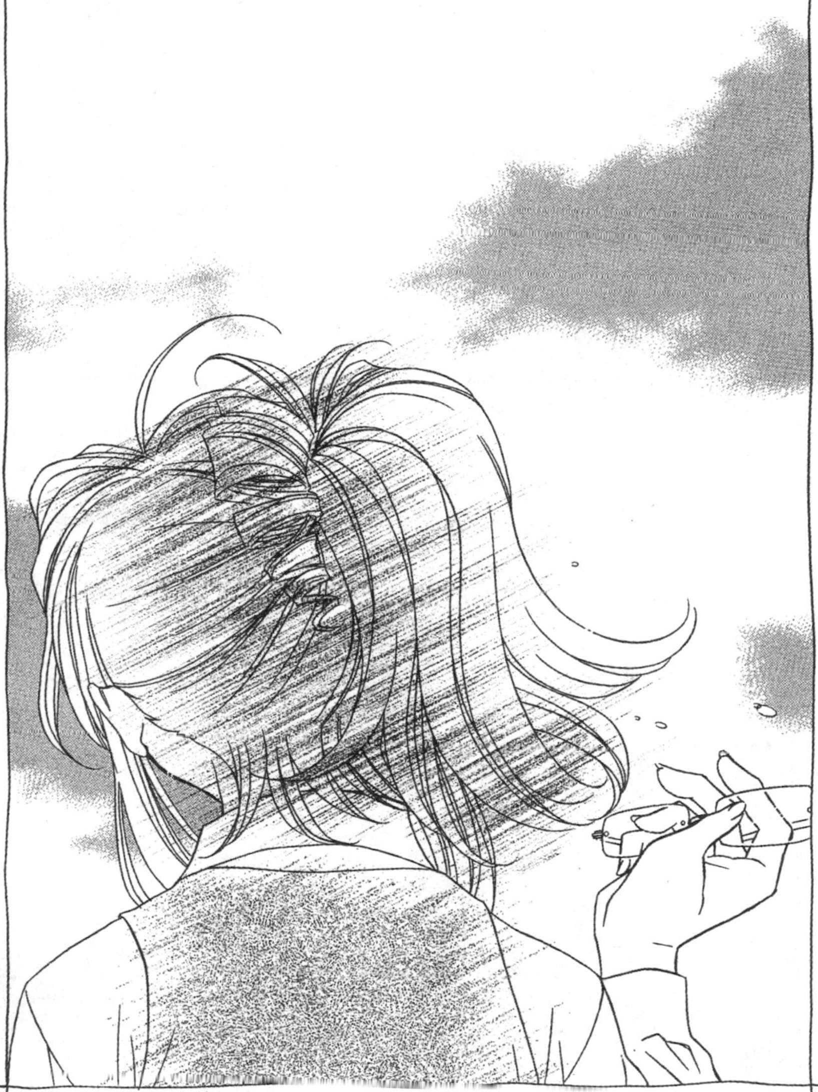

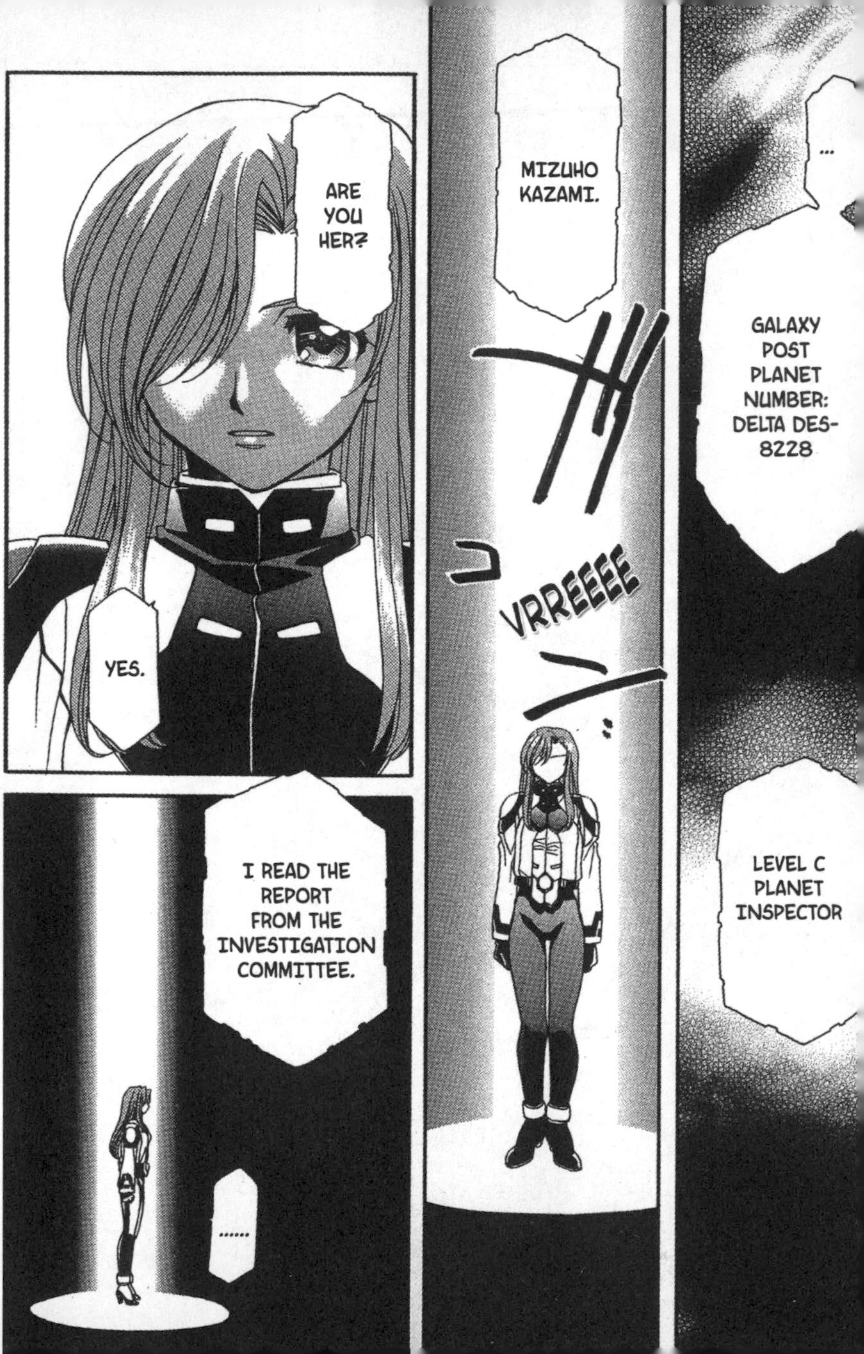
...
GALAXY POST PLANET NUMBER: DELTA DES-8228
LEVEL C PLANET INSPECTOR
MIZUHO KAZAMI.
VRREEEE
ARE YOU HER?
YES.
I READ THE REPORT FROM THE INVESTIGATION COMMITTEE.
......

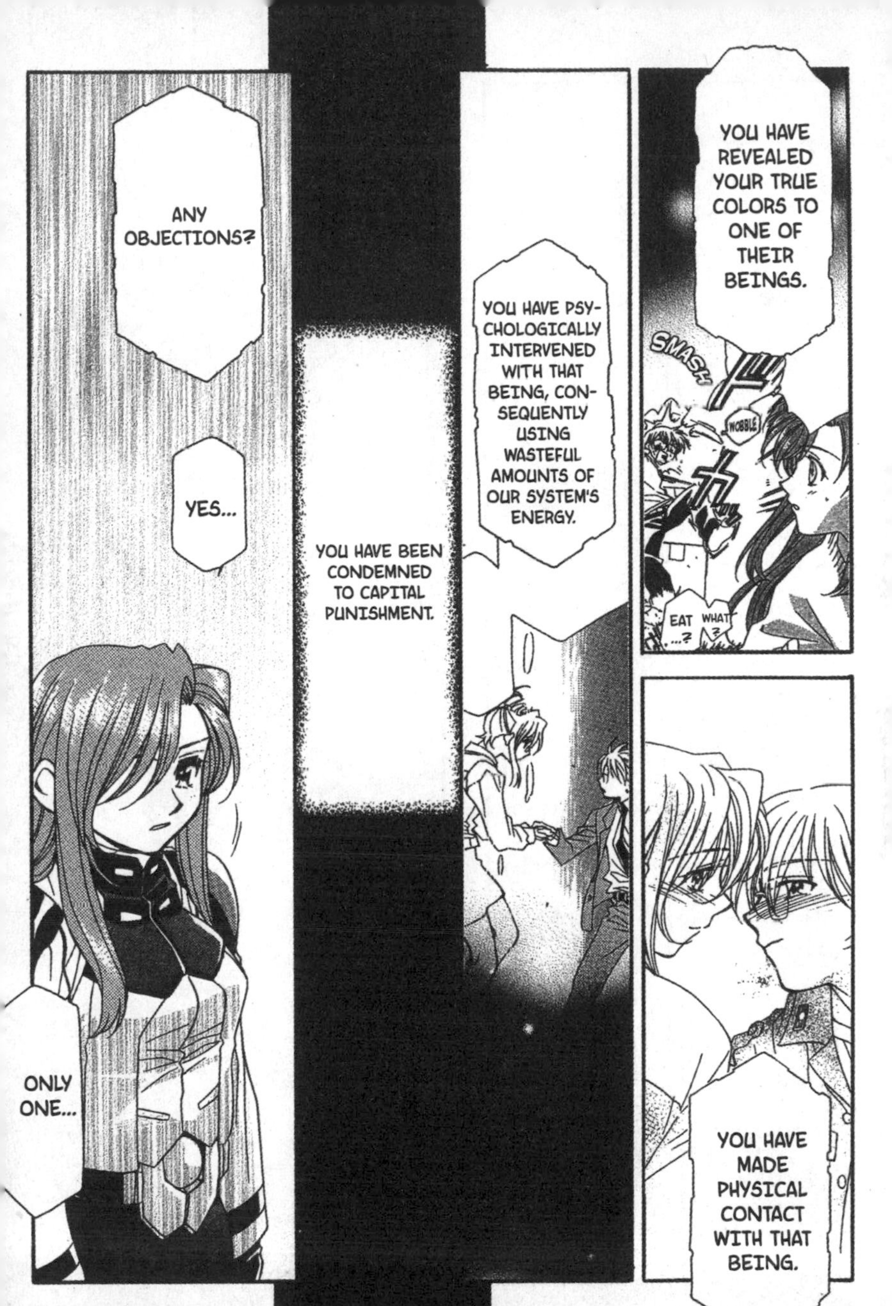
YOU HAVE REVEALED YOUR TRUE COLORS TO ONE OF THEIR BEINGS.
SMASH
WOBBLE
EAT ...?
WHAT ?
YOU HAVE MADE PHYSICAL CONTACT WITH THAT BEING.
YOU HAVE PSYCHOLOGICALLY INTERVENED WITH THAT BEING, CONSEQUENTLY USING WASTEFUL AMOUNTS OF OUR SYSTEM'S ENERGY.
YOU HAVE BEEN CONDEMNED TO CAPITAL PUNISHMENT.
ANY OBJECTIONS?
YES...
ONLY ONE...

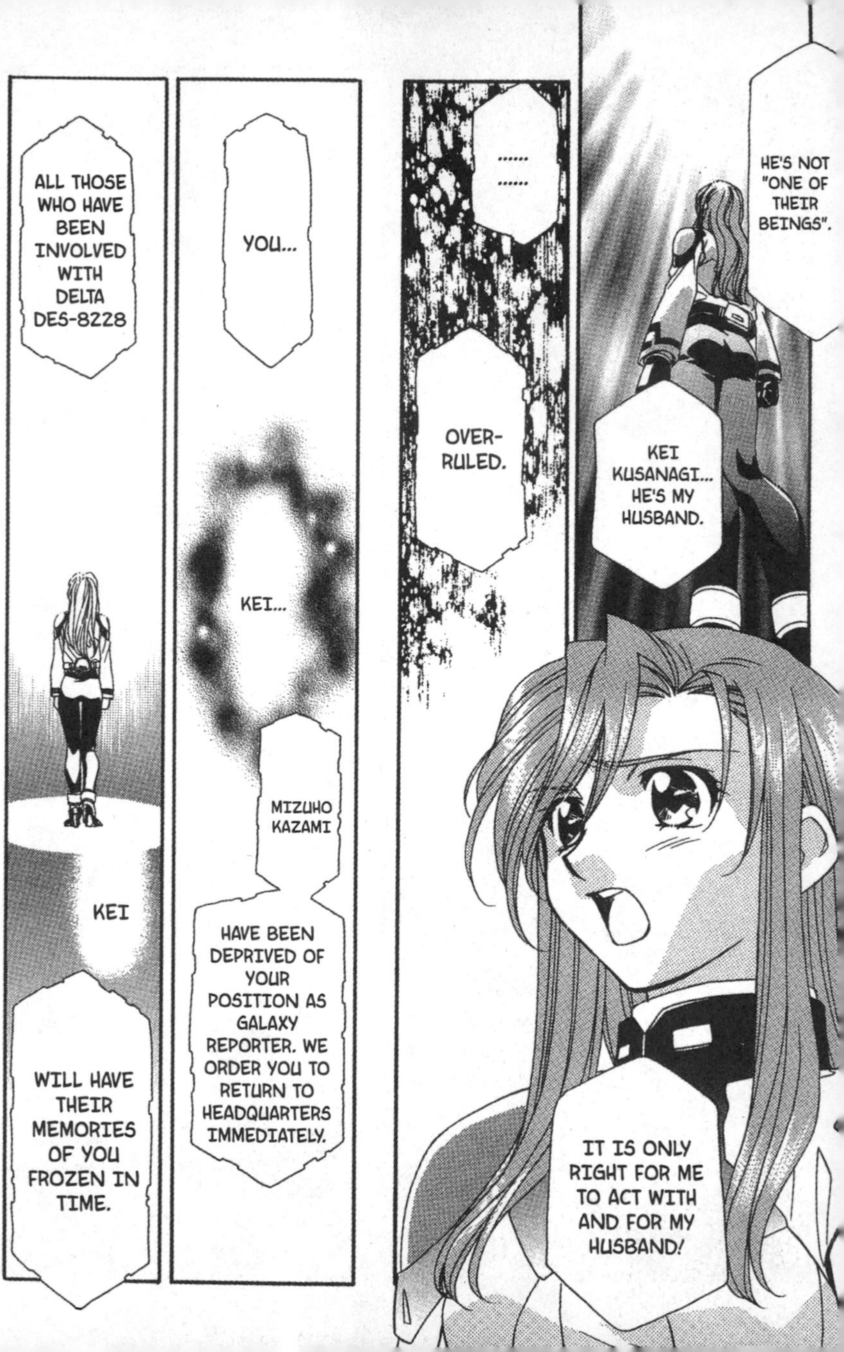
HE'S NOT "ONE OF THEIR BEINGS".
KEI KUSANAGI... HE'S MY HUSBAND.
IT IS ONLY RIGHT FOR ME TO ACT WITH AND FOR MY HUSBAND!
......
......
OVER-RULED.
YOU...
KEI...
MIZUHO KAZAMI
HAVE BEEN DEPRIVED OF YOUR POSITION AS GALAXY REPORTER. WE ORDER YOU TO RETURN TO HEADQUARTERS IMMEDIATELY.
ALL THOSE WHO HAVE BEEN INVOLVED WITH DELTA DES-8228
KEI
WILL HAVE THEIR MEMORIES OF YOU FROZEN IN TIME.

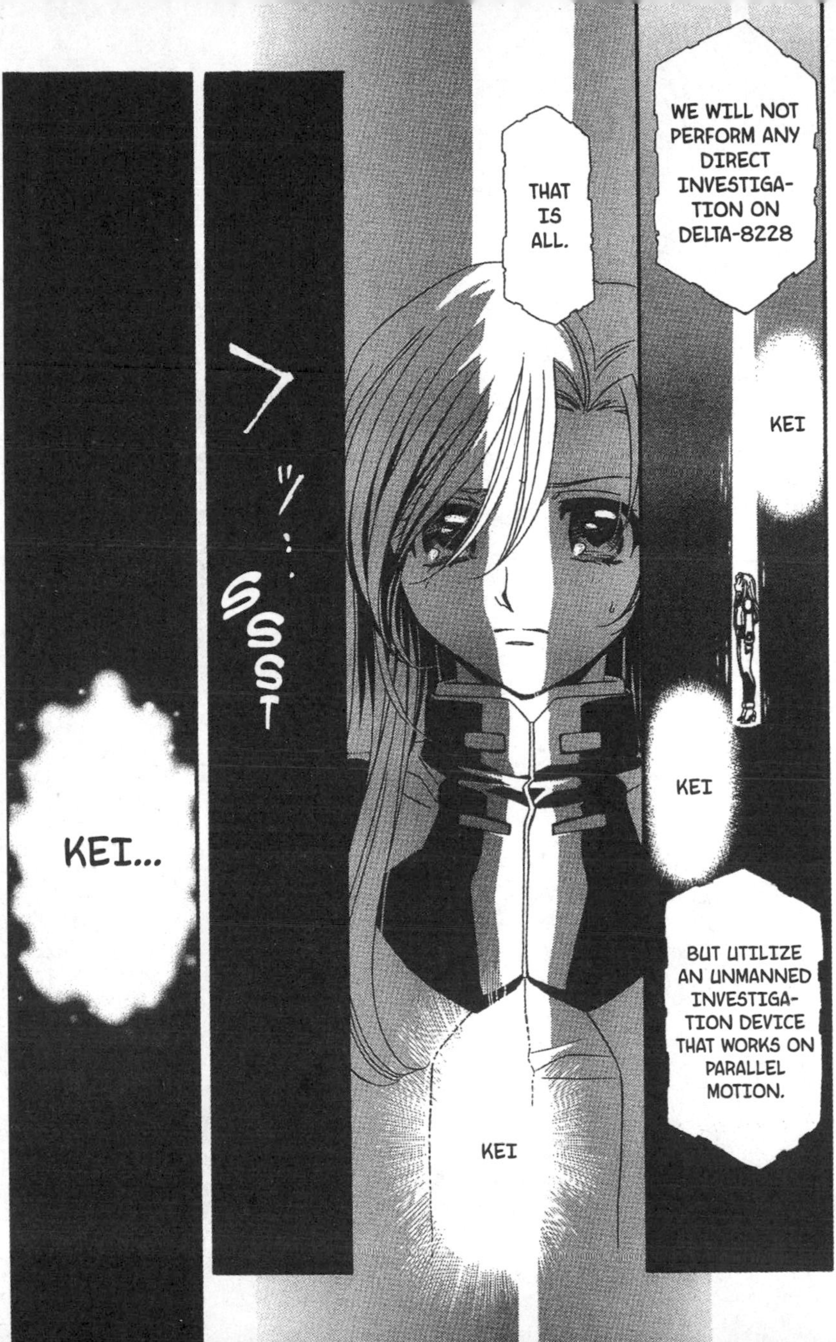
WE WILL NOT PERFORM ANY DIRECT INVESTIGA-TION ON DELTA-8228
KEI
KEI
BUT UTILIZE AN UNMANNED INVESTIGA-TION DEVICE THAT WORKS ON PARALLEL MOTION.
THAT IS ALL.
KEI
SSST
KEI...

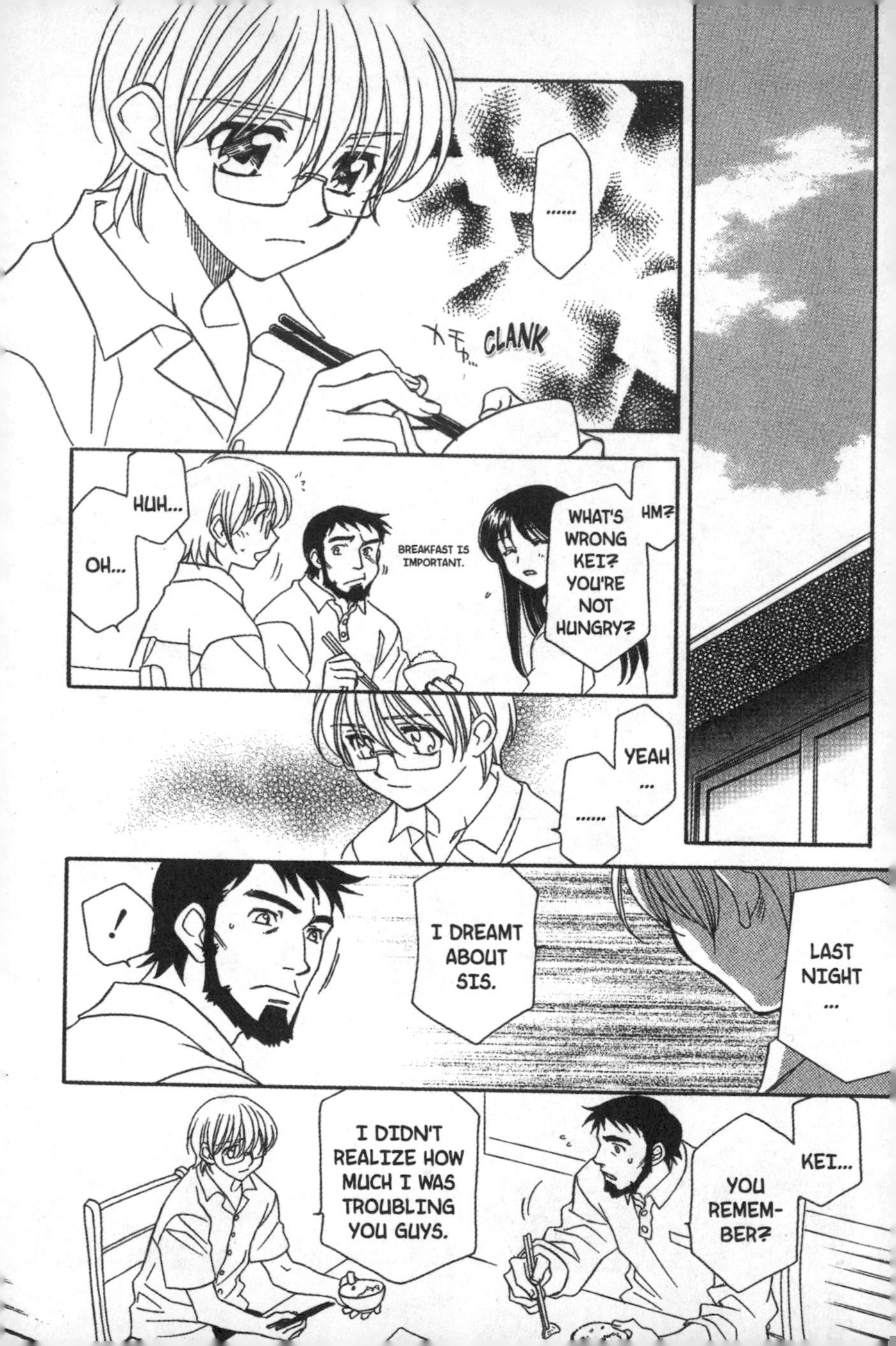
......
CLANK
HM?
WHAT'S WRONG KEI? YOU'RE NOT HUNGRY?
BREAKFAST IS IMPORTANT.
HUH...
OH...
YEAH ...
......
LAST NIGHT ...
I DREAMT ABOUT SIS.
!
KEI...
YOU REMEMBER?
I DIDN'T REALIZE HOW MUCH I WAS TROUBLING YOU GUYS.

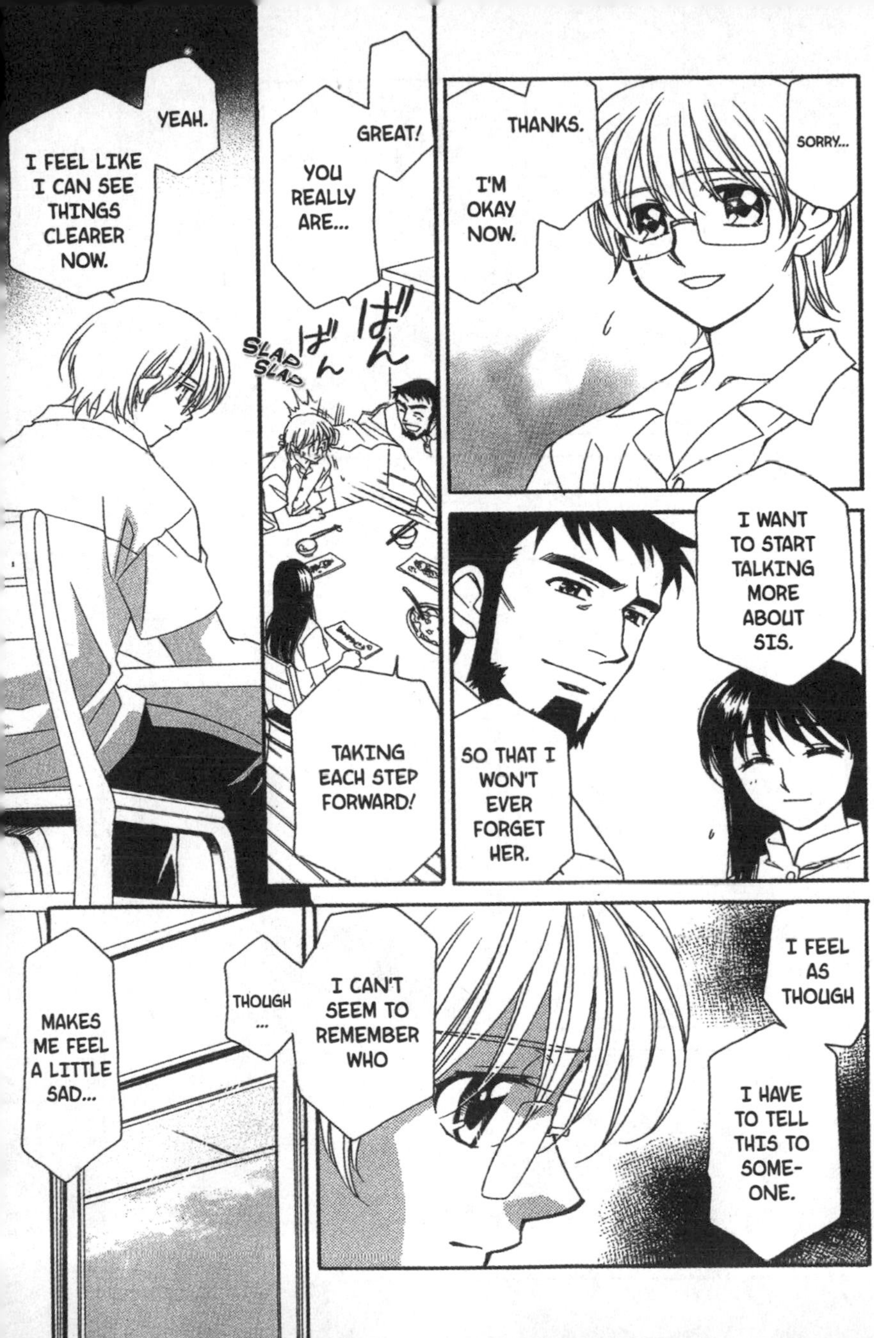
SORRY...
THANKS.
I'M OKAY NOW.
I WANT TO START TALKING MORE ABOUT SIS.
SO THAT I WON'T EVER FORGET HER.
GREAT!
YOU REALLY ARE...
ばん ばん
SLAP SLAP
TAKING EACH STEP FORWARD!
YEAH.
I FEEL LIKE I CAN SEE THINGS CLEARER NOW.
I FEEL AS THOUGH
I HAVE TO TELL THIS TO SOME-ONE.
I CAN'T SEEM TO REMEMBER WHO
THOUGH ...
MAKES ME FEEL A LITTLE SAD...

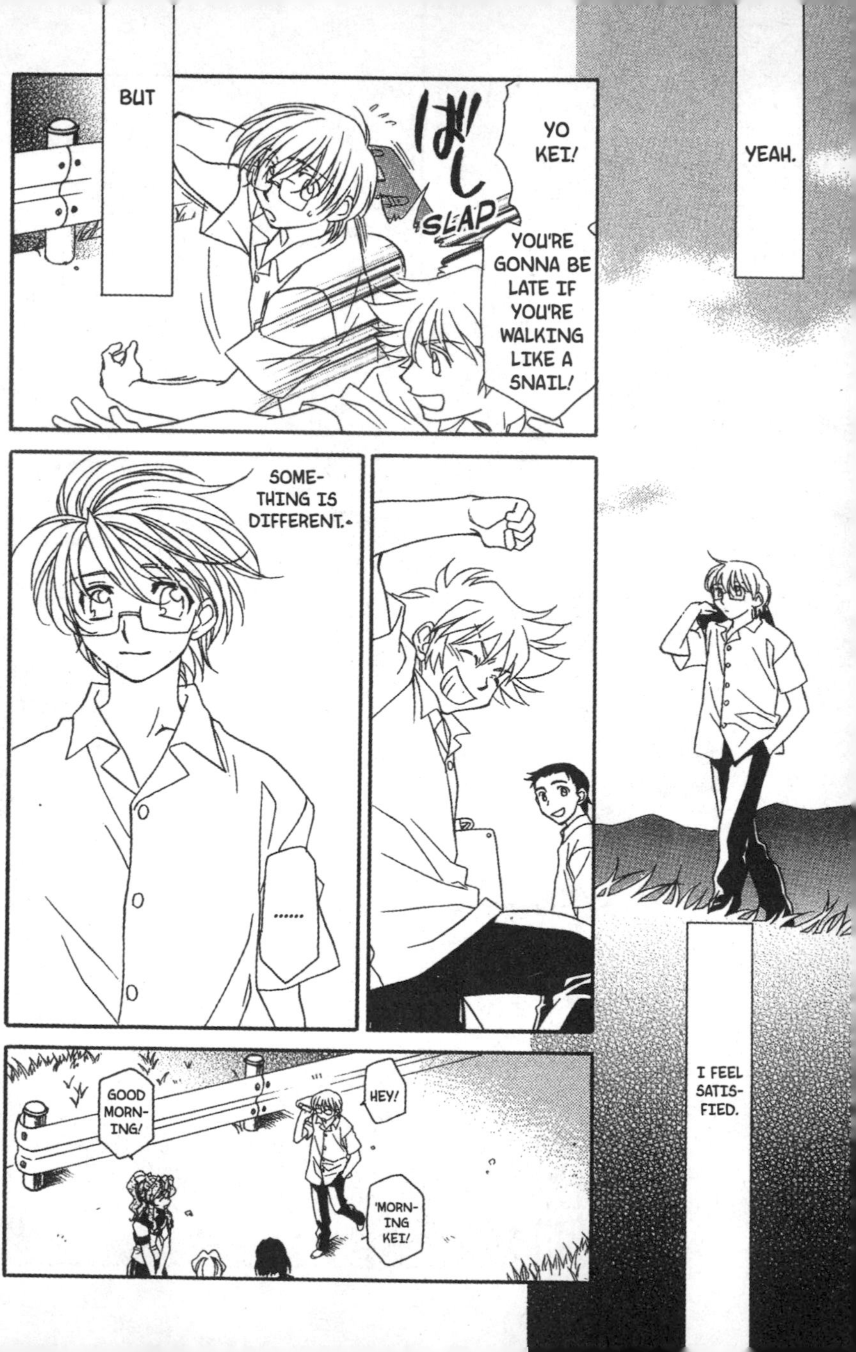
YEAH.
I FEEL SATISFIED.
YO KEI!
ばし
SLAP
YOU'RE GONNA BE LATE IF YOU'RE WALKING LIKE A SNAIL!
BUT
SOMETHING IS DIFFERENT.
......
HEY!
GOOD MORNING!
'MORNING KEI!

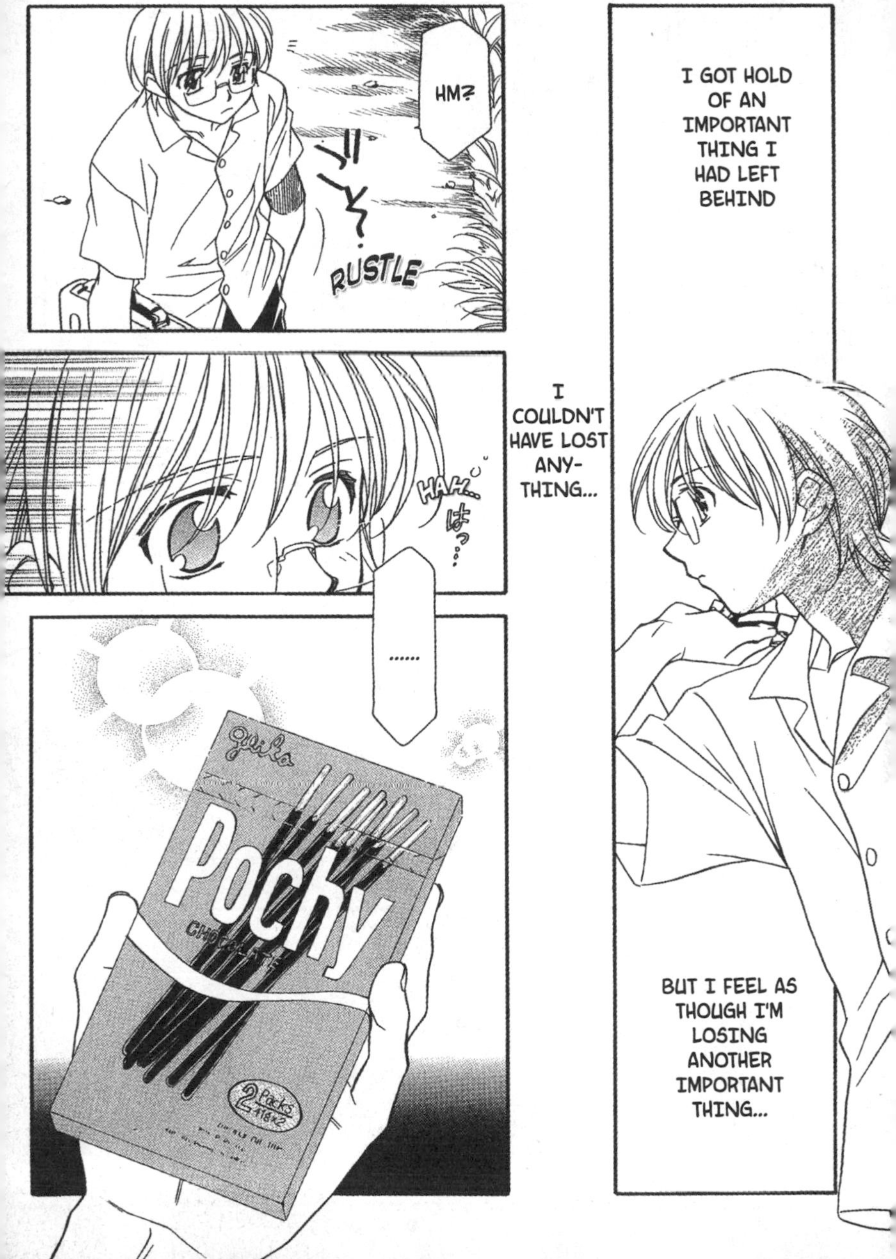
I GOT HOLD OF AN IMPORTANT THING I HAD LEFT BEHIND
BUT I FEEL AS THOUGH I'M LOSING ANOTHER IMPORTANT THING...
HM?
RUSTLE
I COULDN'T HAVE LOST ANYTHING...
HAH...
はっ…
......
Pochy
2 Packs

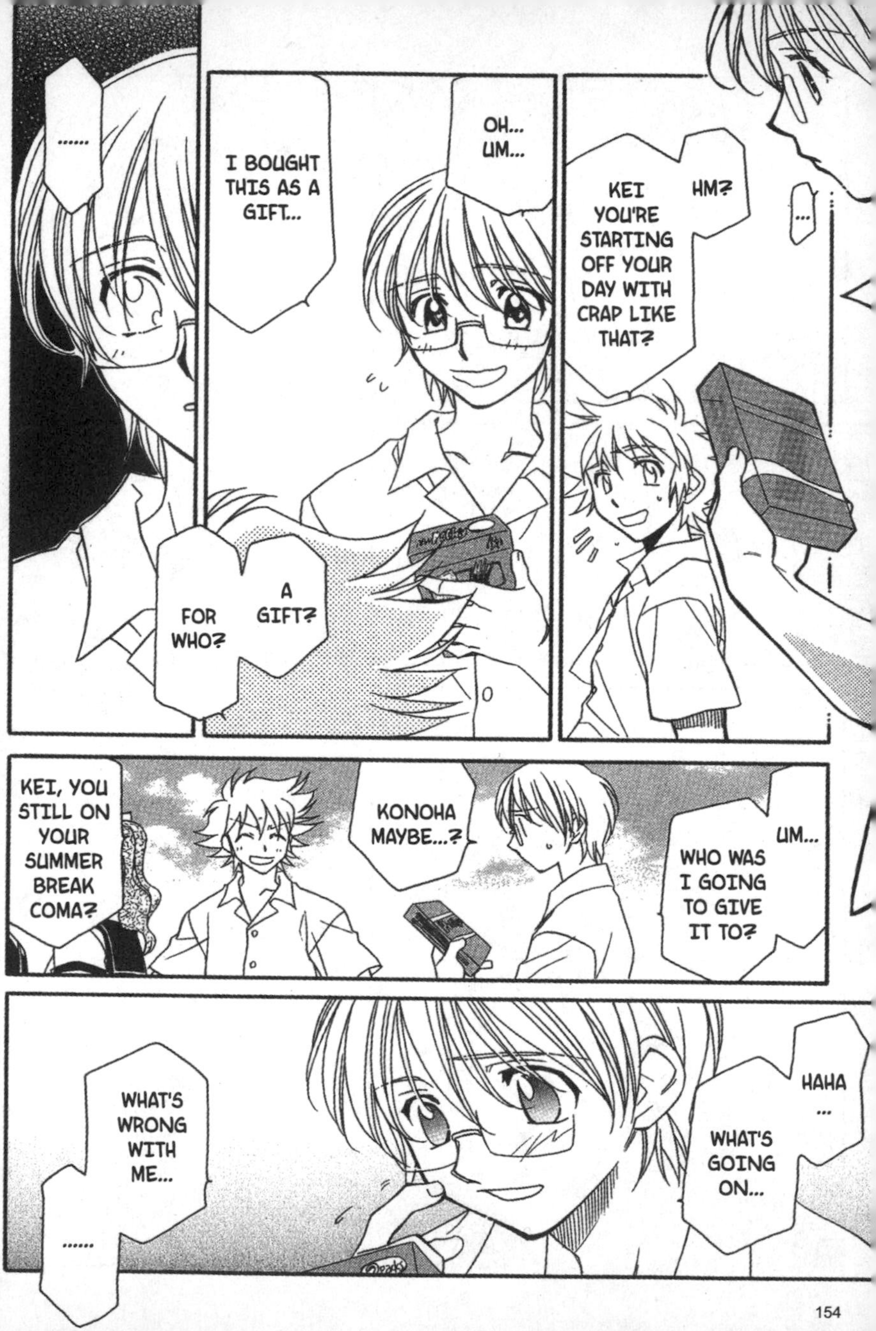
...
HM?
KEI YOU'RE STARTING OFF YOUR DAY WITH CRAP LIKE THAT?
OH... UM...
I BOUGHT THIS AS A GIFT...
A GIFT? FOR WHO?
......
UM... WHO WAS I GOING TO GIVE IT TO?
KONOHA MAYBE...?
KEI, YOU STILL ON YOUR SUMMER BREAK COMA?
HAHA ... WHAT'S GOING ON...
WHAT'S WRONG WITH ME...
......

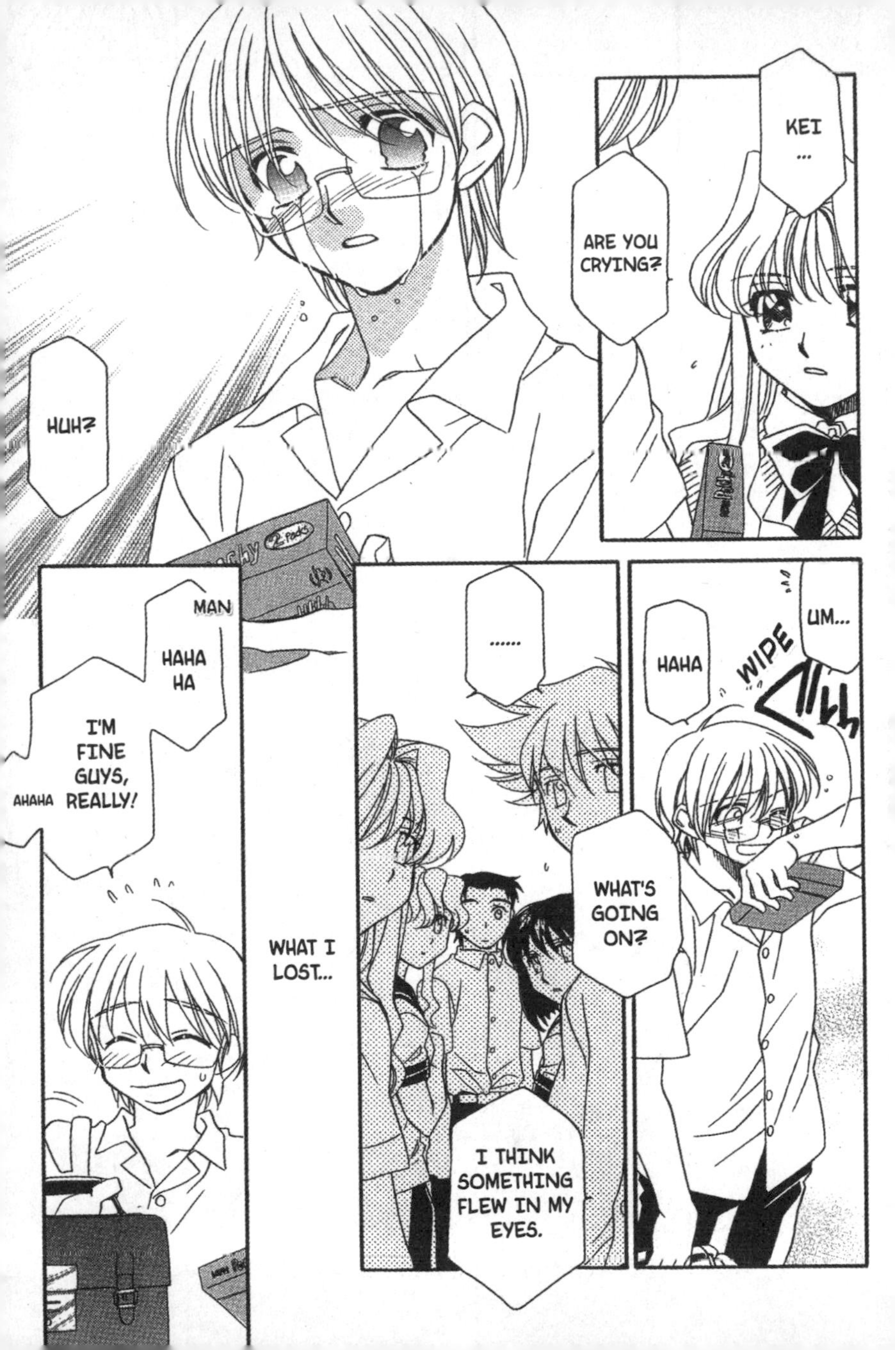
KEI ...
ARE YOU CRYING?
HUH?
UM...
WIPE
HAHA
......
WHAT'S GOING ON?
I THINK SOMETHING FLEW IN MY EYES.
WHAT I LOST...
MAN
HAHA HA
I'M FINE GUYS, REALLY!
AHAHA

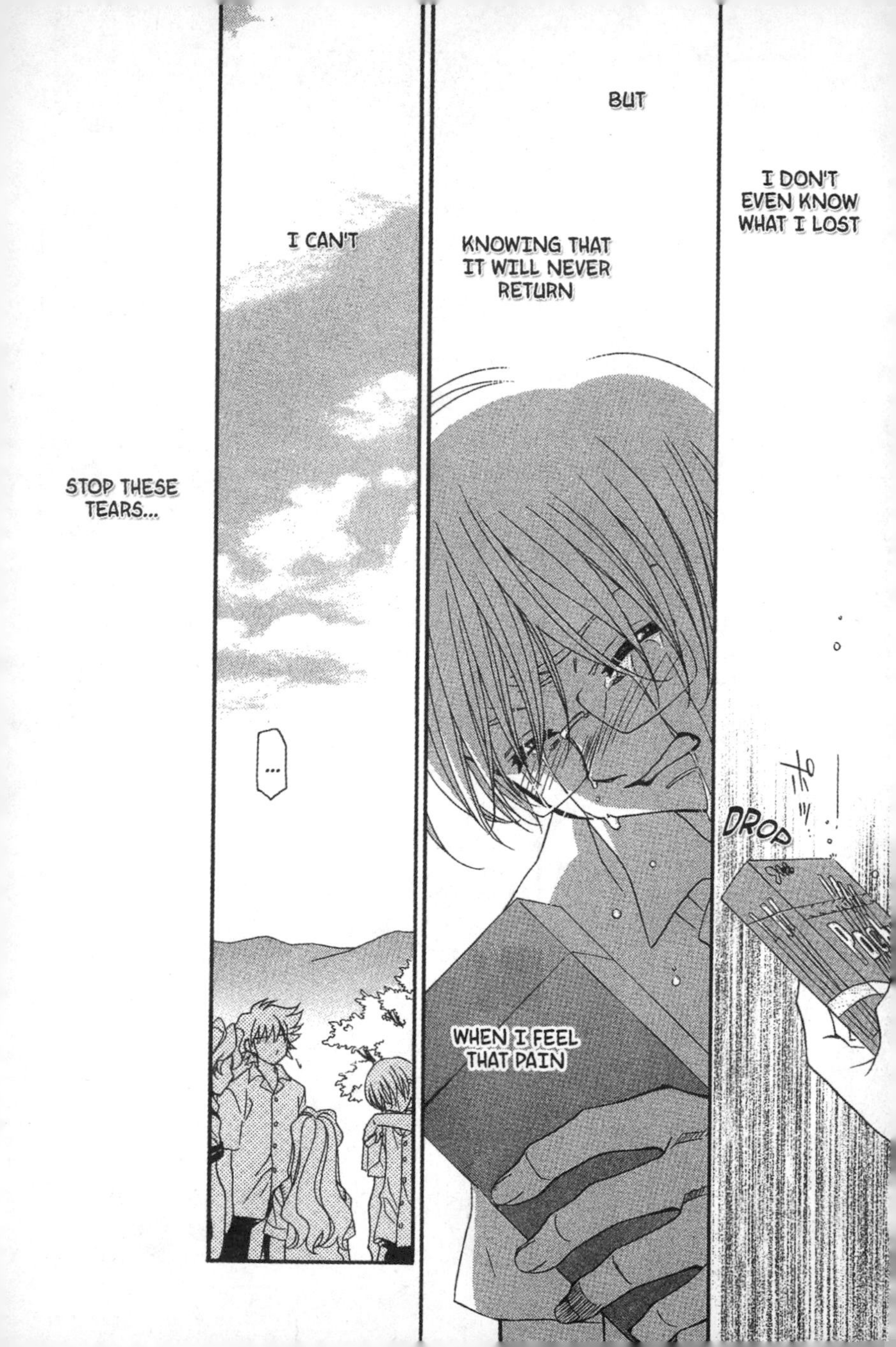
I DON'T EVEN KNOW WHAT I LOST
DROP
BUT
KNOWING THAT IT WILL NEVER RETURN
WHEN I FEEL THAT PAIN
I CAN'T
...
STOP THESE TEARS...

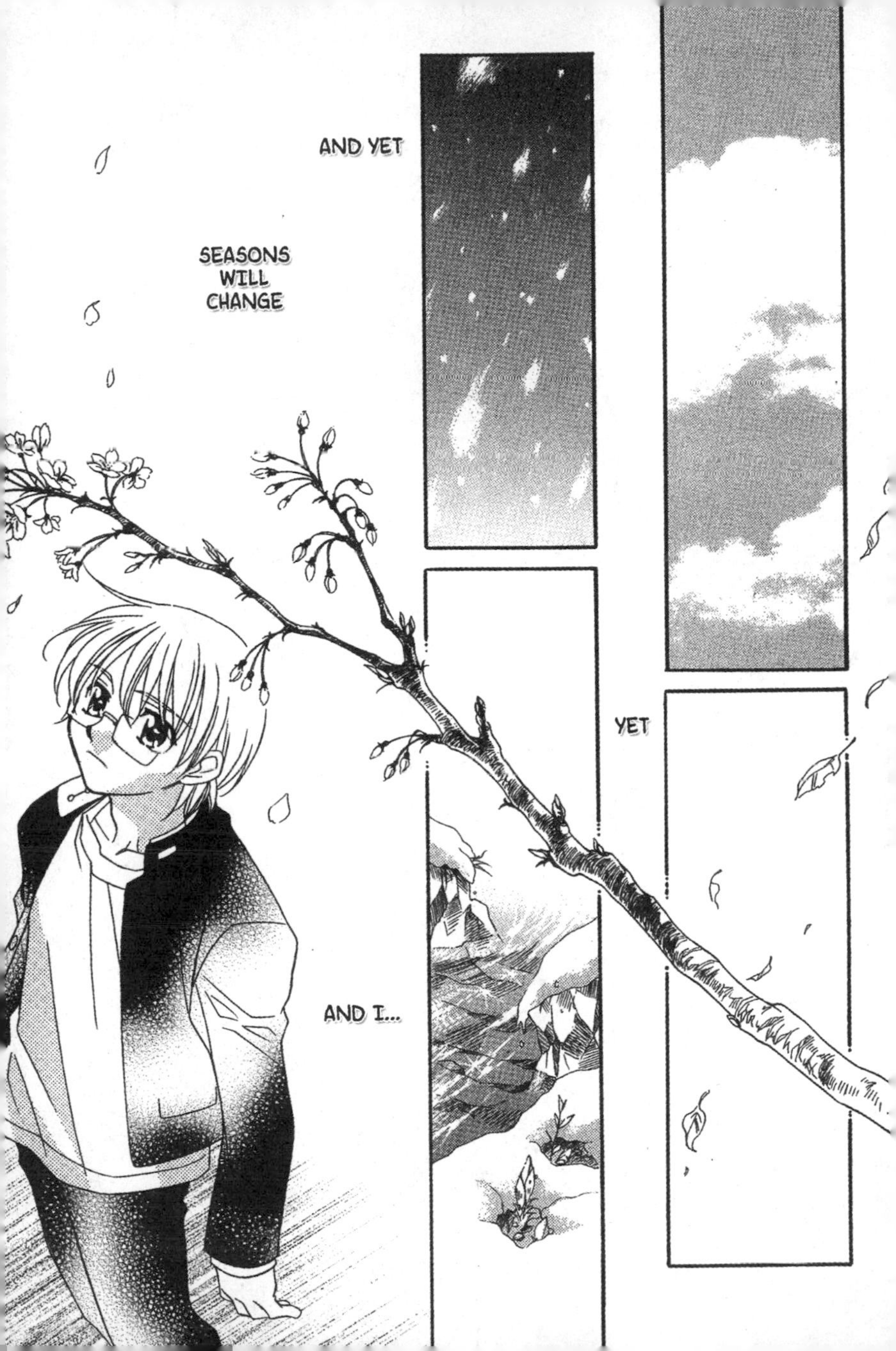
AND YET
SEASONS WILL CHANGE
YET
AND I...

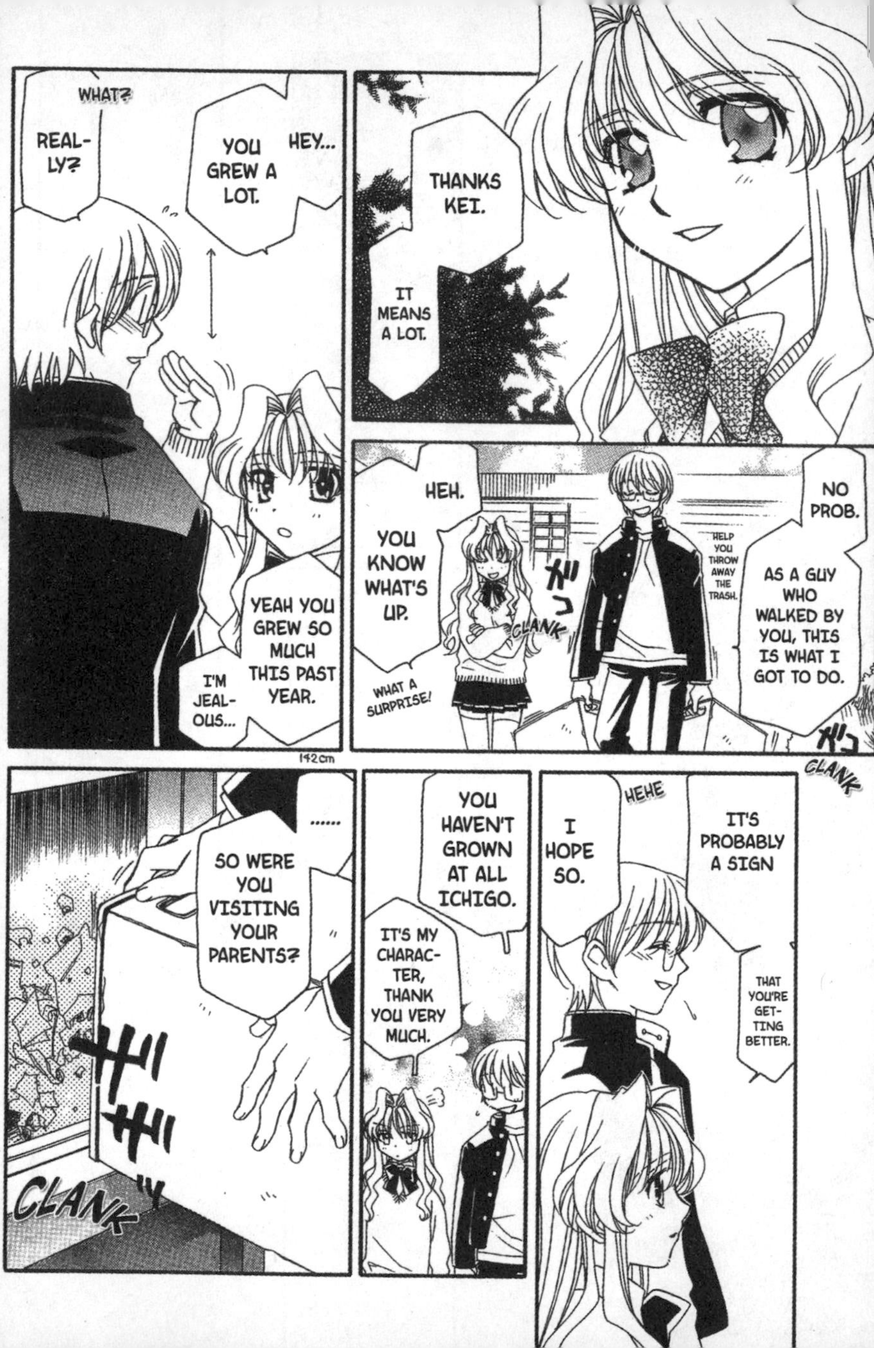
THANKS KEI.
IT MEANS A LOT.
NO PROB.
AS A GUY WHO WALKED BY YOU, THIS IS WHAT I GOT TO DO.
HELP YOU THROW AWAY THE TRASH.
CLANK
HEH.
YOU KNOW WHAT'S UP.
WHAT A SURPRISE!
CLANK
HEY...
YOU GREW A LOT.
WHAT?
REAL-LY?
YEAH YOU GREW SO MUCH THIS PAST YEAR.
I'M JEAL-OUS...
142cm
IT'S PROBABLY A SIGN
THAT YOU'RE GET-TING BETTER.
HEHE
I HOPE SO.
YOU HAVEN'T GROWN AT ALL ICHIGO.
IT'S MY CHARAC-TER, THANK YOU VERY MUCH.
......
SO WERE YOU VISITING YOUR PARENTS?
CLANK

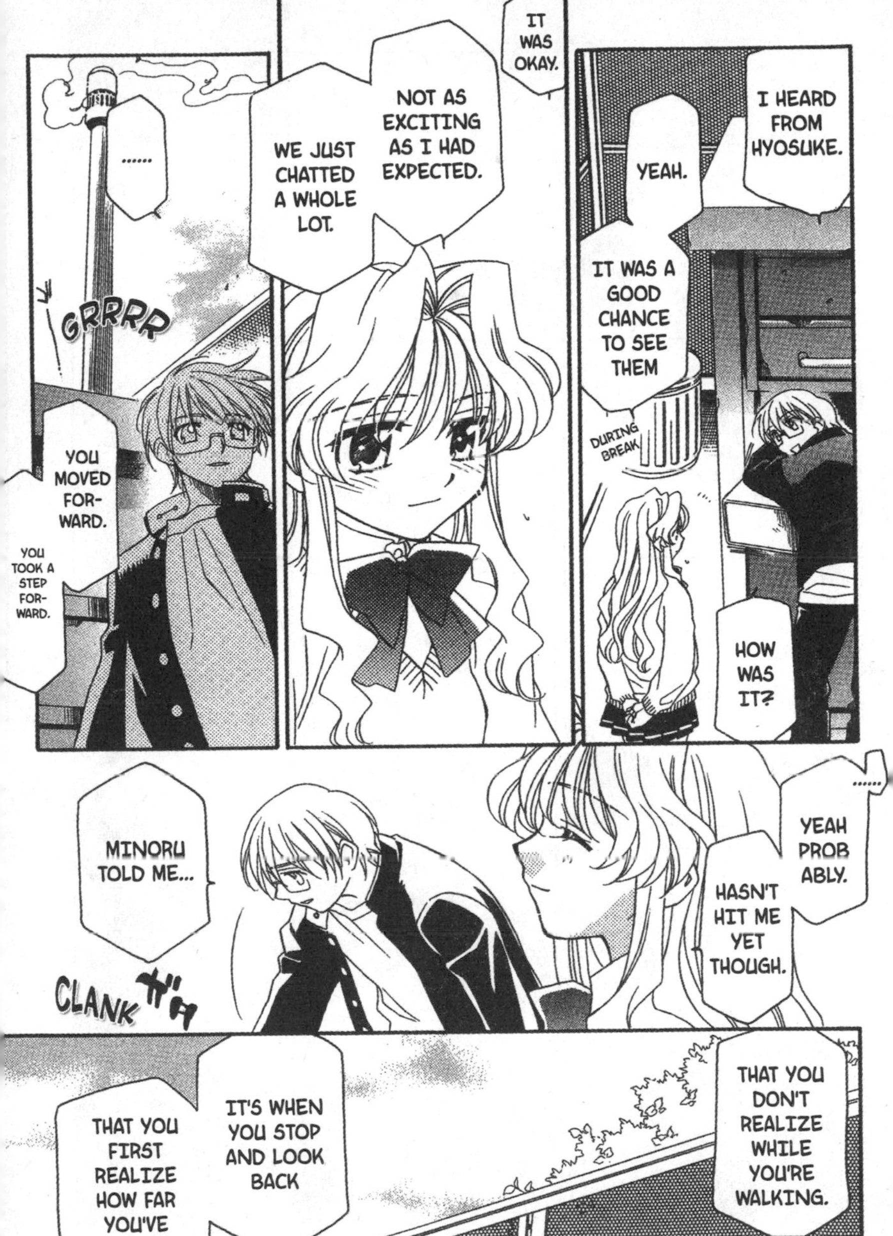
I HEARD FROM HYOSUKE.
YEAH.
IT WAS A GOOD CHANCE TO SEE THEM
DURING BREAK
HOW WAS IT?
IT WAS OKAY.
NOT AS EXCITING AS I HAD EXPECTED.
WE JUST CHATTED A WHOLE LOT.
......
GRRRR
YOU MOVED FOR-WARD.
YOU TOOK A STEP FOR-WARD.
......
YEAH PROB ABLY.
HASN'T HIT ME YET THOUGH.
MINORU TOLD ME...
CLANK
THAT YOU DON'T REALIZE WHILE YOU'RE WALKING.
IT'S WHEN YOU STOP AND LOOK BACK
THAT YOU FIRST REALIZE HOW FAR YOU'VE TRAVELED.

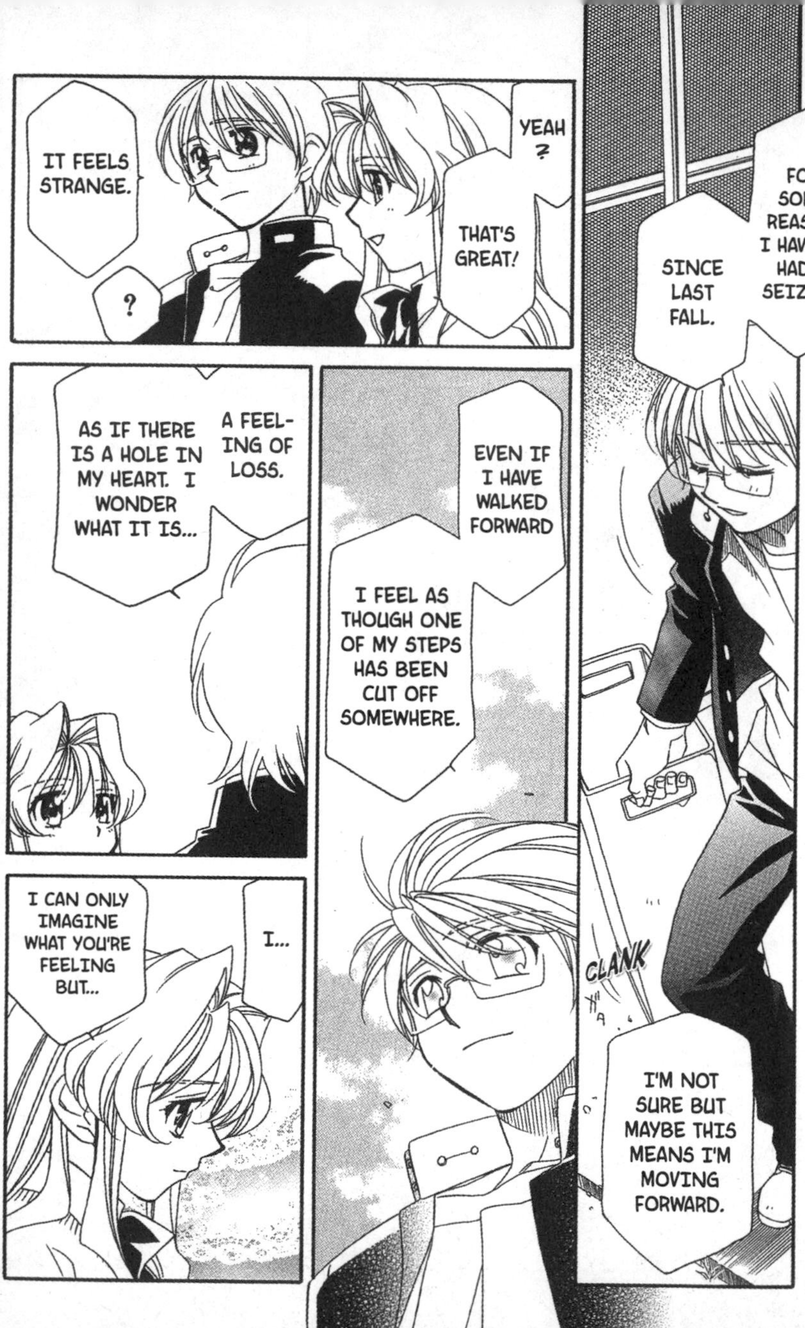
FOR SOME REASON I HAVEN'T HAD A SEIZURE
SINCE LAST FALL.
CLANK
I'M NOT SURE BUT MAYBE THIS MEANS I'M MOVING FORWARD.
YEAH?
THAT'S GREAT!
IT FEELS STRANGE.
?
EVEN IF I HAVE WALKED FORWARD
I FEEL AS THOUGH ONE OF MY STEPS HAS BEEN CUT OFF SOMEWHERE.
A FEEL-ING OF LOSS.
AS IF THERE IS A HOLE IN MY HEART. I WONDER WHAT IT IS...
I...
I CAN ONLY IMAGINE WHAT YOU'RE FEELING BUT...

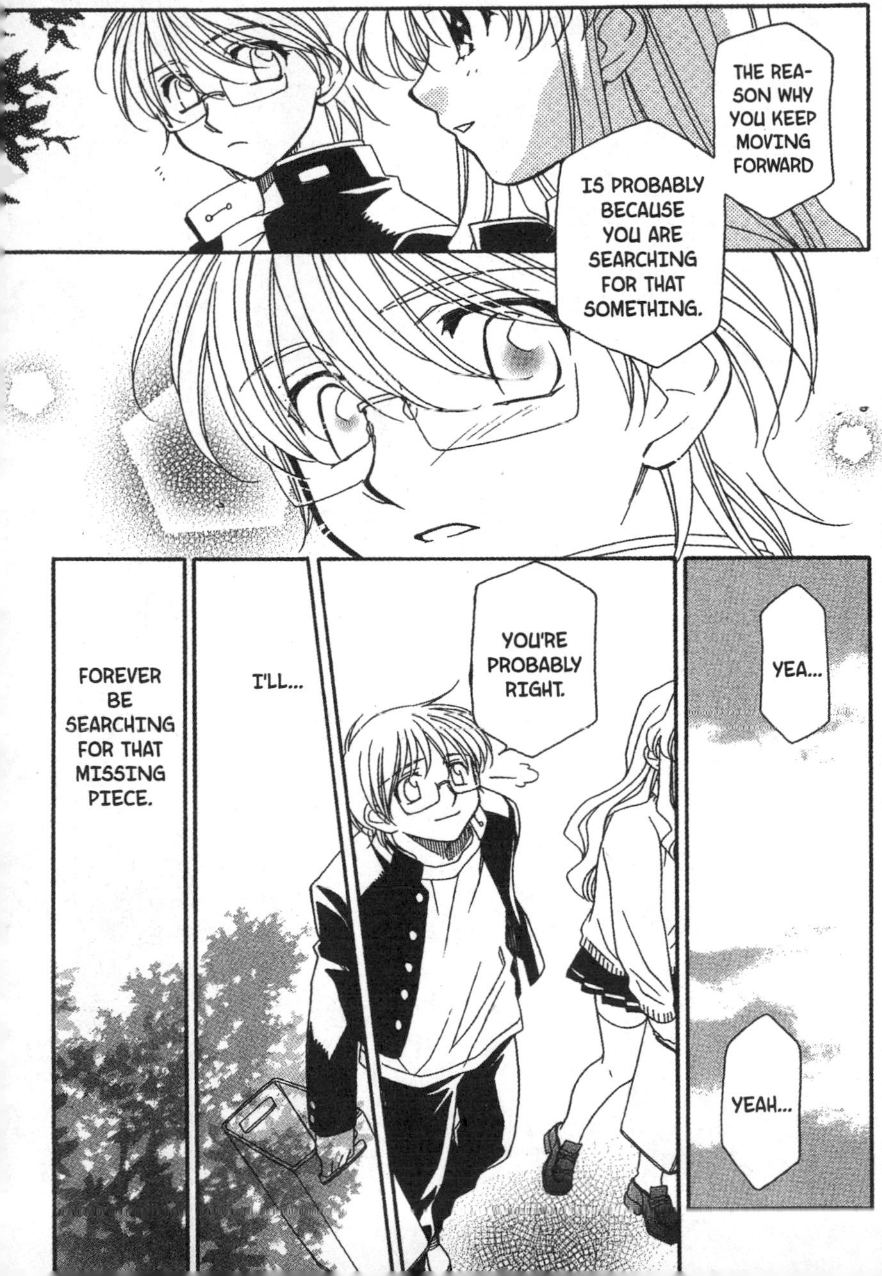
THE REASON WHY YOU KEEP MOVING FORWARD
IS PROBABLY BECAUSE YOU ARE SEARCHING FOR THAT SOMETHING.
YEA...
YEAH...
YOU'RE PROBABLY RIGHT.
I'LL...
FOREVER BE SEARCHING FOR THAT MISSING PIECE.

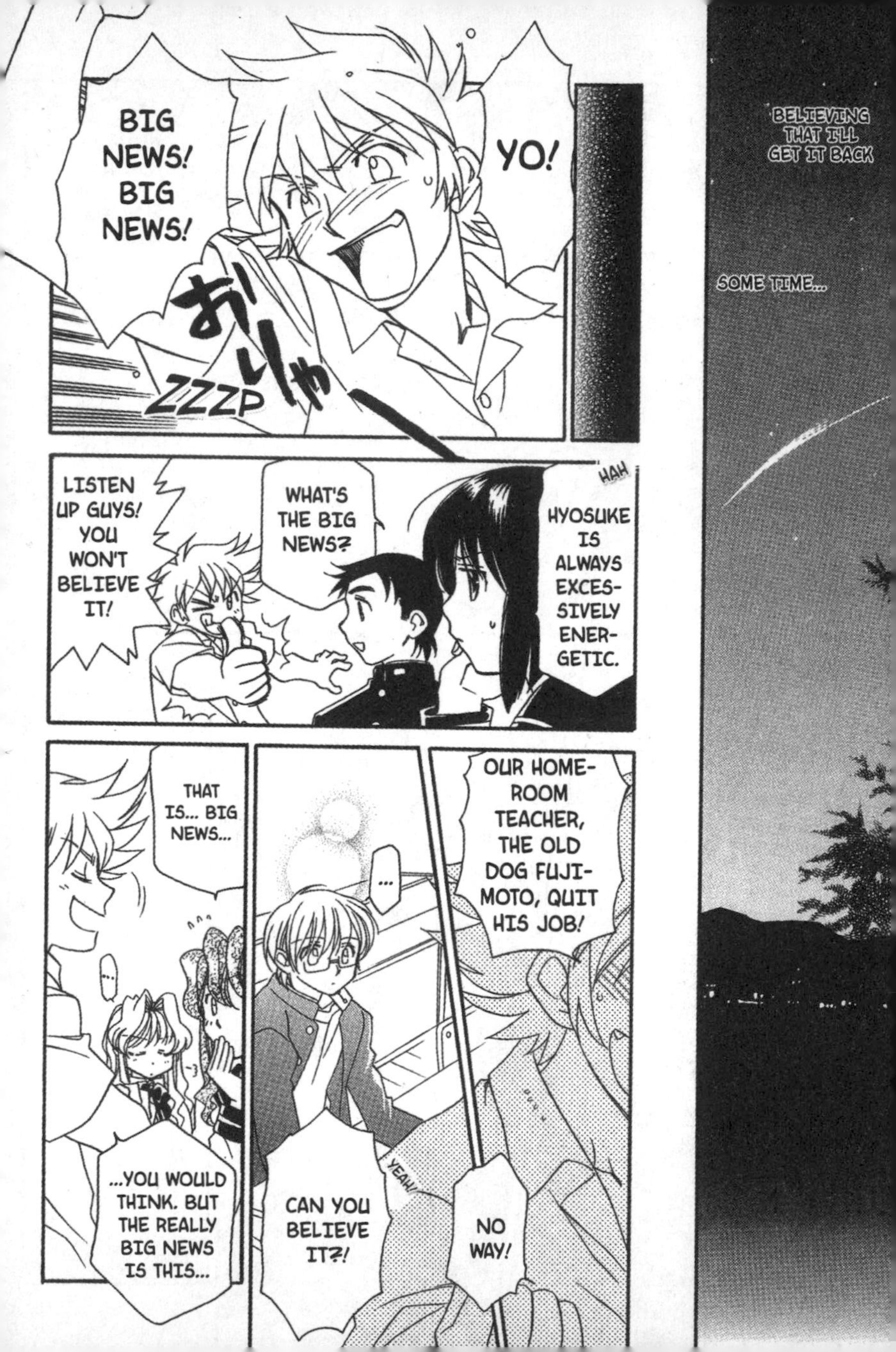
BELIEVING THAT I'LL GET IT BACK
SOME TIME...
YO!
BIG NEWS! BIG NEWS!
おしゃ
ZZZP
HAH
HYOSUKE IS ALWAYS EXCES-SIVELY ENER-GETIC.
WHAT'S THE BIG NEWS?
LISTEN UP GUYS! YOU WON'T BELIEVE IT!
OUR HOME-ROOM TEACHER, THE OLD DOG FUJI-MOTO, QUIT HIS JOB!
NO WAY!
...
YEAH!
CAN YOU BELIEVE IT?!
THAT IS... BIG NEWS...
...
...YOU WOULD THINK. BUT THE REALLY BIG NEWS IS THIS...

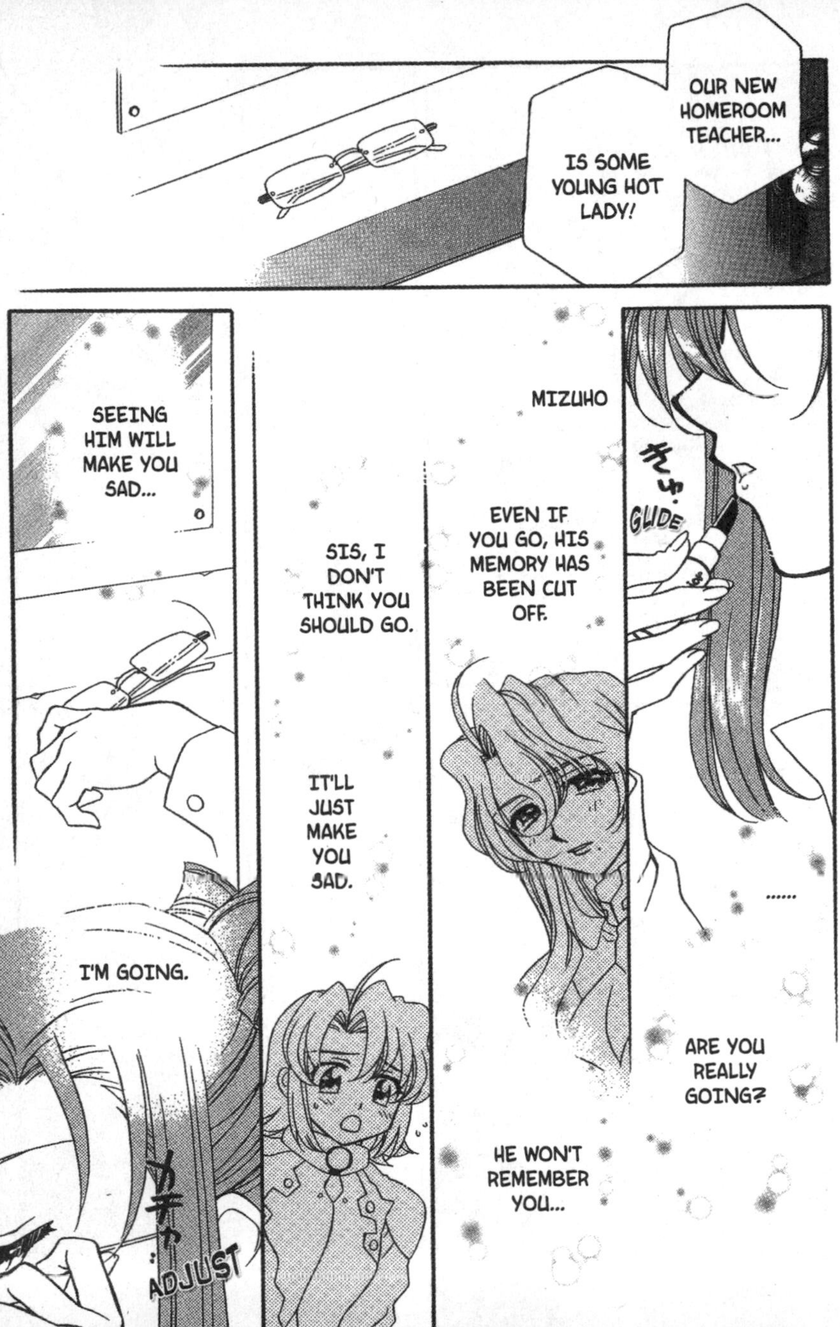
OUR NEW HOMEROOM TEACHER...
IS SOME YOUNG HOT LADY!
MIZUHO
きゅ
GLIDE
......
ARE YOU REALLY GOING?
EVEN IF YOU GO, HIS MEMORY HAS BEEN CUT OFF.
HE WON'T REMEMBER YOU...
SIS, I DON'T THINK YOU SHOULD GO.
IT'LL JUST MAKE YOU SAD.
SEEING HIM WILL MAKE YOU SAD...
I'M GOING.
カチャ
ADJUST

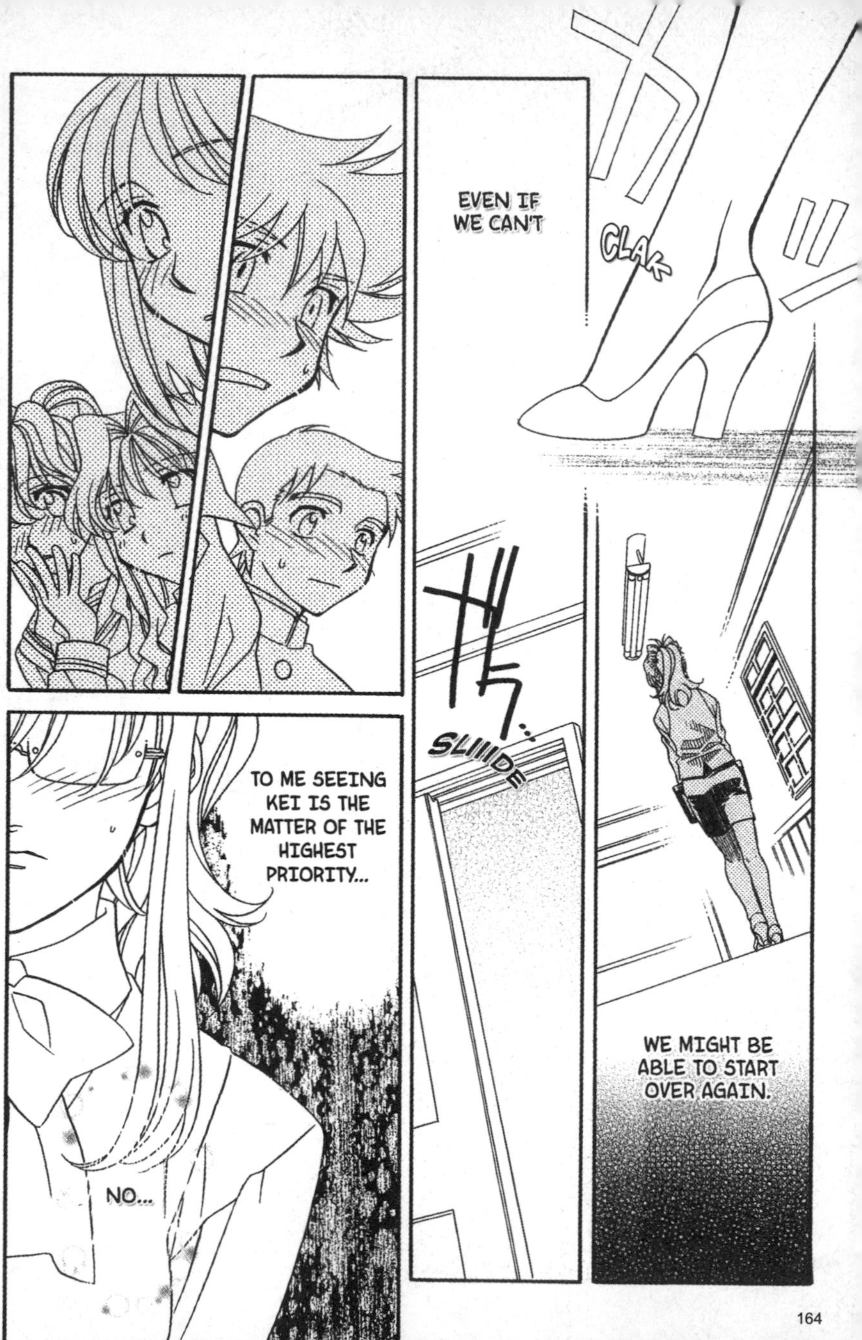
CLAK
WE MIGHT BE ABLE TO START OVER AGAIN.
EVEN IF WE CAN'T
SLIIIDE
TO ME SEEING KEI IS THE MATTER OF THE HIGHEST PRIORITY...
NO...

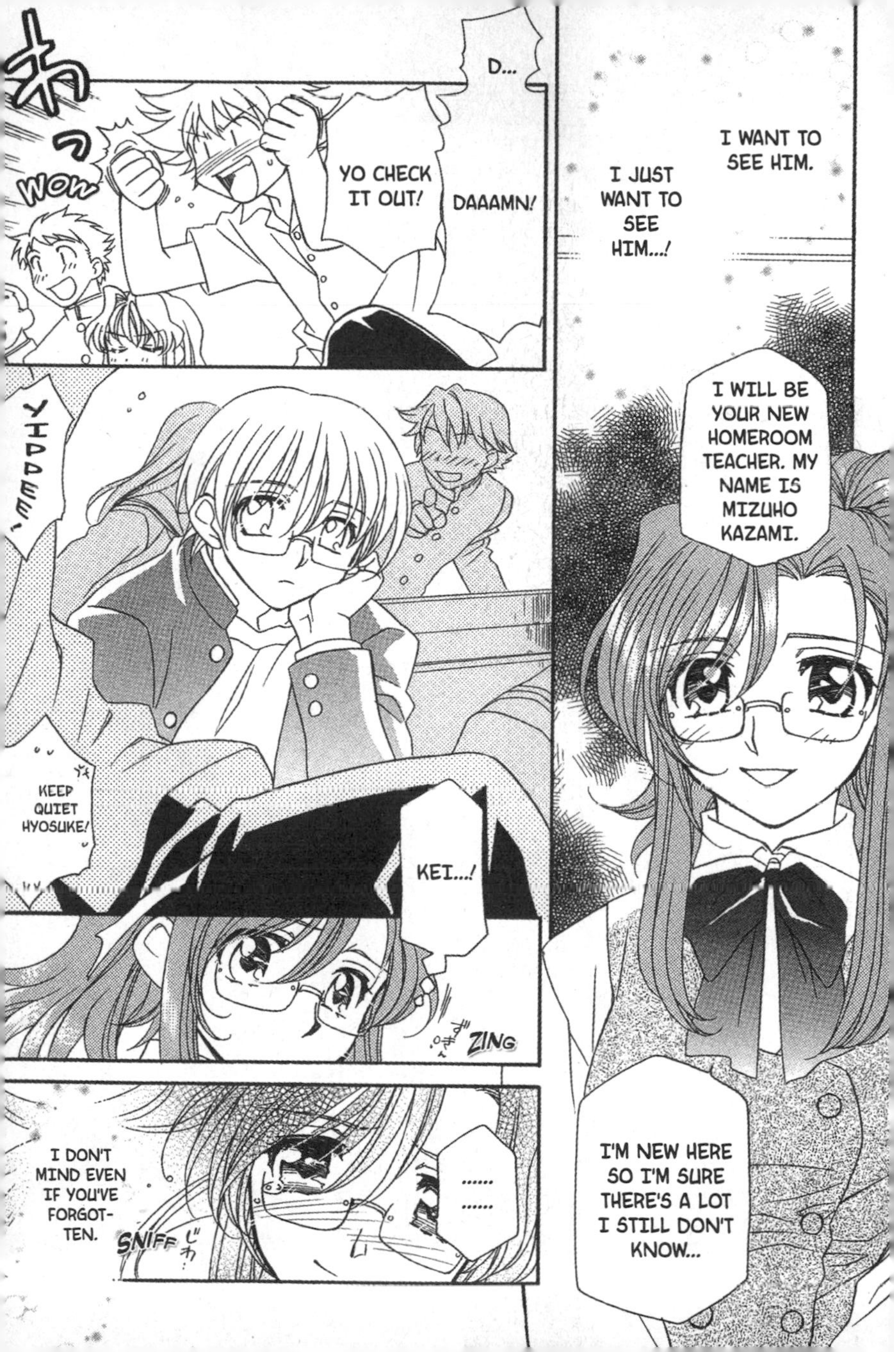

I WANT TO SEE HIM.
I JUST WANT TO SEE HIM...!
I WILL BE YOUR NEW HOMEROOM TEACHER. MY NAME IS MIZUHO KAZAMI.
I'M NEW HERE SO I'M SURE THERE'S A LOT I STILL DON'T KNOW...
D...
DAAAMN!
YO CHECK IT OUT!
WOW
YIDDEE,
KEEP QUIET HYOSUKE!
KEI...!
ZING
......
......
I DON'T MIND EVEN IF YOU'VE FORGOT-TEN.
SNIFF

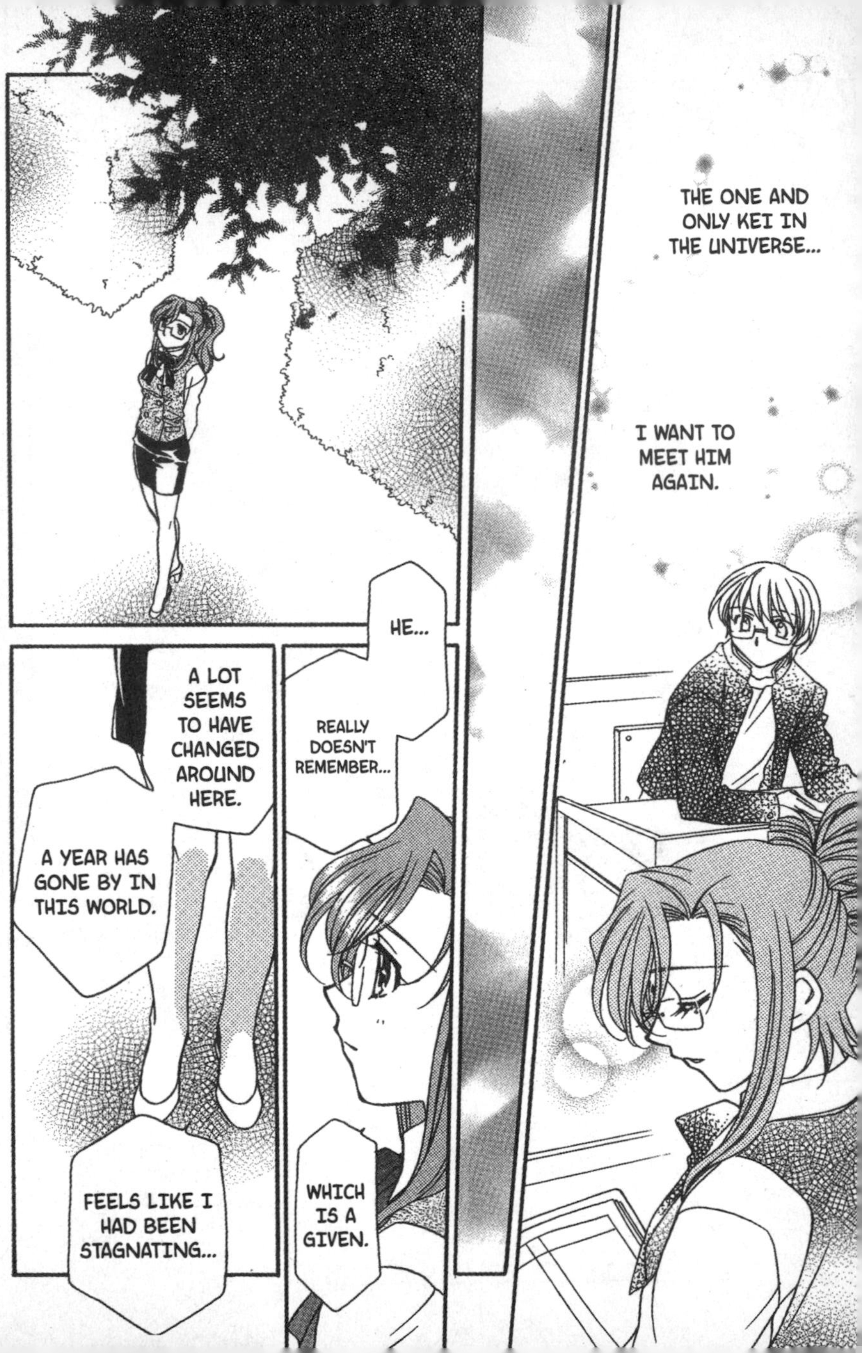
THE ONE AND ONLY KEI IN THE UNIVERSE...
I WANT TO MEET HIM AGAIN.
HE...
REALLY DOESN'T REMEMBER...
WHICH IS A GIVEN.
A LOT SEEMS TO HAVE CHANGED AROUND HERE.
A YEAR HAS GONE BY IN THIS WORLD.
FEELS LIKE I HAD BEEN STAGNATING...

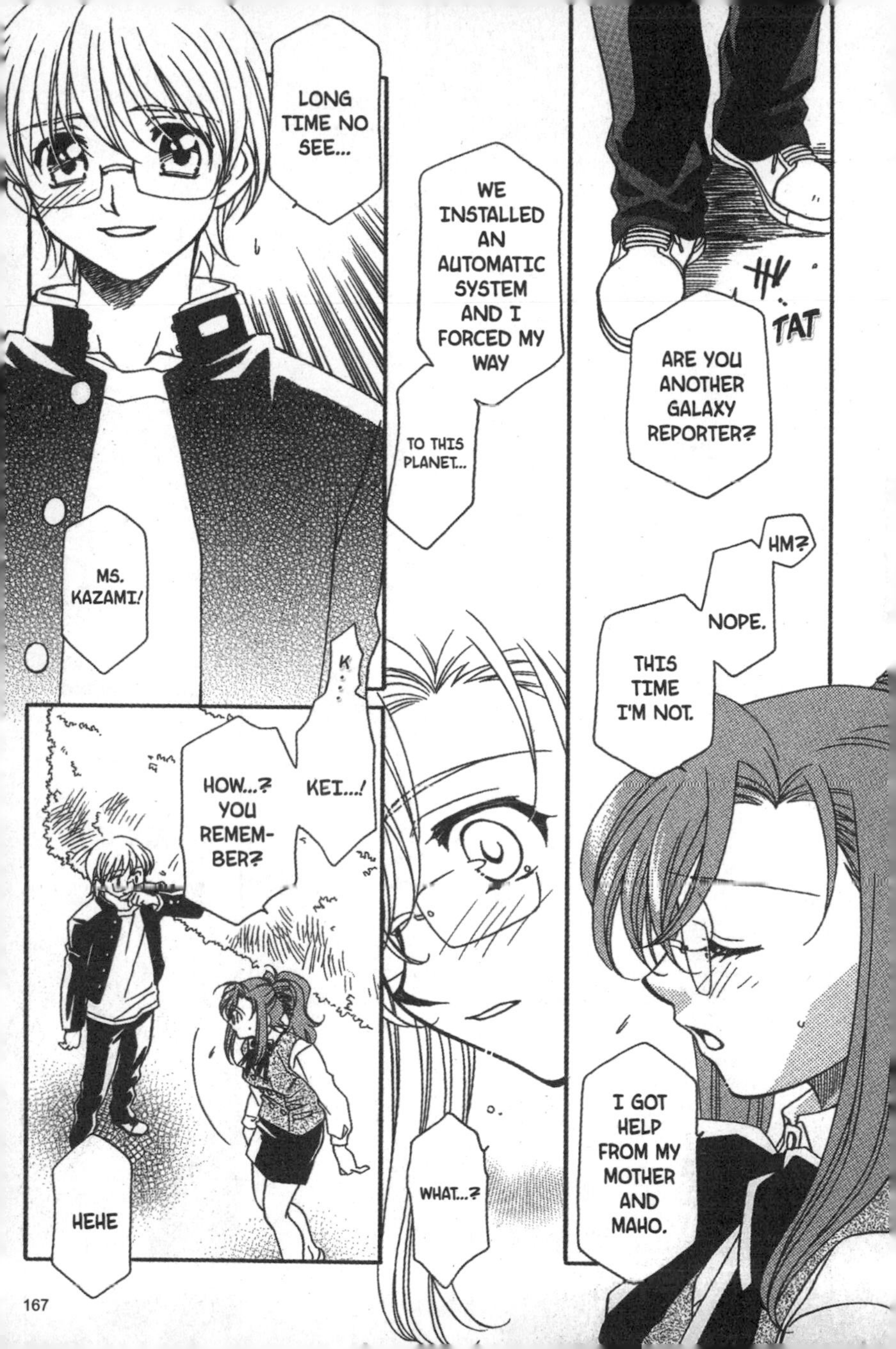

LONG TIME NO SEE...
MS. KAZAMI!
K...
KEI...!
HOW...? YOU REMEMBER?
HEHE
WE INSTALLED AN AUTOMATIC SYSTEM AND I FORCED MY WAY
TO THIS PLANET...
WHAT...?
TAT
ARE YOU ANOTHER GALAXY REPORTER?
HM?
NOPE.
THIS TIME I'M NOT.
I GOT HELP FROM MY MOTHER AND MAHO.

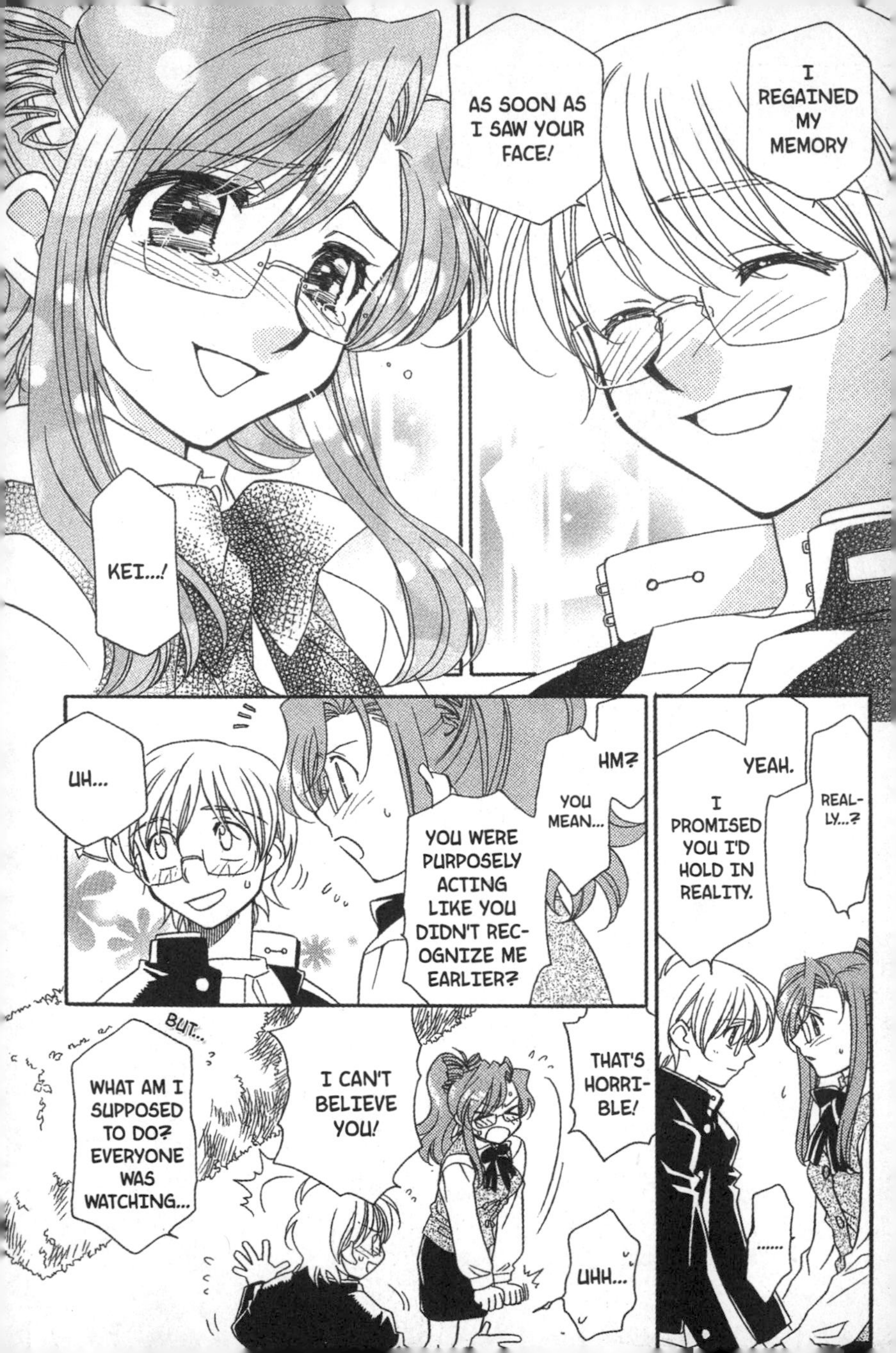
I REGAINED MY MEMORY
AS SOON AS I SAW YOUR FACE!
KEI...!
REAL-LY...?
YEAH.
I PROMISED YOU I'D HOLD IN REALITY.
......
HM?
YOU MEAN...
YOU WERE PURPOSELY ACTING LIKE YOU DIDN'T REC-OGNIZE ME EARLIER?
UH...
THAT'S HORRI-BLE!
I CAN'T BELIEVE YOU!
BUT...
WHAT AM I SUPPOSED TO DO? EVERYONE WAS WATCHING...
UHH...

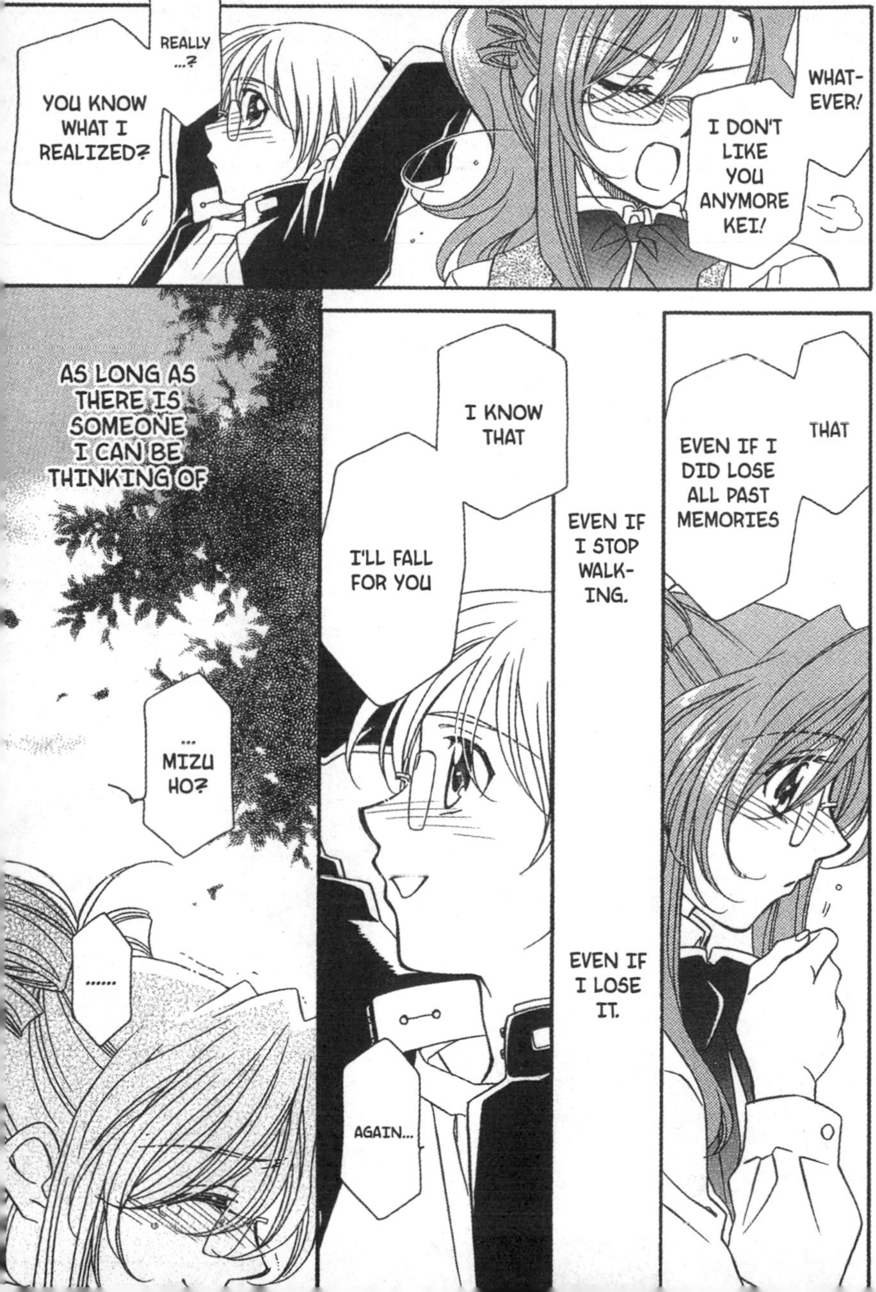
WHAT-EVER!
I DON'T LIKE YOU ANYMORE KEI!
REALLY ...?
YOU KNOW WHAT I REALIZED?
THAT
EVEN IF I DID LOSE ALL PAST MEMORIES
EVEN IF I STOP WALK-ING.
EVEN IF I LOSE IT.
I KNOW THAT
I'LL FALL FOR YOU
AGAIN...
AS LONG AS THERE IS SOMEONE I CAN BE THINKING OF
... MIZU HO?
......

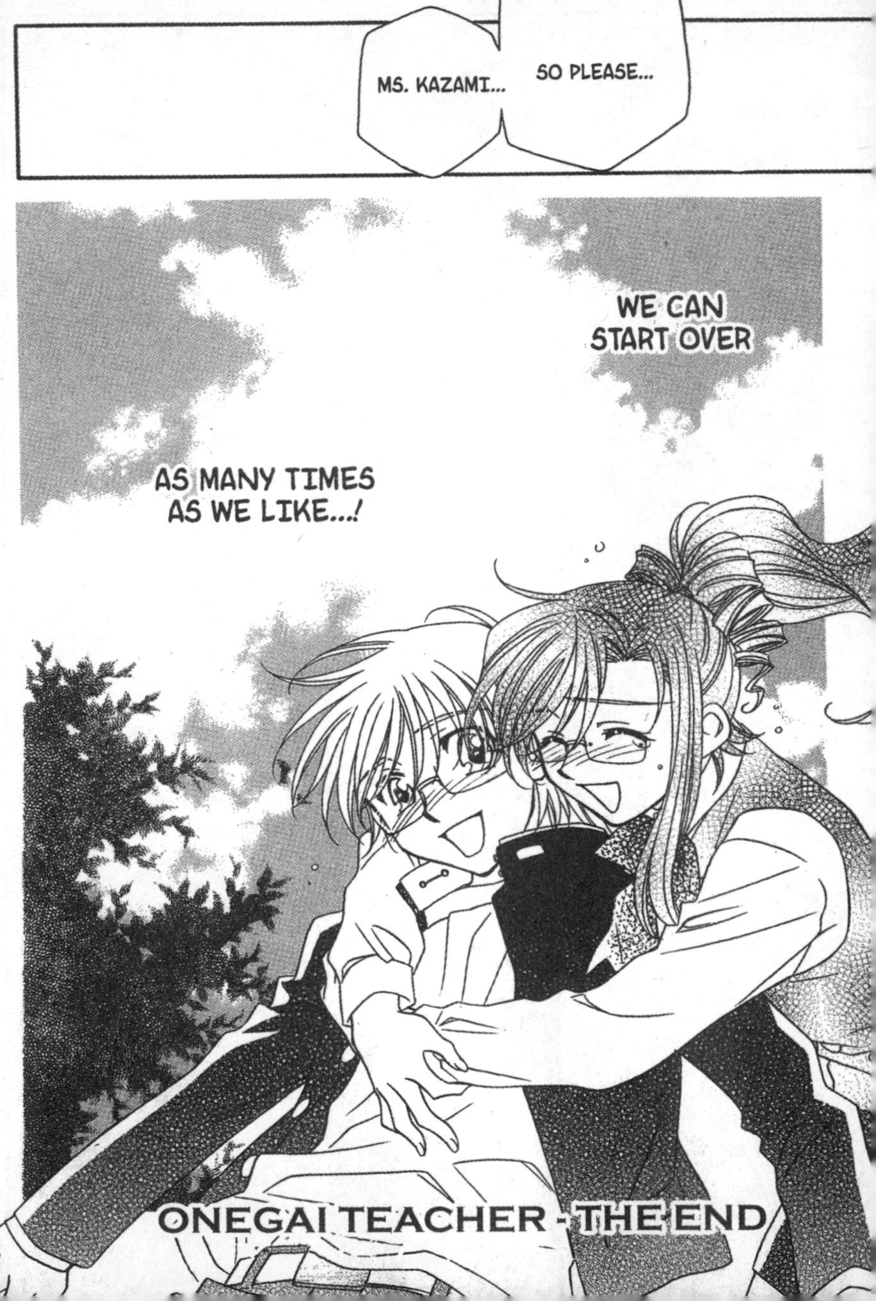
SO PLEASE...
MS. KAZAMI...
WE CAN START OVER
AS MANY TIMES AS WE LIKE...!
ONEGAI TEACHER - THE END

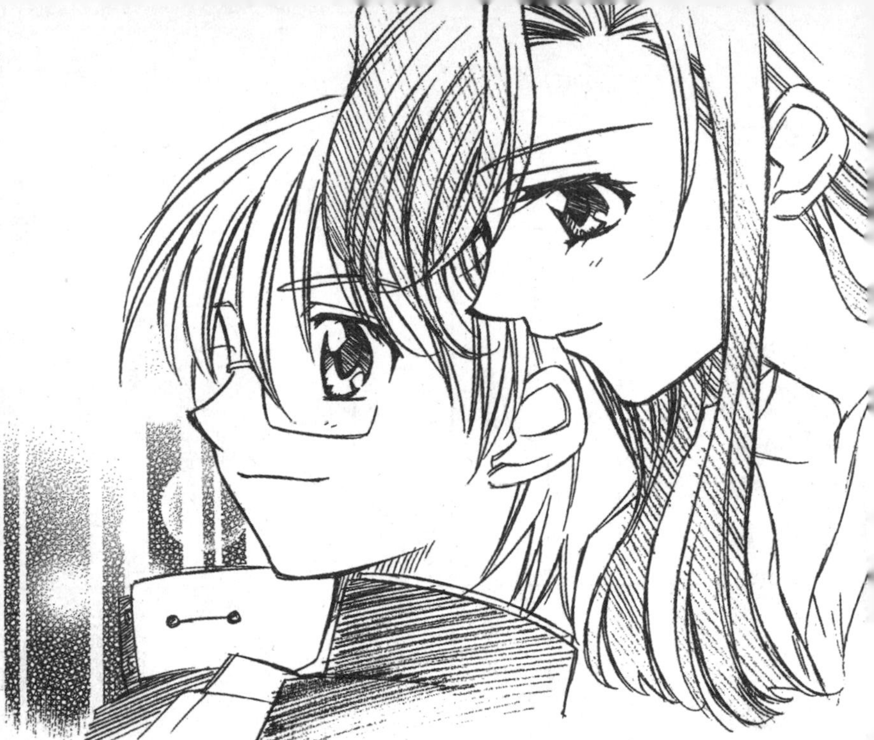

I HOPE YOU ENJOYED IT! SO THIS IS THE END OF HAYASHIYA'S VERSION OF PLEASE TEACHER. THANK YOU THANK YOU...!!! I WANTED TO TAKE ADVANTAGE OF THIS LAST PAGE TO TELL YOU GUYS SO MUCH BUT... NOW THAT I'VE ACTUALLY COMPLETED THE STORY I CAN'T THINK OF WHAT IT WAS I WANTED TO SHARE. WELL ANYWAYS! AS I MENTIONED IN THE PREVIOUS VOLUME, WRITING THIS COMIC HAS BEEN A GREAT LEARNING EXPERIENCE FOR ME IN MANY WAYS. BUT I'VE BEEN VERY SELFISH IN MANY WAYS, DOING THINGS THE WAY I PLEASE... SORRY AND THANK YOU! OF COURSE MY THANKS GO OUT TO ALL THE FANS! SORRY FOR SUDDENLY CHANGING THE SUBJECT... (PAINFUL LAUGH) <-- IT AIN'T FUNNY... ANYWAYS! I HOPE TO SEE YOU ALL AGAIN SOON!

SHIZURU HAYASHIYA, JANUARY 2003

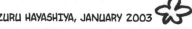

P.S. LAST BUT NOT LEAST, MY ASSISTANTS! WELL, MORE LIKE MY PARTNERS! : REIKO MAKISE AND SATARO SATO. THANKS A BUNCH! AND OF COURSE MY ACCOUNT EXECUTIVE MR. RED. THANKS A LOT!

Relationship Chart

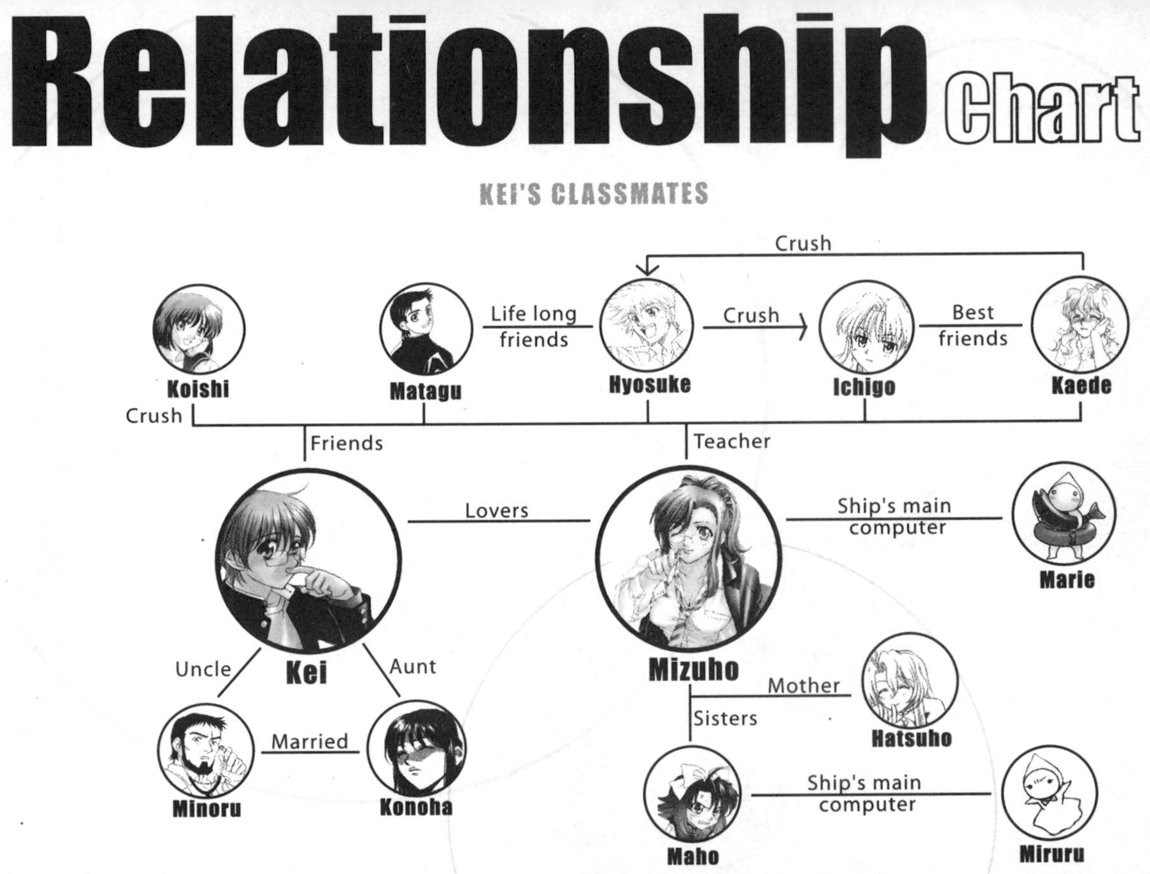

KEI'S CLASSMATES
Crush
Koishi
Matagu
Life long friends
Hyosuke
Crush
Ichigo
Best friends
Kaede
Crush
Friends
Teacher
Lovers
Ship's main computer
Marie
Kei
Uncle
Aunt
Minoru
Married
Konoha
Mizuho
Mother
Hatsuho
Sisters
Maho
Ship's main computer
Miruru

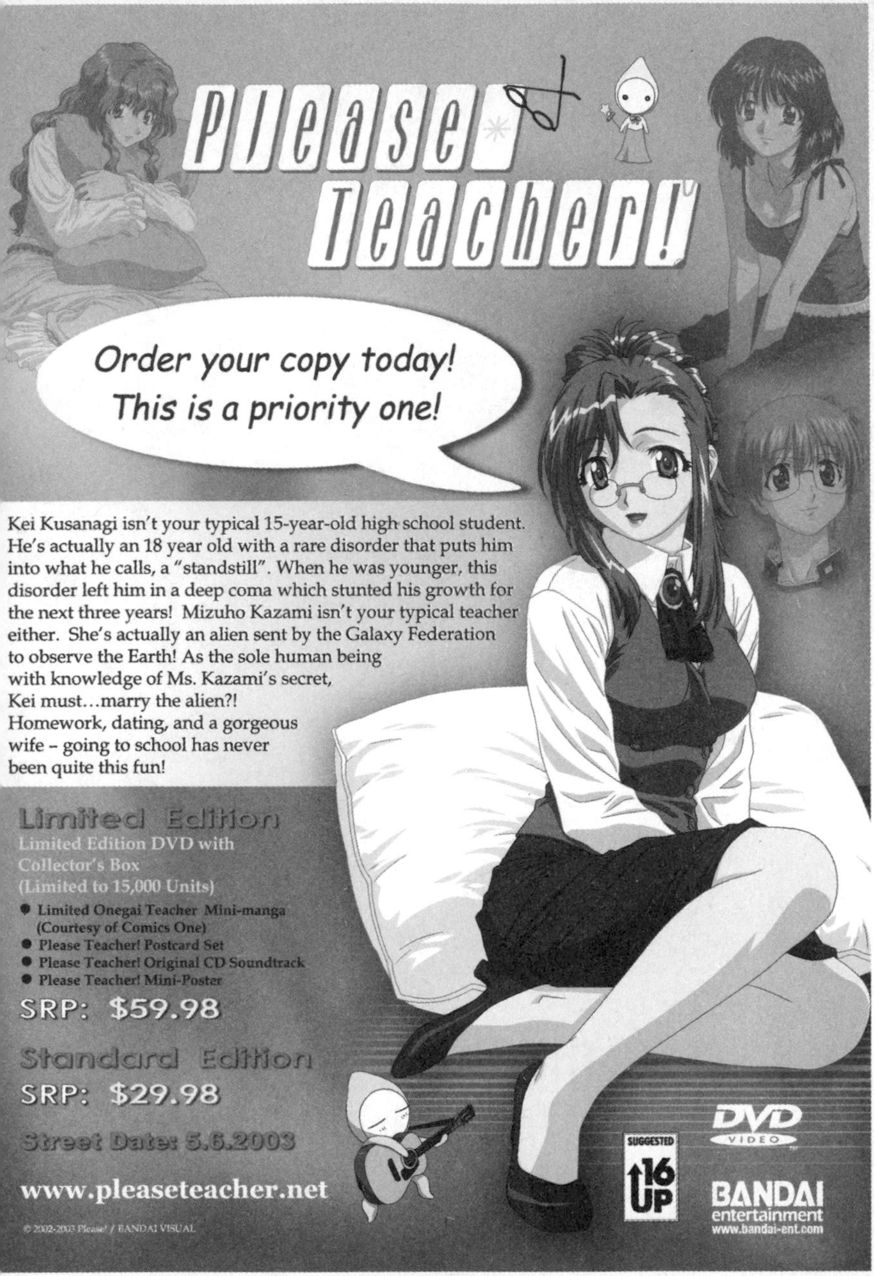
Please Teacher!
Order your copy today!
This is a priority one!
Kei Kusanagi isn't your typical 15-year-old high school student. He's actually an 18 year old with a rare disorder that puts him into what he calls, a "standstill". When he was younger, this disorder left him in a deep coma which stunted his growth for the next three years! Mizuho Kazami isn't your typical teacher either. She's actually an alien sent by the Galaxy Federation to observe the Earth! As the sole human being with knowledge of Ms. Kazami's secret, Kei must…marry the alien?! Homework, dating, and a gorgeous wife – going to school has never been quite this fun!
Limited Edition
Limited Edition DVD with Collector's Box (Limited to 15,000 Units)
Limited Onegai Teacher Mini-manga (Courtesy of Comics One)
Please Teacher! Postcard Set
Please Teacher! Original CD Soundtrack
Please Teacher! Mini-Poster
SRP: $59.98
Standard Edition
SRP: $29.98
Street Date: 5.6.2003
www.pleaseteacher.net
SUGGESTED 16 UP
DVD VIDEO
BANDAI entertainment
www.bandai-ent.com
© 2002-2003 Please! / BANDAI VISUAL

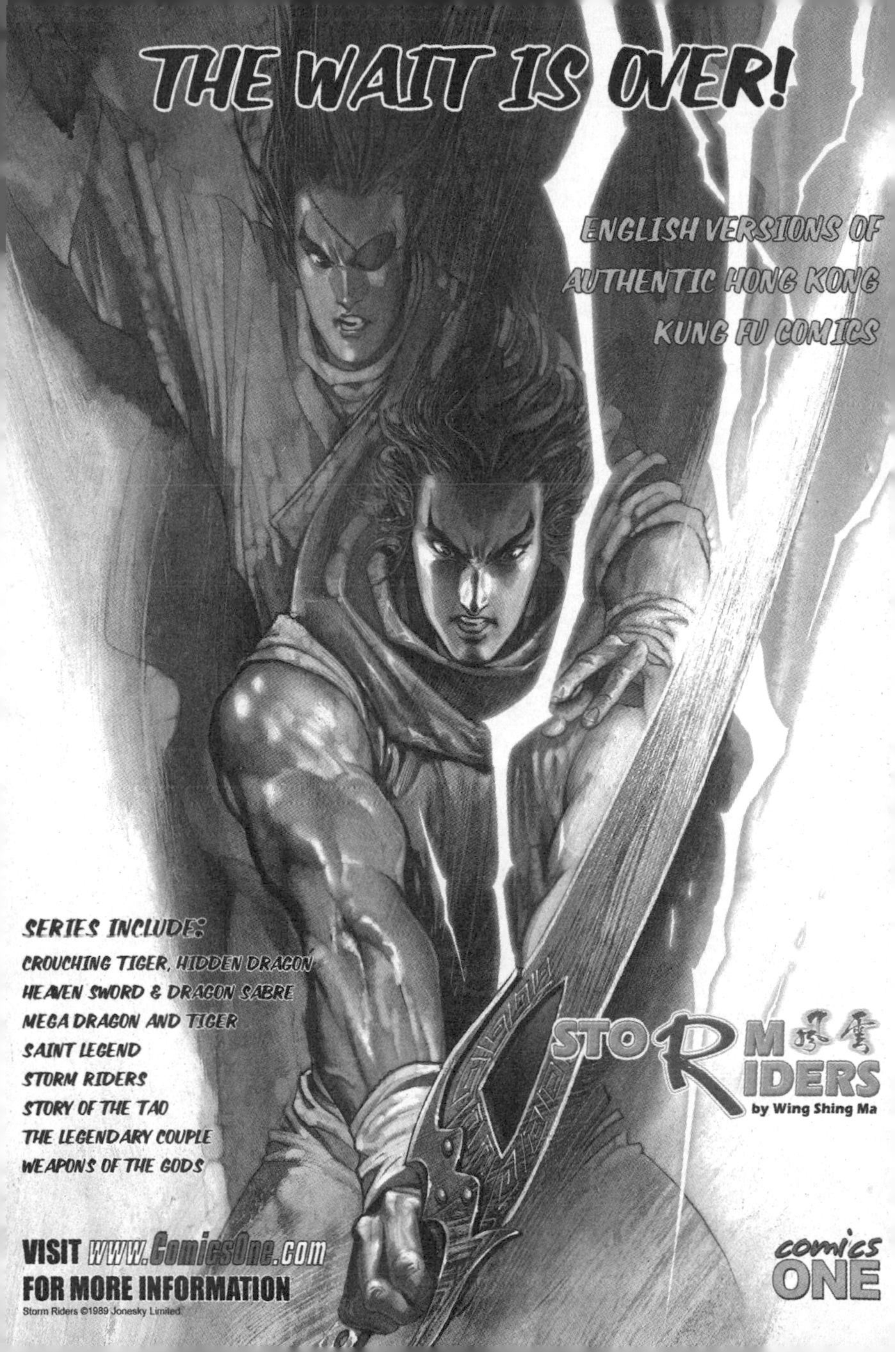
THE WAIT IS OVER!
ENGLISH VERSIONS OF AUTHENTIC HONG KONG KUNG FU COMICS
SERIES INCLUDE:
CROUCHING TIGER, HIDDEN DRAGON
HEAVEN SWORD & DRAGON SABRE
MEGA DRAGON AND TIGER
SAINT LEGEND
STORM RIDERS
STORY OF THE TAO
THE LEGENDARY COUPLE
WEAPONS OF THE GODS
STORM 風雲 RIDERS
by Wing Shing Ma
VISIT www.ComicsOne.com
FOR MORE INFORMATION
Storm Riders ©1989 Jonesky Limited
comics ONE

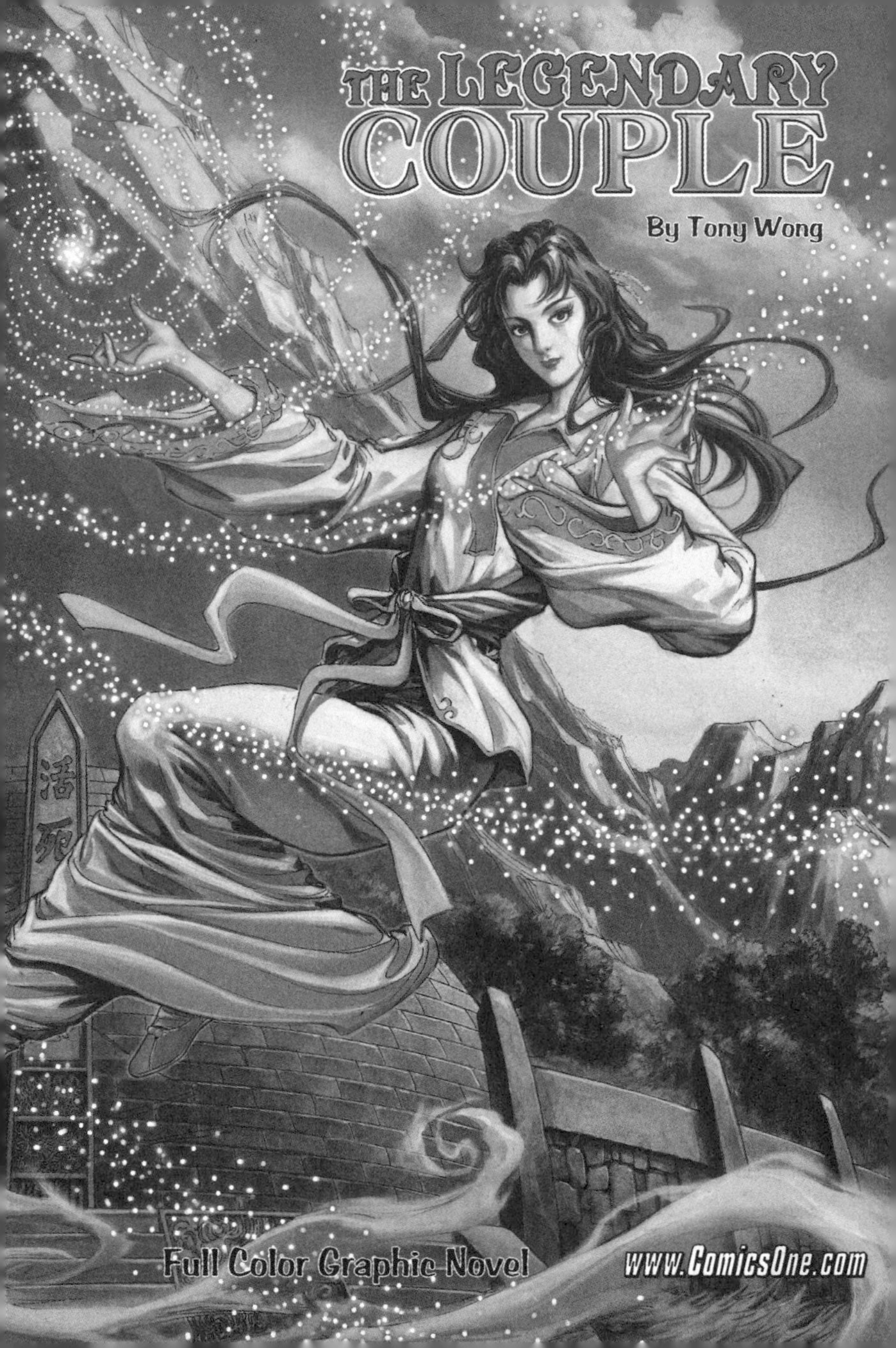
THE LEGENDARY COUPLE
By Tony Wong
活死
Full Color Graphic Novel
www.ComicsOne.com

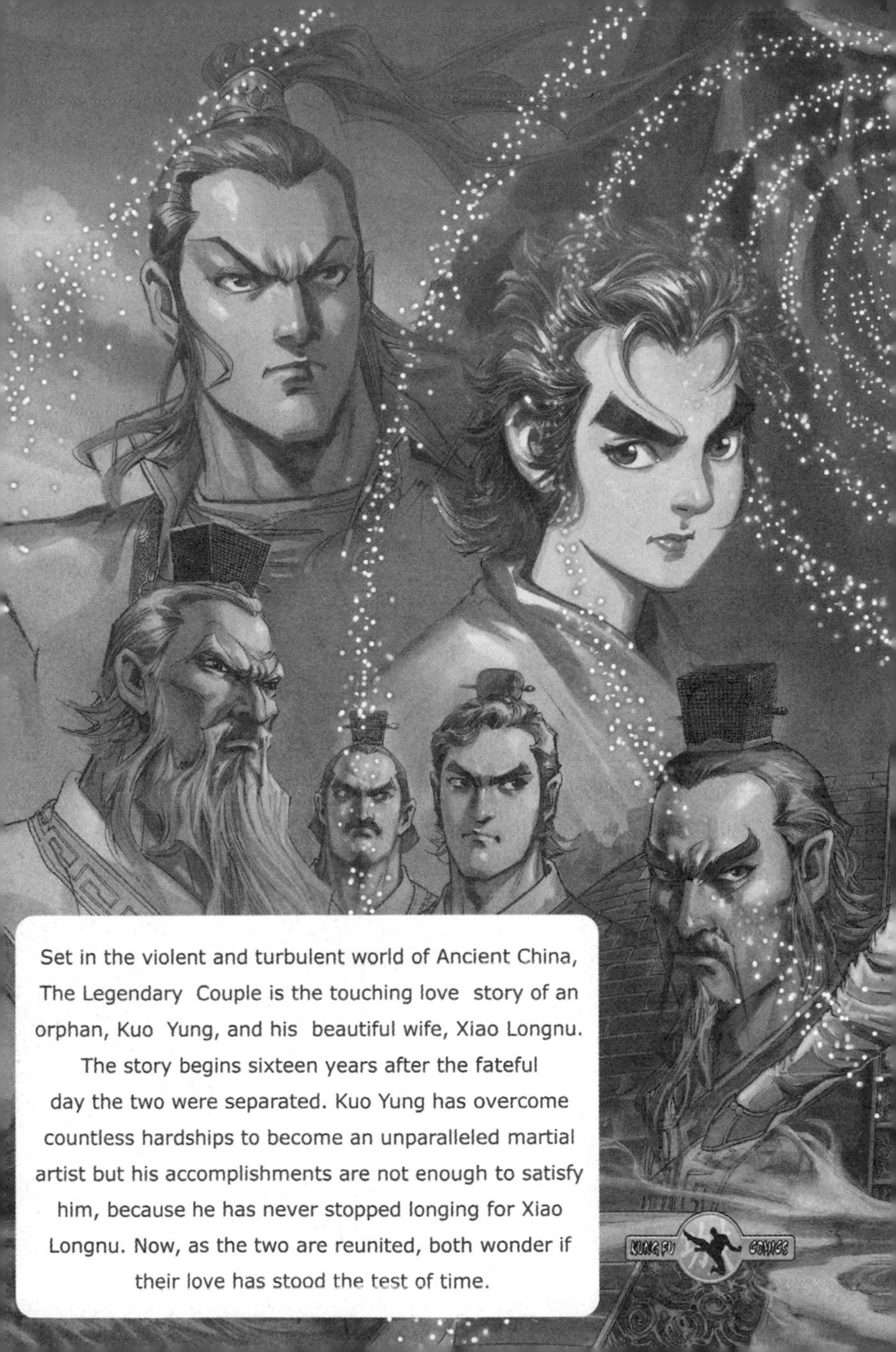
KUNG FU COMICS

Set in the violent and turbulent world of Ancient China, The Legendary Couple is the touching love story of an orphan, Kuo Yung, and his beautiful wife, Xiao Longnu. The story begins sixteen years after the fateful day the two were separated. Kuo Yung has overcome countless hardships to become an unparalleled martial artist but his accomplishments are not enough to satisfy him, because he has never stopped longing for Xiao Longnu. Now, as the two are reunited, both wonder if their love has stood the test of time.

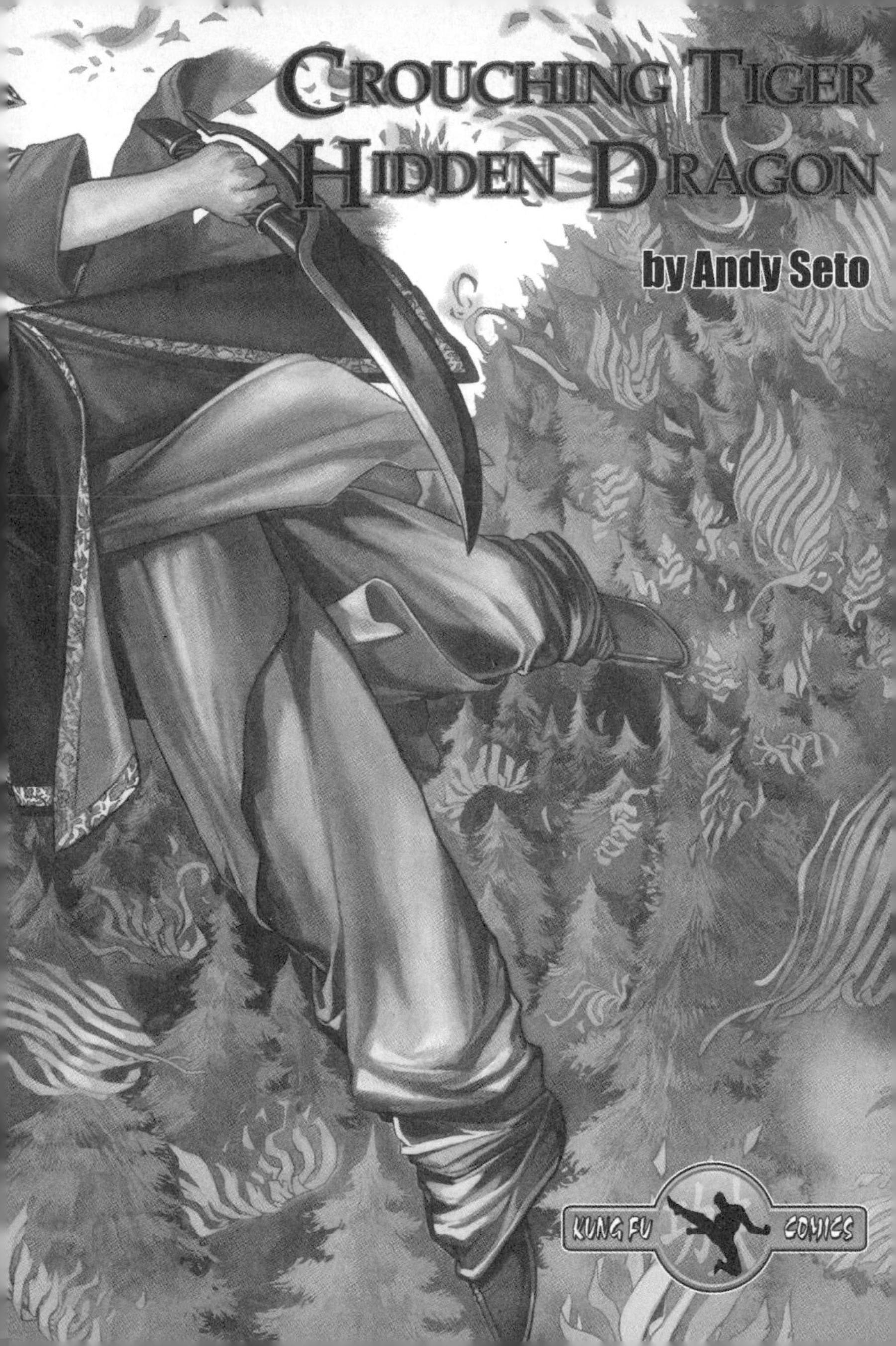
CROUCHING TIGER
HIDDEN DRAGON
by Andy Seto
KUNG FU COMICS

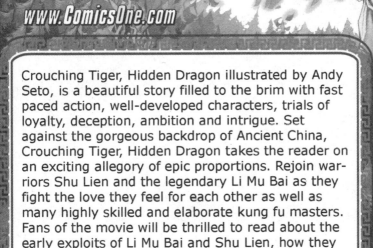

Crouching Tiger, Hidden Dragon illustrated by Andy Seto, is a beautiful story filled to the brim with fast paced action, well-developed characters, trials of loyalty, deception, ambition and intrigue. Set against the gorgeous backdrop of Ancient China, Crouching Tiger, Hidden Dragon takes the reader on an exciting allegory of epic proportions. Rejoin warriors Shu Lien and the legendary Li Mu Bai as they fight the love they feel for each other as well as many highly skilled and elaborate kung fu masters. Fans of the movie will be thrilled to read about the early exploits of Li Mu Bai and Shu Lien, how they got into the emotional entanglement we remember, as well as learning the backgrounds of a host of new and intriguing characters. Not to mention, readers will be privy to the events that follow after the Crouching Tiger, Hidden Dragon movie.

Full Color Graphic Novel

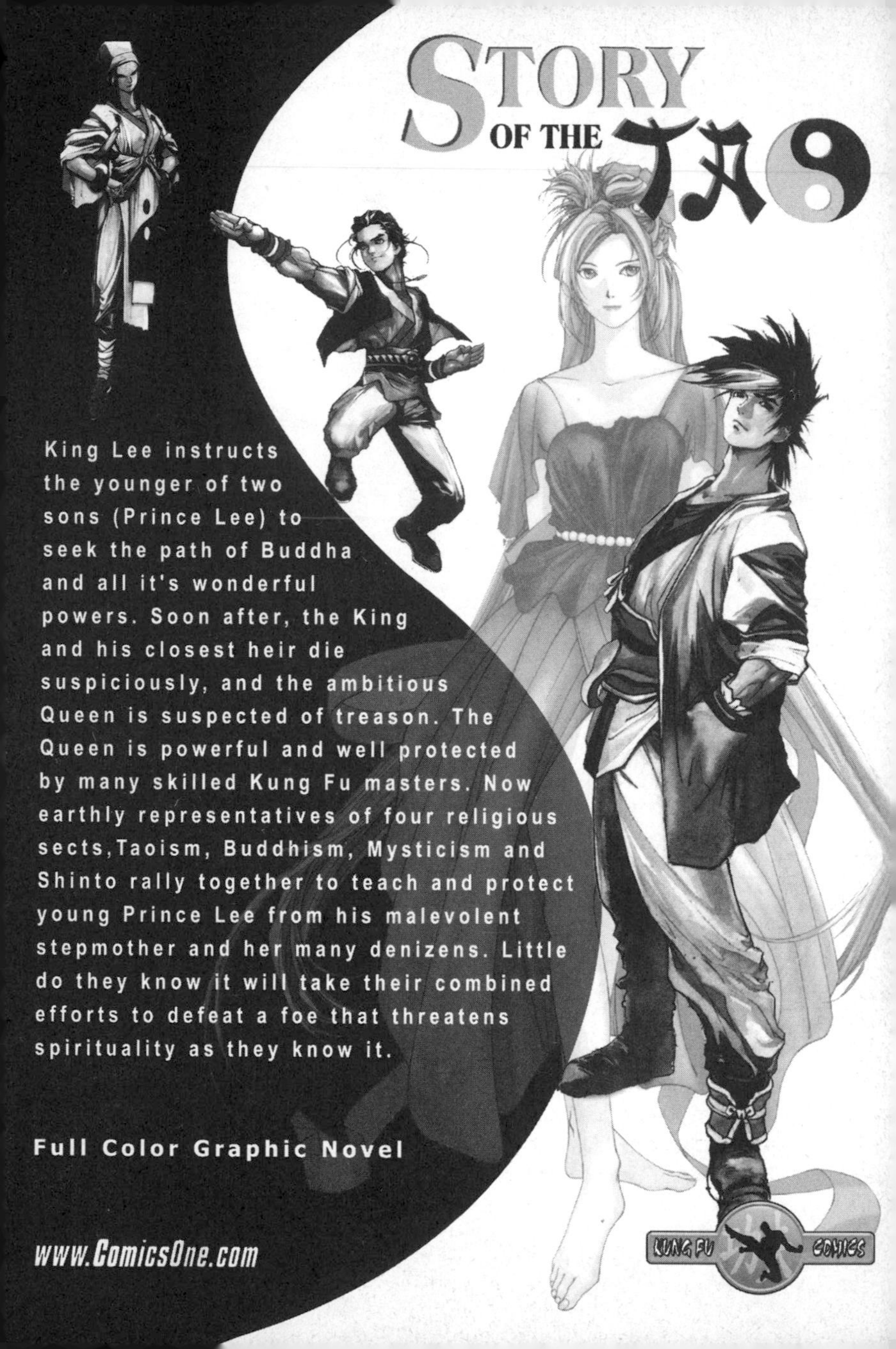
STORY OF THE TAO
King Lee instructs the younger of two sons (Prince Lee) to seek the path of Buddha and all it's wonderful powers. Soon after, the King and his closest heir die suspiciously, and the ambitious Queen is suspected of treason. The Queen is powerful and well protected by many skilled Kung Fu masters. Now earthly representatives of four religious sects,Taoism, Buddhism, Mysticism and Shinto rally together to teach and protect young Prince Lee from his malevolent stepmother and her many denizens. Little do they know it will take their combined efforts to defeat a foe that threatens spirituality as they know it.
Full Color Graphic Novel
www.ComicsOne.com
KUNG FU COMICS

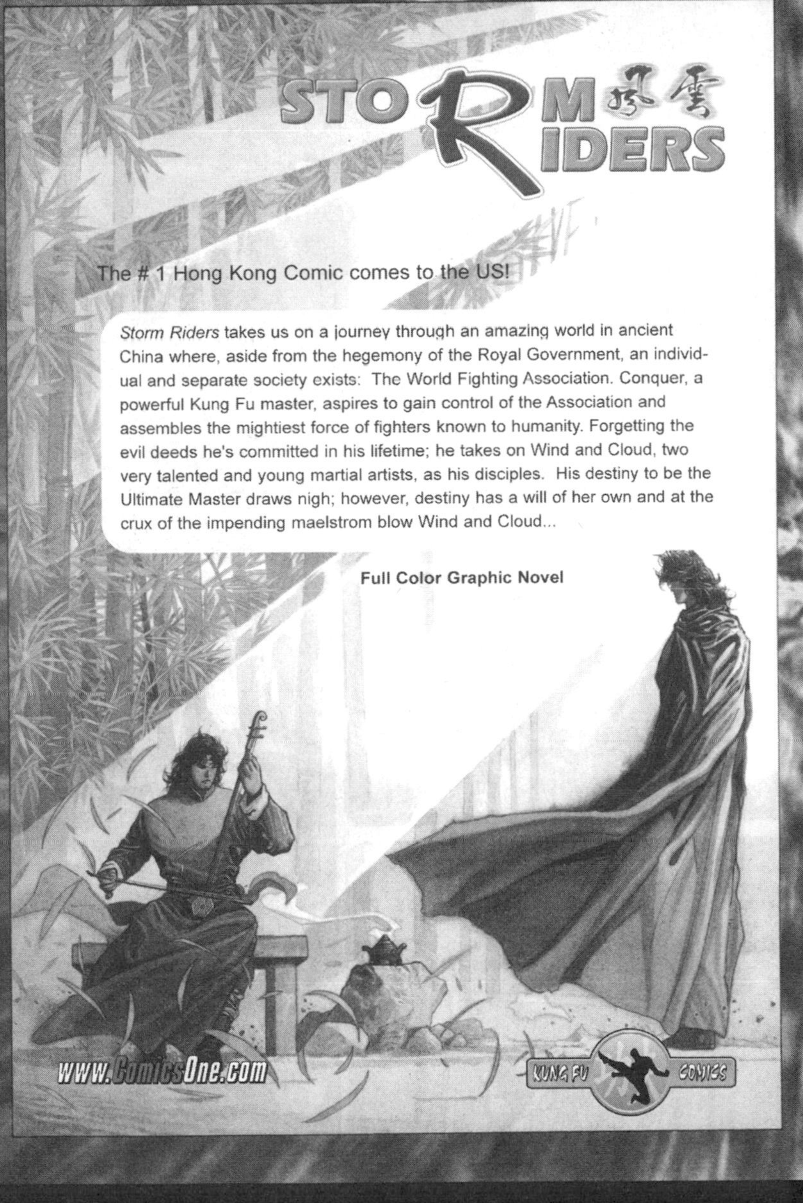
STORM RIDERS 風雲
The # 1 Hong Kong Comic comes to the US!
Storm Riders takes us on a journey through an amazing world in ancient China where, aside from the hegemony of the Royal Government, an individual and separate society exists: The World Fighting Association. Conquer, a powerful Kung Fu master, aspires to gain control of the Association and assembles the mightiest force of fighters known to humanity. Forgetting the evil deeds he's committed in his lifetime; he takes on Wind and Cloud, two very talented and young martial artists, as his disciples. His destiny to be the Ultimate Master draws nigh; however, destiny has a will of her own and at the crux of the impending maelstrom blow Wind and Cloud...
Full Color Graphic Novel
www.ComicsOne.com
KUNG FU COMICS

STORM RIDERS

Merchandise

Hero Sword

Hero Sword: Master swordsman Nameless of the Storm Riders series, passes this potent yet modest sword to his devoted and skilled student Jien-Chen. The straight sword has always been the weapon of the scholar and ComicsOne's 9-inch Hero Sword is definitely a distinguished way of opening your mail. It ships in a fine wood box perfect for displaying and comes with a jeweled scabbard and a red tassel bound to the hilt. Get yours today!

Snowy Saber: One of the most powerful weapons in the entire kung fu world is now available from ComicsOne as one of the most powerful letter openers in the world. Wielded by main character Wind from the popular Storm Riders series, this beautifully crafted 9-inch letter opener is the perfect replica, complete with scabbard and cloth-wrapped hilt. It ships in a fine cherry colored box perfect for displaying. Get yours today!

Snowy Saber

Destiny

Destiny: The perfect complement to the Snowy Saber and Hero Sword, this curved stainless steel blade is 9 inches long and comes with an ornately detailed scabbard. Store this powerful weapon in its decorative cherry box until the time comes to strike down your enemies or open that ever-menacing utility bill. Get yours today!

Mini Snowy Saber

Mini Snowy Saber: From the pages of Storm Riders comes main character Wind's family blade. Our mini Snowy Saber is the perfect trinket to spruce up your key chain and ward off any would be assailants.

Flame Kylin Sword

Flame Kylin Sword: Young Master Duan-Lang inherits the Flame Kylin after his father's tragic demise. This Duan family heirloom comes in two different flavors. Choose from the jade colored scabbard with a bronze blade or the silver scabbard with matching blade. The Flame Kylin Sword is 5.5 inches long and comes with an elegant red tassel. While the Flame Kylin makes a great letter opener, the sword and scabbard can also double as hairpins.

Please visit our web site for order and weapon information at www.comicsone.com or www.comicsworld.com

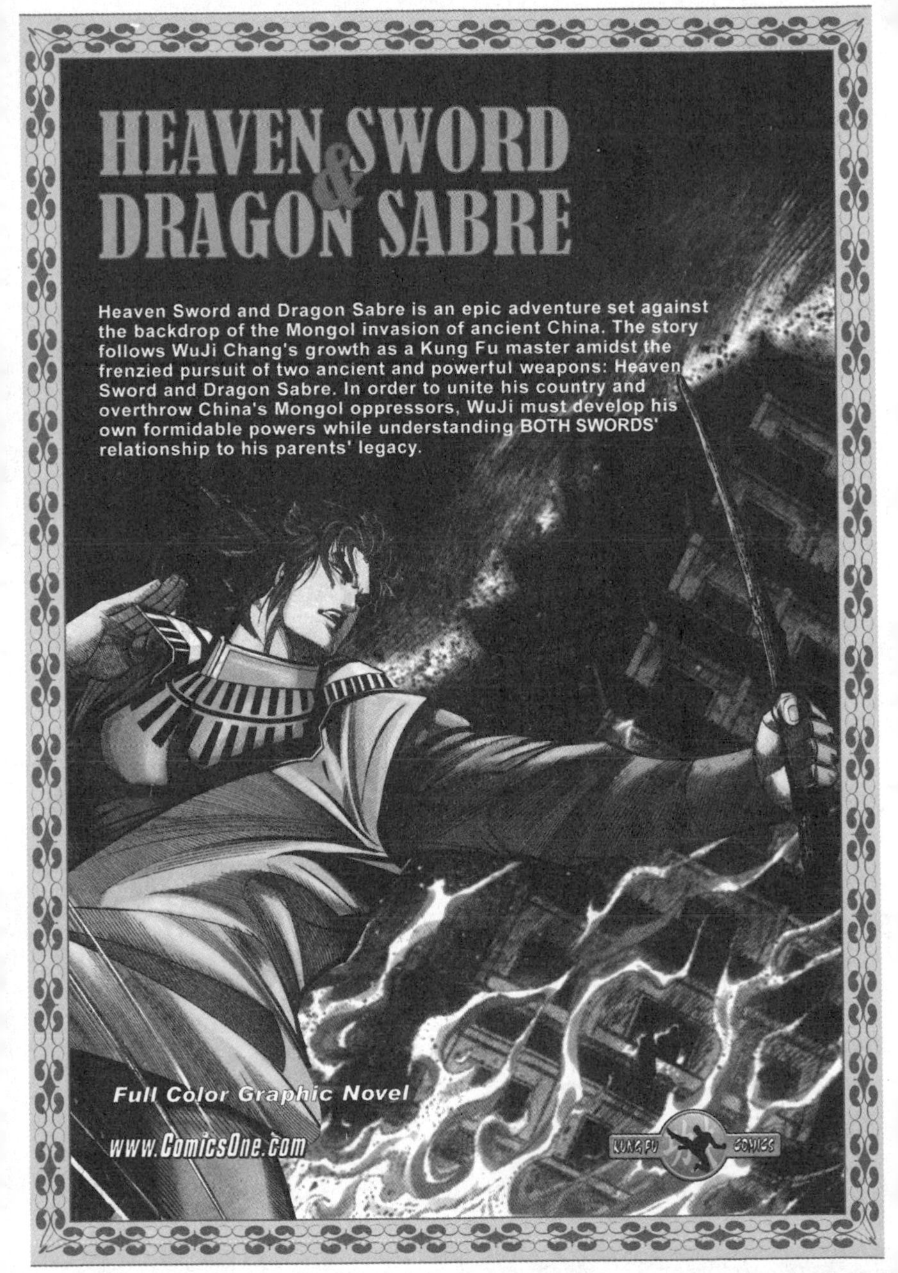
HEAVEN SWORD & DRAGON SABRE
Heaven Sword and Dragon Sabre is an epic adventure set against the backdrop of the Mongol invasion of ancient China. The story follows WuJi Chang's growth as a Kung Fu master amidst the frenzied pursuit of two ancient and powerful weapons: Heaven Sword and Dragon Sabre. In order to unite his country and overthrow China's Mongol oppressors, WuJi must develop his own formidable powers while understanding BOTH SWORDS' relationship to his parents' legacy.
Full Color Graphic Novel
www.ComicsOne.com
KUNG FU COMICS

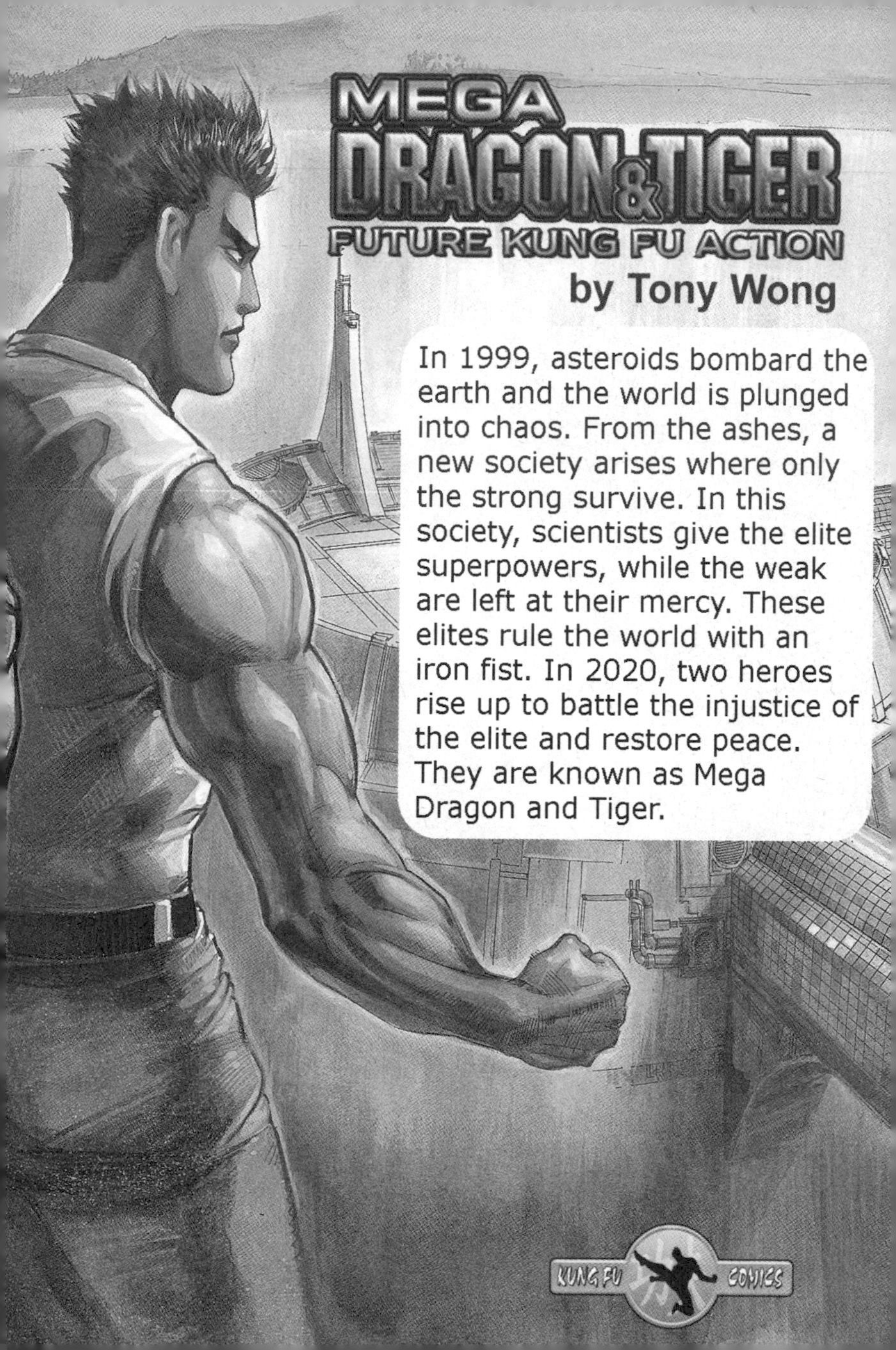
MEGA DRAGON & TIGER
FUTURE KUNG FU ACTION
by Tony Wong
In 1999, asteroids bombard the earth and the world is plunged into chaos. From the ashes, a new society arises where only the strong survive. In this society, scientists give the elite superpowers, while the weak are left at their mercy. These elites rule the world with an iron fist. In 2020, two heroes rise up to battle the injustice of the elite and restore peace. They are known as Mega Dragon and Tiger.
KUNG FU COMICS

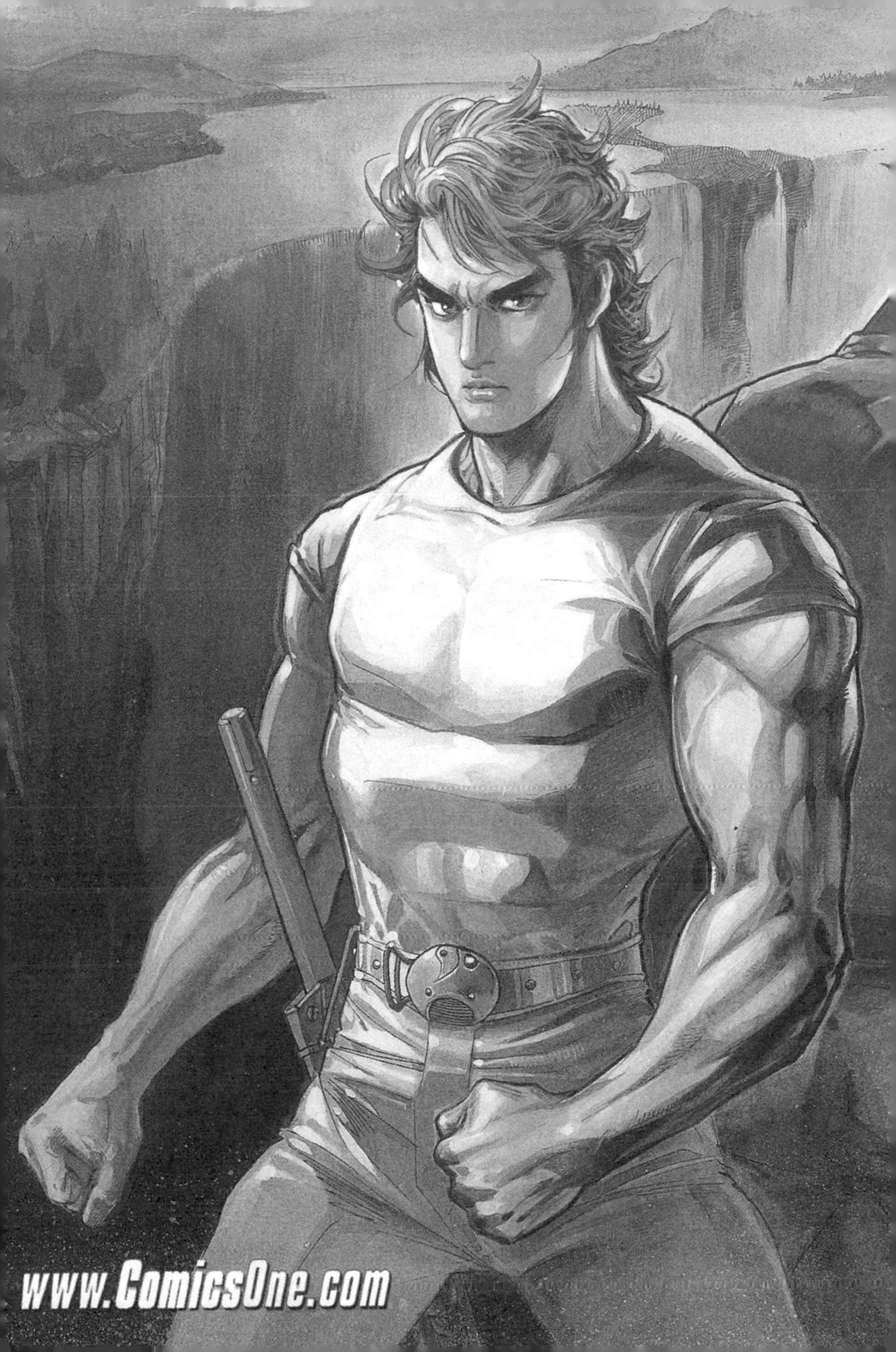
www.ComicsOne.com

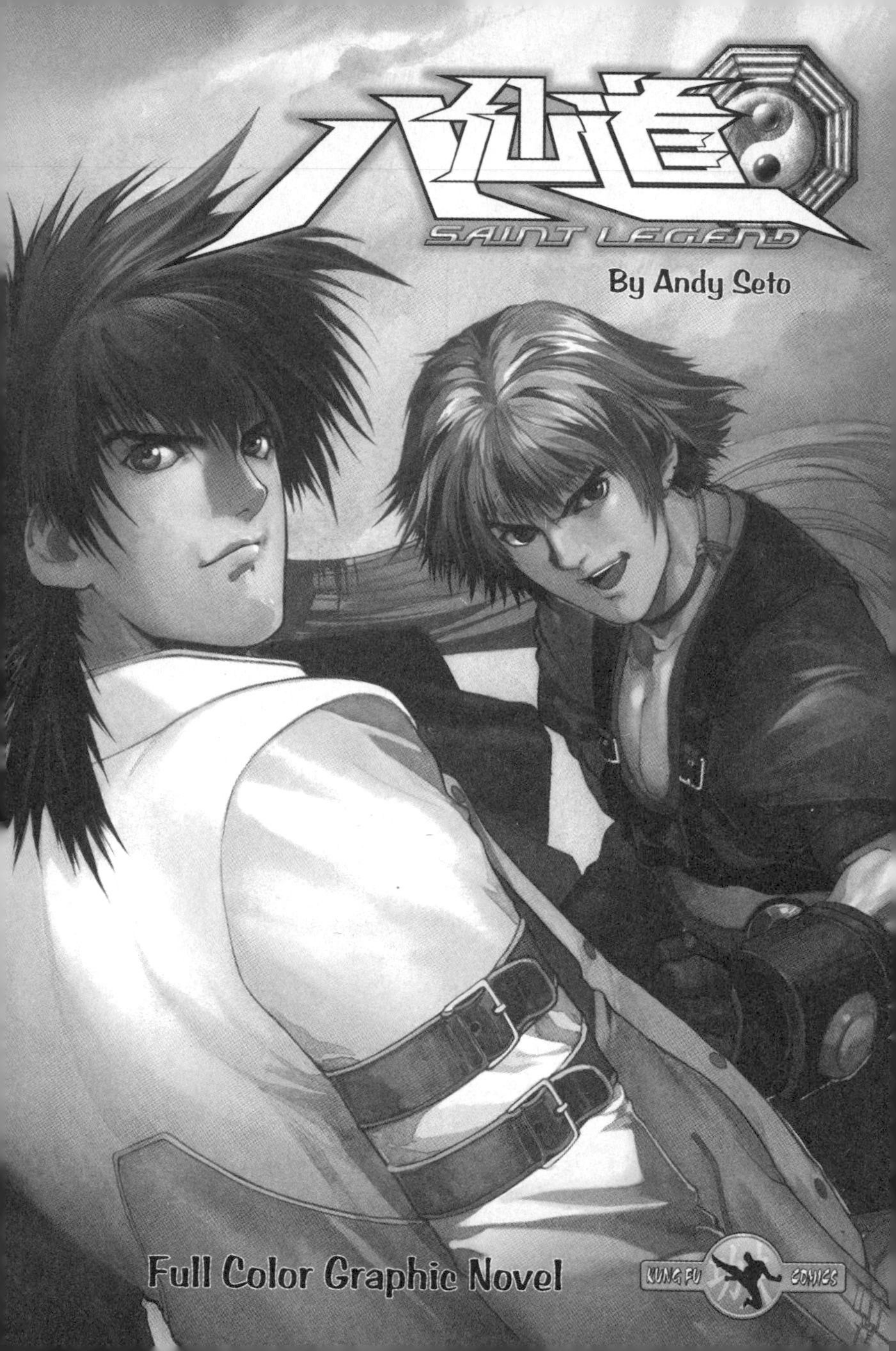
八仙道
SAINT LEGEND
By Andy Seto
Full Color Graphic Novel
KUNG FU COMICS

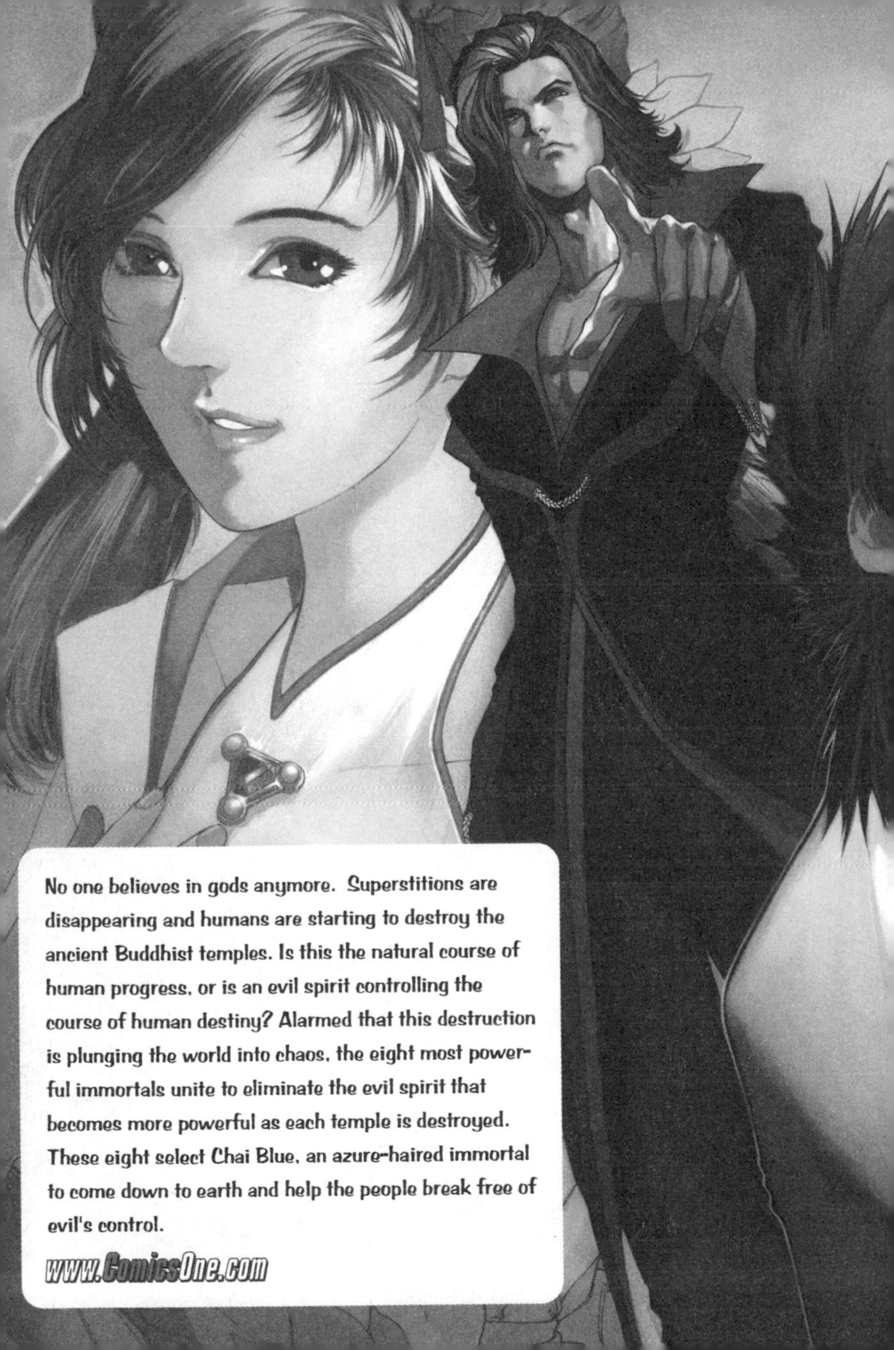
No one believes in gods anymore. Superstitions are disappearing and humans are starting to destroy the ancient Buddhist temples. Is this the natural course of human progress, or is an evil spirit controlling the course of human destiny? Alarmed that this destruction is plunging the world into chaos, the eight most powerful immortals unite to eliminate the evil spirit that becomes more powerful as each temple is destroyed. These eight select Chai Blue, an azure-haired immortal to come down to earth and help the people break free of evil's control.
www.ComicsOne.com

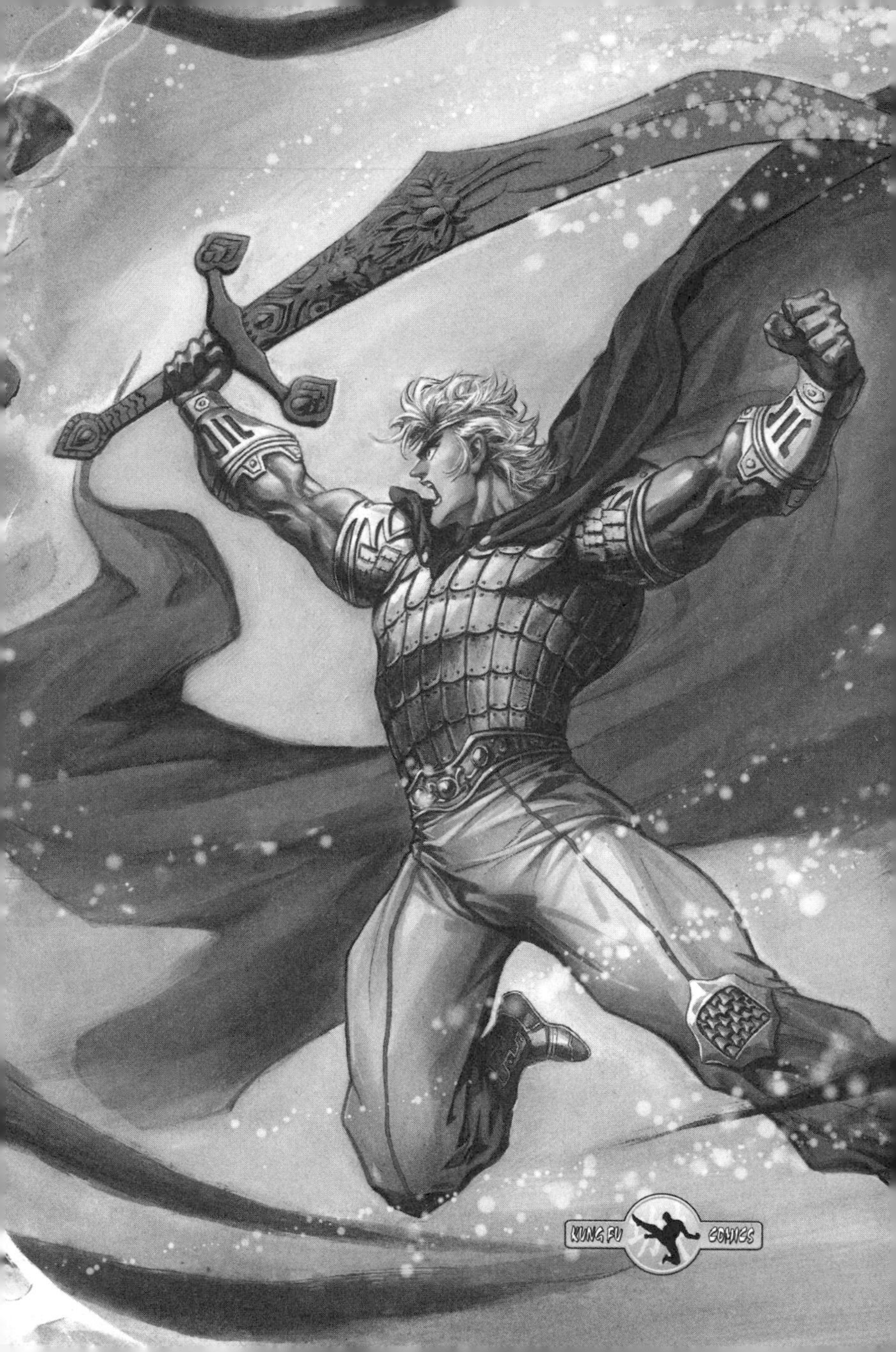
KUNG FU COMICS

In Ancient China, Celestial Goddess was locked in battle with the Dark Spirit. She used five colored stones to create a magical weapon known as Heaven's Crystal. One hundred years later, Heaven's Crystal disappears. Now, evil forces are trying to use Tiger Soul to destroy the world. Our hero, Tian, must search for Heaven's Crystal; only its power can defeat the fearful might of Tiger Soul.

Full Color Graphic Novel

We know ComicsOne Series are good, but don't take our word for it. Here is what others think:

Crayon Shinchan

"People who think that Bart Simpson is over the top and out of control have never seen Crayon Shinchan, and to be honest, it would probably give them heart attacks. For everyone else, though, this graphic novel will have you in stitches... and then you'll end up laughing some more. I'm thrilled that there are a lot of Crayon Shinchan collections on the horizon, because this is the funniest book I've read all year."
Greg McElhatton, icomics, Dec 2002

Red Prowling Devil

"Shimizu's artwork is distinctive with somewhat of a pencil-sketch flair to each panel alongside some nicely dynamic shading. This particular series flaunts his love of flying machines, and the detail and authenticity of each fighter jet is admirable. There's more than enough technical data in this volume to keep airplane buffs interested as the story progresses. And if that doesn't do it for you, there's also a healthy amount of fanservice for the more sex-crazed readers out there."
Pat King, Animefringe.com, Feb 2003

Heaven Sword & Dragon Sabre

"If a pit fight or tournament should be held to determine the Best of the Best of Hong Kong comics, I'm certain that Heaven Sword & Dragon Sabre would emerge from the fracas looking good and utterly victorious."
Patrick Macias, Animerica, Dec 2002

Bride of Deimos

"Bride of Deimos is comparable in formula to Narumi Kakinouchi's Vampire Princess Miyu, but surpasses that manga in inventiveness and charm, achieving the right balance between moody atmospherics and stuff actually happening."
Jason Thompson, Animerica, Dec 2002

Story of the Tao

"This fusion of several distinctly different styles of comic book art melded together with fascinating and relevant story about religion and its pitfalls is well suited to the times we live in. The result of all this is one of the best comics I have read in my life. " **Dr. Brown, Animerica, Jan 2003**

What is THE PRESS Saying?

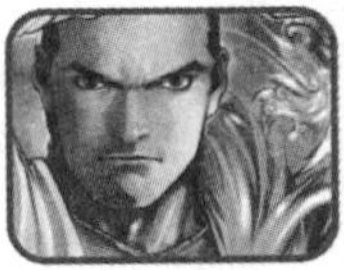

Crouching Tiger, Hidden Dragon

"The artwork in this comic is simply phenomenal. The color is rich without being overpowering, and Andy Seto's drawings are done with very,very fine lines and close attention to detail." **Javier Lopez, NewType USA, Jan 2003**

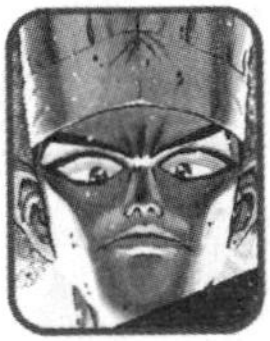

Iron Wok Jan!

"Shinji Saijyo's manga really surprised me because he was able to do something that you don't see in most English comics: taking an off-beat theme like cooking and not just making it into the central point of the series, but making it absolutely enthralling." **Greg McElhatton ,icomics, Jan 2003**

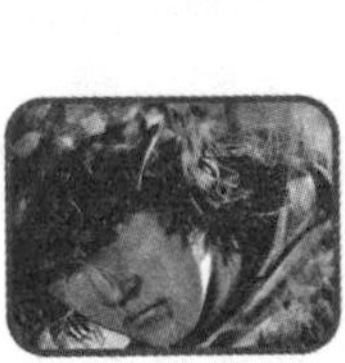

Storm Riders

"The best English treatment of a Hong Kong comic to date, ComicsOne's Storm Riders (originally printed in 1989) is neither fish nor fowl to readers familiar only with American comics and manga." **PULP, July 2002**

Weapons of the Gods

Merchandise

Power Wheel (Silver/Black)

This level 2 Weapon of the Gods was forged in ancient times. Only the most skilled martial artists are able to wield such a treasure. This attractive replica is made from metal and is available in both Silver/Black and Black/Red. Display stand included!

God's Ruler (Special Edition)

For a level 2 Weapon of the Gods this oddly shaped blade has the unique and fantastic power to cure and destroy. This Special Edition model comes in its own forest green display box.

Heaven's Crystal 1:1 (3.5 feet)

This level 1 Weapon of the Gods was forged from enchanted stones of various shades, by the Celestial Goddess herself. Its only rival in the world is Tiger Soul. Our full-sized Heaven's Crystal is the perfect gift and makes a great accessory for nearly any costume. Composed of plastic. Get yours today!

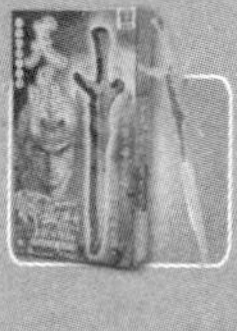

Heaven's Crystal 8" (Glow in the Dark)

Afraid of the dark? Now you can have our glow-in-the-dark Heaven's Crystal to light your way. Comes equipped with a display stand. It also doubles as a stylish 8" letter opener.

Heaven's Crystal 12" (Glow in the Dark)

Beware the curse of Heaven's Crystal: "Those who wield Heaven's Crystal shall be blessed with great wealth and cursed with boundless catastrophe." Yet, don't let that stop you from opening your mail with this snazzy 12" glow-in-the-dark letter opener. Composed of sturdy plastic and includes display box!

Weapons of the Gods (Ultimate Collection)

All of the most powerful Weapons of the Gods can be yours. This collector's set is filled with 10 lead miniatures, and includes its own wood display box.

Visit www.ComicsOne.com to order

comics

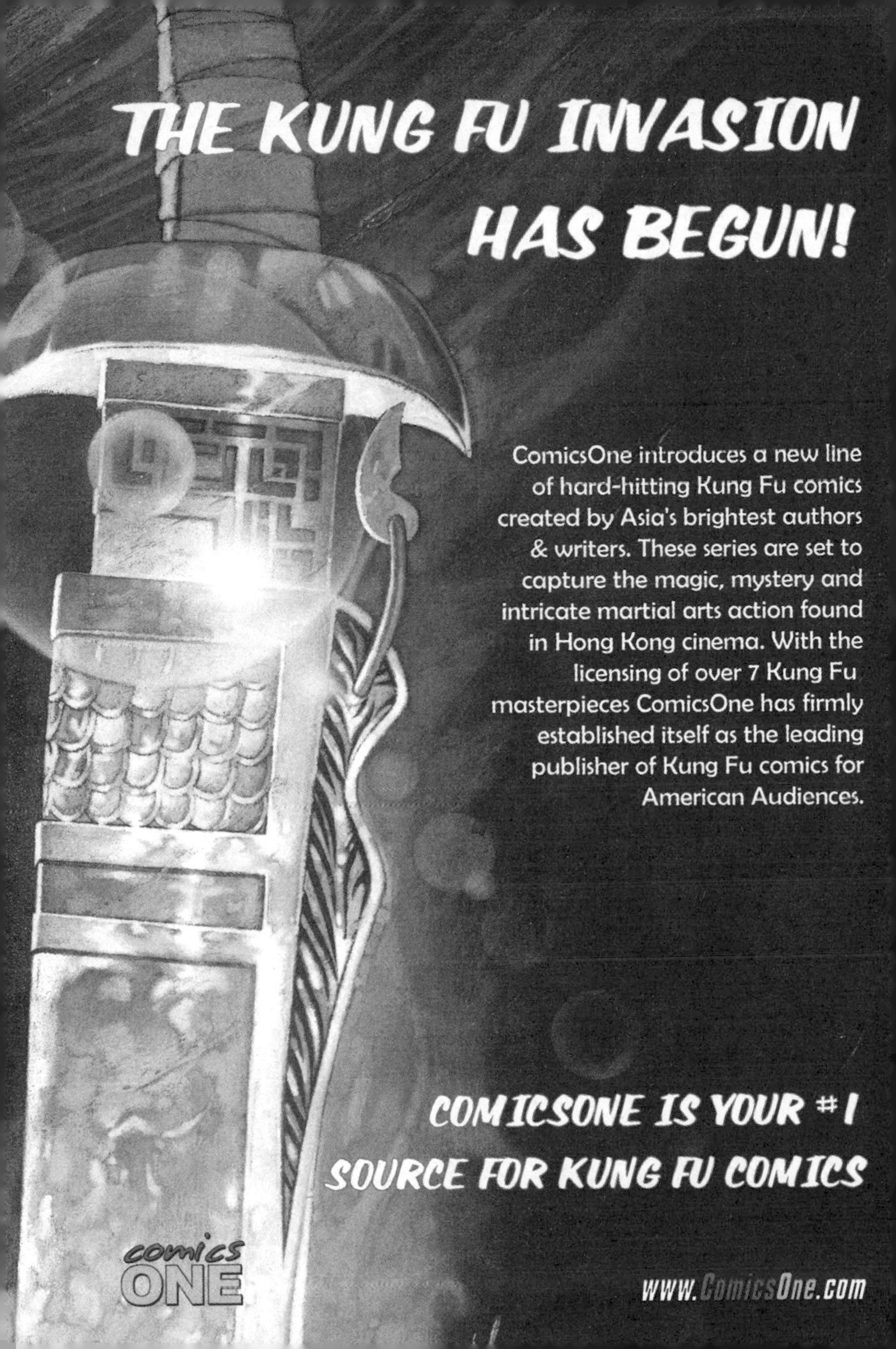
THE KUNG FU INVASION HAS BEGUN!
ComicsOne introduces a new line of hard-hitting Kung Fu comics created by Asia's brightest authors & writers. These series are set to capture the magic, mystery and intricate martial arts action found in Hong Kong cinema. With the licensing of over 7 Kung Fu masterpieces ComicsOne has firmly established itself as the leading publisher of Kung Fu comics for American Audiences.
COMICSONE IS YOUR #1 SOURCE FOR KUNG FU COMICS
comics ONE
www.ComicsOne.com

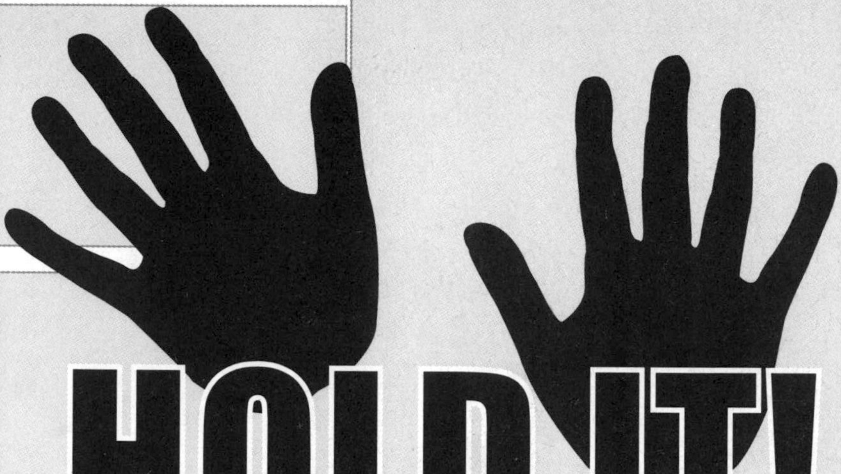

HOLD IT!

This book was printed in the original Japanese format. Please flip the book over and read right-to-left.

NIPPON ¥80

ORIGINAL MANGA